I TATTI STUDIES IN
ITALIAN RENAISSANCE HISTORY

Sponsored by Villa I Tatti
Harvard University Center for Italian Renaissance Studies
Florence, Italy

The

MEDICEAN
SUCCESSION

Monarchy and Sacral Politics in
Duke Cosimo dei Medici's Florence

GREGORY MURRY

Harvard University Press

Cambridge, Massachusetts
London, England

2014

Copyright © 2014 by the President and Fellows of Harvard College
All rights reserved
Printed in the United States of America.

Library of Congress Cataloging-in-Publication Data
Murry, Gregory, 1982–
The Medicean succession : monarchy and sacral politics in duke Cosimo dei
Medici's Florence / Gregory Murry.
pages cm. — (I Tatti studies in Italian Renaissance history)
Includes bibliographical references and index.
ISBN 978-0-674-72547-8 (alk. paper)
1. Cosimo I, Grand-Duke of Tuscany, 1519–1574. 2. Florence (Italy)—Politics
and government—1421–1737. 3. Tuscany (Italy)—Politics and government—
1434–1737. 4. Florence (Italy)—Kings and rulers—Biography.
5. Tuscany (Italy)—Kings and rulers—Biography. 6. Monarchy—Italy—
Tuscany—History—16th century. 7. Divine right of kings 8. Medici,
House of. I. Title.
DG738.17.M87 2014
945'.507092—dc23 [B]   2013022678

To Katie

Contents

List of Figures   ix

Prologue: The Scene   1

Introduction   8

1. The Familiarity of Terrestrial Divinity   16

2. Divine Right Rule and the Providential Worldview   50

3. Rescuing Virtue from Machiavelli   104

4. Prince or *Patrone?*
   Cosimo as Ecclesiastical Patron   133

5. Cosimo and Savonarolan Reform   163

6. Defense of the Sacred   192

Conclusion   243

Appendix: Glossary of Names   249
Sources and Abbreviations   259
Notes   261
Acknowledgments   343
Index   345

Figures

1.1 Giorgio Vasari, *The Apotheosis of Cosimo*   17

6.1 Provenance of priests elected to
benefices by communities, 1546–1550   202

6.2 Provenance of priests elected to
benefices by the ordinary, 1546–1550   202

6.3 Provenance of priests elected to
benefices by Rome, 1546–1550   202

6.4 Percentage of testators demonstrating
belief in Purgatory   233

6.5 Percentage of testators using Catholic identifiers   235

6.6 Comparison of nobles and nonnobles
requesting masses   235

The Medicean
Succession

Prologue: The Scene

THE STORY BEGINS in blood, with the brutal stabbing of the first duke of Florence, the last direct male heir in the Medici line. On Epiphany night 1537, the roguish duke, Alessandro dei Medici, hastily made his way down the Via Larga to the chambers of his cousin and best friend, Lorenzino. For some time, Alessandro had been needling his dissolute kinsman to procure the sexual favors of a highly respected Florentine matron, and that night Lorenzino had promised he would deliver. The prospect was undoubtedly scandalous, but Alessandro undoubtedly did not care; he was convinced his grip on the city was ironclad, and he wantonly made use of that fact to satisfy his reportedly strange sexual appetite, devouring the city's wives, widows, and virgins with little regard for their age or rank.[1] This night's prospect was also undoubtedly difficult, but Lorenzino had proved adept and trustworthy in such exploits before. Thus, Alessandro's mind was probably at rest as he readied himself in the bedroom chamber, removing his armor and sending away his bodyguard, leaving himself just as Lorenzino

I

wanted: naked, defenseless, and completely oblivious to the dangers awaiting him.

Lorenzino had indeed been importuning favors, but not the kind Alessandro expected. Safely hidden in the dark corners of the Piazza Santissima Annunziata nearby, he had just initiated his Hungarian servant into his secret plan to assassinate the unpopular duke. Lorenzino was ready, however, to sink his dagger into his Hungarian accomplice instead should he show any signs of trepidation.[2] If pangs of fear or morality pricked the Hungarian's conscience, he must have kept them to himself. Moreover, it must have come as quite a shock to Alessandro to find it was no beautiful matron Lorenzino had seduced into his bedroom but a hefty and dangerous-looking ruffian. Lorenzino first attempted to dispatch Alessandro on his own, but the unkindest cut proved insufficient, and Alessandro scrambled to his feet, defending himself from Lorenzino with a nearby stool. The young duke even managed to bite a chunk out of his assassin's hand before being laid low, six thrusts later. The wounded Lorenzino panicked. Fleeing the scene, he mounted a horse, rode to the city gates, and talked his way out. The guard let him ride, despite the suspicious-looking cut on his hand.[3]

He did not stop riding until he reached Venice, where he was immediately hailed as a new Brutus by the rich anti-Medicean exile Filippo Strozzi. Though Alessandro may well have deserved the title tyrant, the brooding and sulky Lorenzino was hardly cut out for the salvation of the *patria*.[4] The terror-stricken assassin was little more than the same petulant youth who had once found himself exiled from Clement VII's Rome for knocking the heads off the statues on the Arch of Constantine.[5] Though by his dual blows against monarchy living and dead, he gained a reputation as the slayer of tyrants both ancient and modern, his panic soon proved costly. The Holy Roman Emperor's agent in Florence, Cardinal Innocenzo Cybo, got wind of the murder before the news could spread and prudently kept it quiet.[6] Claiming that Duke Alessandro was sleeping off the previous night's revels, Cybo quietly had the fetid, rotting body secretly snuck out of the chamber and into the nearby family crypt in San Lorenzo. Meanwhile, he sent out urgent pleas for troops, which arrived in due time under the command of Alessandro Vitelli. But by Monday morning, the trickle of disquieting rumors had begun rippling across the city and into its dominion, inevitably lapping over the borders of Tuscany itself. As the news began to spread, so spread the threat from the city's disgruntled republican element. In Venice, Filippo Strozzi was raising troops and cash.[7] In Rome, the Florentine cardinals Niccolò Ridolfi and Jacopo Salviati were drawing up plans for the new government.[8] The excitement was even bubbling over into the streets of Florence itself, where jubilant bands were somewhat prematurely proclaiming the rebirth of republican liberty. The recently restored Medicean principate was facing the largest crisis of its short life; would it survive, or would it be strangled in its cradle like so many other Florentine governments?[9]

On Monday, with an anxious and ominously swelling crowd situated just outside, the Florentine Senate of Forty-Eight nervously assembled to decide the republic's fate.[10] Alessandro's next of kin happened to be Lorenzino, whose treacherous act disqualified him from the succession. Cardinal Cybo hit on the idea of placing Alessandro's three-year-old bastard, Giulio, on the throne; of course, Cybo himself would act as regent, keeping the real power in his own hands. Cybo's plan was extremely distasteful to some of the elder statesmen in the senate, the venerable Francesco Guicciardini foremost among them. However, these men also knew that the rapidly swelling mob would not countenance a naked power grab by the senate itself, for the plebs of Florence seemingly always preferred the voracity of one lone tyrant to the grasping maws of forty-eight little ones. Nor would the Emperor Charles countenance a return to a real representative republic. He knew that the Medici had occasionally proved useful allies, whereas republican Florence had always remained unswervingly pro-French. Cut open the heart of any Florentine, so went proverbial wisdom, and there one would find the golden fleur-de-lis. There was a real danger that Charles would seize the city for his own rather than risk it to his perpetual nemesis, the King of France. Most of the oligarchs in the senate had few fond memories of republican rule anyway, which in the last experiment had turned rather nastily against wealthy and noble alike.

All this was enough to prod the oligarchs in the senate into accepting a compromise candidate. To that end, the pragmatist senators engineered the election of seventeen-year-old Cosimo dei Medici, related to a cadet branch of the Medici family through his famous condottiere father and to the main branch through his mother. The young Cosimo was thought to be more or less disinterested in the city's turbulent political affairs, as he spent much of his time in the soldier's long tunic, hunting and hawking outside the city walls. It was hoped that he would become an absent duke who would leave the real business of running the state to the senate. The oligarchs who supported his election thought they could make a puppet ruler out of him, a figurehead cloaking an aristocratic regime,[11] but the oligarchs had misjudged their man.

Cosimo was the son of Giovanni delle Bande Neri, a brilliant soldier and absentee father, whose liberal-handed generosity and premature death had left Cosimo in a rather humiliating and awkward poverty vis-à-vis his Medici relatives. As such, his mother, Maria Salviati, cherished suitably narrow ambitions for him: hitch his wagon to Alessandro's star and find a suitable dowry; the ducal chair was really never in her purview.[12] His election came as somewhat of a surprise, perhaps not an entirely pleasant one. He was inheriting a desperate situation; indeed, the prospect of taking the reins of an untamed, unbroken Florence was so unattractive that his mother wondered if he should not refuse the offer outright. Since the fall of the last Florentine republic in 1530, Pope Clement VII and the bastard Duke Alessandro had alienated and exiled so many citizens that a veritable army of malcontents had spent much of the last ten years in Rome, Venice, and Bologna, biding their time and dreaming of vendetta. Now that good fortune had just fallen into their lap, and laden with French gold and silver, they were putting together small armies to march on Florence. Cosimo faced them armed only with a depleted treasury, a pittance of an allowance, and no independent fortune to shore up the state's finances. Furthermore, he had no solid assurance of support from the emperor, nor did he even have physical control over the city; that particular card was held by Alessandro Vitello, who had taken possession of the fortress and was not about to let it go without being handsomely rewarded for services rendered. Nevertheless, Cosimo could not pass up the offer of a lifetime. When he entered Florence, he entered alone, without the escort offered by some of his father's doggedly loyal veterans. Later that day Cosimo was sworn in as *"capo et primario"* of the Florentine state. Preferring to support this creature of the senate rather than exasperate the pope and Venice by an outright annexation, the Emperor Charles approved the senate's decision, granting Cosimo formal recognition as head of the Florentine government in September of the same year.[13]

Cosimo did not remain long in such a tenuous position. The seventeen-year-old had precocious political talents, a fact that should have surprised no one given the blood that ran through his veins. His forceful personality blended both the foxlike political cunning of his Medici namesake, Cosimo the Elder, and the iron will of his paternal grandmother, Caterina Sforza, whose fortitude is best recalled by a picturesque episode played out on the battlements of Forli. When a group of conspirators who were camped outside the citadel threatened to kill her captive children if she did not immediately surrender, she impudently flashed her genitalia and called back, "As long as these remain to me, I can make new children."[14] So well equipped biologically and well geared to rule by temperament, Cosimo quickly put his house in order. In the first year of his reign, he won a resounding victory over the disordered and confused bands of exiles who flung themselves into the heart of Tuscany, thereby securing his throne and winning the emperor's respect. His nemesis Filippo Strozzi, who was locked in the fortress, soon followed Cato's example, preferring to end his life on his own sword rather than watch the new tyrant snuff out the last flicker of republican liberty. Two years later Cosimo secured his relationship with the Hapsburgs by marrying himself off to the daughter of the viceroy of Naples with a pomp and bravado that belied just how uneasily the ducal crown yet sat on his brow. In 1543 Cosimo would celebrate his first real propaganda victory, regaining the fortress with a timely payment to the perpetually cash-strapped Emperor Charles. In the early 1550s, he took neighboring Siena in his one and only major military action. In 1569 he convinced the well-meaning but ambitious Pius V to crown him grand duke of Tuscany, a title his heirs would proudly bear until the nineteenth century. At his death in 1574, the compromise duke could boast that he had stabilized the ducal finances, secured his borders, doubled his territory, and attracted a dazzling array of scholars and artists to his court, academy, and universities. Most important, he would claim that he had pacified the perennially fractious politics of Florentine life, presenting himself as the mediator in whom all strife dissipated.

In the self-fashioned image he forged from those inauspicious beginnings, Cosimo presented himself as a unique persona who rose above the class squabbles that had derailed the Florentine republic and who transcended the narrow urban patriotism that had excluded the Florentine dominion from the benefits of empire.[15] Indeed, he was the unique persona who might usher in a golden age of peace underwritten by his own personal power.[16] To this end he cast his propaganda to attract a wide array of adherents, from longtime Medicean clients to that cadre of urban aristocrats long jealous of Medici power; from the rabidly Savonarolan artisan class to the mass of urban and rural poor. Indeed, Cosimo's propaganda was carefully modulated to attract all those willing to compromise: city and dominion; Medicean and republican; rich aristocrats, middle-class Savonarolans, and laboring poor. This study will primarily focus on the way Cosimo's propaganda was directed to Florentines, who were perhaps his hardest sell, since they had the most to lose, the least to gain, and the strongest traditions of self-government. Where appropriate and possible, this study will also examine the issue of trying to build consensus across the larger Tuscan region.

Indeed, building any type of consensus would not be an easy task. Despite Cosimo's success his monarchy reportedly weighed heavily on his subjects' hearts.[17] The list of complaints to which his situation left him vulnerable was long. In the first place, he was only seventeen years old at his ascension, and for many Florentines, the seat of government was no place for a boy.[18] Second, he had little hereditary legitimacy, and for many Florentines, his actions exceeded the little sphere of authority that the senate had actually tried to concede him. And finally, he was a Medici, and for many Florentines the very name reeked of tyranny.[19] Indeed, it seems that even in Cosimo's ducal Florence, republican ideals would not die easily or quietly, for even as Cosimo consolidated his rule, much of the old guard continued to reappropriate memories of the city's republican past.[20] These nagging and persistent problems drove Cosimo's program of artistic, literary, and academic patronage, which attempted to do what neither his name nor his ancestry ever could: legitimize his monarchical government in the eyes of the world and his fellow Tuscans. Failing at this task would mean that he and his line would forever be nothing more than occupants of a blood-spattered throne, inheritors of a power won in siege and assassination. Thus, Cosimo quite consciously set out to make his power not just legitimate but sacrosanct; to make his personage not just regal but divine; and to make himself into not just a prince but a god.

Introduction

COSIMO CERTAINLY must have known that peddling sacral monarchy to Florentines would not be easy, for the Florentine monarchy itself had begun in blood just a few years earlier. A starving and outgunned Florentine republic finally signed away its last liberties to its Medici conquerors only in 1530. Indeed, Florentine republicanism stood in the starkest contrast to ideologies in the rest of early modern Europe. Almost everywhere monarchy was in the ascendancy, and almost everywhere this meant some kind of sacral monarchy. In most Christian polities, the ideologies that equated the prince with a god on earth were a matter of long-standing tradition, woven into the tapestries of mythic and heroic dynastic histories. Paint, canvas, and brush had long been set to work to depict monarchical sacrality, gallons of ink had been spilled arguing in favor of it, and whole quarries of stone had been emptied attempting to immortalize it.[1] Florence was one of the last exceptions to this rule, an island of republican consensus in the swelling sea of monarchy. Florentines thought their republican constitution necessary because they were too noble, too unyielding, and too honor-bound to bend their necks to one-man rule. In turn, they found the source of their own strength and genius in that very same republican constitution.[2] Florentine historians had long made the expulsion of a monarch a defining moment in their patriotic mythology, never hesitating to compare the city's chasing of the tyrant Walter of Brienne to the similar moment in Roman history when the Roman people had expelled the Tarquins. The equation of liberty and republicanism was so deeply engrained in Florentine consciousness that Cosimo's Medici ancestors had rather prudently decided to rule the city under a republican cloak, wielding control in the shadows rather than through legitimate organs of governance.[3] At the end of the fifteenth century, the fiery and persuasive Dominican preacher Girolamo Savonarola had upped the ante, turning republican liberty into holy liberty, a godly ordained constitution providentially appointed to usher in a golden age of peace.[4] Savonarola's fiery death at the stake in 1498 had only served to light the imagination of his many followers, who continued to cherish his memory and message for years after his death. Indeed, when the combined armies of pope and Holy Roman Emperor sat down outside the walls of Florence to starve out the last Florentine republic in 1530, they found a host of Savonarolans peering out at them from the city's battlements.[5]

Born and bred in such unusual circumstances, the Florentine principate is an intriguing test case for studying the construction of sacral monarchy. Unlike other monarchs, Cosimo could not draw on a large body of native political tradition. He took many of his models from more long-standing ancient or foreign traditions, and the idea of sacral monarchy (though not sacral governance) was completely novel for Florence; in fact, it flew in the teeth of the city's most cherished political ideals. Thus, because Cosimo built his sacral image ex novo over a relatively brief span of years, his articulation of legitimacy provides a unique snapshot of the relationship between local religion and r more protracted constructions of sacral monarchy (i.e. France, England, and more problematically, Spain). How then did Cosimo construct a plausible and successful political mythology of Christian monarchy in the very birthplace of "modern" republicanism and Machiavellian realpolitik political philosophy? How did he go from a compromise candidate, whose sole undeniable recommendation was that he was not a Spaniard, to a divine prince? This work argues that Cosimo and his literati primarily utilized and borrowed the models of sacral monarchy that could be inscribed in local religious assumptions. They co-opted the vocabulary of sacral Florence and set it to work for Cosimo's own personal power; they played on traditional assumptions about the place of the sacred in the political order; and they assuaged the populace by modulating propaganda in such a way that it resonated with basic assumptions about the sacred and secular world. In a sentence, Cosimo's grandiose political claims of apotheosis worked because they channeled Florentines' preexisting assumptions about the nature of the sacred. The chapters that follow unearth and explicate the various underlying cultural and religious assumptions that served to bolster Cosimo's political claims.

Chapter 1 argues that the propaganda of Cosimo's princely apotheosis was effective because Florentine religion already directed people to see the immanent manifestation of God in material aspects of the created order. Like many of their early modern Italian contemporaries, Renaissance Florentines generally believed that terrestrial divinity could inhere in any person according to his or her use of reason, exercise of virtue, or participation in the sacramental life of the church. When Cosimo set about trying to convince Florentines of his princely divinity, his claim was simply one more addition to the pantheon. Chapter 2 argues that Cosimo's divine right claims were not absolutist propaganda but the inescapable conclusion of a ubiquitously persistent providential worldview. This chapter argues against a prevailing view of divine right that often draws a false dichotomy between appeals to God and appeals to consent. In both Renaissance and Counter-Reformation Florence, providential thinking was usually multicausal, that is, allowing for the simultaneous action of human free choice and God's guiding hand. Given this basic assumption, Cosimo's image makers could consistently argue that his power was derived from a divine source while simultaneously claiming that he was freely elected by the republic. Chapter 3 argues that Cosimo's panegyrists celebrated his cardinal virtues in ways that were intentionally meant to counter Machiavelli's realist political arguments, using Cosimo's success to argue for the practical utility of traditional Christian and humanist categories of moral virtue. This strategy worked particularly well in sixteenth-century Florence because of a prevalent anti-Machiavellian sentiment. Chapter 4 argues that Cosimo's position in Florence was indissolubly linked to his ability to satisfy his subjects' desires for protection and patronage in the Roman curia, a role long sanctified in Florence but lacking the noxious, autocratic overtones of a more overt absolutism. Chapter 5 argues that while repudiating Savonarola's legacy of monastic intervention in political affairs, Cosimo nevertheless set out to win the favor of the city's considerable Savonarolan element by systematically enacting Savonarola's program of moral reform. This chapter examines this topic under the lens of moral legislation, assistance to the poor, and clerical reform. Chapter 6 looks at Cosimo's utilization of popular piety, arguing that he insinuated himself into the city's sacred life by posturing as its defender. Nevertheless, he was usually careful to accommodate his actions to his subjects' traditional attitudes and desires. This chapter analyzes this dynamic under the lens of sacred office, sacred space, sacred ritual, and sacred power.

Of course, few of the relevant religious assumptions were entirely unique to Florence, so it is no surprise that few of Cosimo's models of sacral monarchy were unique to him. However, the extent to which he and his literati chose only propaganda that could strike root in local assumptions is thrown into relief by examining the models of sacral monarchy he did not borrow; indeed, his mythmakers ignored some of the most potent staples of early modern political discourse. For instance, he did not invite scrofula sufferers to be healed by his touch.[8] Florence had no tradition of political thaumaturgy, and one could not simply be created from nothing. Second, the metaphor of the prince as head of the body politic was conspicuously downplayed, since it would have been a hard sell to republican Florence.[9] Third, Cosimo did not, like some of his near contemporaries, try to effect an apotheosis in which his image was made to stand in as the likeness of the city.[10] Fourth, with one or two exceptions, his literati did not equate divine right with absolutism.[11] Republican traditions dictated that he stress the consensual nature of his power, and in public he respected this exigency, though privately he often wielded power like an autocrat. Finally, his literati had little interest in tracing the Medici line to some more ancient and noble race or to some Wotan-like man-god hidden in the mists of time, for such an attempt would have wounded Florentine and Tuscan pride to the quick. There would be no fictive Trojan lineages, no semidivine founder.[12] Much to the contrary, during Cosimo's age, the autochthony of the house was cherished and celebrated. "Not from foreign and barbarous provinces," eulogized Scipione Ammirato, "did Cosimo draw his origin, but from most noble Italy." Moreover, it was not just from Italy but Italy's greatest province, Tuscany, and its greatest city, Florence.[13] Chasing tales of heroic Medicean ancestors through falsified genealogical tables was not a project that Cosimo's subjects would have appreciated, since the wells of local patriotism ran deep in the relatively small communal territory.

In its immediate historiographical context, this thesis supports a growing consensus among scholars of the grand ducal period that in part, the duke's drastically new type of governance survived by promoting illusions of continuity linking it to the Florentine past.[14] While centralizing power, the duke preferred to utilize old political, cultural, and intellectual institutions for his own purposes rather than abolish them outright, and artistic commissions cast him as the fulfillment of the city's destiny, the end to which all previous Florentine history had been tending. On the political level, he preferred to reintegrate willing republican exiles into the new monarchical system, attracting several illustrious personages back to Florence to work for the new regime. This did not mean, however, that republican thought or ideals simply died out.[15] Well into the ducal period, families continued to shape and reshape memories of their republican, Ficinian, Savonarolan, and Picinian ideals even as they sought to find their place in a changed political atmosphere.[16] Thus, Cosimo's use and co-optation of these icons of the Florentine past played an essential role in attracting an audience of elite and middle-class Florentines in a time of tense political liminality, where old political rhetoric needed to be adapted to a new political reality.

Moreover, the Florentine case opens a window onto more generally applicable points. Much of the work on sixteenth-century monarchy has focused on the dualities of political ideology and political exigency.[17] Historians have asked: from where did rulers draw their models of legitimacy, and what political purpose did these models serve? Insofar as historians have been concerned with the broader relations between political propaganda and the axioms of religious thought, they have almost exclusively directed their attentions to the ways reformed religion helped to desacralize the sacral polity in the later early modern period.[18] Cosimo's case insists on throwing another element into the mix: the Florentine experience foregrounds the extent to which the propaganda of sacral monarchy needed to be inscribed in the matrices of local religious experience. To borrow a popular early modern metaphor, political ideology and political exigency may have supplied the seeds, the sun, and the water, but religious assumptions provided the soil and climate. Specific forms of sacral monarchy could only flower where all these conditions were right. This study seeks to examine this dynamic in the Florentine experience, laying bare the pertinent assumptions and explicating their links to political culture.

In uncovering these assumptions, this book will contribute to the ongoing revision of the idea of a secular Italian Renaissance. In the wake of Charles Trinkaus's and Richard Trexler's pioneering work, historians have come to see the Florentine Renaissance as neither a leap forward into secular modernity nor a jump back into classical paganism.[19] The picture of Florentine culture that has emerged from this and other studies increasingly looks deeply religious, especially in its urge to reconcile classical thought with Christian precepts. This study attempts to go one step further, by integrating religion more fully into the political narrative, a move that many Florentine historians, with notable exceptions, have often neglected to accomplish.[20] Scholars of mid-sixteenth-century Florentine governance, especially Italian historians, have often refused to acknowledge religion as an independent ingredient of political culture, choosing to treat it merely as an instrument of power wielded by cynical autocrats.[21] Thus, this study seeks to fill in some of the gaps in the political narrative by situating the study of political culture more fully within a revised view of religion's place in Renaissance Florentine society, arguing that Cosimo's political propaganda tapped into existing religious assumptions and impulses as a way to establish continuity with Florence's Renaissance past.

Moreover, this work will also point out the ideological links that bound the late Renaissance period to the Counter-Reformation, thereby contributing to Paul Grendler's call to examine the continuities between two periods that had once seemed to "inhabit different worlds."[22] Indeed, the Florentine Renaissance and Counter-Reformation held far more in common than is traditionally assumed. Counter-Reformation Florence continually looked to its Renaissance past in order to uphold the sacred nature of man in the material world, the free nature of man's interaction with the divine, and the place of virtue in the economy of salvation. As the first three chapters will demonstrate, it was on these bases that Cosimo and his propagandists primarily built his sacral image.

As a final theme, this study will insist on a clear distinction between the influences of the Protestant Reformation and the Catholic Reformation on models of political legitimacy. Leaving divine right aside, most scholars of religion have assumed that the Reformation tolled the death knell for sacral monarchy. Now at least one influential historian has identified reformed Catholicism as a twin motor of desanctification, bolstering his claim with the now manifestly apparent reality that Protestant and Catholic reform "tended to have similar social and cultural effects wherever (they) emerged."[23] Catholic and Protestant reform were twins in many ways, but this study suggests that their kinship did not extend to the realm of political theology. If the ordering of the world remained deeply religious, then much of what the Catholic Reformation reaffirmed, including transubstantiation, human merit in salvation, indulgences, the Virgin Mary, and the network of saints, grounded Catholic intellects in habits of thought decidedly more keyed toward locating the immanent manifestation of the sacred in specific objects in the material world. These habits of sacred immanence could not but aid Cosimo's bid for political apotheosis.

CHAPTER I

The Familiarity of Terrestrial Divinity

WHEN COSIMO'S one and only war came to a close in
1555, the truce loosened the strings on his notoriously
thrifty purse just long enough to get the artistic work started
again in the Palazzo Signoria. Shortly thereafter, his favorite
painter and intimate friend Giorgio Vasari began painting over
Leonardo da Vinci's acclaimed masterpiece in the Salone del
Cinquecento, the large hall that had been built to house the
Great Council of the Florentine Republic.[1] The work was part
of a larger ongoing project, designed to turn the palace into a
suitable residence for the ducal couple, and it certainly showed
more delicacy of feeling for the Hall of the Great Council than
previous Medici projects, such as using it as a horse stable. Still,
it is likely that some republicans privately burned with resent-
ment as Vasari's brush covered, stroke by stroke, the images that
had once been meant to sanctify the great symbol of Florentine
republicanism, for the new schema was unquestionably meant
as a propaganda vehicle for the duke. However, when work on
the palazzo was finally completed in 1572, very little of it

FIGURE 1.1. Giorgio Vasari, *The Apotheosis of Cosimo.*
(Courtesy of Alinari/Art Resource, New York.)

would have passed for effective propaganda. The schema was so abstruse and disjointed that Vasari felt compelled to devote an entire volume to explaining the dizzyingly complex imagery of the program. There was, however, one exception to this absurd complexity. The central image in the tondo of the room bore the unmistakable portrait of Duke Cosimo himself. With his bare knee thrust out in the traditional posture of royal clemency, Cosimo peered down regally from the upper reaches of the cosmos as the goddess of Florence placed a wooden crown on his royal head (Figure 1.1).[2] Most visitors did not need to read Vasari's *Ragionamenti* to realize that this most unsubtle of political imagery, which he called the "key and conclusion to the whole work," had one purpose: to divinize Cosimo with the laurel of apotheosis, to cast him in the mold of a god.[3]

Such an attempt sounds audacious to modern ears. Indeed, as the historian Ernst Kantorwicz once remarked: "political mysticism . . . is exposed to the danger of losing its spell when taken out of its native surroundings."[4] Few components of early modern political theology are more exposed to that particular danger than claims of princely divinity. In this most ancient of conceits, the monarch was held to be a god on earth, whose power in the state was a microcosmic reflection of the divine powers that ruled over the universe. Though Christianity's insistence that there was just one God and that worship was owed to him alone seriously threatened to undermine the proposition altogether, Renaissance Christians' insistence on the dignity of creation in general and man in particular codified a far more wide-ranging concept of terrestrial divinity: the apotheosis of man himself. Indeed, man bore the image of the divine in his very being, and a divine destiny awaited him if only he could be raised up to participation in the divine life. This substitute divinity by participation is how medieval and Renaissance Christians made a god out of a man, and though they were often careful to stress the monotheistic unity of the Christian God's essence, they rarely refrained from conflating their own version of apotheosis with the conceits of antiquity or from drawing explicitly on the Roman monarchical tradition to claim godly status for the lords of the earth.[5]

Nevertheless, Cosimo's divinity was a very different kind of apotheosis from the kind claimed by Roman emperors.[6] Despite Vespasian's wry deathbed comments, in which the Roman emperor sarcastically remarked that he thought he was becoming a god, Roman oblations testified to a lively cult of ruler worship; and indeed, some of the less balanced emperors probably really believed themselves to be gods. After all, it would be much easier to be an incarnation of Apollo than the second coming of Christ. Cosimo certainly didn't believe himself to be either one. At times, his princely divinity was left safely in the realm of metaphor; at other times, it was inscribed in a more immanent view of the divine presence in the world. Quite often, the exact mechanics of the process were left conspicuously ambiguous. Whatever the case, his apotheosis was grounded in a local culture in which terrestrial divinity was a surprisingly humdrum affair, deeply inscribed in habits of thought far more widespread than the political arena. This chapter will argue that Cosimo's apotheosis was more easily sold to Florentines because apotheosis was already a long-standing motif in Florentine culture, a motif that potentially transformed any human into a god on earth.[7] While theologians supported the idea with scriptural passages, humanists quoted the ancients. Moreover, since the Eucharist transformed the laity into the body of Christ, the people of God became gods (in a pious sense) at least once a year and with increasing regularity as the Jesuits got their way on the issue of frequent communion. Indeed, though princely apotheosis was a new category, Cosimo's rhetoric was not even the first political apotheosis in Florence; earlier Medici had been called gods by their clients, and the republic itself had long been considered a holy thing. In the fifteenth century, even Archbishop Antoninus had claimed: "the common good of the republic is in a certain sense divine."[8] By the end of the Renaissance, the rhetoric was so diffuse it had become practically banal; saints and ancient heroes were divine, but so were doctors, artists, and magicians. In Florence, princely divinity was just one more addition to the pantheon, and a rather late one at that.

In Resemblance of the Divine Majesty: Cosimo as a Godlike Prince

Cosimo's artists had already conjured up evocations of divinity for him a number of times before Vasari put paint to the walls of the Palazzo Vecchio. Though political historians have generally overlooked this feature of Cosimo's rhetoric, art historians have found it far less easy to ignore, noting that Cosimo repeatedly appeared in the guise of the divinized Augustus and then, like Augustus, in the guise of Apollo as well, albeit in an appropriately allegorical sense.[9] When he entered Siena, he entered like a conquering Jesus riding into Jerusalem, the recently subdued populace waving the palm branches of victory.[10] On medals and engravings he appeared as the semidivine Hercules, laboring to restore the Tuscan state.[11] In his lushly designed gardens he was Neptune, striking his trident into the sea to bring water to the city.[12] Even Cosimo's family appeared in semidivine likeness. Craig Hugh Smyth has argued that Pontormo's portrait of Cosimo's mother was meant to evoke the Virgin Mary, while Gabrielle Langdon has elucidated evocations of divinity in the duchess Eleonora's portraiture.[13] Indeed, the visual evidence leaves little in the way of subtlety or ambiguity; Cosimo was never shy about ornamenting his visual propaganda with divine overtones, and art historians have paid attention.

With some notable exceptions, historians of ducal politics have not paid similar amounts of attention. Despite scholars' lack of interest in them, evocations of divinity were by no means buried in the duke's political, historical, and literary projects, for the medium of print did not limit itself to garbing the prince as a semidivine pagan deity. Whereas canvas and stone transformed Cosimo into an allegorical pagan god, paper and pen turned him into a simulacrum of the God of the universe. A 1547 work dedicated to Cosimo by a client priest-scholar set the tone: "We confess that there is only one God to whom the prince on earth bears resemblance, and thus, I say we must have princes on earth who resemble the divine power . . . in order to keep God in the people's minds."[14] Indeed, even as early as 1547, there was little question on what footing panegyrics to monarchy needed to be grounded. Ducal courtiers, academicians, humanists, and simple aspirants to ducal favor were not far behind in unoriginal repetition of the argument. A 1548 work dedicated to Cosimo and his son Ferdinand insisted that one needed "in [princes] to revere the highest God."[15] In his *Dialogus del Giusto Principe,* which he had revised from an earlier version and humbly laid at Cosimo's feet in 1550, the onetime republican, onetime exile, and always bankrupt Antonio Brucioli suddenly developed a taste for monarchical propaganda, interpolating the following into the revised version: "who does not know that the governance of a just and good prince surpasses all the other forms of governance of which one knows, conforming more to the manner in which God rules over the universe."[16] If we assume that Brucioli was writing with anything other than a mere mercenary pen here, then the ease with which he and so many former republicans could adopt formulas like this testifies to terrestrial divinity's grounding in the axioms of contemporary thought. Twelve years later, the same type of argument came from the pen of another of Cosimo's literati, Giambattista Gelli, a man whose shameless fawning over the prince was probably a good deal more sincere than Brucioli's, though ultimately stoked by the fact that offering his pen to Cosimo paid better than the cobbling trade for which he was otherwise destined.[17] Thus, Gelli's opinion comes as little surprise; he wrote: "As men are obliged to render honor to God, they must in the way that they best know and are able to always honor their prince, who is the simulacrum and true image of God."[18] In yet another work offered to the dedication-hungry Cosimo, the Florentine canon and Medici client Matteo Saminiati married ducal claims of sacral monarchy to absolutist papal claims, noting how appropriate it was that God left his church in the care of a monarch "in whose person the majesty and greatness of the creator is represented on earth. Indeed, all confess that monarchy is such a thing, a fact that is clearly proved from the proportion and similitude that it holds with the governance which God uses for ruling heaven; no one can deny that whatever participates more in that is nobler and more perfect than anything else."[19] The precedents for these arguments were many. They might have harkened all the way back to Plato or to Roman ruler worship. We might chase the paper, or papyrus as the case lay, all the way back to the fertile banks of the Tigris,

Euphrates, and Nile. The precedents may have been drawn from literature closer to hand: Patritius, Vergerio, Castiglione, Giles of Rome, and even Erasmus had allowed the prince something of the divine.[20] The idea's very ubiquity in almost every place except republican Florence makes any single source unlikely. However, it is significant that Cosimo's literati and artists adopted it for their own political purposes with little in the way of apology to what could only be considered a hostile and captive Florentine audience.

Moreover, treatises that divinized monarchy in the abstract were often delivered with saccharine odes to Cosimo's own rule. For instance, when Fabrini prefaced his own volume with the caveat that he had translated it "so that by reading it [Cosimo], as in a vivid and clear crystal, might see there all the holy virtues that heaven has given him and that he has amplified," readers would have been left with little doubt to whom Fabrini's more generalized abstractions were meant to be applied.[21] However, the rhetoric could be far more explicitly directed to Cosimo, even among the less ideologically committed. In a 1549 translation of Aristotle's *Politics,* the ducal functionary Bernardo Segni wrote: "One cannot deny that the Great God has made a great demonstration of his favor, having placed Florence under the same type of governance with which he governs and administers this universe."[22] This republican was no dyed-in-the-wool believer or even a sincere convert. An admirer of Machiavelli, Segni had followed Machiavelli's lead, trading in his republican credentials for a place at the Medici table and earning his bread from the scraps Cosimo threw to him, even though privately he had harsh words for Cosimo's government. Nevertheless, Segni's quote bears the mark of a republican-turned-monarchialist desperately seeking justification for changing his republican colors.[23] Again, the ease with which former republicans adapted themselves to the new ideology is rather striking.

It was not just Florentines who could be won over to such rhetorical flourishes. In a congratulatory panegyric, Leonardo Gini exalted Cosimo into the halls of princes, "who, though mortal, just like gods, preside over and likewise administer all things."[24] A eulogy written for Cosimo made much the same claim, exhorting his crusading order to continue to respect the Medici as their heads, since "the governance of the one is the most similar to God."[25] Indeed, explicitly divinizing Cosimo was never beyond the pale of acceptability.

Concerned as they were with questions of the universal, Cosimo's political writers were less likely to fawn over any particular prince than were his panegyrist poets, who relished the rhetoric of terrestrial divinity with a characteristic sense of overstatement that would have made Plato hanker to evict them from his republic. Fortunately for them, begging the dedicatee to show godlike mercy on the lowliness of the work dovetailed nicely with the false pretenses of humility required of all early modern writers. The Tuscan poet Michel Capri prefaced his volume accordingly, arguing that by prizing the work on the love with which it was offered, Cosimo would "make himself similar (in a certain way) to the heavenly and divine monarch, the great father of the uncreated and to his glorious splendor, to whom both the great and the little lights are acceptable, coming to him from us his tributaries to honor him, if they come from a heart enflamed."[26] The conceit was not limited to laics; the Carmelite poet Niccolò Trivigi made the argument in his own poetic homage to Cosimo's governance, claiming: "If it seems to your Lordship that the duty of lauding you has been too high and difficult an undertaking for my small and weak craft, remember that in every century the creator of the world is greatly pleased to be praised and made known by rude and low intellects."[27] Even Vasari was drawn to follow the divinizing logic of the poets, begging Cosimo to "Accept this my—rather your—book on the lives of the artists of *disegno,* and in likeness of the great God, look more on my soul and good intentions than on my work, taking from me willfully not what I would like to give or what I should give, but what I can give."[28] Indeed, it seems that dedications were as fertile ground for Cosimo's apotheosis as canvas or stone.

Moreover, in case anyone had missed the point in the dedication, the poetry itself was no less direct. Trivigi wrote:

> My soul is warmed by love all the day,
> And there a temple consecrated to your deeds is raised.
> Whence is my understanding alit, and set ablaze.
> By the worth of your deeds, for not but heat is given by
>   their ray,
> Through which sparkle, and show demonstrably
> The good of the highest God all visibly,
> Like in a crystal, one sees the sun, limpid and clear,
> In you the beauty of the universe appears.[29]

Other poets picked up the same concept. In a book of one hundred sonnets to Cosimo, Niccolò Martelli, who fired off praise poems with some frequency, frequently played on the same motif, penning this obsequious ode in praise of his patron:[30]

> How much of heaven's goodness
> Is glimpsed by the one who has seen
> My Cosimo's great, divine, and regal mien
> That greater blessing our age has not witness'd.[31]

In several other passages, Martelli bestowed the title "mio terrestre Dio" more explicitly.[32] But all this was to be expected. If more sober philosophers and historians could not be expected to refrain from bestowing divine honors on Cosimo, how could one restrain the hyperbole of the poets? Moreover, if we pull the lens away from Cosimo, we will see that ascribing divinity to people was so common in Renaissance Florence that panegyrists' pens turned to it almost instinctively when they were set to work to glorify the new Medici monarch.

Terrestrial Divinity: A Staple of Florentine Christian Humanism

Despite terrestrial divinity's rather dangerous tendency to slide into Pelagianism or overenthusiastic celebration of the heroes of antiquity, many found the rhetoric of terrestrial divinity easily reconcilable with monotheistic Christianity. The apotheosis of man had indisputably scriptural foundations, and neither men nor princes were ever understood to be anything other than gods by participation in the divine life. Moreover, it never really constituted a definitive break with the anthropology of the Christian Middle Ages. Fallen, sinful, miserable humanity and glorified, godlike humanity were understood to be not mutually exclusive but the end result of free choice; indeed, humanists and preachers toggled rapidly and effortlessly between descriptions of human misery and human dignity.[33] A sixteenth-century sermon that almost reads as a compendium of the preceding century's dignity-of-man literature paints just this sort of paradoxical picture. Dividing his topic into two parts, the anonymous preacher spent several minutes making the case for the utter misery of man before doing a volte-face and claiming: "The composition of man is the most admirable work that God has made."[34] The exempla he had used to prove man's misery were then turned inside out and used to prove man's excellence instead. If man came naked into the world to show that he came to suffer, then on the other hand, nature arranged his nudity to show the greatness of her artifice.[35] If man was born defenseless and weak, lacking the speed of a deer or the claws and teeth of the tiger, then on the other hand, man needed no defense but reason. Finally, if a continual war raged in the pit of man's being between his reason and his appetites, then on the other hand, the victory of reason might raise him up to divinity.[36] Indeed, far from posing an intractable dilemma, the paradox provided just the type of rhetorical game in which Christian humanists could revel.

Moreover, once the influential philosopher Marsilio Ficino had set to work on translating the Hermetic and Platonic corpus, the ideal found weighty authorities in the voices of antiquity. For instance, the Hermetic author had bequeathed this passage to posterity: "Now the Father of all Beings, being life and light, brought forth a Man similar to himself, whom he loved as his own child. For the Man was beautiful, reproducing the image of his Father, for it was indeed with his own form that God fell in love and gave over to him all his works."[37] Noting the similarities with biblical accounts of creation, humanists of the fifteenth and sixteenth centuries excitedly rushed to proclaim Hermes Trismegistus a prophet on the level of the ancient sibyls, a precursor to the advent of Christ. With impetuous haste, they frequently took to citing his authority on the proposition that man was "an animal to be honored and marvelously formed in the image of God."[38] Having incorrectly dated the early Gnostic text to the time of Moses, the humanists took Trismegistus to be the founder of the Platonic school, since Plato had evinced several similar conceptions about the divinity of man's soul.[39]

Ficino's own glosses on Plato were probably even more influential in this regard. On this account, he had written in the *proemio* to his *Platonic Theology:* "[Plato] considers man's soul to be like a mirror in which the image of the divine countenance is readily reflected; and in his eager hunt for God, as he tracks down every footprint, he everywhere turns hither and thither to the form of the soul. . . . So anyone who reads very carefully the works of Plato . . . will discover among many other matters two of the utmost importance: the worship of God with piety and understanding and the divinity of souls."[40] On these twin foundations, one of them a mistake, quattrocento humanists had laid the basis for the ideal of human apotheosis, and the

Florentine Catholic Reformation adopted this Renaissance tradition as its own, as Cosimo's culture found itself deeply enmeshed in Ficino's questions, sources, and ideas.[41]

Ficino and Pico's circle had almost turned the Platonic and the Hermetic corpus into a new canon, finding in them authoritative classical support for terrestrial divinity. Less adventuresome spirits had only to turn to more familiar sacred books, for Genesis reported that on the sixth day, God sculpted man in his own image and likeness. Thus, humanist apotheosis found a complementary tradition among religious writers, who cited the relevant passage in Genesis with astonishing frequency.[42] Indeed, it was considerably difficult for Renaissance laypersons to escape a sermon or devotional tract without finding at least one reference to man's semblance to the divine.[43] This did not merely mark the influence of paganism on Christian thought; theologians found plenty of perfectly orthodox uses for the conceit. For instance, one preacher used the concept to underscore the wickedness of sin, arguing that the sinner offended not only God and neighbor "but the divine image that is in himself."[44] For another thinker, terrestrial divinity proved the necessity of the real presence in the Eucharist, since as a being with both angelic and animal nature, man needed nourishment both corporal and spiritual.[45] Even a preacher attempting to compete with Luther's pessimistic anthropology could write that man's debt to God was all the greater since God had made man's soul in his own image.[46]

Indeed, the Christian Bible provided its own perfectly orthodox and authoritative justification for terrestrial divinity, but just as often, humanist arguments were advanced pari passu with Christian arguments, with preachers calling on classical philosophy to support scriptural passages and humanist scholars calling on Christian theology to support the claims of the ancients. One anonymous sermon argued: "In the marvelous composition of man, more than in the great edifice of heaven and more than in the power of the elements and more than in the order of the universe, the excellence of God's wisdom is made manifest; as in a most clear mirror, one sees in man the being of God himself and the other secrets of his divinity and Trinity. Part of this was seen by the ancient wise men with the natural light [of reason], since contemplating thus, Hermes Trismegistus said what a great miracle is man, in which great things are seen. And Aristotle believed that man was the end to which all things referred."[47] Plato, Aristotle, Trismegistus, Pliny, Pythagoras: all could be called on to support the godliness of man and the conceit drawn from scripture. Moreover, if preachers were calling on classical models to support theological arguments, then the reverse was equally true, for classicizing humanists were not loath to call on theology. For example, even though Plato had spoken of more than one god, Francesco Vieri found he could use the doctrine of Christian apotheosis to reconcile Plato's paganism with Christian monotheism. To this end, Vieri wrote: "Although in the Timaeus Plato speaks of other gods besides the Father of the World, he does so because he esteemed that they were Gods in virtue of their participation in his eternal and spiritual nature, in similitude to his goodness, and in their ability to enjoy the paternal heredity. Thus, saith the divine scripture that through Jesus Christ the power is given to us to make ourselves Gods and sons of God, first, in the life here below by similitude and then in the hereafter through fruition of the paternal goods."[48] Here the order is reversed; Christ comes to the defense of Plato, and the doctrine of terrestrial divinity is used as a bridge to span the gulf that divided polytheistic Plato and monotheistic Christians.

Sixteenth-century humanists were quite aware that they were not the first thinkers to attempt to reconcile Platonic and Christian philosophy. A very old and very authoritative voice could be conjured up from late antiquity to give sanction to the entire project. Recalling Ficino's own arguments, Vieri declared Plato "the most conformable to the Christian and the divine, a fact that is amply demonstrated by Saint Augustine, one of the first theologians of our holy and Catholic Church in his work *On the City of God.*"[49] Augustine had gone quite a ways in molding the concept of terrestrial divinity into a Christian form. In his *De Trinitate*, the African doctor argued that if man's soul was truly made in the image of God, it must bear the image of the creator, namely, a triune structure. Augustine found the appropriate structure in the powers of the soul: memory, intellect, and will.[50] As Augustine's work was read with relish throughout the period, his arguments were repeated with similar abandon. Many of the humanists of the quattrocento had found it an appealing argument, and not even Savonarola, as pessimistic toward formal learning as he was, shied away from making the connection between the human soul and the Trinity, recasting the argument into peripatetic language and arguing that man is like the Trinitarian God because all creatures are in some ways similar to their cause.[51] In the beginning of the sixteenth century, Savonarola's disciple Antonio Dolciati echoed the master's quotation with these words to his own congregation: "The image of the Holy Trinity is found more expressly in the rational creature, that is, in man. Because when God wished to create man, he said that which is written in the first chapter of Genesis, 'Let us make man in our own image and likeness.' This image can be considered in three ways and the first is how it is naturally formed. And as the Holy Father Augustine says in his *De Trinitate*, 'though our mind is not of the same nature as God, it is there that one must seek the image of him, of whom nothing is greater.' Now our soul is one thing and has three powers of which one is not the other: memory, intellect, and will."[52] We find the same argument in an anonymous sermon delivered toward the middle of the century: "There is nothing that so well represents another thing as man represents God, and mainly in his soul, which is incorruptible, immortal, simple, without any composition, and all in one being, just like God, and in his soul there are three powers (memory, will, intellect) that represent the Most Holy Trinity."[53] In another anonymous sermon delivered

around the same time, the author claimed that when God created man he said: "let him be my image, and adorn him with
three powers: memory, intellect and will."[54] Indeed, hearing the
words of Augustine on the lips of religious and theologians
should surprise no one, but he was on the lips of Cosimo's humanists as well. For example, Cosimo's secretary Domenico Mellini argued for the nobility of the human soul thus: "the human
soul has been created spiritual and eternal by the King of the
Stars in his own image, with three powers (memory, intellect,
will), since he is one essence and one real and true god in three
persons, one and the other truly distinct."[55] What did intellectuals and humanists find so compelling about Augustine's Trinitarian anthropology? No doubt, locating man's divinity in the
triune powers of the soul dovetailed nicely with many of their
own concerns; it was more specifically the last two powers of the
soul with which they were most interested: man's intellect and
his will. Those attributes made man godlike in two of the humanists' favorite areas of human activity: reason and will, especially the will to exercise virtue.

Intellect, Reason, and Wisdom:
The *Communanza* of God and Man

As noted, the powers of man's soul were three: memory, intellect, and will.[56] Since this tripartite soul was thought to be an
image of the Trinity, the use of memory, intellect, and will was
thought to be a participation in the divine nature. This came
with certain caveats, for it emphatically did not include intellect
used for free speculation. Since God was unerring, only reason
exercised rightly could be considered divine. Most early modern intellectuals continued to deny a distinction between religious truth and the truths to be gleaned from natural philosophy;
moreover, they did not doubt that philosophy was primarily
ordered to lead humans to knowledge of God, to inform man's
will of the true nature of the universe, and to guide humankind

toward eternal beatitude. If pagan philosophy could be used as a preparation for attaining truth, so be it. If not, it was to be discarded as folly and error.

Under these conditions, there were no limits to the praise of intellect. There is little surprise that a scholar and medic like Baccio Baldini exalted those who "live in accordance with the intellect, by which man alone is made a kinsman with the divine."[57] However, the point has even more weight to it in the mouth of the age's harshest critic of the human mind: the philosopher Simone Portio. Portio, a Neapolitan Medici client, was both one of Cosimo's readers at the Studio of Pisa and an avowed disciple of Pomponazzi's claim that there was little to separate the human mind from that of the animals; nevertheless, Portio penned this perfectly Platonic prose in 1551: "if the senses are conquered and thrown to earth and the intellect reigns, then the man becomes free from the senses and as the Platonists affirm, almost like a God."[58] Portio then called on Aristotle in defense of Plato's point, allowing Portio to assert categorically: "The nature of man has been called divine because it is endowed with intellect, which is unmixed and divine; those who live according to this intellect do not merit to be called mere men, but friends of God and his most close kinsmen."[59]

For more theologically minded intellects, the ideal of friendship with God was transmuted into the more appropriately Christian category of beatitude. Moreover, Christian beatitude drew its possibilities from man's intellect just as surely as the more exclusively philosophical model had. Moreover, this Christian apotheosis-by-intellect dovetailed nicely with midcentury rejections of Luther's denigration of natural reason. The Florentine canon Francesco Diacceto borrowed an argument from Aquinas when he said in a sermon: "man is in potential to attain the knowledge of the blessed, which consists in seeing God. Thus, he is ordered to his end inasmuch as he is a rational creature created in the image of God."[60] The classicizing Franciscan bishop of Bitonto, Cornelio Musso, who was in Florence in the

1550s, had the same idea. In one of his more important sermons, he claimed: "in order to make us superior to all the animals, the highest father of human nature gives us that divine part of reason which makes us equal or at least similar to the angels."[61] The psalms had declared man to be little less than a god, Christian theology had long made man's soul or spirit the godlike part, and classicizing scholars would most frequently locate divinity in the second power of the soul, the ability to reason.

It was philosophers who had attempted to make a god out of Cosimo and philosophers who attempted to make a god of intellect, so there is little surprise that the same philosophers would bestow the accolades of divinity on the purveyors of reason too, that is, on themselves. One humanist courtier wrote that philosophy linked man to God through wisdom, "the knowledge of things divine and human, in which is contained the common nature (*communanza*) of God and of men."[62] Another quoted Augustine saying: "to philosophize is a divine thing."[63] With that most Platonic of conceits echoing in their ears, the philo-Platonists in Cosimo's circle felt quite justified in prefixing Augustine and his Greek mentor's name with the divine honors.[64] Cosimo's *protomedico,* Baccio Baldini, explained: "Plato, the Athenian, was a philosopher so highly revered among the ancients that he was rightly called divine by them."[65] Moreover, the divine honors bestowed on Plato and Augustine could even be won for philosophers closer at hand. Filippo Sassetti gave just this kind of the praise to the first auditor of the realm, Lelio Torelli, remarking in a funeral oration that his own tear-filled eyes only wished to see the dearly departed "image of the father of reason" sitting among them in the Florentine academy.[66]

This is the intellectual substratum of the Florentine penchant for prefixing philosophers' names with the word *divus.* An offshoot of this ideal made the artist a kind of god as well, since as Vasari pointed out, God was the first artist, and all those imitating the book of nature were just following in his wake.[67] Indeed, if the institution of the principate had no monopoly on terrestrial divinity, then Cosimo himself had no monopoly on divine honors. Any outstanding intellect might win them.

Christomimesis, Sanctity, and Virtue

Renaissance Florentines' fascination with the divinity of humanity did not end with the celebration of the intellect. Reason was primarily ordered to illuminating the other divine attribute of man, the will. Gualandi may have followed Augustine in asserting that "philosophy is a divine thing," but this was only, so the quote ended: "because it orders man to beatitude."[68] In the same spirit the Platonist Verino wrote, in direct imitation of Ficino: "all the philosopher's acts and all his speculation need in the end to be directed to the divine cult of that Lord from whom we have received philosophy, just as we have received all other gifts."[69] Whether treated by classicizing humanist or no, philosophy was still the handmaid to the queen of the sciences: theology. Moreover, if the *communanza* of God and man consisted in reason, then this friendship was perfected by Augustine's third attribute of divinity: free will exercising virtue.

Platonists and Christians found this yet another area of common ground, for in both traditions, virtue was linked to freedom, freedom linked to the will, the will linked to the soul, and the soul linked to the divinity. As Baldini made the case: "The free will is a property of man, and it is a form and perfection that we have from God and from nature. In the sacred scripture we read that when God wanted to create man he said, 'Let us make man in our image and likeness.' Just as nothing can violate or force the will of God, so nothing can force the will of man."[70] It was in freedom that man was created in the image of God and by the free exercise of the will in virtue that he could be made like god, liberated from the determinism of matter and body. The argument was not of course unique to Florence, but it was peculiarly important in Florentine culture, for the influential Pico della Mirandola had made the case in his *Oratio Dignitatis Hominis* nearly a half century before, and the affirmation lived on as a type of manifesto of the Renaissance. The crescendo and résumé of the argument went like this:

> O great liberality of God the father, great and to be admired the felicity of man, to whom is given the ability to have what he chooses and to be what he wants. As soon as they are born, the brute animals bring with them (as Lucullus says) from the womb of their mother whatever they will possess. The higher spirits either from the beginning or soon after are that which they will be for all eternity. At his birth, the father gives man the seed of every kind of life and every type of action. He will develop that seed as he grows and will carry its fruit in himself. If vegetative, he will be like a plant; if sensual, he will be like the brutes; if rational, he will end up a celestial animal; if he lives according to the intellect, he will be an angel and son of God. And if content with the fate of no creature, he will remove himself to the center of his own unity and be made one spirit with God, in the solitary darkness of the father who is set up over all, he will surpass everything.[71]

Pico's gigantic intellectual status assured this argument's continuing popularity. For instance, one midcentury preacher paraphrased the great humanist's claim thus: "Man has all things in himself; thus, he is free to be what he pleases. If he does nothing, he is like a rock; if he gives himself to the pleasures of the flesh, he is like a brute animal; and if he so desires, he can be made like an Angel, contemplating the face of the father, and it is in his will to be made so excellent that he be numbered among those to whom God says: gods you are."[72] Closer to Cosimo's court, Baldini made much the same case, arguing: "If one conquers his evil natural inclinations with the liberty of his will, he is above fate, completely lord of himself, and similar to God. However, if he lets himself be conquered by natural inclinations and obeys them, he becomes the slave of fate and by his own hand loses the liberty of his will, reducing himself to the level of the animals without reason."[73] Later in his *Panegyric to Clemency* he expanded the argument, arguing that when man has been "liberated by the purgative virtues from all perturbations, receiving inside of himself the forms of the naturals things, then looking at himself he understands himself to be similar to God."[74] The ducal functionary Gelli expressed his opinion of heroic and supernatural virtue in the same cultural parlance, as that "which raises men above the human condition and makes them participate in the divine."[75]

Humanists were not the only ones stressing the dignity of man's free will; this humanist discourse was paralleled by a similar tradition among ecclesiastical writers. In the preceding century Francesco Patritius, the bishop of Gaeta and friend to the humanist Pope Pius II, had written: "God is the highest good and the author of every good, and the end of man is none other if not to approach God by similitude, which one can only do with virtue; whence, the stoics are well to say that between God and man there is a friendship given birth by virtue."[76] Thus, the equation of Pico's idea with Christian ideals of beatitude and sanctity was not long in coming, as virtue was stressed as an intermediate means to beatitude. If the dominant spirituality of the day consisted in exhorting pious Christians to imitate the footsteps of the man/god Christ, then this exhortation rested on a theandric foundation, which insisted that God "orders his creatures to beatitude, whom he has created in his image and likeness," and that "the image of God in us asks that we live as Gods on earth."[77] Even Savonarola was captured by the rhetoric of terrestrial divinity, ascribing it to the saints John the Baptist and Paul by claiming that these two were "almost like God[s] on earth."[78]

Indeed, this theological version of apotheosis was a cherished part of Renaissance thought; as the century wore on, its importance only grew as thinkers picked it up and used it as a stick to fend off Reformation opponents. The preacher Musso used it to defend the Catholic doctrine of infused grace and real justification against the Lutheran concept of forensic justification, claiming: "As God took on the pollution of human nature, not outwardly, and not just in appearance or opinion, but really took on the flesh and the soul of a man, just so, the justified, if he becomes a son of God by adoption, is exalted to the divine nature and is deified."[79] Though Counter-Reformation theologians like Musso stressed God's grace rather than will and virtue as the primary agents of deification, not all writers were so careful. The slippage here between classical versions of apotheosis by virtue and Christian versions of sanctity could dangerously skirt the line between orthodoxy and Pelagianism.[80] Even Girolamo Seripando, quite wary of the whole rhetoric of terrestrial divinity, granted that virtue could make one a semigod.[81] In one of his sermons he argued: "The heroes and semigods venerated and so celebrated by the ancients as superior to other men and as saints at a certain grade of divinity (as is written of Hercules or Romulus) won such honor and praises neither by nobility or great riches, but through marvelous works made in benefit, not for their houses and their families, but for all mankind, and through the heights of heroic virtue, with which one is raised from the earth and in turn raises the common condition of other men."[82] The slippage between Christian sanctity and classical apotheosis was more than occasional or accidental. The one was explicitly conflated with the other, by no one more confusedly than by Gelli, who argued that men of superior virtue were, "called by Gentiles demigods or Heroes, and by the Christians, Saints and blesseds."[83] Christian saints and pagan heroes thus found themselves strange bedfellows in early Counter-Reformation thought. Indeed, long before Cosimo's humanists had begun crowning him with the laurel of apotheosis, Florentine culture was already familiar with this other type of apotheosis: the divinity of the Christian saint, or perhaps slightly troubling to more inflexibly minded Catholics, the divinity of the classical semigod.

Apotheosis in Sacramental Theology

Christian scholars may have found their prime source for the doctrine of terrestrial divinity in Genesis, but that was not the only scriptural passage that could by mustered in favor of it. Frequent references were made to the Gospel of John and his claim that "to whomever would accept Jesus and believe in his name, he gives the power to be made sons of God," as well as to Galatians and its claim of divine sonship by adoption.[84] Theological, Christological, and soteriological considerations were paramount here, but preachers readily addressed the message to their flocks in simple terms. "God," one midcentury preacher claimed in a representative statement, "through the merits of his savior son has given you this most great and precious gift, so that by this you become consorts and participants in the divine nature."[85] The cathedral canon Francesco Diacceto put the matter thus: "We say that we are particularly his children because we have received him through faith and obedience, and he has given to us a particular power of becoming his children through adoption."[86] From Antoninus on, a bevy of local preachers reminded Florentine audiences of their own divine sonship so frequently that the idea was never far from a devout listener's earshot, maintaining its place as a centerpiece of Florentine theology in sermons, devotional tracts, controversial literature, confessionals, and other religious works.[87] Moreover, the matter was not just one of abstract or historical speculation on the nature of the incarnation and the saving act of grace; for Catholics, both those moments were immediately present, immanent in the waters of baptism.

However, if baptism and faith gave each Christian a sort of substitute divinity by adoption, the reception of the Eucharist restructured man's being in far more profound ways. It goes almost without saying that Counter-Reformation theologians reaffirmed the real presence of Christ in the Eucharist, but spiritual guides also increasingly informed the laity that they were what they ate. In the words of one Florentine religious thinker, in the Eucharist, "man dresses himself in divinity," in a sacrament that "changes man into God."[88] Or as another preacher put it, "this food is spiritual, celestial, and divine, and because it is the food of our spirit, worthily taking it makes us spiritual, celestial and divine."[89] The local humanist and Petrarchan scholar Lelio Bonsi claimed that the Eucharist was God's greatest gift because by taking it, "we become the same thing as the body of Christ . . . there is no doubt that through this grace and communication of the body and blood of our lord, we transform ourselves into himself."[90] On these grounds, Christian humanists could again appeal to the authority of Augustine, quoting him as saying "whoever eats of me, you will not change me into yourself, but rather you will be changed into me."[91] The Jesuit doctrine of frequent communion gave a gentle push to the rhetoric. Whereas the Jesuits' traditionalist opponents viewed consumption of the Eucharist as the reward of a holy life, the Jesuits argued for frequent communion as an aid to virtue.[92] Thus, the champions of frequent communion had an interest in emphasizing the sacrament's transformative aspects. As it became clear that the Counter-Reformation aimed to match the Reformation blow for blow and that it would highlight rather than downplay theological differences, the practice of vesting sacral power in the Eucharist only heightened.

Moreover, just as the more general forms of terrestrial divinity could be extended specifically to the prince, the philosopher, the artist, or the saint, sacramental divinity could be extended as a special case to the priest. When Florentines were told that Cosimo was a god or a lieutenant of god because he held the place of god in the state, it would have sounded vaguely familiar since the same claim had long been made for the clerical estate, divine beings because they held the Almighty's place in confession. Those confessing their sins were encouraged to see their priest as the living image of God, acting in the person of Christ. Frequent were the exhortations to go to one's confessor as the "vicar and lieutenant of Jesus Christ."[93] As the self-proclaimed hammer of heretics Lorenzo Davidico noted, the priest needed to keep his eyes on Christ crucified: "whose place he holds on earth."[94] Thus, the laity were encouraged to act as if they were confessing not to a man but directly to God, or at the very least to "be attentive that in the sacrament they are in the presence of God, and that one makes confession, not to man alone, but to God first, and then the one who holds the place of God."[95] Again, Jesuit spirituality supplied the impetus for a renewed emphasis on confession, though Savonarola had already anticipated the Counter-Reformation in promoting both frequent confession and frequent communion.[96] Moreover, in both cases the Renaissance ideal of apotheosis found a new skin in a new religious program, for the heirs of the Renaissance found little difficulty in tying the Renaissance ideal of apotheosis to a rigidly Catholic understanding of grace, redemption, and beatitude.

His Hand in His Work: The Divinization of Nature

Terrestrial divinity lived in the Florentine imagination in more than just its princely form, but what was the relationship between princely divinity and the other more general kinds under examination? In fact, there was little qualitative difference it seems, for sanctal, classical, and political apotheosis spilled from the pens of thinkers with little distinction. In a work dedicated to Cosimo, Frate Archangelo, an avowedly Picinian philosopher, defended the ideal of apotheosis thus: "In the Psalter, God is called lord of the gods. God is thus one in essence but many in participation. In another place, the same prophet (David) says: I say you are gods and sons of the most high. When explaining this, Christ said, 'You are Gods, who by the word of God were made.' Elsewhere, Jacob says, 'he brought us forth by the word of truth, and they are gods by participation and by the anointing of divinity.' Then in John it is written 'he gave them power to be made sons of God.' As Aristotle says in his *Ethics,* one is a God by the excellence of virtue. And the same is written about the judges in Exodus, because they hold the place of God."[97] Frate Archangelo included here each of the various versions of apotheosis. More to the point, this monastic author viewed them all as different manifestations of the same phenomenon: godhood by participation. There is no sense that political divinity is in any way special or different from the many other kinds under examination.

Generalized human divinity and princely divinity had more in common than that; indeed, both forms served the same end: to reveal the inner nature of God by the contemplation of his works. One midcentury author explained the dynamic with a metaphor lifted from Pico. He claimed that on completing the construction of a city, an ancient ruler would erect a statue of his own likeness somewhere near the center in order to show everyone who had built the city. God had done the same thing in his creation of the world, so followed the argument, breathing his own image and likeness into man before placing him in the center of creation. Man was God's marker. Man was his statue.[98] At least one of Cosimo's writers made a strikingly similar claim for monarchy: "Everyone can see that the principate has more similitude with the celestial reign than any other form of government; it was left by God on earth in likeness of the celestial court, so that all we mortals might better understand his greatness and incomprehensible power."[99] If humanity in general revealed God as pure intellect and sublime virtue, the prince highlighted God's immense power. Both claims took their starting point from an immanent view of the creator's essence in his own work, God's desire as the divine artist to leave something of his own being in the works of his hands. Thus, the

Catholic reaffirmation of sacred immanence located in specific material objects was an essential underpinning of monarch sacrality. Moreover, the idea of man as a simulacrum of God was itself only part of an even more general search for the footprints of the creator in all of creation.

The argument drew its force from a common epistemological assumption: that humans ascended to knowledge of invisible, spiritual realities through the visible signs of creation.[100] Of course, this was classically Platonic, and Vieri put into Plato's mouth the quotation "one is not able to rise to knowledge of god in this life but in likenesses."[101] But if this idea had an impeccably Platonic pedigree, it was nevertheless shared by the Scholastics. The Scholastically trained Dante, for instance, argued in favor of it in the third canto of the *Paradisio,* and it was primarily on Dante's authority that Cosimo's humanist Domenico Mellini claimed: "it is through the visible creatures that man knows the invisible."[102] If the prince was an image of the divinity left on earth in order that one might better know the power and greatness of the celestial monarch, he was but one image out of many. With Dante clearly in mind, Mellini even supposed that the carnal beauty of the human face had the same function:

> The form is that perfection which truly is the essence of beauty and almost is painted on the human body, and this is a ray of the divine bounty and a splendor that descends from it, which shows itself on the material that is prepared for it and makes of everything around light and desirous with that flower and that vivacity and that grace which he himself produces in the human face and in all the other created things. He brings forth this beauty and enraptures to itself everything that is able to know and understand, so that by benefit of it they be made participants in the divine goodness, which is their true and ultimate perfection. There is no need to remain in earthly beauty and earthly goods, as if they were the highest felicity; from the beauty and goodness of things below it is necessary to raise oneself up through the

intellect to that highest good, which is loved and desired before all things. Rather one should use the things below as a type of ladder that leads to the contemplation of the maker.[103]

The argument was echoed by another of Cosimo's Platonic humanists, Flaminio Nobili, in a similar tract dedicated to the duke himself.[104] Whereas Mellini was seeking the secret alchemy that would transmute his sexual impulses into higher spiritual feelings, Nobili was far more circumspect in using the female face and body as a stairway to heaven. However, he did not, therefore, deny the common wisdom of using visible markers to ascend to the divine. He wrote: "I do not know how necessary of a ladder is feminine beauty to ascend to divine love; it seems to me a far more secure way can be found to the knowledge of the highest beauty by considering the miraculous and ordered effects of nature, the stable movements of the heavens, the vigor of light, and the perfection of the universe."[105] Indeed, sense experience was ladder to the divine not only for humanists but for theologians as well. For instance, the preacher Visdomini affirmed nature's relation to the divine in a slightly less erotic way when he argued that God had made the world "to call it, by natural imitation, to uncover the being of God with its own being, uncovering God's innumerable and infinite virtues with the little semblances and vestiges that serve for it, so that as by a visible ladder, the fortunate contemplators can ascend to know part of the invisible divine virtue, as (for example) his beauty is seen in the sun, his force in fire, his sweetness in air, his stability in earth. Just as God in heaven alone knows his creations on earth, one discovers, as best one can, through his creatures the virtues of the creator."[106] There was here an explicit affirmation of the dignity of matter and its relation to the divine, which the Catholic Reformation sealed on religious consciousness.[107] In a world in which the entire created order served no higher purpose than raising the human mind to the knowledge of the divinity, casting the prince as an image of God was no difficult feat.

Putting the Familiarity of Terrestrial Divinity to Work

So popular a motif was terrestrial divinity that Cosimo's literati did not limit their divinizing panegyrics to his role as prince. If philosophers could win the plaudit of god on earth, then Cosimo's literati would turn the largely unlettered duke into a philosopher, a purveyor of nature's healing secrets in his patronage of medical research. If classical heroes and saints could dwell in the empyrean realm, then Cosimo would be a saint or hero on the old mold. Moreover, if the suffering Eucharistic Christ stood as the quintessence of the man/God ideal, then suffering Cosimo would be the visible means of sanctification for his own subjects. Not only did preexisting categories of terrestrial divinity make Cosimo's new princely divinity easier to swallow, the new princely form ended up swallowing the preexisting categories in the bargain.

When Cosimo's literati made him into a philosopher monarch, striding about the Palazzo Vecchio as if it was some kind of Olympian academy, they were certainly evoking the ideal of the Platonic monarch that the Medici had been cultivating for more than one generation.[108] In his characteristic idealism, Ficino had sought to mold Lorenzo the Magnificent into just this type of Platonic king, a project that later Medici must have known about.[109] However, the brilliant Lorenzo played the part a good deal better than Cosimo could ever aspire to, since Cosimo bore little resemblance to an intellectual. He had to win his philosopher god credentials vicariously instead. This is why his panegyricists lauded his patronage of the Studio of Pisa and the Florentine Academy so profusely and why he licensed a ducal printer to cultivate his image as a patron of letters.[110] It was to speak to this image that he invited Ignazio Danti to decorate the walls of the *sala carte* at the Palazzo Vecchio with maps of the entire known world, a project emphasizing Cosimo's advancement of scientific knowledge.[111] If the *sala* was perhaps too private and too subtle to demonstrate his promotion of reason and philosophy, there was nothing private or subtle about the whale carcass he had publicly dissected just outside the palace in the late 1540s, a very public demonstration of his knowledge of and mastery over the natural world.[112]

Philosophy had wide-ranging connotations in Florence, extending to practical as well as theoretical knowledge. Thus, natural philosophy included one of Cosimo's favorite projects, the medicinal use of alchemy. His scientists concocted various brews in the foundry he established in his own palazzo, and he dispatched them across the European continent. Fancying himself a type of expert, he took special care in licensing the apothecary guild, and in 1544 he established a chair of botany at the Studio of Pisa. In free moments, he descended into the foundry himself to lend a hand in experiments or personally copy and annotate alchemical recipes.[113] The confluence of old Medici ideals and Cosimo's personal interests and ambitions constituted a perfect storm; a little wordplay on the Medici surname linked Cosimo to the healing profession, and a few rhetorical flourishes made him a kind of medic of the state, with a dose of the traditional theology that made Christ a medic of the soul.[114] The end result turned the medical profession into a divine occupation and the medic/prince Cosimo into an image of Christ whose superior knowledge healed the wounds and diseases in natural bodies as his superior science in government healed the wounds in the body politic. Here Cosimo was on familiar Medici ground; earlier Medici, especially Leo X, had already attempted to link themselves to the healing powers of the Christian magi and the Hermetic figure of Ficino's *prisca theologia*.[115] Cosimo's literati were not nearly so subtle about the implications; his own *protomedico* drew the connection most vigorously, arguing that Cosimo's patronage of medicine was "truly worthy of Great princes, since more than any other thing it makes them similar to God. In this way they do the greatest possible benefit for men, rendering them healthy and conserving them in that health without which they cannot truly enjoy any of the gifts that God has given them."[116] If this was too potent a metaphor, another eulogist substituted a pagan one, claiming that everyone came seeking healing from Cosimo as if to an Aesculapian god.[117] Perhaps Cosimo's medical credentials sufficed as a substitute for his lack of thaumaturgic powers. Certainly, he was not the only early modern ruler to draw parallels between healing real physical bodies and healing metaphorical political ones.[118] Alchemy allowed him to play the part of Christ medic via the more scientific and more distinctively Florentine brand of alchemy.[119] Either way, the association certainly allowed princely divinity to swallow up the divinity of the philosopher.

As intellect was ordered to cultivating virtue, virtue vaulted the philosopher into the ranks of godhood as well. Cosimo's literati understood this concept from the start. Evocations of heroic virtue adorned the decorations for Cosimo's wedding festivities, while the closing play highlighted the theme by asserting the rather unproven claim that he ruled his land with "not human but celestial virtues."[120] The fashion never died out. Indeed, the language of heroic and divine virtue decorated almost all of the panegyrics written at his passing. In recognition of his virtue, Scipione Ammirato called Cosimo not a human but a "divine prince," while Bandini claimed: "[his] divine and immortal virtue could not remain hidden."[121] Betti summed the conceit up nicely, writing: "Considering the weakness of my abilities, I do not know how to title him without saying much less than his valor merits, unless I imitate those ancient Spartans who, when they greatly admired some person, called and reputed him divine; if this was said in those times about many great heroes, one can reasonably say it also of the Most Serene Grand Duke. However, those men were admired particularly for some one virtue, but he has collected them all in himself in such a manner that his soul seems that it was the very tree of virtues that are called heroic and divine."[122] Betti proffered this opinion with some (probably feigned) reluctance, but he was at any rate making an appeal to antiquity that was neither new nor objectionable to his listeners. Cosimo's commissioned artwork had already represented him as the heroic avatar of the virtues of ages past: as the divinized Augustus, the furiously anti-Gallic and attractively republican Camillus, the god Apollo, and the demigod Hercules.[123]

The trend even manifested itself in themes ripped from the Old Testament. At various times, Cosimo took on the likeness of Moses, Joseph, Solomon, or David.[124] Here again appears the Renaissance tendency to let the rhetoric of heroic virtue slide into the category of Christian sanctity. For instance, Francesco Verino claimed that the duke was not only, "through his benefice and for all his virtues, divine" but that through his, "true and highest religion, was most holy."[125] In this, Verino was echoing a familiar refrain; Cosimo's client scholars had long been smuggling the language of sanctity and the sacred into all sorts of genres, including praise poems, panegyrics, and even legislation.[126] Indeed, his image lived in the space between ancient hero and Christian saint that the Italian Renaissance found so strangely easy to reconcile.

If pious Christians proffered suggestions of Cosimo's sanctity with trepidation, how much more dexterity did the panegyrist require when comparing him to the Eucharist? How could the prince be equated so directly with the body of Christ without crossing the line into blasphemy? It was a difficult proposition, but one of the more adventurous of Cosimo's panegyrists eventually found his way to it. The argument was laid out delicately, without explicit reference to Eucharistic theology:

> If we consider the matter closely, we will see that the prince is like a second God, and we will know that as God wanted to ransom us with his blood and to liberate his elect, just so, the prince liberates the republic from all the scourges that

hover over it with his thoughts, difficulties, unease, and continuous dangers of death. Moreover, he castigates and corrects the republic, setting it on the road that leads to heavenly glory. Thus, we must declare with Hesiod that the prince is the companion of God, and as God gives to each blessed soul its place in heaven, so the prince leads the people to heaven through ways that are pleasing to God. Since the matter stands thus, should I not call the Prince a god on earth, just as the Roman Senate called those emperors gods who had won glory by some important deed?[127]

As Fabrini still thought the state to be a mere way station on the route to eternity, the prince's most important job was to help procure the eternal salvation of his subjects. Thus, the hardships accompanying the task could, at least superficially, be compared to Christ's saving act on the cross. The prince then became the "visible" means of sanctification through his suffering. However, everyone certainly equated the visible means of sanctification with the Eucharist, which in sixteenth-century Florentine religious thought was primarily conceived as the extension of the sacrifice of the cross through space and time. Indeed, Cosimo's own sculptor had given eloquent testimony to the association when shortly after the Council of Trent's decree on the Eucharist, he began sculpting a *Christo Morto* to be placed on the high altar of Florence's cathedral.[128] In Fabrini's argument, then, the suffering servant-prince could become Eucharistic in function, if not in essence, and Cosimo's princely rhetoric could steal this last and most difficult independent category of terrestrial divinity, just as it had stolen the others.

Conclusion

It has been the argument of this chapter that Cosimo found it easier to pass himself off as a terrestrial divinity because the line between man, god, and man/god was already rather blurry in Renaissance Florence. Florence was not the only such place, especially in Renaissance Italy. In fourteenth-century Naples, King Robert had promoted himself as a divine ruler.[129] In Sforza Milan, the juridical traditions of the "mystical body" and the humanist co-optation of Roman ruler worship had made Galeazzo Sforza into his own type of divine king a century before Cosimo.[130] In republican Venice, Doge Foscari had become a quasi-divine figure as he took on himself the likeness of the state.[131] Of course, the Spanish, English, and French kings all had apotheoses of their own as well. Thus, the very fact that Cosimo was so explicitly equated with god may have been unusual for a political head in Florence, but it was not unusual for Italy or Europe in general.[132] Thus, it would be easy to read Cosimo's apotheosis as nothing more than an importation of foreign political customs. This would be a mistake. Cosimo's apotheosis worked primarily because it dovetailed with the reigning assumptions of Florentine political culture, a point that is thrown into relief by the fact that those same assumptions also dictated which forms Cosimo's apotheosis could not take. Certain foreign importations that were ubiquitous elsewhere were clearly beyond the pale in Florence. For instance, Cosimo's scholars were generally careful to avoid tying his apotheosis to his role as the "head" of the body politic. Insofar as Florentine political tradition had considered the republic a mystical body, Florentines had categorically asserted that it would brook no human head. Thus, unlike other monarchs, Cosimo's apotheosis did not imply either that he was the charismatic center of the body politic or that he took on the "likeness of the state," as did Galeazzo Sforza of Milan or Doge Foscari of Venice, respectively.[133] Indeed, at least on the rhetorical level, Cosimo was careful not to let his own apotheosis swallow up the charisma of the rest of the polity. On the contrary, Cosimo's apotheosis was achieved primarily on the grounds of his "extraordinary" virtue, tropes present and politically useful elsewhere but practically pervasive in the Christian humanist atmosphere of Florentine culture.[134]

Thus, when the rhetoric of Cosimo's divinity arrived at the ears of the Florentine populace, it arrived as a concept familiar enough to make it nonthreatening. The prince may have been a divine being, but so was every man, at least in some small degree. Man had been created in the image and likeness of God. Man resembled God in his ability to philosophize, to reason, and to practice virtue. Man took the place of God in the administration of sacraments. Man could become a son of God in baptism and a god himself by taking the Eucharist. So many things were divine, the ubiquity of the concept made it almost banal.[135] Augustine was the divine Augustine, and Aquinas was the angelic doctor.[136] Moreover, in Renaissance Florence this could be ecumenically extended in all directions. Virgil was the divine Virgil.[137] Augustus was the divine Augustus.[138] Plato was the divine Plato.[139] Even Michelangelo was the divine Michelangelo.[140] One admiring contemporary even went so far as to express a desire to burn incense and devote ex votos to the great artist.[141] When the young duke's son incanted the mass with a solemnity above his years, his tutor was moved to flatter the skeptical duke with the opinion that the little "angel" sung with a voice "not human but divine."[142] The semantic definition of the term could obviously slide into the most trivial of meanings. This was only because the concept of terrestrial divinity was written deeply in the pages of the Florentine Christian experience. It was only a small leap to make the prince a special case.

CHAPTER 2

Divine Right Rule and the Providential Worldview

IN NOVEMBER 1549, the young cleric and Florentine humanist Giovambatista Gualandi acquired the rectorship of the parish church of San Piero a Castra in the rugged, hilly, and poverty stricken diocese of Pistoia, a ruined little church for which the annual revenue was not even enough to restore the place's dilapidated condition. Pondering his dubiously lucrative gain, Gualandi mused: "I think that God has delivered it into my hands so that at least it would not fall into complete dilapidation."[1] In April 1559, Cosimo had a strikingly similar moment. His forces had just mopped up the fragments of the Sienese republican armies when he received the prize he had so ardently and unconvincingly claimed he did not want: the most Catholic king of Spain invested him with neighboring Siena as a fief of the Spanish Crown. Though Cosimo's territory instantly doubled, the broken and battered republic was so devastated that its taxes needed to be remitted for a full ten years. Pondering his dubiously lucrative gain, Cosimo mused: "We certainly believe that for its own salvation and by the will of

God, Siena has come under our power so that according to our custom, justice may prevail over every passion and particular interest; nor will we countenance the oppression of those who want to live free from the power and greediness of others."[2] The two vignettes reveal three important aspects of early modern divine right claims. First, the concept that we now call divine right, the idea that public power derives its legitimacy from the sanction of God, was not just for princes; rather, it was simply one manifestation of a habit of thought that saw God's handiwork in all human events, a habit of thought still triumphantly ubiquitous in Florentine culture and shared in the worldview of Cosimo's courtly circle. The providence that ushered princes and kings to their thrones was no more than a special case of the general providence that guided the daily round of mundane fortune and misfortune, running the gamut from a cleric's election to a small, unimportant, and unlucrative ecclesiastical benefice to a prince's conquering of kingdoms and republics.

Second, because divine right was so closely linked to providentialism, the various manifestations of the former closely followed the variegations of the latter. Early modern Christians had a jumble of providential ideals, and their concerns ranged widely between the here and now and the hereafter. Indeed, we can even talk of two sufficiently distinct modes of providential thought, a situation that gave birth to two sufficiently distinct categories of divine right. The first providence, based heavily on Augustine, posited a transcendent deity whose inscrutably hidden will directed people toward eternal salvation. Blithely unconcerned with mundane matters, Augustinian politics thus counseled the subject to a sort of political quietism born of Christian resignation. On the other hand, a far more potent brand of early modern Christian providentialism imagined a more active God who rewarded good behavior and punished wicked behavior in this world. Nearly pantheistic in his immanence, this God made both his presence and his will starkly clear through the signs of nature. This version of the Christian God required more imagination from Cosimo's literati since they were called on to prove divine favor by signs and successes. The differences in the two providential schemata might ultimately be called differences of emphasis, but theological subtleties eventually spelled radically distinct political ideologies.

Third, because providential thinking was multicausal, divine right did not necessarily imply an attempt to elude the claims of lordship vested in other bodies. Cosimo traced his legitimacy back to God, but God's providence might just as easily flow through the people, through the republic, or through the emperor. For instance, just because he claimed to be duke of Siena by the grace of God did not mean, as Danilo Marrara has suggested, that he was "ignoring the tenor and existence of the act of investiture" or that he did not "consider himself subordinate to any other but himself."[3] On the contrary, Cosimo explicitly affirmed that he took the little republic both because "it was pleasing to God, *and* because it was pleasing to the benignity of the Catholic king."[4] Most Florentines would have found little objectionable or unreasonable in this statement. Up and down the social ladder, early modern people conceived of providence as a multicausal affair; the Lord worked in mysterious ways, but he normally worked through secondary causes, even through the free will inherent in every human. The Reformation debates on grace and works only sharpened opinions on the matter as Catholic theologians and controversialists reaffirmed humanity's active participation in its own salvation. This multicausal divine right was especially important for a prince staking a claim to monarchical power in decidedly republican territory, since it allowed Cosimo's literati a free hand to argue that the duke's power flowed from both God and from the consent of the republic, even that his power flowed from God through the republic. Needless to say, the idea certainly helped to salvage republican sympathies.

Just as divine right did not necessarily imply independence, it did not necessarily imply pretensions of absolutism. As Cosimo had warily remarked in refutation of Pope Paul IV's triumphal absolutism: "Never have I found any principate that does not have some limitation . . . and the papacy does not seem to us to be more absolute than all the others because it was founded by God in charity, poverty and peace; these are the honest limitations set to it . . . as to peace, the papacy must persuade Christians to battle and wage war against the infidel, these are the voluntary limitations introduced by the word of God, which his holiness gives over to the bonfires."[5] Cosimo's rhetorical tug at the bonds linking divine right and absolutism is as telling as it is surprising. By 1556, the prince who had aimed at absolute control over his small state and had perhaps come closer to achieving it than any of his contemporaries had come to the realization that the chimera of absolutism was just that: an illusion.

God's Choice: Cosimo and Divine Right

There is little doubt that Cosimo wanted his subjects to believe he had been ushered to his throne by the guiding and all-powerful hand of God, and his propaganda was not at all averse to drawing these conclusions for his audience. In this, he was little different from his monarchical peers in other states.[6] However, whereas other rulers could base their claims on holy unction, blood charisma, and the divine gifts of their families, Cosimo could not.[7] He boasted neither unction nor an illustrious family. Was his appeal to divine right simply imported propaganda, cynically deployed by a skeptical literati and received by a skeptically unconvinced audience? The answer is almost certainly no. The language of divine election and divine right were so deeply embedded in contemporary consciousness that even those who were indifferent or hostile to Cosimo's success grudgingly admitted the legitimacy of his appeal to God.

This is not to say that there was no concerted literary effort to seed the idea in the Florentine mind. On the contrary, divine right caught on early and never gave up its stranglehold on Cosimo's rhetoric. In 1551, Giambattista Gelli exhorted the city to religious thanksgiving for the gift of such a prince, delivered to Florence from the heavenly realms. He wrote: "Among all fortune-favored realms and happy cities, our city and all its peoples have just as much reason as any city to thank God and to glory in the fact that after so many travails, the giver of all goods has given us you, Most Illustrious and Excellent Lord, for a Prince."[8] Gelli's texts certainly support the assertion of the art historian Henk van Veen that Cosimo's early rhetoric was "shot through" with claims of divine right, but what is remarkable about the rhetoric is its casual offhandedness. Cosimo was just one more gift from the "giver of all good gifts." Indeed, this claim of divine right is embedded in the text more as a mild and uncontroversial assumption than a bold and daring assertion. Indeed, Luigi Paolo Rosello, a Padovan evangelical with ties to Cosimo's court, blandly and unapologetically just referred to the "state which God has given (Cosimo)," and with equivalent mildness asserted that Cosimo's "good fortune and the express providence of God had raised him from the private state to the ducal dignity."[9] For Francesco Altoni, one of Giovanni Bande delle Neri's old soldiers, divine right fell under the more wide-ranging category of vocation. For Altoni, God had "called Cosimo to that high grade in which he found himself."[10] Others linked Cosimo's divine right to their own concerns. Frate Archangelo folded a divine right claim neatly into his own desire for literary patronage; in his version, Cosimo was simply one more Medici raised up to be the instrument by which God protected good philosophy and belles lettres. "Now in what branch can [Pico's arguments] safely nest? By what patronage can they be protected against the cavilers? You alone, Cosimo, in all of Italy embrace the republic of letters and cherish it. Whether by fate or divine providence, it was heretofore a special and peculiar characteristic of the Medici bloodline to take up the patronage of the heredity of belles lettres and to favor men of genius. Moreover it is necessary that what always was ever shall be."[11] The play on the divine providence/fate conundrum was simply that: a game of words. As a student of Pico, Archangelo would have certainly thought fate and providence to be two ways of looking at the same chain of causality.

Indeed, there was more going on here than the simple flattery of Medici client scholars; divine right does not appear as a theme to be propagated but as a matter to be assumed. Indeed, this is simply because divine right was underwritten by propositions that few early modern people could escape. First, God was the creator of the world and giver of all good things. Second, as all-knowing, all-powerful, and all-good, God had ordained every event to lead to some human felicity, whether it be in this life or the next. Third, God's guiding hand cooperated with human will in his eternal direction of natural events. Thus, if anything had happened, it was done at the pleasure of God's providence, it was done for human's own good, and its causes could be equally sought in both the natural and supernatural realms. If Cosimo was duke, then God had willed it for Florence's own good, even if it was done in a perfectly free election. This was no mere propaganda but the inescapable logic of a worldview that saw the same author behind both private fortune and public fortune, and behind both natural and supernatural causation.

What's more, this hypothesis can be tested against the sentiments of less public documents, for not all divine right claims were designed for popular consumption. One such private document, an early advice piece hiding in the voluminous corpus of Cosimo's registers, begins with a familiar bit of flattery: "In the most happy and consequently most fecund birth and nativity of Your Excellency and at so young an age . . . the divine essence has unexpectedly and without any human obstacle promoted and decorated you in the highest grade of this city."[12] The author, probably a member of Cosimo's inner circle, remained anonymous, signing only with a frustratingly ambiguous "Vinc." However, it is clear that in this document we are eavesdropping on the internal conversation of the ducal court, finding that Cosimo's own courtier believed it worthwhile to treat Cosimo's divine election as a matter of private conviction.

If it is hard to explain why the charade would have been played out even in private correspondence, it is even harder to explain away the speech made by the Venetian ambassador Vincenzo Fedeli to his own senate. Though Fedeli admired much of Cosimo's work, his republican and Venetian ideological commitments would not suffer him to give Cosimo his real approbation. Fedeli thought Cosimo's swift and terrible princely justice a close kin to proper tyranny and categorically maintained that the Florentine soul suffered under the heavy yoke of one-man rule. Nevertheless, in Fedeli's opinion, Cosimo was the unfavorable judgment of God on the tyranny of the many and the unfortunate means whereby the Almighty might restore peace to the city and staunch the Florentine penchant for shedding civil blood: "The Lord God permitted that [the Florentines] be subjected to one prince alone, which in the end redounded to the benefit of all because now, with the presence of this tremendous and frightening prince, everything has returned to its first principles. The terror of his severe and sudden justice is so great, and so powerful and efficient is the arm of his justice (which touches all orders, without respect of anyone) that though they are subjects, to their infinite grief and pain, they remain in peace and in quiet. No longer does one hear of disorders and perturbations among them, the Lord God having salvaged from so many detestable evils this one good: each stands securely in his state, though each stands in obedience."[13]

Despite all, God's providential care could not be denied Cosimo. Later in his speech, Fedeli continued in the same vein. "I have wanted to say that this election was made by the divine will alone because neither the people, nor the state, nor the

Holy Roman Emperor wanted him."[14] In this argument, Fedeli started from the exact opposite presuppositions as Cosimo's own mythmakers, for they assumed, as will be shown, that Cosimo had the full support of the Florentine republic and that his election was freely made. Nevertheless, the end result was the same; whatever the circumstances, Cosimo's ascendancy had proceeded according to divine plan. Fedeli had no interest in legitimizing Cosimo to his own senate or perpetuating the myth of Cosimo's free election, yet Fedeli found Cosimo's divine right claims devilishly difficult to resist, ensnared as they were in inescapable habits of thought.

As least one native Florentine document suggests that even republicans found it difficult to avoid glimpsing God's hand in Cosimo's election. One anonymous diarist, whose sentiments reveal him to be both a Savonarolan and a republican, certainly had his own choice words for Medicean tyranny.[15] Nevertheless, like most Florentines, he instinctively sought God's will in both political and natural events. Thus, he simply could not escape casting Cosimo's election in terms of providential right. For instance, he not only noted that the men who elected Cosimo must have been "inspired by God";[16] he claimed that God's providence extended even to the two men who discovered the dead Alessandro's body. "God," he scribbled in his diary, "who is a great lover of our city, wanted that they not raise tumults; rather, inspired by God, they went quietly to Cardinal Cybo."[17] The author may have thought that Cosimo was a tyrant, but at least he was the tyrant God wanted for Florence.

Let us take one more example of the grudging acceptance Cosimo's reign garnered from those who were not ideologically committed. This one comes from the quill of the Sienese Dominican Ambrosio Catharino Polito, who shared little more with the new duke than a fiercely anti-Savonarolan grudge. In a tract that attacked Savonarolan doctrine with a fury that only a disillusioned former partisan could drum up, Catharino criticized Savonarola's proposition that a popular state

was necessary in Florence. This was not an attack on Savonarola's politics; the Sienese Catharino accounted himself an enthusiast of no particular political ideology. This was a Dominican attacking another Dominican's logic, and as such, Catharino took issue with Savonarola's claim that a popular state in Florence was necessary because the people did not want an oligarchy. Catharino countered that if Savonarola was fair, he might as well argue that a popular state was unworkable because the oligarchs did not favor it, and thus the reign should be given to a prince. Moreover, "One sees that in the end, this is what was agreed on, and *God has favored it.* Though I do not want, however, that anyone repute me a partisan of any state . . . that state will always be pleasing to me, whether in Florence or any other city, which will be just and will do justice."[18] Catharino's argument worked for Cosimo, but it could have been applied to any state in any age. Indeed, divine right knew no partisanship; it was simply the expression of inescapable assumptions.

Divine right was not just for propaganda; it was often uttered offhandedly and sometimes found in the mouths of ambivalent or hostile nonpartisans. This fact suggests that the entire program was tied at least as much to the long-standing habit of providentialist thought as to cynical projections of political power. Such rhetoric was the natural and rather inescapable consequence of a Christian humanist thought that saw not just political events but all of life's events as the work of a providential, all-powerful, and all-seeing divinity.

Providential Governance: A Staple of Christian Humanism

But was the providential lens still the preferred mode of viewing reality in the Renaissance? This affirmation will take some proving since it flies in the face of previous claims. Did humanism mean the liquidation of providential history?[19] It is the argument of this work that providential thought was very much alive. The passage of time only served to choke Renaissance fatalism out of existence entirely, since Counter-Reformation ideology obviously could make no place for any anthropology that excluded human freedom.

One of the ways Florentine humanists pledged their allegiance to providentialism was via their preference for Plato. Indeed, Plato's view of causation could be reconciled to the Christian doctrine of providence more easily than any other ancient philosophy. The Stoics had imagined fate as an inexorable chain of causation; thus humans possessed little ability to grab the reins of destiny away from the impassive influence of the stars. The Epicureans had raised a kind of blind materialism to the imperium of the universe, binding man in the inextricable chains of his own pleasures. Plato, on the other hand, had exiled the idea of blind fortune from philosophic discourse altogether, since trusting to the naked power of chance would have been an offense against belief in divine order. According to Plato, the superior man threw off the chains of the body and lived according to the spirit, or so his Renaissance interpreters claimed.[20]

Indeed, Florentine Christian humanists were not the first to slip a Christian hand into a Platonic glove. The most authoritative Platonist in Cosimo's Tuscany almost certainly had the Augustinian lens in mind when he called Plato in to defend the Christian doctrine of providential care.[21] It did not hurt that he could round out his discussion with a couple of pithy paraphrases from Holy Writ, for example: "God has diligent providence over us, so that even the hairs on our head are known to him, nor will one hair fall to the earth apart from the will of the celestial father," and if God has care, "even for the birds, so much more will he provide for us, who are so much more noble."[22] Moreover, though Plato was the obvious pagan champion to defend that sort of Christian rhetoric, Aristotle's thought could be contorted to fit the Christian viewpoint as well. Whereas Aristotle had absolutely upheld the doctrine of fortune, he nevertheless defined its more problematic elements out of existence, concurrently keeping will as an essential aspect of human existence. Thus, Lelio Bonsi, member of the Florentine Academy and knight of San Stefano could make Augustine and Aristotle both right: Augustine with regard to objective reality and Aristotle with regard to subjective reality. Fortune did exist, as Aristotle said, but only insofar as the whole question was considered from the subjective weakness of human vision.[23] Only divine eyes could see the beauty in the divine order:

> The judgment of the sacred theologians is without a doubt more true and more certain than all the others, as it is briefer and easier. Theologians remove the power of chance and fortune, ascribing all the effects of all the causes to the power of God and divine providence; thus, when one considers the effects and particular causes from our point of view, it seems that one should attribute them to fortune and chance; however, considering them from the point of view of God, and in their universal causes, one sees manifestly that they proceed with great order from his infinite wisdom. Moreover, we know that God not only knows all things but cares for them as well, not only celestial and eternal things but worldly and corruptible things. I do not say universal according to the species, but even according to particulars and even to the individual . . . so that not a leaf moves without his knowledge or will.[24]

Aristotle, then, could also be salvaged for a providential worldview.

With the most authoritative church fathers and two great Greek philosophers on their side, Florentine Christian humanists went on confidently expounding the doctrine of providential care, with only few exceptions. Following very closely in the wake left by Coluccio Salutati nearly one hundred years earlier, Cosimo's *protomedico* explained away fate thus: "By the word fate, Tuscans mean the absolute and free will of the best and most great God and the providence that he has over all the universe."[25] Baldini was not alone; the humanist Gualandi dedicated a whole volume to shattering the idea that worldly events were wrought by the blind wheel of the goddess Fortuna.[26] Vincenzo Borghini felt it necessary to note that happiness depended not on the stars but on the maker of the stars.[27] Indeed, Florentine thinkers seemed readily to agree that an omniscient and all-powerful hand drove all the world's events.

Moreover, if humanists on the high cultural level espoused Augustinian views, preachers took up the office of transmitting it to a wider audience. On this point, there was very little difference between the lettered elite who read Verino and Gualandi's learned tracts and the simple churchgoers who listened as Lorenzo Davidico assured them: "God has providential care over each of us, as if he did not have any other care."[28] Constant repetition hammered the point into general consciousness, as devotional authors and preachers explicitly reaffirmed Augustine's worldview for their attentive flocks.[29] Thus, this idea was not only a staple of high Christian humanism but likely filtered down until it penetrated the thinking of most Florentines.

Moreover, Cosimo's client-scholars almost always referenced God's more mundane and general providence explicitly when constructing the duke's divine right mystique. Given his professed belief in the Christian and Platonic doctrines of providence, we can certainly believe that Verino was in earnest when he wrote at the funeral of Cosimo: "Divine Providence has given us Cosimo, not only for a most benign Lord, but also for a loving, just, and most prudent father and most powerful defender of his holy church."[30] Fabrini also anchored his arguments for divine right firmly on the rock of the more wide-ranging category of divine providence, writing: "If one has a pure heart, he must believe that the high and immortal creator of every created thing, who undeniably governs, rules, and orders all the universe, will dispose and order each republic (almost as one of his own members) to that government and order of living that he knows sufficient to maintain it at the necessary time."[31] At Cosimo's coronation ceremony, Salviati made the same claim, inserting his own opinion into the debate on fortune and providence by claiming that Cosimo was not only legitimate but sacrosanct, writing: "the fortune of this prince renders testimony of his virtue, and fortune is the minister of divine providence in his care over all terrestrial things."[32] Cosimo's assumption of the throne was just an event, and he had a divine right to sit on it only because the same God who ruled over the daily round of all events ruled over the political world as well.

Augustine's Providentialism, Christian Resignation, and Political Quietism

Divine right was certainly grounded in providential thinking, but in early modern Florence, providentialism had more than one meaning, both for Christian politics and for life in general. Providence was not some monolithic intellectual structure riding on Augustine's intellectual ascendancy; it was a fractured and tension-riddled hodgepodge of ideas drawn from different lineages. The Augustinian brand of providential thought posited an inscrutable God directing human events from behind the scenes, making the sun shine on both the good and the wicked. The other, perhaps more pagan brand posited a direct link between fortune and virtue; God sent scourges and disasters to the wicked while raining blessings on the devout. The split in this providentialist thought was not an absolute one; even the most committed Augustinian admitted that God sometimes rewarded his servants in this life, while even the most committed material providentialist admitted the superiority of the life-to-come. However, differences in emphases there definitely were, and as divine right was so clearly a byproduct of assumptions about divine providence, these differences tended to manifest themselves in competing versions of divine right. The next two sections will examine the variant political implications of this split. This section will argue that Augustinian assumptions about providence led to Augustinian lessons on political obedience, for Augustine had asserted that even wicked princes were sent by God and, like all misfortunes, should be waited out with Christian patience. Thus, Christian political quietism grew quite naturally from the more familiar category of Christian resignation.

The coexistence of evil with a benevolent, all-powerful, and providential God raised the specter of theodicy in a powerful way, a fundamentally monotheistic problem that absorbed the energies of Renaissance Florentines just as it had absorbed the energies of centuries of Christian thinkers. In general, Christian humanists came to Augustine's conclusion that evil was a result of man's free will and that misfortunes were trials sent to test the virtue of honest men or scourges sent to raise men out of the dust of ephemeral existence. Misfortune was like the loving beating delivered by a father to his wayward son. As Augustine had so resoundingly written more than a thousand years earlier, "as for the paltry goods and evils of this transitory world, these He allotted alike to just and unjust, in order that men might not seek too eagerly after those goods which they see even the wicked to possess, or shrink too readily from those ills which commonly afflict the just."[33] On the level of high culture, the bishop of Hippo continued to be a key referent. Gualandi's 1562 tract on providence was little more than a one-hundred-page elaboration on these Augustinian ideas.[34] Baldini wrote: "The evils that happen in the universe are not caused by God, but he uses them for the conservation and well-being of the universe."[35] Lorenzo Strozzi was more specific, proffering four reasons why God should allow misfortune: to occasion merit, to correct sins, to work some miracle, or to perfect a person in virtue.[36] The proper response, as Strozzi spent the whole tract declaring, was to resign oneself calmly to God's judgment in perfect Christian patience. At Cosimo's own request, Strozzi forced his own sickly body to scribble down the last few pages of the manuscript, which he dutifully presented for Cosimo's approval. Of course, Strozzi did not forget to throw in the appropriate flattery of Cosimo's own practice of the patient virtue of resignation.[37] Here, Strozzi was on good footing, for Cosimo nurtured a healthy respect for his own heroic patience, a fact that he had repeatedly attempted to publicize. At least one of these projects bordered on overkill, as he commissioned no fewer than three translations of Christendom's greatest exponent of resignation, the nemesis of Fortuna and her perpetually spinning wheel: Boethius.[38] Of course, Cosimo got the dedication on all three.

There is nothing to suggest that Augustine and Boethius exceeded the intellectual ability of Florence's exceptionally large pool of common literate men. In fact, these two philosophers' ubiquitous presence in fifteenth-century notebooks suggests quite the opposite, as even nonhumanists copied their favorite passages into a medium they could keep close at hand.[39] Moreover, these Christian ideals could even be propagated to the illiterate. Few media were as effective for this purpose as the sacred play. Not only would many Florentines have seen several of these, many would have acted in them as well.[40] The themes of divine providence crept into several sacred plays, but perhaps into none as comprehensively as the one I shall now place under examination, the *Rapresentazione di Abataccio*, republished in Florence in 1547. The play opens with a general discussion of the relation between fortune and providence:

> O you who seek to know
> The secret mind of God
> Oft take good as woe
> But judge with a vision flawed;
> Because truth is hidden
> You forget justice but
> You will see today if you are intent
> How we need to stand content.[41]

With the moral prematurely revealed, the play proceeds to make theological didacts out of its adolescent cast. The first actor to come on the scene is a merchant, dressed in the occupational garb quite familiar to all Florentines. This first actor loses a sack full of money at a well, which is in due course found by a second actor. Having found and kept the treasure, the second actor exits the stage. A third man arrives at the well just in time for the merchant to return and demand his money. When the wrongly accused third man fails to hand over money he does not have, the merchant strikes him dead. Enter an old hermit who has observed the whole messy business. Disgusted that he has spent his whole life doing penance as the dupe of a God who would allow such injustice to flourish, he renounces his profession, his faith, and his vows to give himself over to pleasure. On the way to his future debaucheries in Alexandria, he is met and accompanied by an angel disguised as a man. The hermit immediately takes this angel for a robber and villain, a conceit that is only confirmed when the angel steals a holy man's prized vase and drowns the beloved son of a generous host. When the two travelers knock on the door of an abbey, the fat and greedy abbot refuses their request for shelter, at which the angel hands the greedy abbot the holy man's vase. At this point, our hermit is sure that he is traveling with no mere bandit but with a demon in the flesh.

However, the angel now manifests his true being and illuminates the hermit's dull vision, explaining the ultimate justice of all events. The merchant whose loss had occasioned the hermit's crisis of faith was no honest banker but a thief who had lost nothing but ill-gotten loot. The second man, who found the bag, was a just and poor man. By giving the treasure over to him, chance had ensured that the money would see its way into the coffers of the poor. The man whose death at the well the hermit considered so unjust was actually in the habit of delivering occasional beatings to his own father, and his death at the well was little more than just retribution. *Abataccio* thus incorporated the ideal of earthly misfortune for earthly misdeeds. However, the play's real message lay in showing God's direction of man to final felicity. The holy man, whose prized vase had been stolen by the angel, had been entirely holy except in this one thing: his attachment to his precious vase, which robbed him of zeal in prayer and tied him down to earthly life. By stealing the thing, the angel removed the one stumbling block on the holy man's path to heaven. Whereas the holy man had his vase for a stumbling block, the innkeeper had his son, and his charity had flagged lately as he had begun to hoard up his wealth as an inheritance for the beloved heir. Indeed, he loved his son too much, so that he even went to the lengths of making illicit contracts in order to secure his son's future wealth. Finally, the angel claimed that he had only given the ill-gotten vase to the abbot in order to speed him on his way to hell. However theologically suspect this last assertion may have been, the message was clear enough: the apparent triumph of injustice is an illusion, as is the triumph of misfortune, when viewed under the teleological lens. This was high Augustinian theology produced for an illiterate populace.

But did the underlying message really penetrate minds? The evidence is too scanty to say for certain, but we do have some lines penned by an anonymous chronicler suggesting the lesson did work. When one of Cosimo's taxes on milling grain occasioned a general muttering among the populace, this anti-Cosimian diarist wrote: "There was great murmuring against the prince by everyone. Nonetheless, one needs to accord oneself with the will of God, who allows these things for some end, and thus it follows that whoever wants to eat needs to pay."[42] Indeed, it would be difficult to believe that having soaked in the message from birth, Florentines would not at least occasionally translate the Christian ideal of resignation into real political inaction, especially when Cosimo's propagandists so frequently reminded them of their religious duty.

Moreover, Cosimo clearly bought this ideal of Christian resignation himself, for this was the pose he repeatedly struck
when suffering the slings and arrows of misfortune. When his
beloved duchess took ill and died with malaria, he wrote these
deeply Boethian lines to his son Francesco: "Worldly actions
are such that every day, according to the will of the great mover,
our imperfect bodies are moved now in pleasure and now in
displeasure, but he that cannot err [God] disposes of us and our
life and death in such a way that is pleasing to his great goodness. We must always think that it be for our benefit."[43] Giving
advice to his son, he wrote: "Be consoled then, and thank God
for everything that is his will; serve him and pray to him that he
directs you to conform to his will and gives you consolation in
all these events, as only he is able to do, for I have not found
any consolation in these cases other than that which God has
given me."[44] This posture, and it seems that it was more than
just posturing, was not isolated to this incident; such an attitude was Cosimo's usual response to misfortune and the advice
that he repeatedly sent out to friends on the deaths of their own
loved ones.[45] These deeply Augustinian lines came to Cosimo
straight out of contemporary religious literature; for instance,
the tract Strozzi sent to Cosimo exhorted its readers not to complain when relatives die, since God moves us, now in pleasure,
now in displeasure. "It is a stupid thing to go against the will of
God, knowing that he elects the best time for us to die," Strozzi
wrote; rather, whoever murmurs against their misfortune, "de-
nies God's providence and goodness."[46]

Indeed, this everyday duty of patient suffering and heroic
trust was doubly important since it underwrote the political
implications of Augustinian providentialism, which amounted
to political quietism. Princes should be good, but the wicked
prince was like any sort of misfortune, whether that be the loss
of a child, an earthquake, or some less dramatic ill. Cosimo's
literati were not loath to attach the political message directly to
the more mundane religious one. Indeed, Cosimo himself posed

as the model. When he ostensibly demonstrated his usual cold resignation on the death of his mother, Varchi's funeral oration drew out the implications for his subjects. "Among the sweetness of life, it is very true that good subjects need to be content and happily receive all that which is pleasing to the prince and their lords, just as good princes and lords, of which our prince is undoubtedly one, need to receive happily everything that is pleasing to God."[47] Cosimo's resignation to his misfortune at the hands of God was here made a lesson in political quietism as well as a demonstration of his masculinity, politically useful in this case as proof that he possessed a "manly" control over his passions, which otherwise might adversely affect his ability to rule.[48] Deity mimesis was stretched to its logical conclusion, but only insofar as it resonated with an ideal already cherished in Florentine life.

Indeed, the ideal of political quietism was always made with reference to God's more mundane governance over all misfortunes. Fabrini's work tied the strings of Christian resignation and political quietism up nicely:

> How true is this opinion of so many poets, briefly I will prove to you. God is most wise; he knows future things, like the present and the past. What's more, he is most just and unchangeable, and all the things that are, are by his will. If thus, all the things are by his will, and he is just and wise and unchangeable and having always before his eyes the future, as if it were the present or the past, it follows that what he orders to happen from time to time cannot be otherwise than what he has ordered, nor could it be better, neither could it be changed, whether by others or by himself, because if others changed it, it would be more from God than from them, and if he changed it, he would be mutable and thus, not just, or at least not wise, not just because if he had ordered things justly, justice would be obtained, and not wise, because if he changed them himself because he had not ordered them well, it would be a sign that he had not seen correctly.[49]

Fabrini's characteristically mind-bending prose was nothing more than a convoluted way of saying that the rule of divine right and political quietism was a specific case of a more general providence and Christian resignation. Another Medici courtier, Cosimo Bartoli, Cosimo's fawning polymath ambassador to Venice and one of the century's most enthusiastic Platonists and anti-Machiavellians, as well as the architect of Cosimo's take-over of the Florentine Academy, wrote that without the will of God "no Prince has their supreme powers" and that all citizens were therefore called to conform themselves to God's will by "living quietly."[50] Finally, Gelli used this conceptual language to exhort Cosimo to punish those malefactors who had rebelled against him and thereby "against the will of God."[51] Thus, the first category of divine right quickly became little more than the de facto legitimization of any status quo and the duty of Christian citizens to suffer political woes as they should suffer any misfortune.

Pagans, Astrologers, and the Old Testament: God in the Signs of Nature

Augustine provided a clear, indisputable, and easy legitimation of Cosimo's principate that no doubt was seized on with vigor. Augustine had his limits, however. Many, if not most, early modern people preferred a God whose will was slightly less inscrutable, a God who was a little less patient in his justice. Nor was everyone ready to swear fealty to any tyrant who had waded to his throne through rivers of bloodshed. If God sent the prince to do justice to a crooked and degenerate race, then could he not also send an avenging rebel to enact his justice against a tyrant? Tyrannicide was still a concept in play, and the age, both Italian and European, was one fruitful in civil and religious disobedience.[52] Moreover, Christianity's explosively revolutionary streak was rarely so strong as in Florence, whose popular and learned culture celebrated both the martyrs and tyrannicides of antiquity with equal approval. Thus, simply appealing to the divine will was not enough. A prince, and especially a new prince, needed to demonstrate some concrete sign of divine favor. This chapter will first explain the underlying conceits of this material providentialism and then show how Cosimo's propaganda tapped into it.

Any Florentine seeking support for material providentialism had no need to cast about too far. The idea had an illustrious pedigree that essentially predated Christianity. Germans and Celts alike had blamed natural disaster on the gods and were quick to make their king their scapegoat in times of economic scarcity.[53] The ideal had such legs that even in 1527 Cosimo's contemporary King Gustavus Vasa of Sweden had noted that his population blamed him personally for the kingdom's bad weather, exasperatedly remarking: "It is as if they did not realize that I am a human being, and no god."[54] The idea had no less illustrious a Roman pedigree, for Renaissance historians were well aware that both the Greeks and the Romans had attributed material blessings to the direct intervention of their gods.

Thus the pagan led neatly into the astrological, and the astrological forged an essential link between transcendent monotheism and material providentialism. In the early modern schema, God was linked to nature as creator, sustainer, and first mover in a great chain of causation. Link by link, the power of God descended from his seat above the stars down to the natural world below. First, the prime mover communicated his power to the intelligences that ruled over the celestial heavens. The intelligences then moved the stars themselves. The stars themselves generated intelligences that linked to the elements of the world, and the elements directed natural events here on earth, especially the weather.[55] Causation, as even the fiercely antiastrological Savonarola claimed, was like an onion with layers enveloped within layers.[56] Cosimo's *protomedico* argued that this chain of causation was identical to what man commonly called fate. This schema salvaged fate as a concept by putting God at the top of the pyramid and excluding man's will wholly from fate's dominion. In that case, fate was really nothing else than a name for nature, and defined that way, it was both an ancient and ill-conceived pseudoscience and a strikingly modern view of nature's mechanistic processes. Moreover, it legitimated searching for God's providence in the signs of nature, since the Almighty set the whole works in motion and ruled over its operations. Thus, the fundamental tenets of this worldview reinforced what many Florentines almost instinctively believed: lightning strikes, comets, earthquakes, good harvests, bad harvests, and all other naturally occurring events were auguries sent by God to warn, to chastise, or to admonish.

Astrology and paganism were not the only streams of thought that drew links between the ruler's conduct and the favor of heaven. Renaissance thinkers found plenty of precedents in Christian thought as well. One of the earliest and most read Christian historians, Eusebius of Caesarea, had altogether too gleefully sought God's providence in the excruciating deaths meted out to the emperors who had persecuted the early church, thereby inaugurating the long line of Christian historians who attributed material disaster directly to sin.[57] Thus Renaissance Christian thinkers frightened audiences not only with examples drawn from the Greek, Roman, and other pagan worldviews but also with the same type of historiography that medieval thinkers had used to educate people on providence, as well as the unmistakably similar type of providentialism chronicled in the Old Testament. As with so many other things in Florentine religious life, Savonarola had set the tone for this, since the old firebrand had drawn his material heavily out of the Old Testament, never hesitating to draw lines directly between those books and contemporary political events.[58]

Savonarola's style persisted. Citing a string of Old Testament examples, Visdomini explained that the immovable and benevolent God of the philosophers nevertheless strikes like the jealous

God of the Old Testament because he "cannot tolerate (sins) with his honor, though it is true that unhappily and against his every intention (speaking humanly), he is forced to show his justice and vendetta."[59] Toward the beginning of the century, the Savonarolan Dolciati reminded his audience that Saul's impious persecution of David had earned him an inglorious death in the field at the hands of the Philistines.[60] Of course, the most pertinent Old Testament exemplar was the city of Sodom, whose toponymic vice had ignited the immediate disaster of fire and brimstone. Sixteenth-century preachers did not shrink from threatening Italy with the same fate.[61]

It is hard to say just when church and state got a handle on this dangerous fashion of fiery and apocalyptical preaching, but Florentines of the midcentury had been born and bred to such sermons, and old habits died hard.[62] For instance, Paradisio Mazzinghi, a former republican reading at Cosimo's Pisan University, could not refrain from the old style: "The Great and Living God, Our Lord, has in his infallible vision, ordered everything from the beginning of the world until today . . . that when he desires some change or innovations, he gives us mortals some sign beforehand, permitting the people to dispose themselves to penitence."[63] God, indeed, sent signs, and astrology told Florentines right where to look for them: up. Running the gamut of examples from the Old Testament and Christian history, Mazzinghi ended on a note of terror, the well-worn example of Jerusalem's destruction and the strange astronomical phenomena that reportedly preceded it:

> When God wanted to destroy and annihilate the royal city of Jerusalem by the means of Titus and Vespasian, he desired to provoke the Jews to penitence with great terror and celestial signs. As Josephus, the author of *de Bello Judaica*, and Eusebius the historian write: a star in the form of a knife hung over the city for one year; the comet's flames were seen to burn; the moon was eclipsed for twelve nights continually; and the gates of the temple, though stopped

with a great weight, were opened in the middle of the night. At dawn on the 21st day of May, chariots of armed men were seen to combat (in the sky), and many other signs were sent that I cannot relate. After this, there was great mortality, hunger, pestilence, and agony so that the city was totally eradicated.[64]

In passages like these Renaissance astrology could prop up old medieval views of history.

Sermons were not the only way that material providentialism was infused into more general consciousness—if it even needed infusion. The sacred play did the trick as well. The Florentine religious stage, concerned as it was with the martyrs of antiquity, quickly familiarized the sight of the Roman tyrant whose persecution of Christians provoked immediate vengeance on himself and his people. Sant'Agata's merciless foe, Quintilian, represents the type well. In the midst of her torture, the ingeniously complicated stage machinery that Florentines constructed with relish was called on to produce an earthquake, a sign that the Roman populace immediately recognized as God's judgment on Quintilian. Massing against the governor, they uttered these imprecations:

> O Quintilian, what do you think this has meant
> If not that you are wrong to give Agatha such torment
> And each of us feels the punishment
> And are disturbed and languish malcontent
> If you do not leave off, heeding the sign that is sent
> All your senses will have cause to lament
> For you are the reason this earthquake draws near
> And holds all the people in the grip of fear.[65]

Indeed, the scene of the tyrant split on the rock of the fearless martyr thereby made its gruesome way into general consciousness. Augustine's message of eternal felicity and misery is not left out here; the demons did drag Quintilian's soul to everlasting torment after all. However, the terrifying consequences of his actions most pointedly included material disaster as well. If the erudite conception of the heavenly rotations was too advanced for the common person, then this more simplified medium served to underscore the same message.

The ideal of course swung the other way; if impiety caused misfortune, then only virtue could assure God's material blessings.[66] How then did Cosimo set this axiom to work for his own propaganda? If the ruler's virtue secured the goodwill of God and the goodwill of God secured the city's fortune, then Cosimo would give his people both virtue and fortune. This axiom of providentialism is the context lurking close behind Cosimo's favorite *impresa*, "Fortuna sequester virtu": fortune follows on virtue. Cosimo put these lines on artwork and decorations whenever occasion called for such sentiment.[67] On one occasion, the message of material providence that the *impresa* contained was proclaimed in the shade of his own palace by one of Florence's most important boy confraternities, which staged a triumph of David outside the Palazzo Signoria on the antevigil of the Feast of John the Baptist. Of all Old Testament exemplars, none was more often or more emotively used to underscore the links between piety and fortune than David. Moreover, if the play's contemporary political message was lost in the flair of the drama, it would have been hard to ignore the closing lines, uttered while Cosimo watched approvingly above from the comforts of his own chambers:

> Now You, illustrious and honored Prince
> By whose great valor, beautiful Florence
> Forgetting its past ills
> Happy and joyful, remains in peace
> Follow then, the style begun
> For whoever fears God first
> Turning his eyes to him, and honoring his laws
> As do you, glorious and happy,
> To a felicitous end, will lead all undertakings.[68]

Events like this probably caught the widest audiences, but Cosimo's literati expounded on the terse *impresa* in several ways.
G. B. Adriani, one of Cosimo's seemingly endless supply of republicans become courtiers, delivered his judgment on Cosimo's
virtue up to the God of battles, claiming that "having faith in
God and in his clear conscience, [Cosimo] always got free of
every danger and conquered his enemies often."[69] The luck Cosimo lived by might even smile on his subordinates; the poet
Symeoni assured the secretary Concini that he need not

> Fear death, difficulty or pain.
> Because the eternal and Greatest God
> Favors the just undertakings of all good Lords.[70]

Salviati made much the same point when he claimed: "Cosimo's
fortune bears witness to the fact that he was not only legitimate
but sacrosanct."[71] Late in the reign Francesco Verino came to
the point with all of this, arguing that subjects would obey religious lords simply because they know "their prince is with piety
conjoined with the Lord who is Lord of Lords and King of
Kings, from whom all aid comes to us in dangerous times and
every good in this present life."[72] Verino drove home the overall
point: the devout prince should be obeyed because God would
rain material blessings on the devout prince's people. Indeed,
the most authoritative Christian voices had been arguing for
centuries that fortune was better called the providence of God.
Florentine humanists had been repeating that in earnest for
almost two hundred years. Little wonder that when Cosimo
chalked up his success to divine favor, few stood to dispute him
on the point.

Moreover, it is fairly clear that Cosimo was not selling a
claim to which he lent no credence. Indeed, he could no more
easily escape the habit of providential thought than any of his
contemporaries. In private as well as public discourse, he was
fully assured that "God had given him the victory in the battle

of Scannagallo."[73] On the victory of Montemurlo, he asked one of his rectors to "seize that happiness and comfort that we do here in Florence and render most devout thanks to the divine bounty from which all graces and gifts proceed."[74] Indeed, Cosimo was as tuned in to the signs of fortune as any; when he wanted to convince the pope to lend some scudi for the emperor's coming war with the League of Schmalkald, he pointedly instructed his ambassador to tell the pope: "The emperor has found an almost incredible amount of gold and silver in the Indies (Mexico and Peru), whence one knows that God wants to help him, and thus, you should help him too."[75]

Indeed, prevailing beliefs often emphasized the idea that fortune smiled on God's dearest friends. Cosimo's client scholars thus had only one move to make: demonstrating the links between Cosimo's fortune and his piety. Mario Matasilani tried just this by arguing that the bizarre coincidences between Augustus's and Cosimo's lives were "signs truly sent from God," so that the people of Tuscany might be sure that Cosimo's ascension had happened by the will of God.[76] No sign was so repeatedly utilized as Cosimo's Capricorn ascendant, represented wherever appropriate places could be found for it.[77] According to the wisdom of Cosimo's circle, the heavens had arranged the ascendant for one purpose: to link Cosimo to his Roman type, Augustus, who had sported a similar horoscope. The idea was to represent Cosimo's ascent as the final triumph of that traditional Hesiodian and Virgilian emblem that the Medici had been cultivating for decades, the return of the golden age.[78] Cosimo would restore Tuscan peace and glory just as Augustus had done for Rome. Matasilani summed up the sentiment, writing: "as Augustus was sent to Rome 'by the disposition of heaven' in order to quell the discord of civil war, so God sent Cosimo to Florence in order to quell the turbulence of that city's factional politics."[79] This was no mere turn of phrase. Matasilani was truly convinced, as were many other educated men of the day, that God had made heavenly bodies his "means" to communicate with man.[80]

Indeed, early modern people gazed at a sky vastly different from the one we perceive today. Their heavens were far more meddlesome: the divinely ordained influxes of the stars constantly intervened in everyday affairs, especially in the weather. God sat atop the heavens, and the heavens sat atop the movements of nature. This perception made it far easier for early modern people to find connections between the moral and physical universe, and in case Florentines needed any encouragement, preachers readily supplied it, repeatedly articulating the perceived connection between Christian virtue and the state of the natural world. In this favored metaphor, sin was a kind of winter of the soul; Christ, the sun of justice, was the harbinger of springtime. As the Savonarolan devotee Angelo Bettini claimed in a sermon: "The winter has passed, the rains have left and gone away, and flowers have appeared on earth, signifying the renovation of the times. In the rainy and windy and cold season, nothing is well, but with his coming, Christ our God, the Sun of Justice, has taken away that season, and as he nears he has begun to heat the earth of our hearts. He has renewed the season and brought back the florid spring in which all things begin to grow and the flowers give hope of subsequent fruits, odoriferously flaming flowers showing the renovation of old man. This signifies in us the fragrance and beauty of the celestial grace."[81] Bettini's sermon may be read in an entirely metaphorical key, but other preachers did not draw so tidy a distinction between metaphor and reality. Mazzinghi preached: "I was subjected to the power of the devil, and I did not know your holy name. The clouds were tied up so that they gave no rain, the trees gave no fruit, the flocks wandered, and the fish went away from the sea. . . . But now my Lord, I have known your holy name, I have repented of the multitude of my sins, and I want to remain always in your grace. I want always to obey your commandments, gratefully praying and beseeching that you give me your most holy love which is everlasting good. By your mercy I pray that you break the bouquet of clouds so that your rain may descend over the earth, the trees give their fruit, the mothers give birth with ease, and children suckle at the breasts of their mothers."[82] The rest of this sermon strongly suggests that it was intoned in the midst of a local drought. Thus the linkage between fecundity, grace, sin, and virtue was not always left safely in the abstract realm of spiritual metaphor.

Moreover, our scanty diary evidence suggests that this tendency to seek God's will in the heavens, in personal fortune, and in nature was no purely intellectual or religious conceit, unabsorbed by the populace.[83] Consider this passage from the diary putatively ascribed to a certain unknown Marucelli:

> On the 24th of January 1543, around the 17th hour, a great eclipse of the sun took place, lasting an hour and a half. Many stood in complete awe of it because it was so dark you almost could not even see the man next to you. In truth, I was one of those because I did not know what this frightful thing could be, but then I thought that it must be a great sign sent by the great God so that we wretched Florentines [would] convert ourselves to a new life. I thought this because one sees and has seen many things in similar times. Many greater signs have appeared in the heavens than these, especially in impudent and useless Italy, and all has happened according to the order of the great God, so that we be ready when the scourge comes.[84]

Even those less ready to run to confession were nonetheless accustomed to seeing the heavens mirroring the political world. In his famous autobiography the sculptor Benvenuto Cellini claimed to have seen a huge beam of fire lingering over the city on the night of Duke Alessandro's death, an augury of that great political event.[85]

Moreover, if Cellini saw auguries in the sky, he could just as easily find God's will in the more mundane features of his own life. For instance, when a man who had quarreled with Cellini's father suffered a catastrophic fall, Cellini attributed it to the "the sheer mightiness of God."[86] When he somewhat impetuously ran into one of his many enemies' houses, stabbing the unfortunate man through the doublet, he credited his escape from said house to the fact that "sometimes God mercifully intervenes."[87] Finally, with his characteristically narcissistic braggadocio, he chalked up Pier Luigi Farnese's death in battle to that prince's personal unfairness to him, giving out this ominous warning: "Let then no prince, however great he be, laugh at God's justice, in the way that many whom I know are doing, and who have cruelly maltreated me."[88] Could men who thought as Cellini did deny that their princes' conduct affected God's providence over political fortune when they were so sure that their own conduct did the same? Indeed, Cellini was not the only Florentine who saw the hand of God in political events. Commenting on a rout of Huguenots in 1569, the Florentine chronicler Giuliano Ricci had these words: "One can know by effects that Our Lord God never fails to aid his own when they are most abandoned by every human aid and at the most desperate hour, he intervenes with his most holy hand, in accordance with the promise made by the Holy Spirit through the mouth of David."[89] Indeed, set against this backdrop of opinion, Cosimo's own claims strike one as eminently credible to his contemporaries.

However, as much as men and women saw God in their own private fortune or misfortunes, it was always nature that struck the divine will's most terrifying blows. For instance, when shortly after Cosimo's election a great wind blew down the Apennines, destroying property and striking fear into local hearts, an anonymous diarist recorded that all the populace considered it an "augury of most great things."[90] When a huge earthquake rocked the Scarperia in June 1542, the courtier Bernardo Segni remarked: "the people thought that so many unusual and rare signs had not just come by chance but that they must have been signs of some great [impending] ruin."[91] Moreover, the inhabitants did not need to be told how to respond; they immediately organized processions to the Church of Santissima Annunziata in order to "placate the wrath of God."[92] According to one report, the massive votive pilgrimages and confessions were accompanied by the naked and barefoot histrionics of supplicatory flagellation. Such drama was not surprising, since the event had been preceded by all manner of strange portents, replete with an unnatural birth, a celestial battle scene, and an ominously threatening comet hanging over the area in the shape of a knife.[93] Of course, one cannot help but be struck by the way such mass popular hysteria borrowed liberally and specifically from accounts of the destruction of Jerusalem as passed on in sermons such as the one just cited. It seems that when Florentine preachers lingered on the topic of gloom and destruction, they held their pious listeners' attention and captivated their imaginations.

Nor was the Scarperia reaction an isolated response to material disaster. When another earthquake hit in 1559, the diarist Agostino Lapini again attributed it to the scourge of God. An anonymous *ricordi* from the Confraternity of Archangelo had this to say about a 1562 drought: "13 September 1562, the second Sunday of the month. A procession was held to ask for God's mercy since by many signs he has shown himself to be very irate with us: first, because it has not rained for more than six months; second, because most of the world is full of heresies; and finally, because those few Christians who are left are mostly dissolute and improper."[94] To cite one more example of Florentines' reaction to natural disaster, we might add Ricci's reaction to a flood of the Magra River: "Let it be pleasing to God to let these disasters be at an end, and let him not think our sins worthy of greater castigation."[95] In a culture in which plays, sermons, and literature had already embedded the idea that the moral state and physical universe were intimately bound up, the ground was already prepared for a positive affirmation of Cosimo's divine favor.

Thus, there was an essential complementarity between the sermons cited here, elite culture, popular attitudes, and the propaganda that promoted Cosimo's advent as the return of spring and fecundity. A poem by Martelli deftly captures all of the pertinent themes: the return of spring, the signs of nature, the Capricorn/ Augustus motif, and the divine providence that moves it all. He wrote:

> When Clouds have thickened about the sun
> Condensing all surrounding air
> And rain pours, as Capricorn prepares
> As is wont to be often begun
>
> By a miracle of Heaven, it was then undone
> Black wet clouds dispersed by prayer
> And across heaven's face appeared a day so fair
> They will not open at the hour when frost's force is none
>
> For appeared the lord who was elect
> To the honored seat, and let it ever be
> In the memory of the ages to come
>
> To show only that we
> are subject to the will perfect
> of he who moves the stars and sun.[96]

The praise poem ties up the lines of Cosimo's rhetoric quite neatly. The duke's advent is linked to the naturalistic metaphor of the return of the sun (that is, both the return of good weather and the return of Christ). The return of the sun/Christ is linked to the return of spring. The return of spring is linked to the traditional Medici emblem of the golden age and to the earth's natural fecundity. Finally, the whole process is ultimately dependent on the will of God. Indeed, Cosimo's sun king rhetoric bears more than passing resemblance to the message of material providentialism delivered from the pulpits. Da Trivigi's poetry made the same sort of connection:

> Giving its rays, that divine light
> Sees that heaven is lit and here resplends
> In the eye desirous of the lord of all
> That he be which he is, which he was, and moves and understands
> With every voice and movement in his ear and sight.
> Through you, a happy serene face to (God/heaven) belongs
> And it has more splendor than before when it was hindered by strong
> boggy humors and black clouds.
> But the dark veil no longer covers it.[97]

The idea was not just limited to the heavens either. Cosimo's panegyrists pointedly extended the metaphor to include the bounty of nature as well, which at any rate early modern thinkers considered to be dependent on the stars. No occasion was better suited to promote Cosimo as a vegetable king of plenty than his wedding, with the natural undertones of sexual potency and fecundity that such an occasion implied. When a series of land goddess avatars had finished laying their gifts in front of the couple, Ceres linked the prince's piety to the land's fecundity by letting the audience know that she "gives most generously the fruits of her breast to those who love her the most."[98] Moreover, when it came time for Cosimo's son Francesco to celebrate his own wedding with Giovanna of Austria, Domenico Mellini opined that perhaps nature itself was celebrating the nuptials by stopping its heavy downpour of rain at the new duchess's entrance.[99] The very public wedding motif was echoed in literature as well. In 1543, Gabrielle Symeoni celebrated some of Cosimo's earliest successes with these verses:

> . . . The place of burdock's and poisonous snakes
> (Thanks to God)
> Shall be taken by flowers, fronds, grasses, shades
> Caves, waves, and soft breezes.

> So that in place of salt and ice
> You will see a rain of such great manna
> On the Tuscan fields
> That there will be a competition to see
> who can sow the greatest quantity
> Ceres, Bacchus, Pan, Pomona, or Pallas.[100]

The linkage between prince and nature could be made to work in the other direction as well, and the same poets who celebrated Cosimo's life as a sunny day in the history of Tuscany also bewailed his death as a dark and cloudy storm, since in this case Mother Nature for once decided to comply with the exigencies of Cosimo's political writers. For instance, Bacelli wrote that on Cosimo's death,

> In the midst of a serene heaven,
> There appeared at a clap, bitter and windy rain
> An unusual fog,
> The waves grew, and the river irate and full
> I swooned as the beautiful work scattered[101]

And in the same mode, Capri eulogized:

> well shows now the darkness, and burning
> stars, the clouds that obscure the sun
> Lamenting of the death of the Great Cosimo[102]

And with those words, Capri sang Cosimo to his rest with the hope he would be received into that most Dantesque of visions: the eternal April. Aldana tied the prince to nature even more explicitly, claiming:

> Full of great sadness is Mother Nature,
> In vain is she saddened, in vain afflicted,
> in vain does she lament
> against heaven, against death, and against Fortune. . . .
>
> Hide then Apollo, your beautiful ardent rays
> Covered by a heaven of darkened horror.[103]

The examples could be multiplied, since with the weather cooperating, Cosimo's poets almost instinctively connected the natural elements to the prince's death.[104]

A passage from an oration given in the Academy of the Travagliati on the crowning of Cosimo as grand duke will serve to end this discussion of the linkage between prince, God, and nature with a final, illuminating example. Recalling the duke's initial election to the governance of Florence, the orator spoke these lines: "One immediately felt that the will of God then began to work for our salvation. By it, Cosimo was called to such an empire, almost as a new Numa, rather to say better, almost a new David sent by God. The first auguries were the plants in his possession, which in so cold a season and against the course of nature, miraculously flowered. One can believe that this occurred by divine providence so that through these means, God might tell the Great Cosimo that in the flower of his most green age, he wanted to put him in the midst of this province, almost as a splendid mirror looking into which each might be able to direct himself to the good."[105] The passage encapsulates material and political providentialism well. Cosimo is likened first to a classical and then to a biblical hero; in fact, the Florentine biblical hero par excellence. God made his favor for Cosimo manifest through a miraculous sign in the natural world. Finally, the whole passage nicely sews up popular theories of providence and the Medici return-of-spring motif. By 1570, the lines of development that I have been discussing had converged into a coherent whole.

The point of this excursus has been to show that divine right was based on habits of providential thought deeply embedded in Florentine, and likely all early modern, consciousness. Indeed, it seems highly unlikely that contemporaries would have seen Cosimo's claims as anything other than an offshoot of a rather typical appeal to providence. Moreover, since there were two modes of providential thought, there were also two types of divine right. Though Christian resignation certainly subdued many into political quietism, many others certainly believed in no such thing. For these, Cosimo wielded the propaganda of material providentialism, and as he leapt from one success to the next, his very fortune became proof of his own divine favor. Though he assumed the role of a pagan king, ensuring the food supply by his virtuous conduct, he assumed that role dressed in Christian garb. Moreover, this garb was familiar to Florentines, who looked for God every day in the slightest shaking of the earth or the lightning bolt from the sky. To all who thought in such a way, republican or not, Cosimo's divine right claims must have been rather blandly uncontroversial.

A Multicausal World: Providence and Free Will

This all brings us to my third point. To understand Cosimo's divine right, we must lay our hands on the mechanics of the providential worldview on which divine right was built. For present purposes, we must insist that providentialism in both its Catholic and humanist forms was multicausal. God might lurk omnipotently behind all events, but he preferred to work through secondary causes. Thus, an examination of Cosimo's divine right supports the case that Francis Oakley has made more generally: that even when the prince traced his legitimacy to God, that did not imply that legitimacy came *exclusively* from God.[106] In definitive contrast to modern science, which generally aims to reduce variables in order to isolate singular causative elements, early modern thinkers were far more comfortable with multicausal analysis and thus were quite comfortable attributing events equally to God's guiding hand and to the free exercise of human will. Aristotle was the key text here, but two phenomena made multicausal providence exceptionally important for Florentines: the Renaissance's fight against prophetic astrology and the Counter-Reformation's reaffirmation of human cooperation in salvation. Moreover, as the heir to a monarchical title in a republican city, Cosimo found it uniquely important to ground his election in both the will of God and the will of the people. Florentines' multicausal habits of thought lent the claim considerable credibility.

We have seen how critical astrology was to divine right. The artistic use of astrological motifs in Cosimo's court has been excellently studied elsewhere by Janet Cox-Rearick, but that analysis has ignored one critical point. Cox-Rearick argues that Cosimo utilized learned astrological conceits to advance the idea that his rule was preordained destiny, carefully fostering the notion of its "inevitability."[107] She then claims that in order to salvage astrology for Christianity, Renaissance astrologers placed God at the top of the hierarchy of causation.[108] Putting God at the helm of heaven's wheel was indeed an essential ingredient of Christian astrology; however, this was not sufficient to Christianize astrology if it still posited the ideal of an inevitable destiny directed by the stars.

Cox-Rearick's general discussion of Renaissance astrology is missing a crucial distinction that contemporary intellectuals would have thought to be of the utmost importance: the distinction between prophetic (or judiciary) astrology and nonprophetic astrology.[109] Prophetic astrologers were the fortune-tellers of the early modern world, scanning the heavens to predict the future. Despite the fact that the practice rested on widely shared assumptions concerning the stars' influence over nature, this type of astrology was beyond the pale. The problem, so argued the orthodox, was that the future could only be gleaned from the stars if man was included in rather than excluded from the great chain of causation. That would make man unfree, an unquestionably heretical proposition. Rather, human freedom threw a wrench into the whole system. Verino's tract let Plato speak for Christianity, arguing that the stars may determine a person's inclinations, but the future cannot be predicted on that basis alone. He wrote: "Though by examining heaven, one can predict what man will be inclined to, as by a remote cause, still a number of more proximate causes compete with that universal cause and render the judgment fallacious. The most important of these competing causes is within us, that is, our will, which is a free power."[110] Thus, any astrology that had recourse to the "inevitability" of events was useless for Cosimo. Prophetic astrology titles went on the Index of Forbidden Books right along with heresy and necromancy, and Cosimo leant the inquisitor his aid to root them out.[111]

Thus, astrologers who claimed to be able to predict the future were clearly seen as heretical, and even much that did not fall strictly within the realm of prophetic astrology was condemned by such thinkers as Antoninus, Savonarola, and Pico.[112] But as Verino's passage suggests, astrology that merely used natal charts to predict inclinations could still be reconciled with Christian orthodoxy. Indeed, Aquinas himself had on several occasions admitted that the stars and planets could affect the makeup of corporal bodies, even human bodies.[113] Moreover, the vehemence with which Savonarola railed against natal charts suggests that they were in widespread use among both noble and poor alike.[114] These sorts of predictions were the realm of nonprophetic astrology, which used natal charts to give information about one's virtues, vices, habits, and inclinations, as well as with whom to be friends and from whom to stay away. Ficino even argued for astrology's use in determining auspicious days and auspicious numbers, though others ridiculed the idea. Nevertheless, it is clear that orthodox opinion, given the authority of Aquinas himself, could at least hold that though stars did not have power or influence over the soul, they did have dominion over the body. So as dualistic beings, humans were at least partially subjected to the influx of the celestial orbs.

Cosimo's medic, Baldini, could even go so far as to say: "the soul of man is constrained by fate since it is conjoined with the body, over which fate is lord, just as fate is lord over all bodies."[115] It was thereby thought that peoples' natural compositions and dispositions could be determined by an examination of the natal chart. So long as this information was not used for predictions, it was acceptable, since it was possible to hold to this type of astrology without necessarily challenging either the doctrine of providence or the doctrine of free will. Indeed, Marsilio Ficino himself practiced medicinal astrology and argued for the use of natal charts in his *De Vita Triplici*. Nevertheless, he emphatically rejected astrological schemas that tended to deny free will.[116] Thus, only on these conditions could astrology and the concomitant doctrine of fate be accepted as compatible with Christian theology. Only on these conditions did Cosimo make astrology a part of court life. Only on these conditions did he promote his Capricorn ascendant. Only on these conditions did he establish a chair of astrology at the Studio of Pisa.[117] And only on these conditions did he have his own horoscope cast.[118] Astrology was fine, just so long as it left room for human will.

As astrology went, so went the idea of fate. God's providence may have guided both natural and human events, but providence intruded in human events far more gently than in natural events. Whereas the celestial processes over which God presided controlled nature outright, providence simply directed the souls of men. The very old paradox of providence and free will had already been thrashed about and settled by the Christian fathers, but because of the debates on astrology, it had to be resettled to the satisfaction of the humanists again in fifteenth-century Florence, by insisting on the individual will's cooperation with fate and providence. For instance, Ficino had claimed that "the soul is above fate through the mind. . . . Thus the soul is placed in the laws of providence, fate, and nature not only passively but as an actor."[119] Salutati had spelled the argument out more clearly: "If we call God or the providence of God by the name of fate . . . it is not unsuitable to account our wills as subordinate to fate. This does not mean that they are deprived of their liberty (for then they would not be wills at all), rather, they are free and unbeholden from any necessity of compulsion, and acting freely, they cooperate with God. The only acts that we call voluntary are those in which the will is a coefficient cause."[120] Savonarola had railed against prophetic astrology and fate with similar vehemence at the end of the fifteenth century "Things without reason are moved by God toward their end by natural instinct, sooner conducted and lead by others than governed by themselves, but man, who has free will, can have providence over himself, and though he is moved by God toward his end, yet he moves himself as well, working together with God. Thus, it is proper to man to seek diligently his ultimate end, to which he has been ordered by divine providence, and to seek the necessary means to arrive there. . . . Divine providence, through the moral virtues, moves all men, but since they have free will, they always are moved freely. If they will consent to the push of divine providence, they will doubtlessly arrive at their desired end."[121] Thus Baldini had a prestigious legacy to draw on when he set about arguing. "All the effects (of nature) lead to their own end by their own nature. However, men are simply directed rather than forced by divine providence."[122] In both the original formulation and the resettling, the cooperation of wills was of paramount importance. The upshot dictated that God might foreknow humans' destinies and guide the way with his omnipotent hand, but destiny could only be brought to fruition by human cooperation. It is fairly clear, then, why the idea of "inevitable" destiny must be excluded from our discussions of Cosimo's propaganda.[123] The duke's literati could argue that God had designed him for rule. He may even have inspired men to make Cosimo prince. However, the consent of the republic was absolutely free and therefore absolutely contingent.

By the time the Florentine Academy came around to lecturing on fate in the mid-sixteenth century, the fight against prophetic astrology had already lost much of its heat. The case against it had already been made and won several years earlier by a host of illustrious names, a list that reads like a who's who of Florentine thinkers: Dante, Salutati, Pico, and Savonarola. However, reforming Protestants rekindled Italian interest in multicausal elucidations of the will's cooperation with providence. Luther and Calvin had denied that humans possessed the freedom to prepare for salvation through prevenient grace and to assent freely to saving grace. Thus, they left little room for active participation in justification and denied man's coparticipation with God in the event of salvation.[124] A host of native traditions, including humanism, Florentine Neoplatonism, and the preceding centuries' antiastrological rhetoric made both Luther's radically fallen man and Calvin's double predestination difficult concepts to swallow. Thus, when the debate over grace and salvation came to Italy, Catholic controversialists already had a template for response ready to hand. For example, in a work published in Florence with Giunti as early as 1521, the Sienese controversialist Ambrogio Catharino explained man's cooperation with the divine using a familiar Aristotelian example, that is, by imagining an artist painting a picture.[125] Just as the painter arranged his canvas and materials, so man must prepare to receive grace. This was the material cause. Just as the painter had an idea of what he would paint, so the soul itself was the form of justification. This was the formal cause. As the painter physically putting his brush to paper brought about the picture, so Christ's death on the cross brought about salvation. This was the efficient cause. Finally, just as the painter painted for some reason, whether for pleasure or a commission, salvation was accomplished by the will of God. This was the final cause.[126]

When the Council of Trent gave their own answer to the question, they canonized this multicausal way of looking at justification. The council affirmed that preparation and cooperation were both essential elements of justification, which was nevertheless effected gratuitously from on high. The fathers thereby held to a middle ground between Lutheranism and Pelagianism when they wrote:

> They who by sin had been cut off from God may be disposed through His quickening and helping grace to convert themselves to their own justification by freely assenting to and cooperating with that grace; so that while God touches the heart of man through the illumination of the Holy Ghost, man himself neither does absolutely nothing while receiving that inspiration, since he can also reject it, nor yet is he able by his own free will and without the grace of God to move himself to justice in His sight. Hence, when it is said in the sacred writings, "Turn ye to me, and I will turn to you," we are reminded of our liberty; and when we reply: "Convert us, O Lord, to thee, and we shall be converted," we confess that we need the grace of God.[127]

The council then went on to enumerate their own gaggle of causes, though they pointedly deviated from a strict Aristotelian demarcation. Nevertheless, the council gave official sanction to this multicausal way of looking at God's action in the world.

Not all multicausal analysis rested on Aristotle's weighty authority. Recall that most Renaissance thinkers conceived of natural processes as a chain of causes, one enveloped in another. Savonarola had preceded the Reformation controversialists in using the distinction between universal and proximate causes (and primary and secondary causes) to answer the prophetic astrologers. The Florentine preacher Lorenzo Davidico borrowed Savonarola's stick to parry the "Lutheran"[128] doctrine of predestination, arguing: "though God works in all things, this nonetheless does not exclude secondary cause, rather experience teaches that he normally accomplishes things through secondary causes."[129] In a work dedicated to Cosimo's majordomo

Pier Francesco Riccio in 1544, Basilio Lapis upheld the doctrine of grace cooperating with will in the same way: "He who made you cannot save you without your cooperation. God's work is to call, man's work is to believe or not believe, which is placed in the choice of our free will, the gospel says no less . . . moreover, it is right to say that free will has some operation even in good works."[130] Though following the argument through its highly involved orthodox formulation, Lapis's prime concern was to uphold human and divine cooperation. The Franciscan Cornelio Musso had much the same take: "God moves everything gently, according to its nature. Man is a rational animal with free will. Thus, he is moved in accordance with his freedom. It is necessary that when he is moved, he is moved by himself. He is not a branch, he is not a stone; he is a man. He operates as a man; he consents, or he dissents. If he dissents, he will never receive grace because God does not force men. If he consents, he is made worthy of God and receives him."[131] Visdomini, another influential Counter-Reformation preacher, put the matter thus:

> God operates as the universal cause of whatever is done down here; however, what he does from his side, he does not do *of necessity* like those works that he does by his most holy, powerful, and most free will in respect of the many unchangeable, natural, concurrent, secondary causes . . . which, modifying the general influx from the first cause, still produce many effects that necessarily emerge, like heat from fire, the courses of the rivers, the light of the sun, the propagation of the animals, and the life of plants. However, God works differently in man because both God's will and man's will are free causes (as he says there is no will without liberty). Thus, the effects occur completely freely and contingently without any sort of necessity. Since God does not in any way want to destroy the order of his creation in his creatures, he needs (with the due of his benignity that theologians call the due of promise) to conserve man free and to let him freely operate and freely arrive at his end.[132]

Visdomini thus granted God the absolute imperium over the entire universe—absolute imperium, that is, for everything except man. Man's actions were always contingent, salvation included. Thus, as mentioned at the beginning of this chapter, just as Cosimo concluded that he had been given Siena because it was "pleasing to God and pleasing to the benignity of the Most Catholic King," Visdomini could similarly conclude that salvation was effected because it "is pleasing to God, and pleasing to the saved."[133]

Cosimo could share this strikingly similar turn of phrase because Visdomini's multicausal providence was no paper phantom. Cosimo and his court shared this habit of providential thought, and it bubbled to the surface for both mundane and important events. Births, safe travel, illness, death, even love: though the proximate causes for these events were plain to see, Cosimo's Renaissance court found little trouble in attributing them concurrently to God. Birth, of course, was an occasion to reaffirm the deity's imperium over the mundane. At the birth of each of his children, Cosimo rendered due thanks to God for his wife's abundant fecundity.[134] Of course, this thanks could not possibly have been meant to exclude the secondary causes for her pregnancies, causes the duke knew as well as any. The habit was catching, or at least, it was simply standard. On the birth of Cosimo's third child, the cardinal historian Paolo Giovio sent Cosimo this congratulatory note: "It is a great sign and more than clear and manifest that the soul of your Excellency is right and just in public and private actions and of a temperate government and religious life that is very dear and acceptable to Our Lord God, since having made proof of your resolute constancy and patience when he raised to paradise your immaculate lamb so quickly, he has desired to restore her and expiate every trace of the sickness of the flesh with such a beautiful gift of a child born without difficulties."[135] The immaculate lamb was Cosimo's illegitimate daughter Bia, who had died in February of the same year, and though the letter was private, the private ideal had public utility, echoing into official propaganda. In his *Commentari,* a work begun under Alessandro and finished under Cosimo, the longtime Medici client Filippo Jacopo Nerli compared Cosimo's many children to the special grace granted to Abraham.[136] Indeed, births affirmed God's providence over both human and political affairs.

Births were not exactly ordinary affairs, but references to providence could be uttered on less important occasions. For instance, on journeys, early modern peoples saw God in the winds that pushed their sails, the weather that graced their travels, and the bandits who did or did not attack their caravans as they rode through lawless lands.[137] Given the dangers involved, it is no surprise to see travel correspondence filled with casual references to providence, and Cosimo's court was no exception. For instance, he wrote happily in 1537 that it "had pleased God to bring (Averardo Serristori, his Roman ambassador) safe to Nice."[138] He wrote the same to his auditor Vintha, who had just dispatched a courier to Germany. "Let it be pleasing to God to give your courier good fortune since we hear that the roads in Germany are very dangerous."[139] Indeed, references to providence occur so frequently that we would be tempted to see them as meaningless figures of speech were they not uttered in more desperate occasions.

No occasion was more desperate than illness, nor does any other life event better illustrate the complexities of early modern providential multicausality. As David Gentilcore has shown for Naples, wellness was both a physical and spiritual affair. Etiologists not only tracked down the effective physical agents of disease but also sought to lay bare the primary moral causes lurking behind them. Gentilcore writes: "Physicians could concentrate their own efforts on natural secondary causes, while allowing that these ultimately derived from divine primary ones."[140] This was certainly the attitude Cosimo himself took when illness struck, as he sought out the natural remedies prescribed by his doctors while simultaneously attributing his cures to the grace of God. Indeed, just like all manifestations of earthly providence, physical and spiritual remedies were meant to work cooperatively. For example, one letter from court, reporting on one of Varchi's life threatening bouts of fever, ended on the line, "we hope for the prudence of the doctors by the grace of God."[141] Indeed, response to illness reveals just how easily early modern Florentines discovered the cooperation of human and divine agency in daily events.

Moreover, love struck from above just as surely as illness. We are not surprised to hear Cosimo call his own monumentally bad decision to marry his daughter to Paolo Giordano Orsini as "pleasing to God."[142] But he also claimed the will of God in marriages quite a distance more removed from his own political interests. For instance, when one of his soldiers married a certain lady-in-waiting of the Marchessa Caterina Cybo, he attempted to secure the lady's dowry for the adventurous and rash young man with the appeal to God's providence over marriage. "Since he needs the dowry, he has asked that I recommend him to your Very Reverend Lord (Innocenzo Cybo), and it seems that I should not fail in such an office for one who is in my service. I pray your Very Reverend Lord that since it is the will of God that he marry this lady, let it please you to favor him so that he receives the dowry, which he tells me is in the hands of the Marchessa."[143] After all, marriage was a sacrament and thereby sanctified by providence in a special way.

The models for multicausal providential election did not just come from the daily round of life events. The ideal was already a familiar political spectacle, enacted behind locked doors every few years or so in Tuscany's neighbor to the south, for the papacy was the early modern elective monarchy par excellence. Like the Holy Roman Emperor and like Cosimo, the popes owed their position to an election—in their case, the push, pull, and sometimes outright simony of papal conclaves. Nonetheless, popes wielded a God-given absolute power and prefixed their names with the title *providentia dei*. Cosimo understood that only multicausal providentialism could make sense of this papal claim. For instance, after the divisions in the imperial party had somewhat disastrously brought the antiimperial Paul IV to the papal chair, Cosimo made the best of the situation, writing privately to his ambassador Alessandro Strozzi: "With all the divisions and controversies in the imperial party (which we have heard about from yours and others' letters), one can say that these have caused the election of the Cardinal of Naples to the pontificate; nonetheless, we recognize his election to be from the first cause, which is Our Lord God, and we hope from him those holy works to the universal benefit and conservation of the Holy Church."[144] Perhaps there was a bit of wishful thinking on Cosimo's part here, and there was certainly a bit of rhetorical pandering, but the sentiment was underwritten by a mind clearly familiar with the political uses of multicausal providence.

The Divine and Republican Prince

Conventional historiography has long made a fairly strict distinction between models of legitimacy: kingly legitimacy based on divine right or republican legitimacy based on the consent of the people. Reinhard Bendix posed the question in his very title: *Kings or People?* Of course, Bendix's work naturally assumed that legitimacy derived from God and legitimacy derived from the consent of the people were mutually exclusive.[145] Nor is Bendix alone. John Neville Figgis explicitly excluded consent from the divine ordination of monarchy.[146] And Walter Ullman traced an entire conceptual framework of medieval political thought based on the competition between the two theories of government: one popular, consensual, secular, nonsacral, and rooted in classical and pre-Christian civilization; the other authoritarian, divinely ordained, theocratic, and sacral, the blame for which is laid squarely at the feet of Christianity.[147] More recently, Helmut Koenigsberger and Mack Holt have lent their authorities to the same dichotomy.[148] Studies of Cosimo's personal rule have followed the more general trend. One recent study on Cosimo has even made this distinction an overarching theme, positing a divine right absolutism that gave way in the 1560s to a republican citizen-prince model.[149] However, such an argument incorrectly assumes that divine right monarchy was incompatible with all appeals to republican consent. On the other hand, Francis Oakley has pointed out that it is wrong to assume that the "conceptual relationship between forms of kingship rooted in the divine and those rooted in popular election and limited in some sense by popular will must necessarily be one of opposition or contradiction."[150] Cosimo's Florentine experience proves Oakley's point in a way few other early modern examples could. Republicanism was a going concern in Florence in ways it was not in most other states, and Cosimo needed legitimation by popular will for many reasons: to blinker his people by preserving a facade of republicanism, to escape from outright vassalage to the Hapsburgs, and to filch the republic's prestige for rights of precedence in foreign courts.[151] Providential multicausality thus reveals its critical importance; with it, Cosimo could be a divine and republican prince.

Had it not waited on publication until the eighteenth century, Benedetto Varchi's official history would have given elegant testimony to this exigency, for nowhere did it exist more forcefully than in Varchi's mind. Varchi was born and bred a republican, and in 1537 he had welcomed the new duke with a spew of vituperative anti-Medicean verses.[152] He ended up nesting in Cosimo's court less for ideological reasons than for personal ones. Varchi had been tutor to the Strozzi children, Cosimo's archnemeses and the last best hope for a republican Florence. However, the Strozzi had cast Varchi out of their house when he formed an undue affection for their youngest son.[153] When Varchi quarreled with Piero Strozzi over a debt, Piero had him publicly beaten in a Padovan piazza, sending him a note: "I have sent you part of what I owed you, and you can consider me in debt for the rest."[154] Shortly thereafter, Varchi found new employment with Cosimo, whom he certainly found a more cordial employer. Cosimo officially commissioned Varchi's history, giving the star poet a free hand to compose a surprisingly frank treatment of the republicans and the Medici. Perhaps that is why it never saw the light of its own day. At any rate, Varchi was somewhat uncomfortable with sacral monarchy, and thus he cast Cosimo in the role of reluctant prince, assuming his throne only because lifted to it by the acclamation of the people. When others tried to convince him to refuse the senate's offer, the young Cosimo found these words put into his mouth by his biographer: "As a principate should not be sought with evil ways, so it should not be refused when offered justly, for such an act would go against both human and divine precepts."[155] Varchi left little doubt; divine right rested explicitly on legitimate forms of consent. For the former republican, *vox populi, vox dei.*[156] In this case, divine precept was made manifest by the suspiciously unanimous set of favorable beans that the senate cast in support of Cosimo. With this trick, divine right was neatly married off to a lingering consensual republicanism.

Cosimo needed republican legitimacy not only for controlling homegrown republicans but also for his prestige in foreign courts, terrified as he was that the world would rebuff him as the upstart scion of a usurious bloodline. Soon after his ascension, Cosimo's fears erupted in a precedence clash with the duke of Ferrara, Ercole d'Este, who was heir to far more impressive feudal titles but ruled over a far less impressive state. Among the many reasons Cosimo's literati advanced for his preference was that by his election he had been made heir to all the dignities of the republic. As the reader may suspect, this popular election was not meant to exclude his calling from God but to complement it, embellishing it with right and justice. His advocate in Rome, Ferrari, made the case thus: "From his first ascension, he surpassed so many other princes in the rightness and justness of his power. Indeed, this point is true and worthy of

all acceptance and can be proved by the authority of the law of
our Christ, when he said that those who did not enter the sheep
fold through the gate are robbers and thieves; however, those
who do enter through the gate, the true door, are pastors. The
pastor going through the gate is nothing but a type for the just
vocatio dei of princes to principates by those who have the
right to call them to it."[157] Ferrari proceeded to illustrate this bit
of creative exegesis with a few religious and classical examples.
Having drawn his text from the New Testament, he then drew
an exemplum from the Old Testament. God's direct intervention, Ferrari claimed, had made the Hebrews a free people; by
signs and portents God brought them out of the land of Egypt
to plant them as a tender shoot in the land of Israel. However,
in free council they had handed over their rule to Saul, derogat-
ing their God-given power to a king. Heaven had smiled on this
free election, as God had immediately granted the gift of prophecy to the new king. In this way, man's will and God's will had
both cooperated in Saul's election.[158] In a 1551 tract, Lucio
Paolo Rosello made much the same claim: "The true election is
that which is made by souls that are neither forced, nor corrupt,
but free, as in truth, was seen at the advent of Duke Cosimo,
and if we examine this election by the notable and virtuous successes of Cosimo, we will see that a higher power governed the
souls of those who made such a holy election."[159] For Rosello,
only the people's election could be a divine election.

The dual election ideal not only attended on Cosimo's political needs in his own lifetime, it even followed him to the grave.
As Carmen Menchini has pointed out, eulogies for Cosimo were
generally unapologetic in referencing the election.[160] This, however, did not mean that divine right was absent from them either. For instance, Scipione Ammirato claimed that the election
of Cosimo was itself "freely made" and then by divine providence "approved."[161] Bernardo Puccini remarked, or at least
planned to remark: "Cosimo was given by God to the world,
putting his election into the hearts of those citizens who held

the highest authority of the republic in their hands."[162] Eulogists neatly elided the problem of the senate's own legitimacy by conflating the forty-eight handpicked oligarchs who comprised the senate with a more slippery, ethereal "universal will of the people." The former republican G. B. Adriani pulled off the trick by claiming that on Alessandro's death, "the light and fame of that noble youth . . . came *almost divinely [corse quasi divinamente]* to the eyes of the people, he who alone seemed to be able to heal the wounds of his country."[163] Bernardo Davanzati was even less ambiguous. "The Greeks and the Romans attributed fortune to their gods," he declaimed: "but [for the origin] of Cosimo's so great success, one must not seek the gods of the Greeks or the fortune of the Romans, but the divine will of the Great blessed God, who makes him worthy of it. To say better, in his never erring judgment, God chose this man, who is pleasing to his heart, and raised him to great fortune by miraculous means, so that by his miraculous virtue, he might govern two peoples."[164] Davanzati left no doubt what those miraculous means were: "just as was done in ancient times, the people spontaneously elected a king."[165] Thus, Davanzati could write: "In his eighteenth year (as he who is the dispenser of all things human and divine wanted) Duke Alessandro died, and all eyes turned toward Lord Cosimo, and immediately he was made head and then Duke of the Florentine Republic."[166] The people's will was thereby made an instrument of God, a fact we should not find incredible, since early modern Florentines saw God's hand behind all secondary causes.

All that remained to be seen was whether God positively desired Cosimo's election for the benefit of the republic or simply allowed the election as a convenient way to purge the republic's sins. At this point, Cosimo's heroic virtue made another appearance, now materializing as a visible sign of God's favor. Moreover, heroic virtue concurrently provided yet another occasion to stress the consent of the republic. This time the conceit was supplied by political philosophy speculating on the primitive formation of society. In yet another dedication to Cosimo, Gio-vambattista Capponi imagined the scene. Some primitive men of uncommon virtue "had found things beneficial to human-kind." Lifting a page from Saint Augustine, Capponi imagined the stupefied primitives accounting these superior inventors god-like beings.[167] Thus, when it came time to form a civil society and live by laws, men naturally turned to these god-men, acclaiming them by common consent. This sort of system naturally tended toward the identification of a singly heroic individual, "so much so that after a long time, one individual arose, whom it was supposed was a god and merited to be exalted above the others; this one was proposed as head over all the others since the primitives knew that unity and monarchy are a unique and di-vine thing."[168] Rosello imagined the birth of primitive society in much the same way. "When one man is found who is so com-pletely furnished with virtues . . . then such a man is born to be a prince. We know too well that the first princes were elected only through the fame of their virtue, since the people, without expecting any gain or loss, elected those whom they reputed most able to keep the common peace. In the Old Testament, the people of God, not confiding at all in themselves to know how to elect a just and wise prince, asked one of God."[169] The lines between these fanciful flights of imagination and Cosimo's own election could not be more obvious.

Thus, Cosimo's client scholars waged an unrelenting cam-paign to link his virtues to his election, casting his natural abili-ties as a divine sign properly interpreted by the people who elected him. For instance, Varchi remarked that the Almighty had given Cosimo an innate knowledge of how to rule along with the reins of Florence's government. Thus, long before the events of Epiphany 1537, God's foresight had been forming Co-simo's political abilities, providentially grooming him as a spe-cial favor to the Florentines.[170] Betti echoed the sentiment, claiming that Cosimo's God-given heroic virtues had "made it clear that he had been born, not to live privately, but to rule and to rule a most great people and state. As one knows, when he was still young, he was by divine council elected, and since the people were united in it, he assumed the governance of the state after the bitter death of Alexander."[171] One final example should suffice. Francesco Verino tied Cosimo's double election to his virtues as well, arguing: "this man was born to govern the most flowered part of Italy for so many years so well."[172] Though he was born to rule by the action of "Divine Providence" he was nevertheless "made duke, lord of the Florentine republic, by his own citizens."[173] This message could be easily inserted into the often-repeated axioms concerning the cooperation of man's free will and God's providence: providence had endowed Cosimo with virtue so that Florentines might grope toward the divine plan through their own inclinations.

Thus, divine right waged no war with republican consent in Cosimo's Florence. Both mythologies found ample berth for play, and such a dynamic brought a favored motif to the fore: Cosimo's dual election by God and the people. The throne was thereby secured "by the divine will, by (the Medicis') merit and prudence, and by the benevolence of their subjects."[174] In this case, multicausal habits of providential thought let Cosimo have divine right and consent simultaneously.

Conclusion

Beyond question, Cosimo believed himself a divine right monarch from the very first, even from that very first night, which he spent hiding in the fortress as the mob, in emulation of the Roman populace, which had a tradition of sportingly invading the residences of newly elected Popes, sacked his house and stole his precious few possessions. He believed himself a divine right monarch simply because, like most of his contemporaries, he assumed God's omnipotent guidance of all human events. Thus, Cosimo's divine right was uncontroversial. However, based as it was on a fractured providential worldview, his divine right fractured into two complementary and competing divine rights. Finally, because Florentine tradition had long attempted to reconcile providence and free will, Cosimo did not need to follow the lead of some of Europe's other kings, undergoing a quasi-sacramental unction with a holy oil flown mysteriously to earth by the miraculous intercession of God's angels.[175] Florentines' staunch upholding of the immanent sacrality of nature and man, God's guiding hand over natural events, and the special providence that God held for human events all did the trick just the same. Indeed, in place of the French king's miracles, Cosimo's literati stressed a more human manifestation of providence: the senatorial election, which was consciously sanctified as a moment of divine intervention, the hand of God guiding human events. This was all sublimely important for a monarch dealing with the urgently pressing claims of his city's republican legacy. However, it turned out to be rather easy in a place that took its providence so seriously.

CHAPTER 3

Rescuing Virtue from Machiavelli

COSIMO'S BIOGRAPHERS have rarely spared him either undeserved praise or outright villainization; for nearly five hundred years now he has appeared in the historical annals either as the savior of the *patria* or a Machiavellian monster, wading to the throne through the blood of his countrymen. Even for an age of scandal and intrigue, Cosimo has frequently cut a particularly sinister figure. For instance, one chronicler suggested that he assassinated his own father-in-law, the viceroy of Naples, when his wife revealed her father's alleged plot to take over Florence.[1] At least one modern historian found he could still report Cosimo's alleged poisoning of Cardinal Ridolfi in the middle of the 1555 papal conclave.[2] A number of parties reported, in all good faith, that on learning that his son Garzia had killed his son Giovanni, Cosimo himself had immediately taken vendetta justice by slaying Garzia on the spot; on which news, his beloved duchess died of grief.[3] It was even whispered around that after her passing the lecherous old he-goat had taken both his niece and his granddaughter into his bed.[4]

Though modern historians have dismissed much of this as the gossip of enemies,[5] Cosimo continues to appear in the annals of historical literature as a perfect incarnation of amoral Renaissance power politics, as if he had simply stepped out of the pages of Machiavelli and onto the Florentine stage.[6] No doubt, Cosimo would be sorely distressed to hear the spin that posterity has put on his accomplishments, for he and his propagandists spent a considerable amount of energy trying to do exactly the opposite by distancing himself from Machiavelli's characterization of princely virtue.[7] If Machiavelli had set a number of hares running into Florentine and European political thought by questioning the practical utility of the traditional categories of virtue, Cosimo's literati presented him as Machiavelli's living riposte, proof of why traditional virtue guaranteed political stability. Indeed, Machiavelli may have subsequently achieved immortality as an original and modern thinker, but no prophet is accepted in his own country. Florence was the first to produce a Machiavelli, and consequently, the first to produce the slew of anti-Machiavellians whose gaggle of unoriginal political tracts provided a far more compelling model for early modern European thinkers.[8] This chapter argues that Cosimo's projection of virtue was born in antithesis to a powerfully unpopular set of reflections recently advanced onto the Florentine stage by the infamous Florentine secretary.

Machiavellians and Anti-Machiavellians in Duke Cosimo's Florence

The study of Machiavelli's influence in Italy is hamstrung by one major difficulty: unlike later French and English writers, who were only too happy to drag the famous secretary's reputation through the mud, sixteenth-century Italian writers could fill whole tracts with point-by-point refutations of *The Prince* without ever referring to Machiavelli by name.[9] Of course, from the 1550s on, Machiavelli's work was on the Index of Prohibited

Books, so this is not inexplicable. However, it is clear that Machiavelli was in the forefront of cultured men's minds as they composed their panegyrics and tracts on princely behavior. Three points make this clear. Many of the authors cited in this chapter can be demonstrably identified as anti-Machiavellians in ways that do not rely exclusively on their own writings. Second, even when authors did not refer to Machiavelli by name, it is often clear that they were dealing with problems set forth by him. Finally, even at this early stage, the *speculum principis* and panegyric literature swirling around Cosimo's court had already developed one of the key features that historians have identified as central to anti-Machiavellian rhetoric: the court's writers were attempting to defend traditional virtues like clemency, justice, and religion on the grounds of practical utility rather than just with reference to teleological and moral ends.[10] In a word, Machiavelli had made it more imperative for political thinkers to reconcile the good and the useful, so we see a sustained attempt to promote Cosimo as an example of the political utility of virtue.

It seems quite likely that anti-Machiavellian feeling was rife among Cosimo's most important literati. According to Giovambattista Busini, the attitude was nothing new. In 1549, Busini categorically asserted that in Machiavelli's own day Florentines already loathed him for *The Prince,* even though that little work was only in manuscript.[11] Busini may have been describing his own age better than Machiavelli's, but the assertion was certainly strengthened by the most important arbiter of intellectual taste in Cosimo's Florence: Paolo Giovio. Among other more virulent attacks, Giovio's work made Machiavelli out to be a "mocker and an atheist" who mixed "poison" in with the "sweet honey of his eloquence."[12] After Giovio's death, his place at the apex of Florentine culture largely passed to Benedetto Varchi, who was only slightly more charitable toward Machiavelli than his predecessor had been. In his *Storia fiorentina,* Varchi had this to say about *The Prince.* "It is truly impious and should not only be condemned but expunged, as Machiavelli himself tried to do after the changeover in government, since it had not yet been published."[13] However, despite such judgments, Machiavelli remained a rather ambivalent figure in Florentine life; almost everyone acknowledged that he had been an indisputably talented author and political mind, but according to Varchi, in spite of the rare virtues for which he was worthy to be praised, his infamy was well deserved.[14]

This combination of admiration for Machiavelli's genius and hatred of his most scandalous assertions underwrote much of the feeling toward him in the mid-sixteenth century. After all, he had been a man of undeniable genius and a Florentine patriot to the core. However, it is clear that many of Cosimo's literati felt as Varchi: whatever Machiavelli's merits, his thought was wrong and dangerous, and it needed an answer. One of the earliest and most explicit responses to Machiavelli came from the quill of Lucio Paolo Rosello, a Padovan evangelical who had intimate links to Cosimo's court. Rosello's title could hardly be less subtle: *The Portrait of the True Government of a Prince from the living example of the Great Cosimo.*[15] Indeed, the work is a point-by-point refutation of Machiavelli's opinions, using Cosimo to rebut the Florentine secretary on issues such as liberality, cruelty and clemency, love and fear, keeping faith, and using counselors.[16] Machiavelli does not appear by name in this script, but his opinions are inserted into the dialogue at numerous points. Consider this near paraphrase of chapter 17 of *The Prince,* inserted into the dialogue only to be refuted a few paragraphs later: "If all men were good, everyone would acknowledge the benefits received from the prince, and thus, it would be better for him to be loved than feared. Since, however, we see there are more evil than good men, ungrateful men than grateful men, flighty men than stable men, dissimulators than those who tell the truth, more that are unfaithful than faithful, and the greater part of mankind loves its own profit more than that of the prince, indeed since most men promise much and deliver nothing or little, it seems that the prince is better off with his people's fear than their love."[17] Rosello may have been absorbing much of this secondhand, but there is little question of the ultimate provenance of this quote. Nor is there any doubt that his refutation, as I shall demonstrate, sought to challenge Machiavelli on his own ground.

Many of the other writers cited in this chapter had even more explicit debts to Machiavelli, though like Rosello, they often found it prudent not to mention them explicitly. For instance, Cosimo Bartoli's *Universal History* was, in the judgment of Judith Bryce, "pervaded by Machiavellian themes" even though it did not once mention Machiavelli by name. In the draft copies Bartoli named Machiavelli several times, but in the final version the name was repeatedly expunged, replaced by the moniker "il nostro Historico Fiorentino."[18] Scipione Ammirato used the same circumspection, replacing Machiavelli's name in his *Discourse on Tacitus* with the phrase *alcuno autore;* nevertheless, Ammirato's work was intentionally designed to answer Machiavelli's *Discourses on Livy* point for point.[19] Even those who had been Machiavelli's friends felt compelled to answer him; Antonio Brucioli dedicated a set of dialogues to Cosimo that "took issue with Machiavelli" as well.[20] Others were more explicit in their hostility. One of Cosimo's readers in the Studio of Pisa, Baccio Baldini, reportedly considered Machiavelli's work so disreputable that he had all the original copies removed from the shelves of the Laurentian library and held under lock and key so that no one could consult them.[21] Though Cosimo kept a copy of *The Prince* on his own shelf, it was dutifully marked *P* for prohibited.[22] All of this suggests that even by Cosimo's time, anti-Machiavellianism was a going concern among the duke's intellectual circle.

Thus, it is certain that a band of writers were explicitly engaging Machiavelli in the middle of the century. However, while writers sought to do so, they were almost invariably shaped by him, especially in that they repeatedly found themselves forced to play the game of political philosophy on his own ground by insisting that their categories of traditional Christian virtues were not only good but also useful. Moreover, it is on this point that one can see the attraction of the anti-Machiavellian model for Cosimo and his writers. On the one hand, upholding the traditional categories of justice and clemency against Machiavelli's claims bolstered Cosimo's legitimacy. On the other, ascribing both virtue and success to Cosimo was a convenient way to parry Machiavelli's arguments about the cleavage between political and Christian morality.

Virtue: Machiavellian, Humanist, and Christian

It is not difficult to understand why Machiavelli's Florentine brethren found him so objectionable. By unmooring political ethics from its teleological underpinnings, Machiavelli had thrown into confusion the long-settled categories of moral virtue and undermined an entire system of thought. Indeed, moral virtue had a definite meaning to sixteenth-century Christians and humanists alike; most educated or pious listeners understood virtue as the four cardinal virtues of prudence, justice, temperance, and fortitude, as well as some of the endless subsets that moral philosophers loved to parse, such as liberality, clemency, and religion.[23] Indeed, the moral virtues were hard to escape, in Florence as elsewhere. While preachers hammered home the ideal of Christian virtue from the pulpit and saintly bishops entrusted it to their confessionals, humanists made it one of their favorite themes, and Florentine artists continued to find it a convenient theme for allegorical representation.[24] The ideal even trickled into popular culture, as the perpetual war between virtue and vice made its appearance on the piazza during the running of the buffalos, a festival in which the hulking beasts were fashioned into suitable allegorical representations of various vices and then run through the Piazza of Santa Croce, hotly pursued by humans similarly fashioned as avatars of virtue stinging them and beating them with rods.[25] In political terms, a long tradition of *speculum principis* literature had made the moral virtues and their concomitant subsets essential elements of political wisdom.[26]

Indeed, these moral virtues were so broadly accepted that we can intelligibly speak of them as Christian humanist virtues. Theologians did not shrink from acknowledging the humanist contribution to the study of prudence, justice, fortitude, and temperance.[27] Christian theologians also agreed with humanists over the ends to which the moral virtues were directed: the perfection of the civil life.[28] This thinking was quite specifically focused on a peaceful existence "in this world."[29] Nor was this attitude a novelty in the sixteenth century; such conflation of Christian doctrine and civic spirit had been a marked feature of Antoninus's preaching in fifteenth-century Florence.[30] Moreover, for all the activism of humanism, virtue was still primarily a preparation for beatitude.

Moreover, traditional virtue was more than just the means to a healthy society; it was a participation in the divine life itself, a type of deity mimesis.[31] One of Cosimo's panegyrists spelled it out directly when he wrote: "Your people see that you appear similar to God (as much as man can). As he rules the universal orb with highest care, highest wisdom, highest justice, and highest piety, just so, everyone knows and experiences your great vigilance, wisdom, justice, and piety."[32] Since God was the perfection of all virtues, any direct attack on them constituted an indirect attack on divine governance. Moreover, Christian theology packed an added punch. Since theologians asserted that there was no difference between God's essence and his existence, God did not simply "have" justice, he "was" justice. He not only "had" peace, he "was" peace. He not only "had" prudence, he "was" prudence.[33] To impugn traditional virtue was a bit too much like a direct challenge to the Almighty himself, and thus, despite the classicizing overtones of Machiavelli's version of virtue, most humanists found his thought as objectionable as the theologians did, for his attack on moral virtue threatened their intellectual edifice just as surely as it threatened the Christian one.

Indeed, Machiavelli did use the word *virtù* frequently and emphatically, but he rarely meant it in the traditional Christian or humanist sense. Thus, much ink has been spilt trying to describe just what his concept of virtue was. Though subtle differences abound in describing Machiavellian *virtù,* scholars are in substantial agreement that it was not in accord with the traditional moral virtues as his contemporaries understood them.[34] As Quentin Skinner writes: "Hitherto . . . it had generally been assumed that the possession of virtue could be equated with the possession of all the major virtues. With Machiavelli, by contrast, the concept of virtue is simply used to refer to whatever range of qualities the prince may find necessary to acquire in order to 'maintain his state' and 'achieve great things.' "[35] Felix Gilbert's reading is quite similar, arguing: "The meaning of [virtue] in his writing has many facets, basically it was an italianization of the Latin word virtus and denoted the fundamental quality of man which enables him to achieve great works and deeds. . . . Virtù was not one of the various virtues that Christianity required of men, nor was virtù the epitome of all Christian virtues."[36] Indeed, for Machiavelli, the virtues as traditionally understood might turn out to be vices if followed scrupulously, and the logical conclusion was that a prince might find it necessary to use the traditional *vices* occasionally instead. Machiavelli almost reveled in the paradox: when one held practical utility rather than traditional standards of morality as the official yardstick, vices might turn out to be virtues and virtues might turn out to be vices.[37] Moreover, what was considered good (morally) might turn out to be bad (politically) if viewed under an appropriately searching lens.

Why did Machiavelli feel the need to discard the traditional meanings of virtue and overturn long-standing ideas about morality? For starters, he felt more acutely than his predecessors and contemporaries the gap between the ideals of the good and the dictates of particular necessity. Though he acknowledged that justice, clemency, and religion might be good in the abstract, the corrupt nature of the actual world dictated to him that they should not always be followed, since they are not beneficial in every situation. He most famously wrote: "A man who desires to do good in all things paves the way for his ruin among so many men that are not good. Thus, it is necessary that a prince, wanting to maintain himself, learn to be able to be not good."[38] Later in the same work he wrote: "You must understand that a prince, and especially a new prince, is not able to observe all those things for which men are normally regarded as good, being often necessary in order to maintain his rule to work against faith, against charity, against humanity, and against religion. . . . [One ought] not depart from the good, if possible, but being necessary, one must know how and be willing to do the bad [*male*]."[39] Thus, for Machiavelli, necessity was the ultimate arbiter of political decision-making, and necessity often dictated that *vices* take precedence over *virtue*. Moreover, Machiavelli was quite frank in suggesting that reconciling conflicting attributes such as love and fear in one prince was nearly impossible. Thus, princes would always be presented with a choice, and when they were, they should choose to be more feared than loved, practice cruelty more than clemency, and put more stock in warfare than religion.[40]

At most, Machiavelli argued, rulers need only appear to have the traditional virtues. Since men know what a prince says but not what he does, this was a task easily accomplished. Princes could cloak their misdeeds under a guise of justice, religion, and virtue, while surreptitiously performing the necessary misdeeds of state.[41] This advice, of course, makes it exceedingly difficult to tell just which princes actually felt themselves just and religious and which were simply following Machiavelli's advice to appear so. Here we wander into the realm of individual conscience, a dangerous ground for the historian. Was Cosimo a

Machiavellian hiding behind a show of virtue? He probably did not think himself so, even though he was occasionally vindictive and cruel. As I will show, Cosimo himself disputed Machiavelli's precepts just as vehemently as his literati.

Given moral virtue's honored place in learned and popular discourse, there is little wonder that Machiavelli's concept of virtue found so little traction in Florence. Indeed, his plea for political realism had the opposite effect, swelling into a backlash of anti-Machiavellianism, a pervasive Florentine trope that Cosimo's client scholars mined to its full extent. To do this, they attempted to recouple Machiavelli's dichotomies in the personage of Cosimo. Whereas Machiavelli had claimed that it was impossible for a prince to be both loved and feared, Cosimo's literati presented him as a prince both feared and loved. Whereas Machiavelli had favored severity over clemency, with little regard for justice, Cosimo presented himself as a prince who was severe in his justice yet loved for his clemency. Whereas Machiavelli had dictated that a prince could either be bellicose or peaceful but not both, Cosimo posed as the bellicose yet Christianly pious prince whose manly fortitude was ordered to securing the higher end of peace. Moreover, Cosimo's literati used his success to argue that Machiavelli had been wrong in ascribing practical utility to such vices as cruelty, injustice, and acquisitive warfare. In many ways, Cosimo as the answer to Machiavelli worked because Machiavelli's themes were so recognizable and because Florentines so desperately wanted to believe Machiavelli was wrong. Thus, the third leg of sacral monarchy was built on yet another space of intellectual reconciliation between Christianity and humanism.

Fear and Justice

Was a prince to be more loved or feared? Machiavelli had answered Seneca and Cicero's famous question in a most unusual way. Since most men act from fear of punishment rather than from love of the good, he claimed, the prince must seek first to make his subjects tremble. For Machiavelli, subjects' love was desirable but unnecessary and practically impossible to couple with fear. But just how scandalous was this bold assertion? Almost everyone would have agreed with the underlying principle: most people act more from fear than love. Almost everyone would have agreed that a healthy dose of fear was necessary for civic harmony. And almost everyone would have agreed that civil governments were responsible for inculcating it. Machiavelli's scandal did not lie in his admonitions concerning fear but in his indifference to using cruelty and injustice to achieve the desired effect. In his *Discourses on Livy,* Machiavelli famously quipped: "Where the safety of the country depends on a resolution, no questions of justice or injustice, humanity or cruelty, should be allowed to play a part."[42] In *The Prince* he wrote: "A prince, so long as he keeps his subjects united and loyal, ought not to mind the reproach of cruelty."[43] As tract after tract demonstrates, early modern thinkers found it quite acceptable, even praiseworthy, for their governments to make them afraid. However, they found it quite unacceptable to be so frankly cruel or unjust about it.

How could this thorny knot be untangled? Cosimo's intellectuals responded by recoupling fear to its counterpart, love, as well as to its appropriate virtue: justice. Moreover, they answered Machiavelli by arguing for the practical utility of tipping the scales away from fear and severe justice and back toward love and its concomitant virtue: clemency. Thus, justice legitimized fear as an instrument of government, and clemency won the subjects' love. Moreover, as unamiable a figure as the stern duke was, he found it essential to stake his claim to his subjects' love, at least on the rhetorical level, for both the prince's justice and the peoples' love lay at the very heart of early modern myths of political legitimacy, as well as of Cosimo's image as a citizen prince who ruled by consent.

Cosimo never lacked the stomach to turn to the rhetoric of fear, so long as he could convincingly argue that it was coupled to justice. Indeed, Savonarola himself had said: "there is no animal more evil" than a man who lives without fear of the law.[44] Cosimo agreed. He even allowed his own legislation to be punctuated with language that hewed close to Machiavelli's, beginning one law with this passage: "His most illustrious and excellent lord Duke is aware that men of modern times abstain from doing evil more from the fear that they have of the penalty than for any virtue or any other respect that moves them."[45] The law then went on to shore up the loopholes of justice so that more rigorous justice would produce more effective forms of fear. This rhetoric was apparently not just for public consumption. An anonymous unpublished advice piece also counseled Cosimo to do the same, and he obliged, frequently instructing his rectors to kindle the dread of justice in their subjects' hearts.[46]

However, Cosimo was well aware that he could not successfully legitimate his real Tuscan state in the way Machiavelli had legitimated his imaginary one. Cosimo took his cue from Augustine instead. Augustine had acknowledged, while giving play to his frequently pessimistic ponderings, that all polities eventually rest on a foundation of violence and had rather pointedly tagged them all with the title "robber states."[47] For Augustine, only justice could salvage their legitimacy. As in so many other areas of Christian thought, as went Augustine, so went Florentine humanists. Cosimo's functionary Giovambattista Capponi took the line for his own legal tract, a work that was of course dedicated to Cosimo. Capponi wrote: "Justice is the way to conserve human and political intercourse without which all the monarchies, republics, reigns, and empires would not be civil intercourse but truly robberies [*latrocini*]."[48] Here the influence of Augustine trickled into the very language with which legitimacy was articulated.

Cosimo needed no such tract to inform him that the Augustinian principle of justice provided a far more compelling model of legitimacy for his subjects and functionaries than Machiavelli's pragmatism. Justice did hold an honored place in Cosimo's own discourse from the beginning and was on his lips at every important moment of his reign: at his election to the ducal chair, his wedding ceremony, and his consecration as grand duke.[49] Shortly after his ascension, he sent a circular to his local rectors promising to "keep justice in its honored grade," while to others he claimed that justice was, "above every other thing, desired and venerated by us, since we know that it is the principal foundation of every good and so acceptable to the lord our God."[50] The rhetoric of justice was not just for Cosimo's propagandists; he knew how to speak that language as well.

However, there was no propaganda value in justice unless it was equitable justice. Even unbiased accounts are in agreement that Cosimo's sword fell relatively equally on the heads of all, with no respect to wealth, rank, or title.[51] The closer the relation, the better the propaganda value. The idea had its precedents. Florentines celebrated the just exemplars from classical antiquity primarily for delivering up those closest to them, even for casting their own children into the jaws of the law.[52] Cosimo certainly played at that type of justice on paper. For instance, when trying to confirm his son Giovanni as archbishop of Pisa, he once wrote to the pope: "I am most resolute that if Giovanni does not hold to the life that is suitable for a good priest, I will not only not let him continue to advance in that vocation, but rather completely remove him from it."[53] On occasion, Cosimo had to put words into practice. Early in his reign he sent his imperial ambassador Giovanni Bandini to his dungeons as punishment for sodomy.[54] Years later he sacrificed another one of his own to justice, Giovanni Tovaglia, when he caught him pilfering money from public accounts.[55] During the 1560s, he gave his secretary Pietro Carnesecchi up to the Inquisition on charges of heresy.[56] When his auditor Torelli delayed a case involving a poor widow who had a suit against Cosimo's majordomo, Cosimo railed: "This gives us cause to think that you do not esteem my honor much, which consists in doing justice equally; and moreover, it is a heavy charge against you since everyone should say that you do not expedite the case because it concerns my majordomo. Rather get on with it, and give justice to whomever it rightfully belongs. Also, remember to terminate those cases that concern my servants with more speed than you have heretofore done . . . doing justice to whomever it belongs, without respect of persons."[57] Thus, it seems that Cosimo's political rhetoric did match political reality and that this was why his eulogists applauded his stubborn refusal to play favorites as his most singular heroic virtue.

Justice not only legitimized, it divinized as well. As Gualandi argued, the prince was like the scalpel in the hand of God's vengeance, drawing the lineaments of divine law on earth.[58] To that end, the prince needed to conform his own law to the divine law. As Gualandi quoted Augustine: "every law is an inane censure if it does not bear the image of the divine laws."[59] Malaspina eulogized: "Much luckier are those who (like those under Cosimo's rule) are ruled with good and right laws, and the author of those laws should be lifted high with the greatest praises. With good reason the ancients called lawgivers sons of Gods because by law, man is rendered more similar to God, for God is the principle of every order and every right."[60] So lawgiving was another form of divine imitation, and Cosimo did not refrain from mimicking the deity in his legal judgments. For instance, while writing to explain why he was denying the request to have goods reinstated to the family of a certain rebel, Cosimo seized on this stance of deity mimesis, retorting:

> We have responded on this subject in the past days at more length to Bernardo your brother on the same headings that are contained in your letter of the sixth of September. Thus, with this we will only say that as we have not let ourselves be conquered by the courtesy and friendship of he who has faithfully served and obeyed us, so it seems to agree with the dignity of our office to proceed with justice against others who in breaking the divine and human laws have sought to offend not only their lord but also their fatherland and

relatives, as did Alberto your brother. And since in so wickedly committing his act, God has given his person the penalty that he merited, so all the more is it clear that we are
right to give sentence against his memory. Since he has been
justly condemned, his goods and property will be applied to
our fisc.[61]

Soon after this incident, Cosimo's auditor Polverini wrote legislation making the confiscation of rebel goods standard practice.
Cosimo pursued this law in the teeth of his counselors' wishes,
and in fact, the idea was strictly contrary to the Machiavellian
injunction against putting one's hands on the goods of one's
subjects.[62]

Perhaps it was inevitable that Cosimo would flaunt justice as
a central piece of his self-fashioned identity; justice had been a
legitimizing trope long before either he or Machiavelli arrived
on the scene.[63] However, Machiavelli had changed the game,
and by the mid-sixteenth century it had already become imperative to show that justice was not only good but also useful in
maintaining power. Few anti-Machiavellians were ready to dismiss Machiavelli without attempting to carry the battle to his
own ground. Of all the things for which justice was given credit,
none was more important than the inculcation of civility. This
was a category to which Machiavelli had paid little attention
but was increasingly being stressed as a most peculiarly human
institution and even an intermediate end toward salvation.
Where there was no justice, there could be no civility.[64] Where
there was no civility, there could be no trust. Where there was
no trust, there could be no economy. Where there was no economy, the prince had no security. Quoting Cyprian, Gualandi
wrote: "The justice of the king is the peace of the people, the
safeguard of the *patria*, the immunity of the plebs, the furnishing
of goods of the people, the care of the feeble, the joy of man, the
mildness of the weather, the serenity of the sea, the fecundity of
the land, the solace of paupers, the inheritances of sons, and
even the hope of future beatitude."[65] Natural and supernatural

elements were inextricably bound up here, but justice's importance to commerce, industry, and wealth is displayed here entirely on the ground of practical utility. This purely natural utility was echoed in Ammirato, who wrote of Cosimo: "His justice allowed you the ability to go freely through his dominion, day and night, not finding any who would give you trouble, impede your way, or hinder you. It gave men the power to enjoy their goods without fear of soldiers, courtiers, judges, and notaries."[66] Thus, the justice of the prince was the wealth of the land. The wealth of the land was the security of the throne. Justice, in defiance of Machiavelli's assertions, had an absolutely useful function.

On another account, Cosimo's political philosophers countered Machiavelli by upholding the prohibition against cruelty and injustice, arguing that these practices were the surest way to a prince's ruin. The formula was simple: cruelty and injustice led to the people's hatred, and hatred led to the loss of the realm. Antonio Brucioli gave cruelty pride of place in his reasons why rulers lost their realm.[67] Gualandi wrote: "The reign is transferred from person to person on account of injustices and injuries."[68] With more explicit reference to Cosimo, Bernardo Puccini eulogized: "Cosimo had justice always as a companion, rather as a guide and lord. Indeed, prudence, which sees the causes for which reigns and lordships are kept or fall, would be worth nothing if justice did not appropriately retain or chase those things away so that one lives reasonably, justly, and legitimately."[69] Rosello expressed his own opinion in dialectic form: "if you cite me six hundred examples, you will never be able to persuade me that cruelty is a better way to conserve reigns than clemency. If you will examine history, you will find few who have succeeded by using cruelty, like Cambyses and Sulla." In that light, he justified Cosimo's rigor by claiming: "I will not say he used cruelty but severe justice." In such a way, continued Rosello, Cosimo made only his few enemies fear him, while the majority loved him.[70] Thus, there was little support among

Cosimo's writers for the idea that cruelty and injustice could ever be constituent elements of a successful reign. At least in the version provided by his propagandists, Cosimo provided the counterexample, a man feared by his enemies for his justice but not for his cruelty.

Clemency and Love

Though the anti-Machiavellians might have ceded Machiavelli's point about the usefulness of fear, they did not so readily cave on his point about love. Whereas he had said it was quite difficult to be both feared and loved and that for practical purposes fear was the better option, his antagonists argued just the opposite; love and fear were essential elements of the reign, and for the sake of both legitimacy and practical politics, love was the more essential element. Returning to the deeply engrained tradition of Seneca, Cicero, and Renaissance humanism,[71] the anti-Machiavellians in Cosimo's court took Machiavelli squarely by the horns on this point. For the republican Brucioli, legitimacy could only be won by the love of the subjects: "A secure and just dominion is a clear and manifest sign that a king has been constituted and loved by a people because the people have submitted willfully, and they neither can, know [how], nor want to be ruled in any other way or by any other dominion, being thus accustomed to obey and be governed. Only these two can truly be called principates, and all the other types of perpetual domination are unjust tyranny."[72] Rosello wrote: "When the prince does not injure his subjects, does not steal their goods, and does everything with right on his side, those who want to live peacefully love him with all their heart, and wicked men can do nothing but complain. Then the prince cannot be hated because he does nothing to make himself hateful, even though he is feared because he does not pardon delinquents."[73]

How was this love to be garnered? Rulers were supposed to learn from divine governance. If fear was to be inculcated through justice, then love was to be won by the virtues of mercy and clemency, subsets of the cardinal virtue of temperance. Given that, Machiavelli's injunction to a new prince to be cruel, swift, and bloody on taking the throne struck at the very heart of the juridical basis of the Christian state. In 1562, one of Cosimo's panegyrists cited Seneca directly, arguing: "Nothing is more efficacious in safeguarding the reign and holding it stable, nothing is better or more apt to winning the benevolence of the city and more easily holding it than clemency."[74] Cosimo's ambassador to Venice, the polymath Cosimo Bartoli, took on Machiavelli's challenge more directly, arguing that princes succeed best in keeping their reigns "whenever they resolve to be more loved than feared, and whenever they remember they need to be more benign than severe fathers of their people, because the love they bring to their subjects will give rise to their subjects' desire to benefit them, and this will result in beneficial actions. This will give rise to the universal love of the people toward the Prince and the peoples' desire for the prince's safety and happiness."[75] A 1546 eulogy by one of Cosimo's most trusted humanists for one of Cosimo's most trusted advisors also challenged Machiavelli. Arguing that at the time of the Medici restoration, the dearly departed Francesco Campana had served the new lords well by winning more friends than enemies with his clemency, a eulogist told his audience that Campana had often reminded Duke Alessandro: "If enemies by fearing him hold him in hatred, his friends, loving him, will hope from him every good. Campana often reminded Alessandro of Caesar's opinion on this issue since Caesar preferred to obtain greatness for himself by pardoning those who had offended him rather than persecuting them (as he would have been able) and vindicating every injury."[76] Caesar, of course, was the preeminent example of the magnanimous and clement winner of allies, and his assassination at the hands of so-called friends was a fact quite conveniently overlooked. Finally, Baccio Baldini appealed to clemency's utility in his panegyric to the same virtue, claiming: "from this high virtue are thus conserved the reigns and the provinces, since when the prince bestows clemency on those who have not sinned maliciously, one comes to render the souls of the subjects most devoted toward their princes."[77] Here then Cosimo's humanists took the fight to Machiavelli's own ground, drumming up the same sort of utility for mercy as they had for justice.

The need to make this propaganda explicitly refer to Cosimo was felt as pressing, but it was difficult to do because the unbending duke did not always deal his panegyrists a strong hand. For example, when Cosimo's spies foiled Pandolfo Pucci's plot against Cosimo's life in 1559, no rebel neck was spared. Cosimo's close advisor Bartoli made the event an occasion to remark on Cosimo's clemency anyway, arguing in a rather clumsy sleight of hand that "Though Pandolfo and the others that were taken were made what the due of justice desired, His Excellency nonetheless pardoned the goods of Pandolfo, letting his children have them and the goods of some of the others, with his usual clemency, castigating sooner with clemency than with rigidity."[78] Quite ironically, this pardoning of goods may actually have been one of Cosimo's most Machiavellian moves; Machiavelli thought men would sooner forgive the death of their fathers than the loss of their patrimonies. Nevertheless, Bartoli parlayed the example into an exposition on ruling by virtue rather than mere *astutia* alone. In a dedication to Cosimo, Fabio Benvoglienti made the point again by comparing Cosimo's mercy to Augustus's mercy: "the greater (Augustus) grew, so much more was he tempered and benign: just the same, the greater Cosimo grew in fortune, the more he has used beautiful acts of clemency and goodness."[79] Benvoglienti claimed that in this way Cosimo had obtained to both love and fear; the good loved him, while the evil feared him.[80] By the time of his funeral, the plots against his life had been conveniently dropped from memory, and Cosimo appeared as a legitimate and beloved prince, a fact he repeatedly demonstrated, as Davanzati eulogized, by leaving his "bodyguards and going through the city alone, like a true and legitimate king, guarded by the benevolence of his subjects."[81] In Cosimo's mythology, mercy had won and love had prevailed. Machiavelli had been thrown down from his rhetorical pedestal by the living example of Cosimo's virtue.

Moreover, mercy was just as surely necessary to claims of divinity as justice was. Cosimo's panegyrists and humanists were not long in promoting it. Rosello wrote: "in every way, clemency needs to conquer cruelty, otherwise the Prince would not resemble God, of whom he is the living image; indeed, we see God use pity toward us sinners, whose sin renders us worthy of eternal death."[82] Gualandi wrote: "Can it happen that a clement prince is not loved by all? When he robes himself in clemency, he shows to the citizens (as Seneca wrote) that he wants to act toward them as the gods act toward him."[83] Baldini noted that clemency was "more than human" because "as the Platonists say, with clemency one becomes similar to God."[84] Bartoli weighed in by saying:

> A Prince should not think of anything else but to order his business and comport himself toward his subjects in that same manner in which he would like God to comport himself toward him, and if he wants God to be implacable toward his own errors, even to his ultimate ruin, so then can he be toward his subjects. Moreover, there will never be a prince, nor ever was there one, who was completely shielded from the wrath of God, and if God does not punish the errors and defects of men immediately, but is benign and lets himself be placated, is it not even more reasonable that a prince, who is no more than man, should also pardon those who error? And exercise his power and authority with composed, benign, and tranquil soul?[85]

Justice had its own logic of deity mimesis, and so did mercy.

If severe justice and mercy were two jousting aspects of the divine nature, the real proof of princely divinity was the ability to reconcile the two, since for early modern Florentines the resolution of these two contradictory attributes was a central, if not the most central, characteristic of God. Again and again, pious listeners were told that God's infinite justice and infinite mercy had been reconciled on the cross since Christ's sacrifice paid the due that humans could not effect for themselves.[86] Thus, Cosimo needed to show some similar sort of balancing act. Rosello lent him the rhetoric: "We see Duke Cosimo carry himself in such a guise that his subjects fear him, but they do not hate him, just as God the father is feared but not hated. And he accomplishes this by maintaining a clement and severe justice."[87] Salviati echoed the sentiment. In his oration for the coronation, he remarked that Cosimo was "so just in his clemency, or so clement in his justice," that it was a "divine, rather than human virtue."[88]

In all this, Cosimo's humanists were only echoing his own self-promotion. He knew very well how to strike a clement pose. For instance, he once responded to a supplication written by Cardinal Carpi with this boast: "I have never denied grace to citizens who, having repented of their past errors, had asked it, except for those who willfully had wanted to sin and only had recourse to me when they had no other choice."[89] Indeed, he filled his responses to supplications for mercy with phrases such as this: "we will be satisfied and content that justice always has its due and honored place as long as it always accompanied by some honest and justified mercy and pity."[90] He also knew how to make mercy look like deity mimesis. Informing the Commissary of Borgo San Lorenzo that he would agree to cut a certain offender's monetary penalty in half, he justified his decision with a short passage from Psalm 32, recited in a passable blend of Latin and vulgar: "because the land is full of the mercy of the lord, moved by efficacious prayers."[91] The line had particular resonance in Florence because it was inscribed on the *impresa* that the Bigallo's Mater Misericordia image held in her hands as her cloak enfolded the city of Florence. In appealing to this psalm, Cosimo appealed to a powerfully emotive Florentine trope.

Cosimo even knew how to challenge Machiavelli more directly. Writing on the subject of the punishment of the rebel Sienese in 1547, he petitioned his brother-in-law: "I will not fail also to remind you with due reverence that needing to castigate the delinquents, his majesty (The Emperor), whether he leave that city in its usual liberty or put it in subjection, in either case ought to lean toward clemency and grace rather than the rigor of justice since the thing is such an old case. I do not say then that he should leave unpunished the gravest wrongs and demerits, rather that he castigate a smaller number than he could, because the castigation of a few, beyond being an example to others, will cause them to stand in fear and at least will not incite a general hatred, and then, the remission and grace of the many will generate in their souls a love toward him."[92] There could be no more explicit rejection of Machiavellian cruelty; of the Machiavellian preference for fear over love; and of the Machiavellian platitude that fear and love could not exist together.

No Cause for War but Peace: Religion and the Warrior Prince of Peace

Like all his contemporaries, Machiavelli assumed that the Romans had been profoundly religious. Moreover, like his contemporaries, he assumed religion to be a constitutive part of a stable reign; indeed, he had very good things to say about the service Numa had done for the Roman state by introducing religious customs.[93] To that end, Machiavelli had counseled princes to cloak themselves in religion and support the divine cult in their territories.[94] However, he twisted the received wisdom all out of recognition. Whereas medieval intellects had salvaged the state as a handmaiden to religion, Machiavelli salvaged religion as a handmaiden to the state. Having taken up this principle, he favored a religion of strength over a religion of weakness, a religion of glory over a religion of humility, and a religion that shed blood over a religion that let its blood be shed. In short, his religious tastes tended decidedly toward the pagan more than the Christian.[95] On this matter, he sarcastically quipped: "Our religion, having shown us the truth and the true way, makes us esteem less the honor of the world, whereas the Gentiles esteemed honor much and, thinking glory to be the highest good, were more ferocious in their actions. . . . And if our religion asks that you have strength, it wishes rather that you have the strength to suffer rather than to do great things. It seems to me that this way of living has rendered the world weak and made of it a prey to wicked men."[96] The old pagan rites had bred strong stock, distinguished by feats of war. Bloody rites had inured Roman boys to violence, blood, and destruction, while the admittedly fictitious auguries kept the Roman legions united in fatalistic belief in their own invincibility.[97] For Machiavelli, a healthy republic demanded more masculine and martial religious rites than the type of Christianity he saw around him.

The Christian humanists at Cosimo's court found this highly objectionable, convinced as they were that Machiavelli had mistaken the reason for war, the reason for religion, and for that matter the reason for civil society itself. Traditional Christian politics sought the end of civil society in peace. Peace primarily required instruction in civic harmony, which Christian thinkers thought was best inculcated by Christian religion.[98] Thus, warfare could be justified in the Christian tradition, but only insofar as its ultimate ends preserved peace. This maxim was a difficult resolution of a difficult dichotomy. Gualandi put the case forward with reference to the Davidic ideal: "We do not condemn arms; otherwise, the condemnation would lay on the head of David, the most bellicose prophet king, nevertheless most beloved of God."[99] Gualandi then echoed the just war theory of Augustine, emphasizing that "wars are thus to be undertaken . . . for this reason, so that that when the war was over one might live in peace, for it is certain that wars are justified when waged by a just edict, for recovering territory, or repulsing the causes of injustice."[100] Augustinian warfare still had legs, and with the appropriate caveats, the soldier prince could still be a holy figure, both wreaking justice on his foes and offering a lasting peace to the land.

Machiavelli was far more frank about the reasons for war; according to him, one state made war against another "to become lord over her or for the fear of being occupied by her." Given Machiavelli's assessment of human nature, this statement was only natural. Moreover, though theoretically acknowledging the benefits of peace, Machiavelli argued that in the real world, too much peace would only bring the effeminacy and languidness that would lead to ruin. Indeed, too much peace might very well cause the prince to lose his reign.[101] For Machiavelli, a peaceful nation ready for war was best, but since this was impossible to accomplish, it was better to rely on force of arms. As Machiavelli put it, Rome was fortunate to have both a Romulus, who trained the people for war, and a Numa, who taught them the peaceful customs of religion; however, in the end, the prince who imitated Romulus would put his state on a more secure foundation.[102]

Thus Machiavelli had raised the issue of war, peace, and religion in a particularly damning way for Christian politics. Had the demasculinizing of the old Roman virtue of fortitude and the meddlesome hand of the Roman church made Italy a prey to evil men? Was it essential that the prince cultivate the military arts? Should the old religion be scrapped for a more martial one? How could humanists and Christians alike respond to Machiavelli's seemingly unanswerable critique of the emasculating effects of Christianity? Rather, it was imperative that Cosimo demonstrate himself to be a man of war *and* a man of peace. Moreover, it was imperative that Cosimo show that he only went to war for peaceful purposes.

Indeed, he had little difficulty advancing the idea that he was a man of war. A military lineage, a citizen militia, a crusading order, ducats for emperor's wars, ducats for the French civil wars, and one local war carried to a successful conclusion: all these testified to Cosimo's military prowess, and all these have misleadingly suggested to historians that he was a land-hungry rabble-rouser, willing to offer his sword at any opportunity in order to expand the confines of his own narrow borders. There is no doubt that he relished his role as the new strongman of Italy. Moreover, his bellicosity was continually linked to Christian religion. The eulogies directed to his zeal for war primarily trumpeted religious themes: his formation of the crusading order, his funding of the imperial religious wars and French civil wars, and his participation in the crusade against the infidel Turks at Lepanto.[103] The militant Counter-Reformation religiosity that favored such campaigns cast Cosimo more in the light of a medieval crusading knight than a glory-hungry Roman dux.

However, archival evidence suggests that the cautious duke's image as a religious warrior was balanced by a role he relished even more: peacemaker of Italy. As the Italian wars raged on during the mid-sixteenth century, he spent much more time attempting to tamp down the fires of war than to kindle them. For instance, in 1547 he urged the emperor not to take military action against rebellious Siena.[104] In 1549, Cosimo put his mediating services at the disposal of pope and emperor, hoping to get these old antagonists to reach some sort of accord in Florence.[105] When war threatened again in 1550 between the new Pope Julius III and the departing Farnese, Cosimo counseled both sides against recourse to arms, worried that the ensuing war would set all Italy afire.[106] He then privately cautioned the pope against attempting to play one set of barbarians against the other, hoping to forestall Julius from letting the French get another foothold in Italy.[107] A short six years later, another pope was rattling the saber, this time the anti-Spanish Paul IV threatening King Philip, and again Cosimo suggested the issue be resolved peaceably, offering his own services as a mediator.[108]

Indeed, he wanted to wear both hats, as the warrior prince who could ensure lasting peace.

Never was this posture more important than during his war with Siena. In the first place, he was at terrible pains to show that the annexation of Siena was not his casus belli. He had, in fact, refused to move against the unruly neighboring republic several times before events beyond his control forced his hand in 1552, and even on the eve of battle, he had sought to avoid open confrontation by signing a nonaggression treaty with the French, a move that one particularly unsympathetic biographer has attributed to a kind of Machiavellian cunning but is more convincingly read as reluctance to upset the balance of power by inviting the French fox into the Italian henhouse.[109] Cosimo was not ready to stake his own state on a foreign war.[110] However, war came, and when it did, he acted—probably with more than a smattering of disingenuousness—as if he entered into it with pangs of bitter remorse. He did not pose as bellicose expansionist but as the Italian liberator from the Gallic menace. For instance, he assured a Sienese in a letter: "our end in this war is nothing other than to liberate the city from the oppression and servitude of the French, who under the pretext of liberating states, desire rather to make them their own and hold them continuously at war."[111] Of course, the Sienese firmly disagreed, berating Cosimo for launching a surprise attack, but Cosimo's charge did have some truth to it.[112] Moreover, if it was true that he had not just dreamed up his dislike for French intervention in Italy, his claim spoke to the Christian humanist assumption about war as well: war was meant to bring about the end of war.

In addition to this pose, Cosimo did as much as he could to separate himself from the vindictive bloodshed that his German and Spanish mercenaries wreaked on the Sienese. Shortly after hostilities commenced, he wrote to the Sienese captain and *reggimento* of the people, claiming: "It displeases me much that it is not in my ability to provide that the Emperor's soldiers not come to make prey and damage (as those from Porto Ercole have written me) in their dominion because with the forces at my disposal, I am not able to prohibit them. As for the Porto Ercolanis themselves, let them consider that if it was in my power to restrain the soldiers, God willing, they would know in this what they have been able to know in all my other actions: that I have always desired to do them only benefit."[113] No early modern monarch could control the dogs of war once they had been let slip; however, Cosimo's war correspondence is full of exasperation toward his German mercenaries, and any soldier whose bad behavior came to his attention was threatened with with the loss of their employment, or worse, with the loss of their head. Writing to Bartolomeo Concini, who was off waging the actual war on Cosimo's behalf, he ordered: "It is with great sadness that we have heard of the robbery that the army of the Marchese has made in Casole, from which not even the house of God was spared. We do not want these iniquities; when the army is able to sack a town, the churches must be respected, and we desire that the first who dares to make an insult to churches, monasteries, hospitals, and other such places pays the price of such wickedness with the loss of his head."[114] Cosimo's attempts to disassociate himself were probably unsuccessful in this case, but this and other letters like this speak to his attention to his reputation: the warrior prince of peace needed to keep an eye on the peaceful ends of the war.

His panegyrists set themselves the task of publicizing the message. For instance, Giurgi lauded Cosimo's knowledge of warfare with a disclaimer: "You see how at the time, he knew the occasion to fight, and you conclude from this that if for the maintenance of the peace it was necessary to wage war, he would show himself no less of a general than Pyrrhus."[115] However, Giurgi was not content to stop there. Cosimo was greater than ancient generals in the fact that "conforming himself to the will of Jesus Christ, he only let himself be induced to go to war when he saw that the works of seditious rebels disturbed

peace and justice in his state."[116] Closer to home, Puccini eulogized: "never did he operate against his enemies for any other
reason than to have peace."[117] Puccini's laud was all the more
potent given his role as military engineer during the war of Siena.[118] On the subject of the Sienese war, Baccio Baldini claimed
that Cosimo went to war only after "seeing that the thoughts of
peace . . . which he had tried so long to bring about, no longer
had any place."[119] Finally, Malaspina claimed that Cosimo was
not only like a Romulus, drawing up the military in good order,
but like Numa, who instituted the civil customs of religion.[120]
Thus, Malaspina used Machiavelli's own historical metaphor
to recouple peace and bellicosity in the person of Cosimo.

If Cosimo's panegyrists praised the reticence with which he
went to war, so much more did they praise his manner of waging it. Baldini eulogized: "The Great Prince knowing that one
must not make war for any other reason than to have peace
and there being still in the city of Mont Alcino some of his enemies, he deliberated to conquer them sooner with his clemency
and his goodness rather than with arms."[121] Ottaviano Bandini
noted that he took up the war without wanting it and waged it
"with such prudence and sense that he made his enemies love
him as much as his subjects and made his subjects fear him as
much as his enemies."[122] Apparently, more than one Machiavellian platitude could be taken on at a time. Either way, Cosimo
stands in these eulogies as the living riposte to the war-hungry
Machiavelli.

Conclusion

Even as late as the eighteenth century, Frederick the Great titled
his own political tract *The Anti-Machiavel* in imitation of a
long line of writers who found Machiavelli a useful counter-
point to their own conceptions of just monarchy. Cosimo's political writers seem to have been the first in this long tradition. It
is clear that Machiavelli had sharpened the discourse of virtue,

calling into play a number of long hallowed categories, and his literary legacy lived deeply in Florentine consciousness, even though it lived mainly as taboo, for his most infamous work was rarely named directly. Regardless of what Cosimo may have absorbed from the pages of Machiavelli, his government was not founded on a Machiavellian ideology. Only a choice few found the new political philosophy compelling. On the contrary, most sought to refute his assertions about love, fear, justice, clemency, religion, and peace. At the same time, Cosimo was framed as a living anti-Machiavellian prince, saving Christian virtue for Christian politics.

CHAPTER 4

Prince or *Patrone?*
Cosimo as Ecclesiastical Patron

T HE MERCHANT REPUBLIC of Florence had always needed
to be especially careful about the friends it chose and the
enemies it made. The tentacles of Florentine merchant activity
stretched across Europe, and disturbances in the *patria*'s foreign policies sent economic shivers rippling down the collective
spines of Florentines abroad. Foreign merchants resided at the
pleasure of other governments, and guarantees of security were
hard to come by. Of all the enemies the Florentine republic might
make, few held such potential disaster in their hands as did the
papacy, Florence's neighbor to the south, which brandished the
threat of interdiction with ominous menace. An interdiction
would lead to the suspension of all commerce with other Christian nations and allow foreign governments to extort money
from the Florentines residing in their midst.[1] Though the Papal States were in many ways like any Italian power and engaged in so many secular pursuits, the patrimony of Peter was
no ordinary state. Fortunately, Florence and Rome had often
engaged in close financial and political collaboration.[2] Guelf

in temperament, Florence had occasionally proved one of the papacy's most useful allies. Absent outright treachery or territorial dispute, Tuscany had been content to give due obedience to Rome and play the game of papal politics, invading the eternal city for ecclesiastical posts and growing stupendously rich as papal bankers.[3] During the preceding century, Florentines had allowed control of their local church to go out of their own hands and into the papal curia, although their tight links with the eternal city had suited them for controlling the local church by utilizing their contacts in the papal bureaucracy.[4]

Cosimo, however, got off on the wrong foot with his papal neighbor. Bad feeling between him and Pope Paul III abounded almost immediately, for in Cosimo's first year, Paul snatched away the widow of the duke's assassinated predecessor and married her to his own grandson, Ottaviano, robbing the new prince of his hope of bringing her to his own marriage bed. Paul then proceeded to derogate the patronage rights on some of Tuscany's choicest benefices by wielding the powers of excommunication and to extort a tithe out of an impoverished Tuscan clergy by unsheathing the spiritual sword of interdiction. When Cosimo balked, justly assuming that Paul wanted Florence for his own and justly afraid that the tithe money his priests sent out might return in the pockets of the pope's mercenaries, the pope bullied Cosimo into submission anyway. A few short years later, duke and pope almost came to blows over the duke's expulsion of the Dominican Savonarolans of San Marco. Then the two exchanged hard words over the extradition of the fugitive cardinal of Ravenna, whom Cosimo harbored in his state against Paul's wishes. Obviously, Cosimo was off to a rocky start.[5]

However, Cosimo had no choice but to come to grips with the papacy since the pontiff held the reins of both spiritual and temporal power in one set of hands.[6] This meant Cosimo had twice as much business to conduct with Rome, and his Tuscan subjects' demand for favors in the Roman court would not wait

until the election of a pope friendly to Cosimo. Moreover, Cosimo could not simply arrogate church jurisdictions to himself,
since the tonsured estate let loose howls of protest whenever he
stepped too clumsily on the toes of ecclesiastical liberty. Even
had he so desired, he could not have disentangled himself from
Rome's spiritual authority without cutting the ties that bound
him to Rome's considerable bounty of secular favors or without putting in jeopardy the standing of many of his clients from
the Papal States. In this, Cosimo was at a disadvantage vis-à-vis
greater Catholic powers like Spain. In addition to institutional
agreements that gave the Spanish king great control over his
various national churches, the King of Spain could offer the
Papal States much in the way of money, food, and protection.[7]
Nevertheless, even the powerful Spanish king did not neglect to
cultivate a patronage network among the College of Cardinals,
using his ambassadors to woo cardinals into the Hapsburg camp
and get his own clients favored in matters concerning Roman
jurisdiction.[8] If even the mighty Spanish king cultivated his cardinal network, so much the less could Cosimo afford to ignore
the need to do so. Moreover, if he had less leverage over the
pope than the Spanish king, he had even less ability to be a Reformation prince, for the bonds between Rome and Tuscany ran
too deep, and his standing in Florence was linked to his ability
to keep favors in the Roman curia coming.[9] His people wanted
patronage. They had expected it from the Medici ever since
Cosimo the Elder and Lorenzo the Magnificient's days, when
both Florentines and Tuscans had seen them as intermediaries
who could "smooth the way for those seeking ecclesiastical in-
comes and offices."[10] Thus, this chapter argues that Cosimo
chose the smoother and time-tested Medicean path, seeking to
wield influence over the Tuscan church as a patron rather than
an absolutist. Sanctified by its associations to the heavenly
court and legitimized by long usage, the role of ecclesiastical
patron was not tied to any specific regime type, lacking as it did
the toxicity that a more overt form of absolutism over the

church would have generated. On the other hand, the patronage system generated its own limitations, and the second part of this chapter is devoted to illuminating them. Cosimo may have relied on a system of contacts in the papal curia, but the same contacts could press the directions of his ecclesiastical policies in uncomfortable ways, forcing him to tolerate some of the less attractive aspects of the Counter-Reformation, which he would have preferred to avoid.

Patronage and the Heavenly Chain of Intercession

Florence had never seen a ruler quite like Cosimo, a prince who dared to compare his own office to the rule of God over the heavens. Nevertheless, princely divinity was just one category of many; the state could mirror the sacred cosmos in other ways. Indeed, Florentine political life held more important ties than the bimonthly round of officeholding anyway; ordinarily it was not the officeholders who ruled Florence but the puppet masters who pulled their strings. The key to holding those strings usually lay in playing the game of patronage with the most dexterous hand.[11] Indeed, as Trexler notes, the relationship between patron and client in Florence ran deeper, produced greater trust, and was more stable than governmental relations anyway. In Florence especially, patronage and government had always gone hand in hand.[12] Consequently, it was imperative that Cosimo show himself to be not only a successful prince but a successful *patrone* as well, one who could be trusted to secure favors for an extended *familia* of kin and clients.

Moreover, this extrainstitutional system of favor and privilege had its own logic of sacral mimesis, for the earthly chain of intercession was only a pale reflection of that more glorious heavenly chain, which funneled supplication up to the Almighty through the saints and the Virgin Mary. Cosimo's namesake, Cosimo Il Vecchio, had understood the game with his characteristic perspicacity. Though he could never be a prince, he could be divinized in his role as patron and intercessor, a fact that his artistic commissions sought to stress with paint and canvas.[13] His clients must certainly have gotten the point, for they were not loath to pepper their letters of thanks or supplication with phrases like "you are my god on earth . . . never have I wished anything more in life than to take shelter under the wing of your power and authority."[14] In the fifteenth century, Averardo Medici had been addressed the same way; for instance, Bernardo Alammani wrote to him: "I commend myself to you with all my heart, for my only hope is in you and in God. . . . You are my God on earth and all that I crave in this world is the honor and prosperity which I am confident I will receive by your favor."[15] The motif lived on into the younger Cosimo's age as well, as amateur political theologians continued to juxtapose the categories of saintly and patronly intercession. For instance, Varchi uttered these telling words at the funeral of Cosimo's mother, Maria Salviati: "you should pray to [Maria Salviati] devoutly night and day without end so that, just as she was your secure port in all your tempests here on earth, interceding for you and asking not only mercy and pardon but also the grace and favor of her only and illustrious son for whatever you needed, so now she will certainly succor you in your sins and all your needs, ever interceding for you and asking for you in the kingdom of heaven, not only favor and grace, but pardon and mercy from the most holy and only son of God."[16] This linking of earthly patronage and celestial intercession did not issue from the mouth of some unabashed monarchy man—as the reader will recall, Varchi was a republican. But a patronage network was not a governmental form; it was just as important in the republican system as it had ever been to monarchy. Patronage was a part of Florentine life, so divinizing the patron was not too bitter a pill for a republican to swallow.

Patronage networks were sanctified in the very language used to describe their operations, for the patronage system pilfered words and concepts directly from a more sacred semantic register. Grace was one such concept. Cosimo's own clients conflated the two different types of grace with strategic ingenuity. Consider this request for a vacant benefice to which Cosimo held the patronage rights: "Since the Church of Santa Maria of Stia is vacant due to the death of the rector and since as the patron, your Excellency has the right to elect the new rector, I, not at all confiding in any particular merit or sufficiency . . . but only in your beneficence, which has always been natural to your most illustrious house, and in the bounty of God, which is powerful enough to make grace and sufficiency super abound in all others and in me, have recourse to supplicate you of your grace."[17] The juxtaposition of the prince's grace and God's grace was certainly no accident. The writer could not but have known he was shrewdly tapping into an old tradition of equating patron and deity. Nor would Cosimo have missed the connection, for his own letters borrowed just as heavily from sacred expressions. Like many early modern Italians, he asked his favors as *gratia,* he appealed for intercession (*intercessioni*), and he accomplished the task by praying to (*preghi* or *pregando*) the next person on the chain of intercession.[18] This slippage of language may have sometimes operated just out of the realm of conscious deliberation, but only because Florentine experience had engrained the habit binding heaven and earth in two parallel chains of intercession.

Florence and the Roman Connection

Why did Cosimo have to play this part of intercessor in Roman courts? Simply because Roman favors were highly important to Tuscans. It was Rome's game, and Cosimo played it on Rome's terms. For Rome was no ordinary neighbor. The Papal States, with their strange shape, jutting aggressively northward around the eastern edge of Tuscany, made up an uncomfortably large portion of his border, and the fact that the same set of Roman hands dispensed both spiritual and temporal favors made a working relationship with the papal curia indispensable. Most important, the considerable back-and-forth of peoples, moneys, and offices between these two neighbors dictated that Cosimo develop contacts who could protect his clients' interests in Rome. Cutting spiritual ties, or "going Turk," as Cosimo put it,[19] would have simply put his secular interests in the Papal States in too much jeopardy. Moreover, winning the loyalties of his subjects by getting them favors in Rome was a sine qua non of holding the first position in Tuscany.

What stoked the voracious Tuscan appetite for favors in the papal curia? For starters, Tuscans conducted more than their fare share of civil and financial business with their southern neighbor, often invading the Tiber's banks as foreign bankers and merchants. In litigious early modern Italy, legal issues always nipped hot on the heels of business ventures, and with frequent regularity, Tuscans found themselves standing before Roman tribunals. The whole process could be quite daunting because, unsurprisingly, the ability to get anything accomplished in Roman courts was indissolubly linked to whom one knew, what strings one could pull, and what favors one could call in. As one of Cosimo's supplicants complained, his case had been dragged out for "four months without being able to end it, because of the many favors given to the adversary, a familiar of Reverend Cardinal Trani."[20] A good number of such unhappy litigants had little sense of how to navigate the snaking turns of curial politics. Faced with such bleak prospects, they often turned to the most powerful patron they knew: Cosimo. Cosimo was happy to oblige, putting his clients directly in his debt with little more than the dispatch of a letter. Legion were the occasions on which Cosimo called on his patronage network in Rome to expedite a case or provide legal favors.[21] If Tuscany was to continue doing business with Rome, Tuscans simply could not avoid legal entailments in the Papal States, and they could not prosecute them successfully without a patron. Cosimo had to step into the breach.

Legal favors made up a large part of his patronage business, but there were other favors to be had. For instance, Tuscans who could not find opportunities to ply their trades in a Tuscan post often looked to the church's state. For physicians, lawyers, philosophers, and humanists, curial Rome was a welcome alternative to the duke's notoriously tight-fisted government. However, like legal favors, choice jobs were usually not to be had without connections. So when Tuscans went to Rome, they armed themselves with a credential letter from their duke and patron. As a result, Tuscans' ability to make their way in the Papal States usually depended on what regard the curia held toward Cosimo at any given moment.[22]

Moreover, this flow of peoples was not a one-way street; convivial Florence in its turn siphoned its fair share of the pope's citizens away from Rome. Cosimo encouraged this, enticing such adventurers as Ridolpho Baglioni, Stefano Palestina, Stefano Colonna, Giovan Batista Savelli, and Conte Giovanfrancesco da Bagno into his employ as soldiers of fortune.[23] Ties of blood linked Cosimo to other subjects of the Papal States. For instance, he numbered the Rossi of San Secondo and the Cybos of Massa-Carrara among his kinsmen.[24] Thus, his clients and family kept him entangled in papal politics whether he willed it or no. For instance, in 1549 his Colonna clients goaded him into asking Julius III to restore them to a castle they had held under Clement VII. Cosimo, finding himself Stefano Colonna's heir a few short years later, called on one of his cardinal intercessors to protect the widow.[25] And when Lorenzo Cybo's wife died in 1553, Cosimo wrote on his relatives' behalf to the cardinal legate of Perugia, trying to keep the papal *contado* of Ferentillo under the family's control.[26] Cosimo intrigued to keep the Rossi in their fief of San Secondo during the Farnese wars over Parma,[27] and he got the displaced Perugian rebel Ridolpho Baglioni restored to a new state in the papal territory under the auspices of Julius III's good graces.[28] When Cosimo again got a friendly pope in Pius IV, he tried to use his influence to secure

Conte Giovanfrancesco da Bagno, who had been deprived of his hereditary papal fief by Paul IV, safe passage to Rome defend his rights[29] Thus, friendly contacts in Rome were essential if Cosimo was to protect the interests of clients holding land or titles from the pope.

Cosimo's client network was swamped not only with high-ranking papal feudatories but also with commoners, who got themselves in serious trouble in the papal patrimony with astonishing regularity. Petty vendettas escalated into homicide with such frequency that the history of the age reads as much like an Icelandic saga as the rebirth of Western civilization. When the desperate end of murder was consummated, the offenders often scampered out of Rome and into Tuscany and the safety of a foreign land. Rome pursued extradition only for certain types of criminals. Those exiled guests who could win Cosimo's favor and patronage found that they had won a powerful ally in getting their sentences remitted in the pope's courts. For instance, Cosimo was inclined to help the murderer Bernardo Camaiani, brother of two of his closest confidants, to make peace with the family of his victim and to gain pardon from the pope.[30] Cosimo was also inclined to offer his protection to men like Antonio Barzellino, a Medici client who had killed his wife in a fit of passion when he found her committing adultery.[31] These were the kind of extenuating circumstances that Cosimo thought deserved a little clemency, and his Barzellino client was the type of man whom Cosimo was of a mind to help.

Thus, secular matters snared Cosimo into a Roman net from which he could not have disentangled himself even if he had wished. Rome's dominion over the world of the spirit only doubled its importance. Matrimonial cases, inheritance cases, benefice cases: the Roman church claimed the right to adjudicate over a broad swath of life. The renouncement of any benefice often had to go to the Roman courts, and all dispensations needed to be run through the curial office known as the papal datary.[32] Any priest who found that he did not possess the right qualifications for holding a benefice had to throw himself on the mercy of the curia.[33] To cite just one pertinent example, Cosimo's choice to run the Hospital of the Innocents, Vincenzo Borghini, needed a dispensation because the position required the care of souls, and as a regular he could not exercise that function without release from his vows.[34] Too young, too old, too criminal, too married: any number of reasons might drive a priest to ask for Cosimo's assistance. To exacerbate the issue, the ordinary hierarchy, which consisted of canons, diocesan priests, and bishops, was not the only one beyond Cosimo's control; intervening with the regular orders, which consisted of monks, nuns, and abbots, normally required the use of Roman connections as well.[35] Any number of modest requests might come before Cosimo, and he was expected to put his patronage ties to work as eagerly for the good of the clergy as for his other subjects.

There is little surprise that ambitious clerics came with cap in hand to beg Cosimo's assistance, but he also put his network at the convenience of his own bishops, who had as much business to conduct in the Roman courts as anyone. When a bishop wanted to renounce his bishopric, he needed a dispensation, which occasioned Cosimo's intercession.[36] When a bishop wanted to reform a monastery or punish some troublesome monks, he needed the cooperation of the regular hierarchy, which meant getting Cosimo to unleash his cardinal protectors on the generals of various orders.[37] When a bishop was having a dispute over some pensioned benefice, he needed a legal favor, and Cosimo was the man for that.[38] Even when a bishop wanted a promotion, he came to Cosimo. Not only did he help secure some of his clients a red hat, he even helped two of them to the biggest promotion of all, playing the role of pope-maker in the conclaves that elected Julius III and Pius IV.[39] Ironically, Cosimo may have been helped in this regard by his own relative unimportance. Because he was a relatively minor player in European politics, his clients were not liable to be automatically excluded

as were those of both France and Spain, who continuously ve-
toed one another's favored candidates.[40] Thus, Cosimo was able
to parlay his weakness into a major strength, and when Tuscans
came begging for favors from Rome, he had a powerful network
at his disposal. In fact, he simply could not ignore the Roman
connections.

Winning Friends and Influencing Cardinals: Networks of Ecclesiastical Patronage

Only by building ties to the cardinals in the papal curia could
Cosimo forge the type of patronage network he needed. But
how did he construct this network without the threats or money
used by the Hapsburgs?[41] It is to this subject that I now turn. For
years, the quickest way to influence in the curia had been the
soft underbelly of papal finances. This was how the Medici and
other families had initially gotten a foothold in the church, but
since the Medici bank had folded years before, that route was
closed to Cosimo.[42] Fortunately, other standbys of patronage
networking were still available to him, and he was able to use
kinship ties and bonds of mutual interest to win over several key
cardinals. In so doing, he courted the friendship of high-ranking
ecclesiastics with gifts and posts in his own government, and he
showed himself particularly adept at leveraging his control over
the Tuscan church to win the goodwill of cardinals who had
ecclesiastical benefices and other church related interests in
Tuscany.

Both in early modern Italy and elsewhere, ties of patronage
were frequently knotted together by the bonds of kinship or
marriage, an arrangement that could create new patronage ties
ex novo or could serve as a guarantee that mutual pronounce-
ments of love, devotion, and affection were more than mere
words.[43] Indeed, Cosimo's network of patronage in the Roman
curia could not have been built, cemented, or maintained without due attention to this reality. Thus, the first bachelorhood

that Cosimo sold on the marriage market of Italian nobility was his own, and while he may have chosen Eleonora de Toledo for love, eschewing the notoriously ugly and awkward older daughter of the viceroy of Naples for the stately elegance of the younger sister, the alliance with the family was itself rather coldly calculated. That move not only cemented a Medici/Toledo power block in imperial and Italian politics, it won him one very powerful ally in Rome: the influential Toledo cardinal.[44] As the son of the second duke of Alba, Toledo was brother to the viceroy of Naples and uncle to Cosimo's new bride. Moreover, Toledo was no mere leftover from the days of Medicean Rome; Paul III himself had given him the red hat in 1538, and Toledo had real influence in Roman politics.[45] Cosimo did not waste time in putting his new familial connections to work and leaned on Toledo as a crutch in the curia during the 1540s and 1550s. Whether it concerned the most important matters of Roman patronage, like attempting to get his son made archbishop of Pisa, or the least important matters, like trying to win an inheritance case for a poor client widow, archival evidence suggests that Cardinal Toledo was Cosimo's most important patron in Rome.[46] His marriage to Eleonora thus gained him one powerful secular and one powerful ecclesiastical ally. The marriage, moreover, set the tone for both his secular and ecclesiastical networking policies; the connection to the Toledos bound him tightly to imperial interests, and as I shall show, he cast his lot primarily, though not exclusively, with the imperialist party in the curia.

When his own daughters came of age, he shopped their maidenhood with equal dexterity, selling their nubility for both ecclesiastical and secular profit. In 1551 he promised a marriage to the Del Monte clan that never came off.[47] He gave one daughter as a peace offering to the Este duke of Ferrara, Alfonso II, simultaneously using the alliance to try to forge links with Alfonso's cousin the cardinal of Urbino. In this case, Cosimo was pushing extended kinship to its limits: the cardinal of

Urbino was only a second cousin to the duke of Ferrara.[48] At any rate, more important bonds of kinship were there for the taking. In 1558, Cosimo married off his daughter Isabella to Paolo Giordano Orsini. Had he lived longer, Cosimo would have lived long enough to bitterly regret the choice. For one night in 1576, while feigning amorous intentions and passionately kissing his estranged bride, the ill-mannered and ill-bred Paolo strangled the unfortunate princess to death with a cord that one of his servants lowered through a hole cut in the ceiling.[49] Disastrous as the decision may have been on a personal level, giving his daughter Isabella's hand to a scion of the Orsini clan was ultimately good politics. For in this way he tied himself not only to this powerful Roman family but also to one of his more important ecclesiastical patrons, Guido Ascanio Sforza, better known as Cardinal Santa Fiora. Sforza was a scion of the house of San Fiora, the child of Bozio II, and the uncle of Paolo Giordano Orsini.[50] Cosimo made much of the new ties created between himself and one of his most important ecclesiastical contacts, celebrating their new relationship and receiving the cardinal in Florence in 1559 with great pomp and ceremony.[51] Though Santa Fiora was a somewhat inexplicably committed imperial, he also gave Cosimo ties to the enemy with whom he so desperately wanted reconciliation, for Santa Fiora, whom Cosimo had counted among his biggest supporters long before the ill-starred nuptials, was a grandson of Paul III through the maternal line.[52] It was this lucky connection and nothing else that had won him his red hat in 1534 at the tender age of sixteen. If Burgos was one of Cosimo's crutches in the papal court, Santa Fiora was the other, and Cosimo wrote to him seeking patronage on many occasions.[53] Thus, in the first place, Cosimo constructed and cemented his bonds of ecclesiastical patronage in the old-fashioned way: he married into them.

If he could not break with Rome, neither could he afford to break with his own bishops. Fortunately, he did not need to be so proactive on his own home front. The familial Medici

stranglehold over the office of the papacy had left him a suitable episcopal legacy, as many of his own and neighboring bishoprics were already in friendly familial hands. When he ascended to the throne, the Archdiocese of Pisa was in the care of
Onofrio Bartholini Medici; the bishop of Forli was Bernardo
Antonio Medici; the bishop of Arezzo another distant cousin,
Francesco Minerbetti Medici; and the bishop of Lucca was his
half-uncle Guido Sforza Riario, the child of his paternal grandmother. Volterra should have been in good hands but for the
ambitions of Cardinal Salviati, Cosimo's uncle and onetime
nemesis. Apart from Salviati and his occasional crony (Archbishop Ridolfi, who soon became archbishop of Florence), Cosimo began his reign with a malleable brand of favorable bishops
tied to the Medici house through kinship and friendships. Where
real bonds were lacking, close ties could be ensured through fictive kinship. It was in this way that the Medici had bound the
Martio family to them. Originally descended from a branch of
the Vespucci, Angelo Martio Medici had served under Alessandro and been granted the bishopric of Assisi by Clement VII.
Both Angelo and his nephew, the hyperalliteratively named
Martio Marzi Medici, the bishop of Marsico, served as secretaries under Cosimo and held other important posts as well.
Though not really blood relations, the family was allowed to
add "Medici" to their surname, thus forever binding their destiny to the fortunes of the patron.[54] Absent outright blood ties,
few actions could more demonstrably seal the patron-client
relationship.

Cosimo and his wife were fruitful, but their supply of mar-
riageable spawn was not endless. Kinship networking had its
natural limits, limits often imposed by the tragic deaths of children and young brides. Given that, Cosimo had to find other
ways to make friends—to tie his patrons and clients to himself
with the bonds of *amicizia*. This term covered a much broader
range of arrangements than is implied by the modern English
word *friendship,* in that it included a whole range of formal

client-patron ties that were just as important as the emotive valence we consider an essential aspect of friendship.[55] *Amicizia* might consist in little more than the businesslike presumption that one party would supply access to offices and the other side would supply political support. In this limited sense of the term, Cosimo succeeded in making many of his bishops his ("friends"). For example, his first ambassador to the imperial court was none other than the learned bishop of Cortona, Giovambattista Ricasoli, whom Cosimo later would entrust with the delicate mission of winning Queen Catherine dei Medici as an ally.[56] When Cortona went to France, Cosimo substituted the bishops of Forlì and Arezzo as ambassadors to the imperial court. There were more modest uses to be made of bishops as well. He employed two successive bishops from nearby Assisi as secretaries at his court, and where offices were not appropriate, literary patronage could be substituted. He won a strong link to the Farnese court in his patronage of Paolo Giovio, the bishop of Como.[57] Finally, Cosimo solidified the goodwill of the Minerbetti bishop of Arezzo by loaning him a pile of low-interest money from the Monte di Pietà.[58]

If Cosimo was adept at turning his bishops into clients, he was equally adept at turning his clients into bishops, both in his own and other people's lands. In 1551 Julius III installed Cosimo's secretary and onetime ambassador to Trent, Pietro Camaiani, as bishop in the green hills of nearby Fiesole.[59] On Cosimo's prodding, Alessandro Strozzi was made bishop of Volterra in 1568.[60] Jacopo Guidi, a onetime secretary and future Cosimian encomiast, became bishop of Penne and Atri in 1561, under the benevolent promotion of Pius IV.[61] Of all these, none was as dear to Cosimo's heart as the promotion of his son Giovanni to the archbishopric of Pisa.[62] On Giovanni's untimely death, the archbishopric went to another Medici functionary, the onetime governor of Siena, Agnolo Niccolini.[63] Finally, by favoring the young Alessandro Medici's career, Cosimo assured his nephew's smooth transition to bishop of Pistoia and then archbishop of

Florence on his way to the papal chair. Thus Cosimo was able to bequeath to his successors the support of friendly bishops in the same manner that his family had bequeathed friendly bishops to him.

Early modern people may not have minded the stuffy formal friendships born out of the patron-client bond, but *amicizia* did not always lack more warmly human feelings. In the age of Castiglione's courtier, grace and likeability counted for something. For instance, Cosimo trusted Alessandro Strozzi implicitly not only because of his faithful service but also because Strozzi had idled away more than one afternoon gambling with him at a Medici villa.[64] It was with the desire to cultivate these same kinds of personal ties to his own patrons that Cosimo received Cardinals Burgos and Santa Fiore as his guests in Florence, while unsuccessfully trying to wheedle visits to Tuscany out of both Cardinal del Monte and Paul III.[65] When he visited Pius IV in Rome in 1560, the two reportedly locked themselves together for hours on end, and when Cosimo left the eternal city, he left with a pope largely willing to do his bidding, despite the unease of the Roman citizens themselves.[66] Formal friendships were also sweetened by the exchange of gifts, outward signs of the ties that bound. These gifts could help to create the fictive kinship bonds that replaced biological ones. For instance, in 1551 Cosimo sent Pope Julius III two crystal vases on Christmas with the note that he was observing an old Spanish custom of filial piety in which the son presented gifts to the father.[67] When that pope's creature Cardinal Innocenzo del Monte, racked by gout, requested two mules so as to travel through Tuscany, Cosimo found it wise to indulge him, even though he had to take them from his own duchess.[68] Indeed, less formal emotive ties mattered, and formal friendships could be created or cemented by more informal wooing.

Patronage ties might also be born of mutual interest, often generated by various cardinals' need for legal assistance within Tuscany. The overlapping of secular and ecclesiastical jurisdictions made churchmen who neighbored Tuscany the most highly pliable kind, for their proximity created a situation in which foreign cardinals and bishops often had ecclesiastical benefices in Cosimo's jurisdiction, benefices they could not seize without the ducal *placet*.[69] The archival evidence suggests that this is exactly how Cosimo got two of his more important cardinal protectors into his circle: the cardinal bishop of Faenza, Pio Ridolfo Carpi, and the future Pope Julius III, Cardinal Giovanni Maria Ciocchi del Monte. As onetime legate to the Marche and one time bishop of Faenza, Cardinal Carpi had considerable interest on Tuscan soil.[70] My research affirms that he had at least three Tuscan benefices for which he supplicated Cosimo's assistance, but the number is likely greater than that.[71] In one case, Cosimo had to ride to Carpi's rescue and battle off a rival claimant who was trying to seize the benefice by force of arms.[72] In his turn, Cosimo called on this neighboring cardinal on a number of important occasions. When he wanted to reform the Conventual Franciscans he enlisted the help of Carpi, who was the protector of the order.[73] When he wanted to secure the generalship of the still troublesome friars for his own confidant, he tried to get Carpi to fix the election.[74] Finally, when he was trying to get one of his own secretary's inquisitorial cases expedited, he wrote Carpi an impassioned plea.[75] Of course, these were only the tip of the iceberg. Routine smaller favors begged from Carpi filled up volumes of correspondence as well.[76] In these, Carpi was one of Cosimo's most consistent friends, and their friendship lasted until the prelate succumbed to his gout in 1564.

Carpi was a small gamble. Like Cosimo, he was an imperial anyway, so Cosimo risked little in courting his patronage. The gamble that really paid dividends was the relationship Cosimo cultivated with Cardinal Del Monte, who, in an abnormal turn had sought the duke's goodwill as early as 1542.[77] Here we see that the entry into one patronage network, the Toledos, opened up entry to another within the overarching system set up by the

Hapsburg kings. Del Monte probably first reached out to Cosimo because Del Monte was friends with Cosimo's relative the
cardinal Burgos.[78] However, Del Monte had other good reasons
to do so. Paul III soon granted Del Monte all of the benefices
that had belonged to Del Monte's deceased uncle, many of
them in their native Monte San Sovino in the diocese of Arezzo.
Cosimo's archives show that Del Monte's attempts to turn
grace into revenue quickly degenerated into a mess of competing claims and threats. Thus, Cosimo's friendship was fundamentally important for Del Monte, and Cosimo did all he could
for him, readily giving the agent immediate possession of any
nondisputed benefices, agreeing to Del Monte's possession of
those benefices for which Cosimo personally held the *ius patronato,* and even bullying others into ceding their claims to the
Del Montes.[79] In 1546 Cosimo did Del Monte an even bigger
favor, reserving all cases involving Del Monte's benefices personally to himself, to be heard only by his auditor Lelio Torelli.[80]
Cosimo's gamble did not go unrewarded. Del Monte was Cosimo's lifeline at the first session of Trent, and their relationship
was solidified through the lifelong friendship Del Monte cultivated there with Cosimo's ambassador.[81] It comes as no surprise,
then, that Del Monte favored Cosimo at the papal court in his
precedence controversy with the duke of Ferrara.[82] Cosimo returned the favor; against the inclination of the emperor, the as-
pirant kingmaker pushed Del Monte through as a compromise
candidate in the 1549 conclave.[83] This was an undoubted triumph. Del Monte owed his election to Cosimo, and more important, Del Monte knew it.[84] Cosimo had long suffered under
the ire of an unfavorable pope, and a candidate who owed his
election primarily to him was a welcome change.

In his early years, Cosimo used his control over benefices to
win one more important patron, whom it would be remiss not
to include on this list, for this earliest ally in the Roman court
was one of Cosimo's own: the reverend cardinal Santiquattro,
bishop of Pistoia. He was a Pucci, and as a Pucci he held a num-

ber of *patronato* privileges in Tuscany. Thus Cosimo took Santiquattro's familiars under his own protection. When the new
archdeacon of the Florentine cathedral, Victorio di Imola, got
into disputes over his benefices, the complaints were sent to
Santiquattro in Rome and then to Cosimo, and then were
quickly settled, though Cosimo again had to use force to do it.[85]
For his part, Santiquattro was one of Cosimo's earliest cardinal
friends at a time when it was an undoubtedly unpopular position for a cardinal to take. When Cosimo's refusal to help collect the tithe ended in interdict in 1540, Santiquattro went to
the feet of the pope on Cosimo's behalf.[86] And when Cosimo
wanted to keep the bishopric of Assisi inside his own circle of
familiars (though it was outside his territory), it was Cardinal
Pucci whom he asked to intercede.[87] Pucci was thus a lifeline for
the newly elected Cosimo and his only way to wring even the
smallest concessions from his antagonist in the papal chair.

In the twelve short years between Cosimo's ascension to the
ducal throne and Del Monte's ascension to the papal chair, Cosimo came a long way. In 1537, even his own cardinal uncle
Jacopo Salviati had tried to get rid of him, an outcome that
would have delighted the pope, though he refused to lift a finger to make it happen. By 1549 that uncle had been put in his
place, and even Paul III had made his peace with Cosimo. Indeed, attitudes toward the young duke had palpably changed,
and his ecclesiastical patronage reached to the highest chair in
Christendom. By 1550, Cosimo had put together a very impressive ecclesiastical patronage network, even in the teeth of the
pope's general repugnance. Playing the few cards he had, he
had reaffirmed and solidified the ties of kinship that his family
had left him; he had made new ties of kinship by utilizing his
own marriageability and then that of his children; he had opened
up his tight fist and spent some of his little money on entertain-
ing important ecclesiastical dignitaries; he had granted offices
to his own bishops; and he had utilized his small sphere of ecclesiastical jurisdiction to win over a few key cardinals.

The Counter-Reformation Comes to Florence

Cosimo's ecclesiastical standing was very much tied to a traditional system of patron-client relations, as has been shown. However, the same system that opened the church's doors imposed its own limits and boundaries. Those who did favors in Rome expected to receive them in Florence, and one of those favors included bringing the Counter-Reformation to the Arno's banks. This section will show how Cosimo's differing status as a patron under the pontificates of Julius III and Paul IV contributed to his differing attitudes toward the Inquisition, from the attitude of a staunch promoter of the institution under the papacy of his good friend Julius III to that of a stauncher defender of state jurisdiction under the unlikable Paul IV. Indeed, Cosimo's favorable standing in Rome during the early 1550s put him in a favorable mood when the messy and uncomfortable business of auto-da-fé was suggested to him. By the end of the decade, he was out of credit at the Roman court and had little to lose in the way of patronage. It was then that he showed his independent streak. Only the advent of a favorable pope in Pius IV again brought Cosimo's antiheretical nature to the fore.

It is not out of place to examine Cosimo's own sentiments on heresy, since many scholars of his reign suggest that political expediency alone informed his religious policies, assuming, as they do, that he learned his governance from the pages of Machiavelli.[88] This line of analysis is mistaken; Cosimo may not have been a trained theologian, but not all his religious opinions were marked by Machiavelli's peculiar brand of apathetic indifference. On the contrary, Cosimo had always believed himself safely on the Catholic side of the Reformation divide. For instance, when he exhorted a subject to end a vendetta with the argument that the disputant would thereby "gain merit in the sight of the lord," he thereby affirmed his attachment to the traditional Catholic doctrine on grace and works.[89] Later correspondence reveals this to be no mere slip of the pen.[90] Indeed, even before Roman officials began persuading him, he was pursuing heretics on his own initiative. As early as 1544 he ordered processions in the city for both peace and the conversion of the Lutherans, and in 1549 he had to be begged to send a certain heretic named Francesco Puccerrelli to the galleys, as he had apparently personally wanted the unfortunate man burned.[91] Given Cosimo's highly conservative personality, this is no surprise. He would have looked on the Reformation as a *cosa nuova,* and all new things stoked his suspicions. Moreover, it would have been rather a hard case for a Medici with two popes in the maternal line to deny the traditional Roman authority. In this case, then, personal belief married nicely to political expediency; Cosimo's desire to prosecute heresy proceeded at least partially from an uncynical attachment to the traditional religion.

On the other hand, he did not want the apparatus of Roman repression tramping unfettered through his own backyard. Though he did not always give the Inquisition free play, it was no anachronistic concern for religious tolerance that stayed his hand; it was his distaste for the Inquisition's methods. He wanted his justice quick; the Inquisition was glacially slow. He liked his justice cheap, both for his government and for litigants; the Inquisition was expensive for defendants as it frequently bled them dry while holding them interminably in prison. He strove to make his justice impartial; the Inquisition proceeded, according to him, far too often on baseless and anonymous whispers uttered by jealous neighbors. In 1560, he was even so bold as to write a somewhat impudent letter to the Holy Office, a letter that captures his general attitude in a few choice lines:

> Do not be deceived in thinking that I am not a most zealous persecutor of heretics, such is the zeal that I have always had and will always have toward the Holy Catholic Faith and the Holy See. I thank you for the note that you have given me on the 23rd of the past month, in order to enlighten me about the erroneous opinions spreading in Siena

and of the provisions that you think should be made; however, because it would be unsurprising if in a place like Siena, particular passions or ambitions sought to harm others by some sinister invention, I would desire that . . . you come to some particulars about the business. I will provide in the future against such rebels to the faith of Christ with such severity that you will certainly know what my attitude toward them is. Nonetheless, it does not seem that I should have to proceed in the dark in such important business without a good basis, especially since the business affects mostly honored and noble persons.[92]

Indeed, though he had little love for heretics, Cosimo quite palpably disliked the Inquisition, and he knew his Italian subjects did not like it either. Unfortunately, we possess little knowledge of his early dealings with the Holy Office, thanks to the mob that sacked the hated institution and burned its documents on the death of Paul IV. The darkness only lifts in the early 1550s, when Cosimo was lending the Inquisition the full might of his secular power. In one single day in 1552, Cosimo's officers arrested forty heretics, marching them through the streets of Florence to the cathedral, with penitential garb and lit yellow candles testifying to their shame as excommunicates. On the top of the list was one of Cosimo's own, Bartolommeo Panciatichi, ducal secretary.[93] He was not Cosimo's first sacrifice to ecclesiastical policy and rigorous justice, nor would he be the last. Cosimo did not even spare his own from the Inquisition's dungeons.

Why such deferential treatment to an institution that he so obviously loathed? Simply because his patronage network in Rome wanted it, and he could not hold out against requests from that quarter. Cosimo agreed to the *auto-da-fé* only after the master of the Sacred Palace had exhorted him to the brink of tears. The request almost certainly came directly from the pope, who at this time was none other than his good friend the former Cardinal Del Monte.[94] Cosimo could hardly turn down a pope who had spent the first two years of his papacy shower-

ing his former protector with an ample bounty of Roman patronage. Apart from having given Cosimo the *stocco* and *ber-
retone* in 1551, Del Monte provided secular and ecclesial posts
to Cosimo's clients and gave them considerable favors in their
litigation.[95] Whereas Cosimo had occasionally refused to write
letters to Paul III on the grounds that his recommendations did
more harm than good,[96] now he could send clients back to the
eternal city and to a pope who held him in particular esteem.[97]
Like his Medici forebears, he could even use his relations with
the papacy on a wider stage. As the king of France had once
used Lorenzo as an intermediary with Rome, now the queen of
France used Cosimo's intercession there, allowing him to boast:
"The Most Christian Queen [holds] it as a certainty that my intercession with the Pope can accomplish much."[98] Indeed, Roman patronage had gotten almost too good. Things had reached
such a pitch that Cosimo had to remind others that the pope was
not a puppet with strings pulled from Florence. As he wrote to
his ambassador: "It will do us harm if it seems as if His Holiness moves by our order because in fact, we do not want to
push him but only to remind him and to inform him of everything, so that as a Father and Lord, he might take those expedi-
ents that seem suitable."[99] To a duke who had spent years butt-
ing heads against the inimitably thick skull of Paul III, this new
concern must have certainly been a welcome problem.

The pope was not the only one in Rome turning the screws
on Cosimo. His patron Cardinal Carpi was also part of the Inquisition's machinery, and if the pope and his Del Monte clan
were making demands Cosimo could not refuse, how much less
could he refuse the demands of his relative, the cardinal Toledo? The Dominican Toledo had sat on the inquisitorial tribu-
nal since its inception in 1542 and appears to have been quietly
instrumental in swinging Cosimo to Rome's way of thinking.[100]
The buildup of tensions and threats apparently went on for
some time. Already on March 3, 1551, Cosimo had gotten into
a small spat with one of Toledo's *commendatori,* and when the

dispute had come to the attention of the cardinal, Cosimo wrote to excuse himself. "I would not have shown so little affection," the still slightly irate duke claimed, "if your *comendatori,* to whom you show so much affection, had not imputed me to be little religious, or to say better, imputed that I was a Lutheran; if he had not done that, I would not have treated him as I did."[101] Stale rumors of his own heterodoxy were apparently lingering from his altercations with Paul III and were giving Cosimo pause. He was certainly asking himself if that was why Toledo had just failed him in his bid to secure the *commenda* of San Jacopo sopr'Arno in Florence.[102] Would Cosimo's most important relationship and whole patronage network slip through his fingers if he refused to move aggressively against the heretics in his own state? He did not wait to find out. When one of his readers at Pisa came under suspicion later that year, he assured the cardinal that the inquisitors would be given all assistance to prosecute the unfortunate offender, "Because the inquisitor is here under the authority of the ordinary and hears cases involving similar errors, if anyone accuses him, he can come before them since the inquisitors are not only permitted by me but given every aid to be able to castigate whoever errs, and we will do likewise against him if any heresies are found in him."[103] However, eventually Cosimo needed to back up his tough talk with a little exemplary justice. Eventually, he needed to allow the Inquisition in his own city.

This was the context of Florence's first real *auto-da-fé,* for it is almost certain that Toledo lent his ascendancy over Cosimo to the master of the Sacred Palace's exhortations. Tucked obscurely behind Cosimo's other dispatches to the Inquisition appears a letter from him to Cardinal Toledo, sent shortly after the auto-da-fé, pointing out that Cosimo had now fulfilled all the promises he had made concerning heresy.[104] Clearly, Toledo had been twisting Cosimo's arm to make him comply with the Inquisition. Indeed, with Carpi and Toledo badgering him from the Inquisition's side and Del Monte hectoring him from the seat of Peter, Cosimo could not hold out for long. The request for a more vigorous use of the Inquisition came not only from Rome but from those members of Cosimo's patronage network whom he could not refuse.

All Cosimo's cooperation during the years of the Del Monte papacy is thrown into relief by his largely indifferent attitude to the blandishments of Paul IV, a far more zealous pope who had gradually choked off Cosimo's access in the papal curia. As Paul moved into ever more intransigent antiimperial positions, Cosimo's patronage system broke down and with it the pope's leverage over Florence. With Toledo dead, Cardinal Santa Fiora locked away in Castel San Angelo, and all the imperial cardinals out of favor, Cosimo could hardly expect much patronage from his steadfast supporters in Rome.[105] Nor was the pope personally well disposed to the Hapsburg client duke of Florence; the vitriolically anti-Spanish Carafa reportedly counseled the duchess to begin costuming herself in black, since her husband was the son of the devil.[106] Things had definitely changed. Under the Del Monte pope, clients had flocked to Cosimo's patronage, "having great faith that 'his' intercession could dispose the Pope to do them (a) favor."[107] Under Paul, Cosimo apologetically caveated his patronage with the excuse that he did not know "how well my ink runs in that court in these times."[108] And indeed, his ink did not run well there. As the English ambassador in Rome noted, the hostile Paul knew just where to squeeze, taking out his vengeance against the duke's proimperial policies by proceeding "against many men of (the Pope's) estate who serve the Duke of Florence."[109] Given such tensions, Cosimo's failures as an intercessor with the bellicose old pope were many. Perhaps Cosimo's most vexing failure was his inability to keep his client Eustachio Petrucci, a knight of Malta, from losing his *commenda*. In 1558 Paul ordered all the knights of Malta to ready themselves for combat as the shadow of the Turkish fleet loomed over the dangerously exposed Christian outpost. Cosimo asked a dispensation for the frail and aging

Petrucci but could win neither permission nor forgiveness. When the elderly knight failed to show, Paul III deprived him of his abbey and turned a deaf ear to all of Cosimo's attempts to get it back for him.[110] Paul heard Cosimo's appeals on behalf of the abbot of Galgano with the same deaf ear, as Cosimo repeatedly attempted to intercede to prevent the old abbot from spending his last few days in an Inquisition jail.[111] All efforts were to no avail; Cosimo could offer his clients little more than formal and useless pleas in the Roman courts.

If patronage was the sinew of state, Paul's actions hacked at the very tendons of Medicean Florence itself. On the other hand, with less to lose, Cosimo could afford to be less cooperative with Paul's increasingly pitiless campaigns against heresy. Cosimo played the game more deftly this time, asserting independence while avoiding the outright hostility that had ignited passions during Paul III's papacy. For instance, in December 1557 Cosimo's government firmly rejected the Inquisition's creeping tendency to expand their jurisdictional competencies. Processes for scorn of the divine cult, dishonoring sacred things, blaspheming God and the saints, usury, thefts, sacrileges and other wicked things, Cosimo's government argued, had customarily belonged to the state's jurisdiction and would continue to do so. Moreover, the Inquisition would have no jurisdiction over Jews. Florence, the defiant auditor Vintha sardonically remarked, would not become another Spain, where the Inquisition puts its hands on everything.[112] The timing of the pronouncement was no accident, for Cardinal Toledo had died in September that same year and Cosimo could afford a little independence.

With Toledo gone, Cosimo's government continued to draw a line in the sand against Paul's Inquisition. When Paul issued an ultrarepressive Index of Prohibited Books, Cosimo at first played a waiting game, trying to save the booksellers excessive financial loss by appealing to a stay of execution on some of the less offensive titles. He wrote his auditor Torelli: "Having seen what you write to Concino about the Commissary of the Inquisition, we will be content that he be able with edicts and other actions to move against the prohibited books that treat of religion and sacred things, or of magic, spells, geomancy, chiromancy, prophetic astrology, and similar other matters since we have always been an observer of religion and most fierce persecutor of such crimes, but considering the particular damage to many without any profit because of the orders of His Holiness, we want to suspend until we hear from Rome the order for other books, even those by prohibited authors, unless they treat of religion and faith."[113] Cosimo was almost certainly planning to wait the pope out, hoping that Paul would simply die before the issue came to a head. The obstinate old pontiff, however, refused to comply, showing surprisingly stubborn longevity in his octogenarian twilight. Cosimo still had a trick or two up his sleeve, however, and when Paul pressed him into lighting the bonfires in March 1559, he indulged in a little sleight of hand, instructing his agents to leave nonheretical titles on the shelves and to make more "show than effect."[114]

Even in individual cases, Cosimo dug his heels more firmly into the ground than he had under Julius III. For instance, despite the hostilely indignant requests of the bishop of Bologna, Cosimo refused to extradite the Sozzini heretics to the Papal States, only sending them after the friendly Pius IV replaced Paul IV.[115] In December 1558, he promised to send a Tuscan priest named Francesco to Perugia for questioning, but later correspondence suggests that Francesco's extradition never took place.[116] In January 1559, Cosimo ordered some Spoletini heretics sent to Rome, but his commissary dallied for so long that they were able to bribe their way out of prison.[117] And by the middle of 1559, he was flat out refusing the Inquisition's request for extradition.[118] Indeed, both on the level of grand theory and individual justice, Cosimo's legacy of cooperation with the Inquisition became very spotty during Paul's papacy, for Paul gave Cosimo very little motivation to cooperate, and the pope's advanced age counseled the duke to a policy of Janus-faced quiescence and practical indifference. However, this would not last long. The next two popes were both friends to Cosimo, and both brought the agencies of repression to Florence for good.[119]

If patronage seems to have dictated Cosimo's attitude toward the Inquisition, the same patronage ties dictated his attitude to the other leg of Catholic reform, the Jesuit order. Of course, the two were not entirely distinct. The Roman Inquisition had specifically ordered Cosimo's Jesuit confessor to convince him of the need for the inquisitorial crackdown of 1552.[120] Moreover, the Jesuits themselves would become the prime persecutors of Sienese heretics during the 1560s.[121] The same patrons who had foisted the Inquisition on Cosimo seem to have slipped the Jesuits into Florence as well. For Cosimo did not fully trust the new Spanish order, despite his personal respect for Diego Lainez. Moreover, the Jesuits had powerful enemies, some of whom were whispering poisonous words into Cosimo's ears.[122] Thus Cosimo took his first Jesuits only on the recommendation of Cardinal Carpi, who got the Jesuits a foothold in Florence by gifting two of them to the ducal couple in 1546. Always a good judge of talent, the Jesuits quickly got the right man on the job, for Diego Lainez soon became the ducal couple's personal confessor and won over two of the duke's most influential advisors: Alessandro Strozzi and Giovanni Rossi.[123] The piously devout duchess seems to have been particularly attached to Lainez, as she repeatedly tried to find ways to keep the pope from sending this talented future general away from Florence.[124] Lainez so won over the ducal couple that by 1547 he was giving sermons in the Duomo to what he reported as wildly enthusiastic crowds.[125]

By this time, the Jesuits wanted a place in Florence where they might leverage the court into supporting the order's spiritual work of administering sacraments, converting sinners, and educating talented young nobles, and though the Jesuits may have had powerful enemies, they had powerful friends as well. One of these was Alessandro Strozzi, one of the duke's most trusted advisors on ecclesiastical affairs and a man who knew the ins and outs of ducal politics. When Ignatius asked Strozzi his advice, Strozzi suggested enlisting the help of Cardinal Toledo.[126] When the cardinal's letter arrived, it was accompanied by the more verbal admonitions of Cosimo's father-in-law, Pedro de Toledo. For Lainez reported that when the cardinal's letter was read to the duke, he threw up one last defense. In a final gasp of reserve, he muttered: "Some of these new things are dangerous, and while there may be some good men in the order, perhaps not all of them are. I've heard stories from Pistoia and others from Rome that Jesuits steal the wives right out from under their husbands." Strozzi, Eleonora, and the visiting Pedro de Toledo all then went to work refuting the rumors and breaking down the duke's obstinate resolve.[127] Lainez simply looked on in silent satisfaction. Indeed, between Carpi's politic maneuvering and the heavy-handed lobbying of the Toledos, Cosimo could not but be won over. Against his inclination, the Jesuits got their college in Pisa and a subvention from both Eleonora and Cosimo.[128] A few years later they got the church of San Giovannino in Florence as well.[129] Like the Inquisition, the Jesuits were in Tuscany to stay, bringing with them their educational program, spiritual exercises, and fervent obedience to Rome.

Conclusion

Nearly all of Cosimo's contemporary monarchs found control over patronage to their national churches to be an indispensable element of statecraft. Some found the institutional arrangements to wield control over their respective churches already in place. Others grabbed the reins of power during the transition to reformed styles of church governance. Cosimo could do neither. His geographical nearness and deep ties to Rome left him in a situation in which he had to maneuver within the confines of curial politics. Thus he could not wield ecclesiastical power like an absolute monarch; he had to act in the time-honored fashion of patron. This international exigency dovetailed nicely with Tuscan expectations anyway, for Tuscans were not in the habit of bowing their necks before a divinely endowed prince, but every one of them understood doffing one's cap to a sanctified *patrone*. Moreover, Tuscans simply expected that the Medici would play the part of their protector in Rome. Thus, when there was little to recommend Cosimo to a hostile pope, he appealed to the papal curia. When his subjects had interests that only the curia could satisfy, he turned to the cardinals for whom he could return a favor. When things ran smoothly, Cosimo grew in legitimacy, power, and reputation; it was a network he could not afford to ignore. However, the same patronage system that won him so much legitimacy also put him in its own peculiar straitjacket. There was little he could do. He preferred a friendly pope and hampered range of movement in ecclesiastical affairs to absolute liberty in ecclesiastical affairs and a potent enemy to his immediate south and east. Only when he had nothing to lose in Rome did he show an overweening concern for his own jurisdictional prerogatives. With Jesuits and inquisitors at the gates, Cosimo could do little but huff in annoyance, and then meekly let them into the sheepfold.

CHAPTER 5

Cosimo and Savonarolan Reform

SAVONAROLA had often proclaimed that Florence should have no king but Christ, a slogan that was not long in passing from the pulpit to the piazza to become the mantra of the republicanism of the Savonarolan movement. On the other hand, Savonarola's followers were certain that under Medici rule, Florence would have no king but vice.[1] Lust, greed, vanity, irreligion. Hadn't Florence bred a den of sodomites under the Medici's watch? Hadn't the banking family defiled their own hands with filthy lucre and the detestable sin of usury? Hadn't Lorenzo raided the city's dowry fund to pay for his own extravagances? Hadn't he himself been the ringleader of pagan carnival?[2] Unsurprisingly, Cosimo was no friend to the brooding band of Savonarolan devotees, and he cannot be blamed for his reluctance to bestow favor on a movement that so boldly called for his own head. On the other hand, he nevertheless sought to steal a leg up on the Savonarolan movement by purloining the cowled friar's program of moral legislation point for point, making it a central feature of his own projection of sacral monarchy.

Thus, while Cosimo scotched the head of the Savonarolan element by attempting to expel the monks of San Marco, he cut the legs out from under the movement by implementing a series of morality laws that to any attentive contemporary observer would have looked unmistakably akin to Savonarola's own. Indeed, the friar's campaign against vice had lived on in the memory of his followers, and they almost immediately thrust it on the city as soon as the republicans had gained the upper hand in 1527. Thus, in a moment of sublime historical irony, Cosimo based one of the crucial pieces of his own self-fashioned image on the ideological program of his most determined foes. However, for a prince seeking to reconcile old antagonists rather than destroy them, this was smart policy, for the Savonarolans drew their support largely from the working classes of artisans and guildsmen who had traditionally been the most hostile to Medici rule.[3] Moreover, the Savonarolan program dovetailed nicely with other trends of Catholic reform being enacted all over Italy. Thus the Savonarolan prince could pose very easily under the colors of the Counter-Reformation. For starters, the duke immediately set himself the Augean task of ridding the city of what he considered its moral vices, a project he vehemently pursued with direct reference to Savonorala's own underlying assumptions: that moral criminals would bring the wrath of God down on the whole city, while the punishment for their crimes would be laid on the head of the unhappy magistrate who failed to exact justice. Cosimo took up the friar's mantle in two other key areas: protection of the poor and reform of the clergy. In so doing, he attempted to undermine the argument that the Medici supported vice by picking up the shattered pieces of the Savonarolan tradition of moral reform.

Cosimo and the Wailers

As he lay dying, Lorenzo the Magnificent had called to his bedside the Dominican whose voice had lately been stoking the fires of spiritual renewal in the Florentine populace. About to face his last judgment, Lorenzo reportedly despaired of God's mercy, as his soul was fouled with many sins and crimes. Into the sick man's chamber stepped Savonarola, the steel-willed holy friar of God, who had already shown that he feared no man and no Medici. Here was the making of an epic struggle for the Magnificent's soul. In the gentle manner that marked his pastoral care, Savonarola assured Lorenzo that no sins were beyond forgiveness. "You must do just three things," assured the friar. "First, you must put all your trust in God's mercy." The dying Lorenzo nodded in assent; that could be done. "Second," continued Savonarola, "you must return all the wealth that you have accumulated through dishonest means." Lorenzo showed a touch of hesitation before giving his assent to this proposition as well; it would be done. Sensing that now was the time to capitalize on the dying man's pangs of conscience, Savonarola thrust home. "To win eternal salvation, Lorenzo," he concluded: "only one thing remains; you must restore Florence to its liberties." On hearing those words, Lorenzo turned his back on Savonarola and faced the wall, preferring to die without the friar's absolution.

Or so the story goes. Most likely, nothing of the sort took place.[4] Some lively imagination likely invented the tale to smear Lorenzo's reputation. Invention passed into hearsay, hearsay into rumor, rumor into myth, and myth into history. But rumor flew swiftly on wings forged in a political climate highly discontented with Medici rule. In the end, the story tells us little about Savonarola but much about the movement that came to bear his name. Though he had eventually taken it into his head that he was Florence's personal prophet of republicanism, much of the Savonarolans' anti-Medicean vitriol appeared only after his untimely end on a scaffold in the Piazza Signoria.[5] His cult sprang up almost immediately, even though the Florentine government had done its best to squash it by posting a guard at the pyre to prevent his supporters from gathering up the ashes of his

charred body to use as relics. After the initial shock of the confession and execution, Savonarola's band of devotees regrouped
and began agitating for his canonization. Miracles were recorded, the divine punishments meted out to his tormenters
duly noted, and hagiographies composed; in short, many revered Savonarola as a martyr and a saint.[6] With the return of the
Medici in 1512, the Savonarolan religious movement quickly
married itself to the anti-Medicean political movement, adopting the label "Wailers," which their enemies had invented as an
abusive caricature, as a point of pride. The themes of liberty
and republicanism proffered tentatively by Savonarola became
the war cry of the disaffected political class. His supporters
hailed him as the patron saint of not only church reform but
also political liberty.[7] The embarrassing matter of his unfulfilled
prophecies could be safely postponed to the coming time when
the Florentines would once again chase the tyrant Medici out
of Florence; the Savonarolans thereby welded their immediate
desire for political change to an eschatological religious message. After Alessandro's assassination, they were the most glee-
ful element of the Florentine population, publicly declaring that
the time for fulfillment of Savonarola's prophecies was at hand.
They proclaimed in the streets that "Florence would not only
recoup its ancient liberty but would enjoy it through all eternity
with all those graces and felicities that had been prophesied and
promised to it by God through the mouth of [Savonarola]."[8] The
locus of the entire movement was none other than the Dominican convent of San Marco, where the friars zealously guarded
Savonarola's memory and kept his dream of a godly republic
alive.

Thus Cosimo could not but try to squelch the movement.
However, his first blow did not fall on the monastery of San
Marco but on the *capi rossi* conventicle, a group of laymen
charged with poor relief during the last republic. Alessandro's
government left them alone through the 1530s, but the group
continued to grow more exclusively proletariat and religiously

fanatic, engaging in such annoying behavior (from Cosimo's point of view) as prophesying the imminent apocalypse and actively attempting to undermine the Medicean government. It did not take long for Cosimo's spies to sniff out this increasingly bold movement, whose leaders were then subjected to the ridicules of public shaming. Seating them on an ass and then mockingly attiring them with mitered heads, Cosimo had them whipped through the streets of Florence while the crowd jeered them on. Their leaders were all exiled or sent to prison, their mouths forever sealed to further prophesy.[9]

If Cosimo had had any doubt whether the Savonarolans would be friend or foe, the *capi rossi* had laid it to rest. However, his failure to strike a wide, sweeping blow at the institutions that had housed their conventicle anticipated his caution in proceeding against the city's real hornets' nest of Savonarolans: the convent of San Marco. Cosimo crafted his case against San Marco carefully. In April 1545, he sent a letter to Francesco Romeo, the general of the Dominican order, notifying him that certain brothers were accepting minors as novices, "seizing babies hardly come from their mothers' wombs to make them into friars."[10] Because this practice contravened the "common laws," set a bad example to the populace, and was a source of scandal for the church, Cosimo begged for the authority to remedy the abuse.[11] Over the summer, tensions worsened when one rash friar rather imprudently published a work prophesying the fall of the current regime. Cosimo seized on the publication as a *casus belli*, letting the sword of justice fall on the entire convent. However, the brothers were quickly able to bring enough pressure on him to ensure their release.[12] In August 1545, he tried another tactic, expelling all of the brothers of San Marco from their convent, as well as the Dominicans of San Domenico in Fiesole and Santa Maria Magdalena di Pian di Mugnone and replacing them with more tractable Augustinian friars. International circles raised a firestorm of protest, not least of which came from Rome itself.[13] Since Savonarola had attacked the papacy with more remorseless vehemence than he had ever challenged the Medici, the brothers' appeal to Paul III was fodder for not a little ironical commentary.[14] However, Paul saw Cosimo's transgression as a clumsy infringement of ecclesiastical jurisdiction, and the matter was quickly swept up in the ongoing dispute between pope and duke.

Cosimo cited a laundry list of complaints against the brothers of San Marco: they frightened old men into leaving their goods to the monastery, robbing families of the patrimony; they reverenced Savonarola as a saint; and they even read heretical books.[15] Responding to the charges, the cardinal protector of the order admonished Cosimo to think on what the goodly Saint Antoninus would have thought about the expulsion.[16] To this, Cosimo retorted: "If Anthony were still alive today and saw the way his brothers comported themselves . . . he would throw them all in the river with a rock around their neck."[17] However, realizing that the crime of heresy did not technically fall under his jurisdiction, Cosimo was careful to note that he did not evict the brothers because of their heterodox religious positions but only because of their secular offenses. He claimed that the brothers followed the poor example set by Savonarola by meddling in the affairs of state and inciting the people to sedition.[18] Moreover, the Medici family held the *ius patronatus* of the convent. Writing to his ambassador in Rome in October 1545, he claimed: "We have sent the brothers of San Marco away because of their bad behavior, which does not harm me by way of religion but because of the peace and quiet of this state. And if I had not sent them away already, I would send them away again because apart from the fact that one must do thus in affairs of state, I have sent them away because they live in a convent of our house, and we not only are able to evict them from it but to burn it down every time it returns to us, which perhaps I should have done so that that air will not infect all the others who will live there in the future."[19] On the matter of the state's jurisdiction over treason, Cosimo refused to budge an inch, boldly telling his ambassador to inform the pope: "in affairs of state, not only will I not give special respect to brothers, but even if cardinals will give me cause, I will hang them by the throat without another word."[20] The subtle reference to Lorenzo's execution of the archbishop of Pisa following the Pazzi conspiracy would not have gone unnoticed.

Nor would such brash talk go unanswered by Rome. When rumors began trickling out of the curia that the duke of Florence was a heretic who sheltered heretics in his realm, Cosimo rushed to his own defense, indignant and a bit genuinely bewildered that the pope would support scandalous heretic friars who denied his own legitimacy.[21] Laying his arguments out before the emperor, he claimed that the brothers "do not leave anything in the city on which they do not put their hands, and they maintain in the souls of their followers and of other citizens that intense desire that they have always had: that is, to be under the protection of the French and to govern the city by the people. They conduct themselves in such a manner that if I had not taken the opportune and quick provisions that I did, some disorder or scandal would surely have arisen, and this last reason was why I did all I could to evict them from that monastery, having first searched to make some provision and come to some solution with the general protector of the order."[22] Such an argument was very likely to carry weight in a court that had an overriding desire to keep Italy at peace and France out of Florence, but as the case dragged on into November, it became increasingly clear that the pope was not flinching. In November Paul played his trump card, threatening Cosimo with excommunication if he did not submit the case to Roman jurisdiction.[23]

Cosimo bent his stiff neck to the pontiff's will again, but he was not done with the brothers of San Marco. The dispute with the pope and the Dominicans continued to rage on into 1546. If Cosimo could not evict the brothers, then perhaps he could starve them out by cutting off state subventions to the convent. The pope responded by arresting Cosimo's agent in Rome and seizing his papers, prompting Cosimo to levy five thousand foot soldiers in a show of defiance.[24] However, as much as they enjoyed watching the two sides squirm, neither the Venetians nor the emperor would let the ghost of Savonarola haunt the peace of Italy again; thus the emperor quietly informed Cosimo of the need to come to an accord.[25] Threatened excommunications notwithstanding, Cosimo's laments against the scandalous order continued until well into 1548, and his fight would continue until he had scattered political Savonarolanism to the winds.[26]

Moral Offense and the Wrath of God

While Cosimo repudiated Savonarola and persecuted his legacy, he could not afford to ignore the undeniably magical sway the Savonarolan message seemed to hold over much of his citizenry. Given Savonarola's persistent popularity, Cosimo took steps to win over the city's more moderate Wailers by implementing a program of civic reform and moral legislation that bore the unmistakable stamp of Savonarola's own social program. No contemporary would have missed the fact that Cosimo had made Savonarola's targets his own: blasphemers, sodomites, prostitutes, and gamblers all found Cosimo's legislation a heavy yoke. In this, Cosimo was very different from his Medici predecessors and little different from his Savonarolan ones. Savonarola's attacks against these types of sinners had been frequent, and his calls for their blood had reached a near hysterical pitch as the wolves had closed in around him. In the fateful year 1494 he had frequently railed from the pulpit in tones such as these: "I tell you that God wants justice; I say it again, God wants to see justice, and he wants you to punish the blasphemers, and gamblers, and sodomites, and everyone else that is against him and his government. I tell you that God wants them punished; good government punishes the wicked and chases away the sodomites and the evildoers from the land."[27] It is not

hard to imagine the powerful effect this blend of religious, social, and political ostracism had on the devotees who packed the
seats of the cathedral. Savonarola would have begun his sermons quietly, perhaps elucidating some abstract point of theology, but as he turned from theology to political and moral lessons, the tension would have slowly built, the friar's voice getting
louder, his hands thumping the pulpit with ever more force.
Tears may have streamed from his eyes as he drove the message
home, bewailing Florence for the imminent scourge that hung
over it if its government would not heed his warning and correct these moral offenses. For this was the heart of the matter.
Savonarola was assured that moral offense would call down the
wrath of God not only against the sinner but against the entire
city as well. According to his logic, if the republic left justice
undone, the penalty would be visited on the whole republic instead. This was the state's interest in the matter, and it was on
these grounds that Savonarola urged on the city's government
from his cockpit and pulpit in San Marco. Of course, Cosimo
was well aware of the friar's moral arithmetic, and rather than
suffer the imputations visited on his Medici predecessors' heads,
he adopted Savonarola's moral program point for point, proceeding against blasphemers, sodomites, prostitutes, and gamblers with a fury that even the most dogmatic of Savonarolans
could applaud.

The friar's imprecations against offenses like blasphemy had
not fallen stillborn from the pulpit; rather, they quickly breathed
life into reinvigorated moral legislation. In 1494 the Florentine
republic passed laws tightening regulations against blasphemers, providing for harsher penalties and more stringent enforcement.[28] When Savonarola's spiritual heirs got the reins of government in 1527, they did much the same.[29] Moreover, from the
first, Cosimo showed himself just as stern a taskmaster as the
Savonarolans had ever been. As early as 1537, the Otto di Guardia, by this time the most important criminal court in Florence,
was already publishing edicts against blasphemy.[30] When this

failed to have the intended effect, Cosimo tightened up the laws in 1542, writing this legislation:

> The Most Excellent and Illustrious Lord Duke and his Magnificent Counselors having considered that it is very necessary that any state, besides making opportune provisions and orders for the city and dominion, wipe out vice completely, especially those vices that provoke the wrath of the high and omnipotent God and knowing that blasphemy is a sin that offends His Majesty more than any other, bringing into the world turbulences and unforeseen scourges, and wanting to extirpate it completely, it seems suitable to increase the penalties for such delinquents since people have not been corrected by virtue of the laws heretofore made, which impose light penalties. Rather, they quickly forget divine judgment and continue persevering in vice. Thus, with the opinion of the most wise and prudent citizens, they have provided in the following way . . .

The following way was harsh. Blasphemers caught in the act were subject to a 200 lire fine, deprivation of office for six months, and perforation of the tongue. The second offense involved a 300 lire fine, the amputation of the tongue, and the deprivation of office for one whole year. On the third offense, a 500 lire fine was exacted along with public shaming on an ass, two years on the dreaded galleys, and perforation of the tongue.[31] Since the law deemed it necessary to award perforation of the tongue on the third offense to one who was meant to have had his or her tongue amputated on the second offense, we might doubt that such severe corporal punishment was unswervingly meted out to the offending member.[32] Nevertheless, the severity of the intention cannot be doubted, for the law gave judges the discretion to hand out capital punishment to particularly egregious or recalcitrant blasphemers.

Nor could any Savonarolan doubt Cosimo's commitment to ridding the city of the other vice Savonarola detested: sodomy, an act for which Florentines had a particular reputation. Indeed, Savonarola's calls for the blood of sodomites had been so intense that in modern times even his hagiographers mention it only with considerable embarrassment.[33] When he gained ascendancy in the city, he wasted no time in putting rhetoric into policy, pushing through an antisodomy law on the same day the Great Council was approved.[34] His republic prosecuted the "nefarious vice" with such vigor that on his execution, one newly elected *balia* member reportedly exclaimed: "Praised be to god, now we can practice sodomy again."[35] Such enthusiasm was undoubtedly premature. When the republicans threw the Medici out in 1527, sodomy legislation was on the docket once again. Cosimo certainly knew all this and quite consciously chose to play to that constituency, filling up his own galleys with those caught in the act. As early as 1542 Cosimo had the law drafted that read:

> His Excellency the Most Illustrious Signor Duke and his Magnificent Counselors are aware how much in these recent times people so little restrain themselves from the nefarious vice of sodomy because of the small penalties imposed by the current laws, and he wants to wipe it out completely because of the great offense that it gives to the high and omnipotent God; the dishonor that it brings to the city, mainly to him to whom is given the care, governance, and rule of the people; and so that in his city and Dominion, people live with fear of the Lord's Majesty and with due honesty, which is necessary for political life. Moved by said and other urgent, just, and reasonable causes, they have, with the opinion of the wisest and most prudent citizens, provided in the following manner.[36]

The penalty depended on a dizzyingly complex array of qualifiers and distinctions. Depending on the offender's age, level of participation, and class, he would certainly face some combination of public shaming, whipping, deprivation of office, fines, and/or transportation to row one of Cosimo's galley ships.[37] Indeed, Cosimo's laws put teeth into Savonarola's program of moral reform.

In the pecking order of vice, blasphemers and sodomites were followed hotly by prostitutes. Unlike blasphemy and sodomy, prostitution was not strictly illegal. In fact, reforming clergymen often had a hard time even getting people to frown on it with an appropriate level of distaste. As in many southern European cities, more than a few Florentines considered prostitution a legitimate occupation and useful social service.[38] With their strict set of sexual mores, the Savonarolans obviously could not share that opinion. The last Florentine republic, for instance, had severely curtailed prostitutes' liberty of action.[39] Cosimo quickly followed in their path. To his credit, he did attempt to hack at the root of the problem by providing orphan girls with the skills required to find more honorable employment.[40] But of course, stricter rules on existing prostitutes were a matter of course. In 1553 all active prostitutes were required to leave a fourth of their goods to the Convertite, the monastery where reformed prostitutes mended their lives and ostensibly discharged their troubled consciences. This requirement served a twofold function. Doubtlessly, Cosimo hoped the tax would discourage some from the trade and thus wipe their stain off his census roles. Second, like many religious institutes of the age, the Convertite had fallen into poverty, and it is not hard to imagine what scandals arose from a destitute batch of prostitutes turned nuns, some of whom had obviously not entirely traded in their old ways.[41] In 1561 Cosimo's legislation against prostitutes got tighter, as he stipulated that they could not live nearer than one hundred *braccia* to any female monastery, on penalty of 200 spiccioli.[42] This certainly knocked more prostitutes off the official roles and won Cosimo plaudits from the finger-wagging Savonarolans.

Drunken gamblers were the last category of citizen to see their merry excesses sharply curtailed under Savonarolan and ducal regimes. Indeed, the Savonarolan republic had been so hard on the gamblers that they had reportedly wiped the vice off the streets altogether, with chronic gamblers fearfully retreating to pursue their leisure activities quietly in their homes.[43] By now it should be no surprise that the last Florentine republic had also prohibited gambling altogether, undoubtedly one of their least popular moves.[44] Like blasphemy and sodomy, gambling chanced the wrath of God. For instance, when Arezzo revolted under the Soderini government, the Savonarolans in the *Practiche* suggested the best remedy might be to seek God's aid by more stringently enforcing the antigambling laws.[45] Neither official church doctrine nor Cosimo himself held grudges against gambling per se; Rome was awash in wagers, and the duchess herself had a notorious addiction to gaming.[46] However, when citizens and subjects risked money that they neither had nor could afford to lose, the result could be a social and religious catastrophe.[47] Cosimo was thus a touch more circumspect, preferring only to forbid large wagers or those made with IOUs, the type of gambling that risked wasting a livelihood.[48] In any case, both the Savonarolans and Cosimo struck at gamblers' favored locales; the last Florentine republic had closed the taverns in 1528, and Cosimo repeated the experiment in 1559.[49]

To some extent, Cosimo seems to have been playing to Savonarolan sympathies. But why did he prosecute moral crimes with such vehemence? Why pursue blasphemers and sodomites to their unhappy juridical end? The pricking of his own conscience probably has as much to do it with it as anything, since he shared important elements of Savonarola's worldview. This is why Cosimo's legislation evoked Savonarolan explanations for the secular prosecution of blasphemy and sodomy.[50] More than others, these two sins provoked the wrath of God and called down swift and immediate judgment on the city. The idea was long-standing, but it drew special force in Florence from Savonarola's insistent and incessant cry that justice be done before it was too late. The warning lingered in the new monarchical air.

When Cosimo's faithful humanist Gualandi scanned the Old Testament for examples of God's wrath, he chose as his exempla Sodom and the Golden Calf. Even in the changed government, old assumptions still reigned; what really angered God was sodomy and blasphemy.[51]

Thus Cosimo's Savonarolan legislation was neither cynically conceived nor laxly executed. Rather, the duke pursued moral offenses with the zeal of a true believer. Nor is this altogether surprising. Despite his protestations against the friar, Savonarola was in his blood; for instance, his maternal grandfather, Jacopo Salviati, had been a supporter.[52] His legislation held the promise of the renewal of the Savonarolan spirit, and evidence of his uncynical attachment to the program was not long in coming. Given the relish with which Florentines performed the nefarious act of sodomy, Cosimo quickly discovered that he had to let the sword of justice fall on those whom he would have preferred to protect. Shortly after the inception of the law, Cosimo was even forced to arrest his own secretary Giovanni Bandini and send him to languish in the Bargello prisons for the better part of his life. Bandini was a dubious loss at best. Far more difficult was the arrest of Pandolfo Pucci, the son of Roberto Pucci and relative of Antonio Pucci, a powerful voice in the Roman curia and, at times, one of the few cardinals whose support Cosimo could claim in the papal courts. In his battles against the perennially aggressive Paul III, Cosimo could ill afford to lose the Pucci as allies.

Though Pandolfo eventually beat the charges, a prince with a keener sense of realpolitik would have doubtlessly hushed the incident up immediately, for howls of protest and appeal were not long in coming from the Pucci and their supporters; even the pope himself sent Cosimo a letter.[53] Moreover, the arrest could not have been solely for public relations purposes, since the government kept quiet on Pucci's arrest until rumors that he had conspired against the state forced the government to reveal the true case.[54] Why then take the risk of losing valuable friends in the papal curia by tossing their relative into prison? Cosimo excused himself to the cardinal Roberto Pucci, Pandolfo's father, with arguments that might have just as easily come from Savonarola's own mouth. Responding to his eminent but precarious ally, Cosimo wrote: "I have been forced to do this by the observance of the laws and by the honor of God, whom I do not want to irritate, since he has given me so many graces. From the inception of this holy law, I have sent more than twelve poor men to the galleys for this same offense. I cannot, nor should I, irritate God by not castigating also the noble and the rich. It pains me to the core to know that this unhappy fate strikes you; it strikes me as well, as I have found that Giovanni Bandini has also fallen into the same error. Be comforted though and have patience since God orders all for the best; believe thus that he has ordered this for the best and conform yourself to his will."[55] One can imagine that the cardinal found Cosimo's exhortations to Christian resignation less than comforting, for the relationship between Medici and Pucci was never quite the same. However, this incident does reveal that Cosimo thought the enforcement of these laws was a matter of the highest practical politics, though not *realpolitik* as it is now understood. His moral legislation was not merely or even primarily a salve to Florentine consciences; rather, he was truly afraid of divine punishment being meted out to his state if he did not act. It was a real politics in the sense that early modern men considered the wrath of God a real possibility, saw it acting in worldly affairs, and thought that it could be influenced by their own morality. In this, Cosimo acted as a convinced Savonarolan, even though he would have abhorred the name.

On the other hand, it was not just practical politics. If Cosimo really was afraid of an imminent punishment, he was that much more afraid of eternal punishment. For present purposes, Pucci's case functions as a sort of strange test case, elucidating just how far Cosimo shared Savonarola's view of justice and governance. Writing to his ambassador in Rome he explained himself thus: "I have had Pucci seized, doing it against my own inclination. However, since I had already admonished him several times, I do not want to have to render an account to God for the sins of others, especially since I have already sent many poor and middle class to the galleys, in accordance with the tenor of the law that is well known by all."[56] The sentiments expressed publicly to Pucci were thus confirmed privately to Cosimo's ambassador, with whom he was far more accustomed to speaking frankly. Such words might also have come straight from the pages of Savonarola in his concern to exalt the transcendent over the mundane. The action may have lost Cosimo powerful friends. Despite repeated attempts to win him back, Pandolfo Pucci would not be assuaged. Implicated in a conspiracy to assassinate the duke, Pucci met his end on the scaffold in 1559. This was an unfortunate loss for Cosimo, but a heady cocktail of factors had forced his hand in ways he would almost certainly have preferred to avoid: he found that he wanted for Savonarolan allies, he believed in the imminent manifestation of God's displeasure, and he feared that justice left undone would be his own undoing on the day of reckoning.

Father of the Poor

Savonarola's moral program had not been all about the grim business of persecuting sodomites and putting sharp implements through the appendages of blasphemers. From his first entry onto the Florentine stage, Savonarola had cast himself as the protector of the poor, sheltering the masses from the insatiable and blood-soaked jaws of the city's rich elite. Even if Savonarola had not put his magnetic appeal to work in order to win over the Florentine masses, Cosimo would have found casting himself as the protector of the poor to be an indispensable piece of sacral legitimation. Savonarola had made it even more indispensable. To that end, Cosimo adopted the Savonarolan program of poor reform, enacting sumptuary laws, fighting usury, reorganizing poor relief, and tracking down abuses in the hospital system. More than one Florentine government had fallen when the masses saw it siding with the rich over the poor.[57] Cosimo was determined not to make the same mistake.

In the first place, Cosimo could not dispense with direct government subventions, which in the early modern world still went under the name of charity. Never was he a more severe autocrat than on the question of poor relief. For instance, when one of his familiars ignored an order concerning the distribution of bread, he shot off this dispatch to his agent: "You will tell Mister Bernardo Carnesecchi that he is to remember that our advice is an order, and that whoever opposes it, we repute to be our adversary. We desire that the poor be succored, and we do not want bread to be lacking to them; they are more numerous than the rich and merit from us much regard, for our own interests as well."[58] Cosimo nimbly cultivated his image with the poor by selling grain below market value, targeting grain hoarders, and auditing the account books of illegal exporters. Contemporary Savonarolans would have certainly applauded every intervention that brought the price of grain down. In this case, Cosimo brooked no compromise; he understood the essential complementarity between his own position and his image as father of the poor.

Protecting the poor also meant purging the rampant graft in the provincial hospital system and hunting down greedy careerists who directed endowments into their own pockets. His first action of the sort came during his first year on the job, when he refused to allow the rector of the Hospital of Santa Croce Castello to collect the *entrate,* since word had reached his ears that the rector had been converting the funds to his own personal use.[59] This pursuit of malfeasance lasted the length of his rule; his control over the life of pious institutions was largely secured when he succeeded in getting his own reformist clients appointed to the two arch-Florentine hospitals: the Hospital of the Innocents and the Hospital of Santa Maria Nuova.[60] Moreover, his pursuit of malfeasance did not just end at the rectors' offices. The Spedalingo of the Innocenti was given full power to track down and punish any wet nurses who had defrauded the hospital, while the magistrate of the pupils was explicitly charged to do the same with those who defrauded the orphans under their care.[61] Thus, in his characteristically severe way, Cosimo made protection for the poor into a highly public piece of his government's administration.

Cosimo's adoption of Savonarolan charitable zeal followed less direct lines as well, like his meddlesome control over his citizens' garments and jewels. By the end of the fifteenth century, foreign finery increasingly held the Italian peninsula a slave to the whims of ostentatious fashion; Florentines were no exception, increasingly laying aside their old simple civil habit for the foppery of foreign tastes. Under its best colors, Savonarola had seen the rich brocades and precious gems with which Florentines increasingly adorned their costumes as needless expenditure. At the worst, they were the devil's work, the father of lies playing on the vanity of weak wills. After passing a sumptuary law in August 1496, Savonarola's army of boy followers had browbeaten Florentines into handing over such superfluities, piled them in the middle of the Piazza Signoria, capped the entire load with an effigy of the dark lord, and then lit the whole works as a bonfire of vanities.[62] In its slavish imitation of its progenitor's legislative policy, the last Florentine republic overwhelmingly voted in a similar law in 1527.[63] Cosimo again showed himself a keen student of Savonarola, though with less flair for dramatic pyrotechnics. In 1546, even at the height of the San Marco controversy, Cosimo published a new sumptuary law.[64] These laws were meant not only to encourage the virtue of temperance but to stymie the most visible reason the poor had to envy and despise the rich. The law was seemingly in keeping with Cosimo's own Spartan tastes; indeed, the 1562 draft of a new sumptuary law came from his own quill.[65] More to the point, Cellini's irreverent pen has made posterity the awkward witness to at least one epic battle Cosimo fought with his Spanish wife over expenditure on jewelry.[66] However, the timing of the move, at the height of the San Marco controversy, suggests that the legislation was meant to resonate with that element of the citizenry who still felt attachment to the simplicity of Savonarola's republic.

The pair waged their respective wars on poverty far more directly than just by cutting back the expenditure of the rich. One of the biggest splits between Medici and republican had long been the vigor with which each party prosecuted the usury of Jewish moneylenders. The city's large banking firms had salved their own reputations by making a subtle distinction between usury as a private loan at excessive interest and money recouped in exchange for risking capital, thus freeing their own consciences to demonize the Jewish moneylender. With scruples in the banking capital of Christendom thus sufficiently spared, popular preachers had made railing against usury one of their favored topics. When the fiery Bernardino da Feltre almost incited the populace to riot against the city's Jews in 1488, Lorenzo the Magnificent had stepped in to protect them, curbing the excesses of the city's religious and economic frustrations. Savonarola had very different opinions. Showing his characteristic tendency to let all good impulses run bad, the friar's call for protection of the poor repeatedly degenerated into calls for the expulsion of all Jews from the city. To that end, he prodded the city into the construction of a Monte di Pietà that would fill the breach created by the Jews' expulsion. The Monte was essentially one part charity, one part bank, and one part pawnshop, an institution that encouraged the upper classes to invest liquid capital at a 5 percent interest rate as a form of charity. It then used the capital to give low-interest loans to poor people against the collateral of their possessions. Lorenzo dei Medici had been rather lukewarm toward the project, but Savonarola had pushed it through on the weight of his own charisma, encouraging donations from his bully pulpit.[67]

Cosimo's own attitude toward the Jews of his state was far more complicated. Tuscany's Jews, having been expelled from the city by the last Florentine republic in 1527, did not immediately present themselves to Cosimo as a particular problem. Indeed, Cosimo tolerated and encouraged isolated settlements of Jews in Tuscany throughout much of the 1550s and 1560s, and in some cases gave them license to practice usury.[68] Tolerance of the Jews, however, did not mean Cosimo had particularly "enlightened" views on the commercial activity with which they were most commonly associated. Throughout the early years of his reign, he waged a relentless campaign against usurious and illicit contracts among nonlicensed moneylenders on the grounds that they harmed the poor.[69] The Monte di Pietà continued to function as a crucial piece of this puzzle, filling the lacuna left in wake of the expulsion of Jewish moneylenders. Rather than close the Monte down, Cosimo utilized it as an arm of state finance and a post of patronage.[70] Moreover, by the 1560s his government reversed its policy on the Jews, restricting their lending activities and giving them the choice between exile or the ghetto. His primary charge against them: the Jews who had been given license to conduct business in Tuscany had broken the contract by charging excessive interest rates, practicing fraud, and keeping their shops open on holy days. Like Savonarola's scapegoating of Jews in the preceding century, the charge had little merit; as Stefanie Siegmund has shown, the government's claims against the Jews were not backed by solid evidence of widespread wrongdoing.[71] Nonetheless, contemporaries certainly could not fail to perceive the parallels between Cosimo's expulsion edict and those of the Savonarolan republics.

The image of the monarch as a fatherly defender of the poor was no novelty in the mid-sixteenth century. The dictates of Christian politics had long made this a duty of any Christian monarch, and the Medici themselves had, to a limited extent, rode to power on a wave of populist demagoguery.[72] However, the forms and institutions in which Cosimo carried his program forward were deeply imbued with a Savonarolan spirit; the friar's voice echoed through the decades and into Cosimo's own legislation. If Cosimo was father of the poor, Savonarola had been their grandfather.

The Reform of the Religious

By the sixteenth century, the poor state of the secular and regular clergy had persisted for several generations as a rankling fester on the body politic of Christendom. As a result, anticlericalism was an endemic feature of early modern life, whose reoccurrence repeatedly manifested itself in virulent outbursts of satiric verse and prose skewering greedy abbots and lascivious friars. Before the Counter-Reformation, few brands of writer gave the wayward clergy quarter; if the clergy could dismiss Boccaccio's anticlerical vignettes, they could not escape Antoninus's fatherly admonitions. Clergy were supposed to form the moral backbone of the republic, yet everywhere their misdeeds gave cause for scandal. Everywhere their flocks went without their shepherds. Deeply convinced that the contemporary church was a ruin whose scourging by God was imminent, Savonarola brought anticlericalism to a fevered pitch, directing shaft after shaft at tepid and avaricious prelates. Savonarola was sure of this single fact: the causes of all ills in society descended from the bad example of princes and prelates. A 1496 sermon laments: "If the princes and prelates were good, all the world would be good as well. O tepid, o evil princes and priests, O Sammaria, you are the cause of the impending scourge." In the lens through which Savonarola viewed his whole world, the age's priests and princes were alike to Old Testament idolaters, human sacrificers who handed over their flocks to eternal destruction in pursuit of the idols of ambition, lust, and greed. With that in mind, Savonarola called for a general renewal of the priestly class.

Starting with his own monastery, he began a reform of monastic discipline that spread all over Tuscany. He also urged on the necessary complement, making calls to cut the wheat from the chaff and remove the unreformable.[73]

Cosimo quickly set out to prove that monarchical rule could deliver on the promise of Savonarola's clerical reform, tracking down scandalous priests and nuns and punishing them with characteristic severity. His intervention into cathedral politics was so frequent that at least one Savonarolan chronicler could grant: "If the duke had not frequented our Cathedral as much as he has done, it would be worse than a whorehouse because of the immoral prelates. They are so afraid of Cosimo and hold such account of him, that were it not for him, the evil priestly sect would have reduced our beautiful cathedral into a simple country church, which are constantly despoiled in order to give the blood of Christ to prostitutes."[74] As this declaration implies, religious reformers were perhaps overweeningly interested in the sins of the flesh. And little flesh was more fussed over than that of Tuscany's nuns, whom Cosimo spent considerable energy trying to keep chaste and docile behind their convent walls.[75]

Here Savonarolan reform and Tridentine reform merged into a singular movement, as Savonarola's concern for the clausura of female monastics dovetailed nicely with Tridentine strictures.[76] Both of these reform measures aimed to avoid the type of sexual scandals relatively common in both Tuscany and elsewhere, scandals caused, no doubt, by the common practice of depositing younger daughters in the monastery to avoid the higher dowry they would require on the marriage market.[77] These scandals created a problem for the church, the state, and the nuns' families, as their respective senses of honor were all deeply tied up with the chastity of their mutually shared daughters.[78] Indeed, the third session of the Council of Trent would attempt to enforce strict enclosure across all of the Catholic world in the 1560s.[79] Cosimo, however, had already anticipated the Council of Trent's clausura restrictions by enacting legislation in 1545 that theoretically submitted to state control all Tuscan convents except for those few controlled by bishops. This move neatly tied up Counter-Reformation desires for greater supervision over female religiosity, his own administration's desires for order, and the nuns' families' desire for control of institutions over which they felt some proprietary rights. Thus, the legislation established *operai* who were to oversee the temporal administration of the sisters' lives. The *operai* were normally locals, and Cosimo specifically enjoined that they be of good reputation and, if possible, related to the nuns themselves.[80] To coordinate the work of the local *operai,* the duke set up a council of three deputies, thereby linking local administrators to his own personal will. However, the paucity of business conducted by the deputies suggests that the bonds to the center were weak; the deputies were only called on for problematic cases. Thus, Cosimo did not set up a bureaucratic structure in which he could micromanage Tuscany's convents (no three people could, especially since they all had other jobs); rather, he solidified local elites' control over their own daughters' enclosed lives.

The real work of the deputies was directed less toward centralization than toward keeping lecherous friars away from the brides of Christ, that is, providing a structure that enabled Cosimo to break the bonds that existed between female and male monasteries, bonds that led too often to scandals of the sexual kind.[81] This was the concern that constituted the bulk of the deputies' work; indeed, most of their early letters were no more than curt dispatches ordering a number of male religious houses to have no further commerce with their dependent sisters. The local commissaries were put on guard, strictly enjoined to let no one visit the convents without license, especially the former father confessors.[82] The deputies even inspected the walls of female convents personally to make sure that easy access could not be had. On one occasion they ordered the podesta of Barga to find some remedy to the fact that the prior of Ortignano's house was just high enough to see into some of the many windows on the convent of Saint Andrea di Bibbiena. On another occasion they asked the local rector to intervene in order to stop the nuns of San Lorenzo Outside the Walls from changing their habits for street clothes and leaving the convent.[83] All this suggests that Cosimo was trying to show that Florence was no longer willing to wait until the regulars put their own houses in order; as Savonarola had tried to do before him, he would drag them along if he had to.

He accomplished this in two primary ways: the first and most successful was to promote his own reforming candidates into key positions of authority over the Tuscan church.[84] The second was to use his networks of patronage to drag the ecclesiastical hierarchy on board with his programs. Indeed, it was no accident that his clients were so successful in climbing the ladder of the ecclesiastical hierarchy or that the names of his secretaries so often appeared later in the ranks of bishops. The majordomo Pier Francesco Riccio, a zealous reformer and maybe even secretly a Protestant, was named the provost of Pescia in 1547. In 1548, Cosimo wrote to Cardinal Gaddi asking him not to employ the reforming priest Francesco Incontri in his bishopric of Cosenza so that he could remain as the vicar to the bishop of Cortona.[85] Cosimo also tried to get Cortona moved to the vacant bishopric of Pisa in 1555 so that he could get Alessandro Strozzi or Paolo Niccolini elected to oversee reform in that diocese personally.[86] Indeed, Cosimo's attempts to get men of character in his bishoprics occasionally backfired. He fell out with Camaiani, the bishop of Fiesole, in the third session of the Council of Trent over the issue of episcopal residency, and his attempts to get his absentee enemy Cardinal Ridolfi replaced as archbishop of Florence by someone more reforming miscarried when Ridolfi handed the see over to Cosimo's archrepublican enemy Antonio Altoviti.[87]

As he used his bishops to conquer the secular clergy, so he exploited the same patronage network to conquer the regulars, working through the generals to chastise their naughty monks and adopting the bully pulpit to persuade regular congregations to put reforming generals at their head, preferably Tuscans.[88] Indeed, Cosimo simply could not keep his hands off the monastic elections. In 1551 he unsuccessfully attempted to swing the election of the head of the Franciscan order to his own man. Undaunted, he sent a vicar to a Camoldesi synod in 1552, asking them to elect a reforming general and preferably a Tuscan.[89] In 1553 he wrote to the synod of Servites:

> Having heard that the general of the Servite brothers, who was an Aretine, is dead, and desiring that that grade of our fathers of that Religion of Tuscany not go to a non-Tuscan and wanting particularly that our convent of the Annunziata be honored as a place so famous and which for an infinite amount of years has never had that dignity in its house, all these reasons have moved me to write to you at present so that you with our Lord the protector of this religion, which we understand to be the most Reverend (Cardinal) Santa Croce, asking his holiness to honor the convent of the Annunziata and to elect the Venerable Father Antonio Zaccheria, our Florentine, and a person very religious and of good judgment, lettered and of exemplary life.[90]

The frequency with which Cosimo pestered the religious orders certainly testifies to the pressing urgency he felt about clerical reform, as well as his desire for tractable generals. There is no doubt that he felt he needed Savonarola's reforming credentials.

It would be wrong, however, to end the discussion of reform here. Cosimo did not simply drag a recalcitrant church trippingly along behind him. He was not always the main impetus behind reform, and as the creaking gears on the motor of Catholic Reformation groaned to life, Cosimo was just as often the ally as the initiator. For instance, the first project to enclose female monasteries on Tuscan soil came not from Cosimo but the bishop of Arezzo, to whom Cosimo gave secular aid for the project as early as March 1537. Cosimo's generosity in loaning aid to the secular arm continued unabated, as he sent his commissaries, vicars, and *podeste* piles of credential letters for reforming projects initiated by the church.[91]

As in other areas, it is clear that Cosimo's motivations here were profoundly imbued by Savonarola's assumptions: that is, the assumption that the scandalous lives of priests negatively affected the civil comportment of his subjects. For instance, having arrested a priest for carrying arms, Cosimo tried to appease the bishop with an argument frequently made by Savonarola, arguing that a priest "should not be better off than laics, for which reason they need to be corrected; one should not suffer that those who should be an example of obedience and good morals do the contrary."[92] As it was for Savonarola, so it was for Cosimo, and so it was for Cosimo's Counter-Reformation, a top-down and overarching reform of society starting with the reform of the clergy. At least one of Cosimo's handpicked bishops agreed with him, attempting to set the standard of obedience for his flock himself. He was, so he claimed, not about to inform on those who carried arms surreptitiously or spoke ill of the name of the prince, but "for love of the patron, I will remind them of the rights my patron holds in the bishopric."[93] Thus, subservient and reforming priests could be used to extend control and pacify the dominion. In this case, then, religion was clearly being used as an instrument of rule.

However, one should not make religious reform all about utility. For Cosimo was serious about the state's teleological functions. Civil society was supposed to be not so much an end in itself as a helpmate on the way to beatitude.[94] It was an ideal Savonarola and Cosimo shared with most early modern thinkers. The government had the duty to help remove bad priests, to honor the divine cult, and to set the populace on the road to salvation. Cosimo's concern seems to have been real, littered as his correspondence is with references to the well-being of his subjects' souls.[95] Eulogies picked up on this theme. On this ac-

count, Betti claimed: "The monasteries of sacred virgins and
other places that are dedicated to the divine cult that had been
built, maintained, embellished, restored, and helped by the great
piety of this Prince are a testimony to his religion. Is it not well
known that he has often fulfilled the office of a most vigilant
and loving pastor, nurturing them and making sure that diligent
care was kept of them? Not long ago, a most reverend religious
told me that he had seen entire letters in the hand of the grand
duke, written to those who had care of the monasteries located
in the furthest reaches of his state, in which appears the rare
goodness, rather I will say it, the sanctity of this prince."[96]
Thus, the state had an interest in religion for dual yet complementary ends: the stability of the reign and spiritual well-being
of subjects. We need not assume that one necessarily excluded
the other.

To the reasons already adduced, we might add one more.
Religious reform was a matter of Tuscan pride, playing into the
myth of a religious Florence and a religious Tuscany, a myth
with which Savonarola had so deftly mesmerized and manipulated his audiences.[97] Like any number of other early modern
polities, Florence wanted to be both the New Jerusalem, the
shining city on the hill, and the new Rome, light to the barbar-
ian world. Since the city had no empire, their peculiar little light
could not be political. Florence's special mission had to be cultural or religious. Savonarola's passing had not tempered the
fashion. Leo X deliberately married the ideal of Tuscan religiosity to the evocation of the Roman Empire.[98] Cosimo's humanist
Gualandi was still bragging about it years later, citing Sallust
with this quote: "The Etruscans were, he says, very great in supplication of the gods, neglecting their own houses to magnify
those of the gods."[99] Even after Etrusco-mania had reached its
height in Cosimo's early reign, the Arch of Religion, designed
for the wedding *apparato* of 1565, was emblazoned with this
inscription:

For inventing grain learned Athens is famed;
Rome for being fierce at war and powerful in empire;
But this our mild province of Etruria is known
for its divine practice and superior worship of God,
Which they say uniquely possessed the skills of honoring
the deity and teaching sacred practices;
now it is the site of true piety and from it
this reputation never will be taken any time.[100]

Indeed, the religiosity of Tuscany and Florence was a matter of patriotism and thus the reform of the clergy a matter of national pride, hearkening back to a mythic Etruscan past forged by overenthusiastic antiquarians associated with the Florentine and papal courts. Cosimo found this Etruscan myth quite useful, at least temporarily, seeking as he was to create a unified state out of the disparate little communes and republics that had come over to the dominant city's control over the course of the centuries.[101] In this, he was puffed up with the same local pride, peppering letters with self-congratulatory language. "Florence is perhaps more than most dutiful in religion," he wrote to the College of Cardinals, "and our cathedral is the most well administered in the world.[102] Indeed, Florentines had been trying to live up to their self-imposed reputation for quite some time. Cosimo held out the promise that he could finally bring about that achievement.

Conclusion

Cosimo was not the only Counter-Reformation prince to tie his legitimacy to his moral legislation. His program, however, was aimed directly at Florentines and Tuscans clinging to an imagined past in which a cowled friar had inspired the city to moral rectitude, for Cosimo stole the Savonarolans' thunder almost point by point, leaving no area of their moral program unresurrected. Whether Cosimo acted thus because he shared a substantial part of their worldview (and there is evidence that he did) or because he was savvy enough to realize that accommodation to this most potent of Florentine traditions was politically wise, his system of moral legislation was writ deeply into the political consciousness of his Florentine subjects. He knew that a large segment of the population would judge him a tyrant if he did not make some effort to improve the city's morals, and he knew that justice demanded an evenhanded application of these laws. His usurpation of the Savonarolan system did not, as Henk van Veen has argued,[103] have to wait on some tardily discovered republican principles but was a key piece of Cosimo's self-identity, at the same time that he was casting Savonarolans out of the bosom of his city. Moral reform was part of his princely identity, a princely identity, nevertheless, that he liberally borrowed from one of Florence's most cherished republican heroes.

CHAPTER 6

Defense of the Sacred

U NLIKE MOST OTHER European monarchs, Cosimo did not come to a throne replete with the trappings of sacrality. Whereas most monarchs had wide-ranging prerogatives over appointments to church benefices, Cosimo had surprisingly little influence over ecclesiastical property.[1] Whereas most monarchs were the heirs of dynasties that had monopolized sacred space with regal pomp, Cosimo's ancestors had limited their dynastic patronage projects to their own neighborhood churches.[2] Whereas most monarchs came to a reign already associated with sacred festivals, miraculous signs, and other forms of sacral power,[3] the Medici had very little sacral tradition associated with their relatively new dynasty. This, however, does not imply that Cosimo had nothing to work with. The sacred had always occupied a privileged position in Florentine political life; indeed, sacral politics had been a far more potent element of republican government than they had ever been of Medicean government.[4] However, the question remained: how could Cosimo use native

Florentine and republican traditions to satisfy his own very different political needs? This chapter will argue that Cosimo's intervention into Florentine piety followed a fairly consistent pattern: he insinuated his presence and control over the traditional forms of the sacred by posing as their defender. However, careful not to use his power unwisely, he usually sought to accommodate his control to his subjects' traditional desires. Thus, because his tenuous hold on Florence amplified his need to accommodate religious control to popular sensibilities, his example hints at an important but often overlooked dynamic of early modern rulership.

First, this chapter will examine how Cosimo handled appointments to sacred office, arguing that he made himself a zealous defender of his subjects' ecclesiastical patronage rights in order to control the process. Nevertheless, he went to great lengths to respect his subjects' primary concerns: communities' desire for local priests and lay patrons' desire to keep benefices in the family. The second section will make the same argument on the grounds of sacred space, arguing that Cosimo's patronage of churches followed accepted traditions of citizen patronage. Though as a duke he publicly patronized a wide range of Florentine temples, he limited his own private projects to neighborhood and familial churches. The third section will outline Cosimo's policies toward sacred time and sacred festival, arguing that he used his indirect influence over the sacred calendar to set both sacred time and festival at the service of his own personal power. The final section will argue that Cosimo quickly took up the defense and control of manifestations of supernatural power, specifically indulgences and miracles. In his handling of these manifestations, he again proved that he had a finger on the pulse of popular piety, showing himself in all cases adept at using traditional attitudes toward the sacred to adorn a ducal chair bereft of sacrality. As the *defensor sacris,* he took control of sacral life; as a prudent accommodator, he kept it.

Sacred Office: Cosimo and Ecclesiastical Benefices

In early October 1548, the parishioners of San Lorenzo a Campi gathered nervously and silently in their little medieval church on the outskirts of the small Tuscan town of Campo Bisenzio. Perhaps foreseeing his impending mortality, the old rector had called the parish together to elect a successor. There was nothing unusual about the motley assembly of poor provincials and rich Florentines gathering to cast their votes for their future pastor; indeed, many Italian communities possessed the right to present a candidate to the bishop for confirmation, a right known as the *ius presentandi*.[5] However, this particular election came with some added dramatics. In recent weeks, a powerful Florentine noble named Piero Tournabuoni had been inviting local peasants to his house to dine on some pretext or another and then bribing, cajoling, and even threatening them to vote for his own handpicked candidate. Though he had done all he could to keep word of his underhanded tactics from the ears of the community's more influential members, the current local priest caught wind of the matter and called on the aid of a powerful intercessor: Francesca Salviati, Cosimo's maternal aunt.

Not content to let the benefice slip out of his grasp so easily, Tournabuoni showed up at church on the day of the election in the company of a band of armed retainers, who entered with a boisterous and cocksure bravado, intimating to the frightened parishioners that they were "more ready for combat than to elect the new priest."[6] When Tournabuoni insisted that the parish vote on his candidate first, most of the peasants prudently held their tongues. However, another Florentine citizen by the name of Bernardo di Zaccheria Strozzi arose to protest. Strozzi dared to argue that his own favored candidate, Ser Cresci, should be accorded the first ballot, since Ser Cresci had been born in the commune and was well liked by the parishioners. On the other hand, Tournabuoni's candidate was "completely unknown to many."[7]

In response, the threat of violence boiling under the surface erupted: Piero's uncle strode up to Strozzi and struck him a resounding blow across the face with his fist. "How dare you speak to your elders with such arrogance," the uncle thundered, and while he delivered this rebuke he gently fingered the blade concealed under his cape. Strozzi did not back down, retorting that he came to speak for his interests in the parish. At this, the uncle replied: "Are you willing to fight and die for those interests?" Strozzi took a quick glance at the majesties of the altar and thought better of it. "I've not come to fight and kill," he said. "I came to elect a priest." Though Francesca Salviati downplayed her own role in her account, one can only speculate that it was she who interposed her authority (and perhaps her own armed guard), sending all the Florentine citizens ignominiously out into the piazza. The candidates drew lots to see who would be voted on first, and Ser Cresci made good on his patron's claims, winning his neighbors' vote of confidence and the election on the first vote.

Tournabuoni's antics do not represent the only questionable ways various interested parties tried to steal benefices away from unwitting local communes and poor patrons. Parish rectors renounced benefices to their friends without the patrons' permission; well-connected individuals arranged to have patronage rights derogated in Roman courts, where poorer claimants could not afford to litigate; and wealthy claimants often bled their antagonists out of legal battles by dragging cases out in eternally prorogued lawsuits. If all else failed, determined individuals could take the same route as Tournabuoni, using violence to bully frightened peasants into submission. For instance, disputes over hospital benefices in Pistoia had stained the streets of that mountain community red with civil blood, as the law of vendetta impelled the contending parties into ever more unspeakable atrocities. Pistoia represented an extreme case, where ancient grudges exacerbated new conflicts, but everywhere vacant benefices remained a potent source of unrest and conflict, a situation largely exacerbated by the violence and interminable litigiousness of the age. A quick review of the archive of the Auditor of Jurisdiction and Ecclesiastical Benefices bears this out, as the records of this magistracy illuminate Cosimo's attempts to put an end to the chaos, slowly bringing the situation into focus.[8] In 1546, the first year for which the licenses of possession to benefices are preserved, some 22 percent of the Auditor's business involved disputed cases. Moreover, the contending parties resorted to violence in at least three of those forty-five cases.[9] Indeed, the situation was ripe for the intervention of the secular authority.

Thus, threats of violence and conflict provided Cosimo with his *entrepôt*. Appealing to a right exercised by previous Florentine governments, he quickly set himself the task of administering all benefices that went vacant on Tuscan soil, with this legislation: "Since experience demonstrates that scandals and disorders frequently arise on account of vacant benefices . . . it seems appropriate to bring our attention to the matter and provide . . . that in the future these scandals no longer occur. Thus, let the old agreements signed between the Apostolic See and this city be observed, which provide that a representative of the city take possession of vacant benefices in order to render them to whomever canonically has the right to them. This ought to stymie the ambition of those who would intrude on them by force of arms."[10] The extent to which Cosimo was grounding his claims in Florentine tradition is abundantly clear, for apart from appealing to the city's agreements with Rome, the text of his statute basically echoed a similar law promulgated in 1466.[11] Moreover, unlike so much other early modern legislation, Cosimo's decree was no idle threat; it merely applied universally what he had already been doing on a case-by-case basis.[12] When the news of a priest's death reached the administrators of the territories, Cosimo dispatched an agent to the local church to seize the goods. Most of the time, Cosimo's agent would stay around to determine to whom the *ius patronato* belonged. If it belonged to the community, his sword would guarantee order in the election. If the benefice remained vacant for a long time, the territorial rector would make sure that the spiritual needs of the populace were taken care of.[13] Having put such authority to use, theoretically Cosimo had wide-ranging powers over the Tuscan church; in fact, he had little will to use such powers arbitrarily.

Thus, Cosimo's lack of control over the Tuscan church left him with little recourse but to beg the *patronato* rights of others. To make matters worse, he was heir to a permanently poor treasury, so the granting of benefices functioned as a vital cog in financing a government that had a number of clerics on its staff.[14] Of course, European monarchs had spent centuries raiding the church's coffers to pay their officials, but relative to other monarchs, Cosimo possessed precious little control over his local church. As heir to the *Signoria,* he had inherited the right to appoint rectors to any benefice that had belonged to the captain of the Guelph Party, that is, all the patronage rights that had been seized from exiled citizens. However, in a nod to the virtue of clemency, Cosimo had restored the goods of many exiles in 1537. Thus the sum total of these benefices did not amount to much. Moreover, he did not always get to appoint his own candidate; political tact often limited him to the perfunctory act of confirming a renouncement. In the first ten years for which records are preserved, he nominated rectors to only eighteen posts, less than 1 percent of all benefices and less than two posts a year, not nearly enough to feed the voracious appetite for benefices at his perpetually cash-strapped court.[15]

The obvious solution to such a problem might have been to take the benefices by force. However, Cosimo would not make his monarchical power extend to usurping ecclesiastical liberties. As a secretary related, Cosimo once responded to a request for a benefice by referring the requester to his Toledo relatives with this frustrated comment: "I do not know who better can give a benefice than Cardinal Burgos or Don Francesco (Toledo) because I am the duke, and the duke does not give benefices or

ecclesiastical goods."[16] On another occasion, when an agent of
the cardinal of Tournon requested a sinecure in Florence, Cosimo refused the request with the explanation that all the sine-
cures in the city were filled, and he would not touch an occupied one. "I cannot," he declared, "be accused of any violence
or of putting my hands on ecclesiastical property on my own
authority and without the express order of His Holiness."[17] Cosimo was neither the French king nor the Spanish king, both of
whom had won wide-ranging patronage rights from previous
popes. His conscience and deep ties to Rome denied him the options of the English king, who arrogated the jurisdictions to
himself. Nor would he do as the dukes of Milan, who frequently
imposed their own candidates over the objections of subject
communities.[18] In that case, only one option was left.

To collect patronage rights without endangering his image,
Cosimo had to ask for them politely from those who held them:
guilds, cathedral chapters, popes, bishops, lay patrons, and especially local communities. Local rectors were Cosimo's blunt
edge in this awkward and unpleasant task, as Cosimo occasionally instructed them to cajole communities into naming him
their procurator. In the early days of his reign, local rectors received such instructions with a marked regularity, though it is
unclear how often they succeeded.[19] Complying with the duke's
request certainly had its benefits; for instance, when a community's patronage rights were endangered, ceding their voice to
Cosimo gained them a powerful and zealous ally, and when rival factions threatened to tear the community apart, Cosimo
could help find a candidate suitable to all.[20] In this he was again
following a well-worn tradition, since communities in the *contado* had long been accustomed to go directly to the Medici to
solve their factional conflicts.[21] By the 1550s, Cosimo had developed such a good reputation that his aid was actively sought.[22]
However, it seems that at times all he could offer a community
was his own goodwill, a pledge that the community might never
find the chance to redeem. Communities knew they could po-

litely ignore Cosimo's request, and some did, even if his mace-bearer had taken up residence in their parish church.[23] When communities rebuffed him, Cosimo could have theoretically exercised his de facto power, but as noted, he was loath to do that when it was not accompanied by sufficient justification.[24]

Thus the limit of Cosimo's control over benefices becomes obviously clear. In order to get cooperation, he needed to accommodate. He needed to gain a reputation as a judicious procurator for local communities, one who could be trusted to respect local wishes. Moreover, there is little doubt that communities had very definite plans for their benefices; by and large, they preferred local and diocesan priests over *forestieri* (foreigners).[25] *Forestiere* did not necessarily mean non-Tuscan; it could refer to a priest from outside the region, outside the diocese, or even outside the commune. The reader will recall that the community of Campi rejected Piero Tournabuoni's candidate on the grounds that he was a foreigner to the commune, while Ser Cresci had been born in the parish and was well known to the people. A dispute between the stubborn mountain community of Calamecca and the bishop of Pistoia demonstrates that "too foreign" might simply mean a priest from a neighboring diocese.[26] Though both Cosimo and the bishop had exhorted the community to elect the bishop's candidate, the community protested, claiming: "it is not that we find him unworthy of our parish, but because he has been in your (the bishop's) service, we do not want others to think we are punishing our own diocesan priests by giving our benefice to one of your domestic servants."[27] Cosimo and the bishop had no choice but to give the community what they wanted since the *patronato* rightfully belonged to them.

If anecdotal evidence alone strongly suggests that communities wanted local priests, statistical evaluation confirms the impression. Between 1546 and 1550, communities freely electing a rector to a parish were substantially more likely to elect a local priest than were the bishop or the Roman curia.[28] Sixty percent of the rectors elected by parishioners were members of the local community. On the other hand, the ordinary appointed a local priest only 40 percent of the time, and Rome appointed a local priest only 35 percent of the time. If communities could not find a suitable local priest, they usually preferred a diocesan one; the same statistical pool demonstrates this even more starkly. Eighty-four percent of all rectors elected by communities were diocesan priests, compared to 52 percent elected by the ordinary and 58 percent elected by Rome.[29] Many bishops came from outside the diocese and were not resident anyway. Because they used the benefices to pay for their households, their choices did not always match the communities' desires. Thus, legal battles between communities and ordinaries were not infrequent. To any prince paying attention, it was clear what communities wanted.

Cosimo certainly was paying attention and eager to avoid the type of rancorous dispute his bishops often found themselves in.[30] A case from 1554 illuminates his sensitivity to local feeling. When the bishop of Lucera tried to steal the *primierato* of the Aretine cathedral for his nephew, Cosimo set his powerful Roman patronage network in motion to protect local interests. Writing to the adopted papal nephew, Cardinal Del Monte, he claimed: "It has come to my attention that our Aretine citizens find it a very bitter pill that the first dignities and offices of the Aretine cathedral are exercised by foreigners [*forestiere*] who are neither suitable nor accepted by them, and it seems to me that I have a right to complain since I have tried to settle the litigation between Niccolò Gamarrini of Arezzo and the nephew of the bishop of Lucera on the *primierato* of that cathedral two times. I cannot fail . . . to entreat Your Holiness a third time that he make that bishop dispose himself to accept a fair pension and to let Gamurrino enjoy the *primierato* in peace since he has already resided twenty months and is well liked by the all the clergy and the city."[31] In this case, Del Monte wrote to the bishop, the bishop wrote to his nephew, and within the month the matter was settled.[32] For the price of three letters and one favor from the Roman curia, Cosimo was able to ride to the rescue of the most important Aretine temple and present himself as the champion of local prerogatives.

Thus, he understood that there was more to promise a community than simply finding a "discreet person, who was suitable for the divine cult."[33] Communities wanted a local if possible, and he tried to oblige. Because his court and administration included Tuscans from all over the dominion, he found ample opportunity to give communities what they wanted by consistently matching his clients with their own hometowns. For instance, in 1548 he gave the *prepositura* of Prato to his Pratese tutor and majordomo Pier Francesco Riccio.[34] In his capacities as heir to the captain of the Guelph Party, he gave two benefices in Arezzo to his Aretine secretary Pietro Camaiani.[35] With less success, he tried to get his secretary Agnolo Dovitio a benefice near his hometown of Bibbiena.[36] In 1555, San Piero and San Pagolo in Cortona went to Giovambattista Vanucci, a Cortonese.[37] Indeed, of the twenty-four times that Cosimo appointed a rector to a benefice between 1546 and 1559, he presented diocesan priests nineteen times and local priests thirteen times, numbers that approach the percentages of local communities themselves. Whenever possible, he seems to have matched priests with localities as closely as he could (Figures 6.1, 6.2, and 6.3).

Cosimo gave in to the sensitivities of local feeling at other times as well. When the community of Pescia ceded him their right to elect the archdeacon of the cathedral church, he made sure that it stayed in the hands of a native Pescian.[38] When the pope granted him the Hospital of San Lazzaro in Volterra, he gave it to his Volterran secretary, Jacopo Guidi.[39] When the Capponi family presented the Hospital of Altopascio to one of Cosimo's secretaries, he gave it to the secretary with the closest hometown: Ugolino Grifoni of San Miniato. Even when trying to influence others, he exhorted them to match man with locality, whether seeking to get his familiar Guasparre di Prato elected

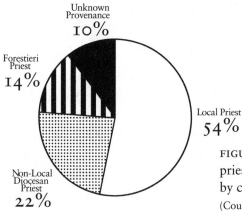

FIGURE 6.1. Provenance of priests elected to benefices by communities, 1546–1550. (Courtesy of Daniel Lewis.)

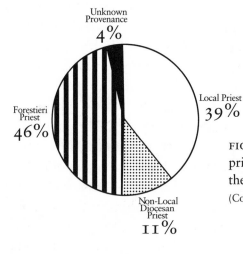

FIGURE 6.2. Provenance of priests elected to benefices by the ordinary, 1546–1550. (Courtesy of Daniel Lewis.)

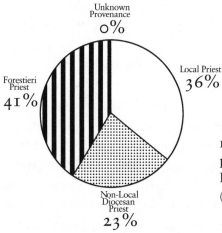

FIGURE 6.3. Provenance of priests elected to benefices by Rome, 1546–1550. (Courtesy of Daniel Lewis.)

and confirmed to benefices in his native town, asking the arch-
bishop of Volterra to nominate his Volterran client Vincenzo
Riccobaldi to a Volterran benefice, or trying to get a client
named to a vacant benefice in his native Castello di Santa
Croce.[40] As a patron, Cosimo intervened to keep the bishop of
Vasona from contesting a benefice held by the son of his auditor, Jacopo Polverini, in the Polverini stronghold of Prato.[41]
When the men of Cecina gave their voice to Cosimo, he elected
a local priest named Piero Vincenzo to the rectorship of San
Giovanni di Evangelista. This case gives us a clue to why local
communities might hand over their own rights to Cosimo. When
another party challenged the *patronato* and appointed a nonlo-
cal priest to the benefice, Cosimo rushed to the defense of his
own candidate.[42] Moreover, when Cosimo's intimates renounced
their own benefices, it seems that he encouraged them to renounce them to locals.[43] Whenever he could, he tried to pair his
courtiers with benefices in their native towns. It was a win-win
situation. The clients found their towns easier to rector, the
communities preferred the locals, and Cosimo avoided conflicts. Since he did not get many chances to nominate rectors on
his own rights, he made sure to accommodate this intensely felt
desire of his subjects.

Communities were not Tuscany's only patrons; individual
laymen had amassed a healthy percentage of the territory's ecclesiastical patronage rights as well. Cosimo was just as zealous
in their defense, though not quite as importunate in begging
their rights.[44] Moreover, he lent a sympathetic ear to their concerns as well, the primary one being the desire to keep benefices
in the family. From 1546 to 1550, 53 percent of all lay patronage benefices, either by election or renouncement were given to
someone who shared the patron's last name.[45] Thus it was not
long until patrons began coming to Cosimo claiming their rights
by familial lineage and begging him to make sure that those familial rights were not derogated in Roman courts.[46] When the
stakes were high enough, he would bring his Roman machinery

clanking to life, littering his letters to Roman contacts with supplications on behalf of his familiars, relatives, and bishops.[47]

Thus, Cosimo followed the republic's lead by intervening in
the regulation of the most lucrative aspect of the sacred: sacred
office. By protecting the *patronato* and accommodating feelings
in local communities, he was able to strengthen his own control
over Tuscan benefices, something he refused to do on an assumed
monarchical authority. Thus, on the subject of church benefices
Cosimo found a way to accommodate policy to popular feeling.

Sacred Space

The widest and arguably most beautiful street in Florence, the
Via dei Calzaiuoli, runs from the Piazza Signoria to the cathedral square, linking as it were the mind and heart of the early
modern Florentine republic. On one end stood the seat of political power, the palazzo tower silently jutting above the city
skyline and keeping vigilant watch over the city's peace. On the
other end stood the Florentine cupola, one of the largest in the
world, standing as a testament to what Florentine tour guides
love to explain as the sheer audacity of Renaissance peoples'
belief in their own powers since the architects planned and built
the base of the church before the technical ability to finish the
dome even existed. In the middle stood the Church of Orsan-
michele, once the city's grain market, then transformed into a
house for a sacred image of the Virgin Mary, the exterior decorated by the city's major and minor guilds in demonstration of
religious, civic, and professional pride. The Calzaiuoli is thus
elegant testimony to the intimate linkage of the political and
religious, for in the early modern world, the two spheres were
connected not only conceptually but also spatially.

Thus, in the articulation of political power, religious space
could not be ignored; indeed, as Edward Muir and Ronald
Weissman have pointed out, every Florentine regime laid claim

to legitimacy by utilizing the city's vocabulary of sacred space.[48] Cosimo's Medici ancestors had been masters of bolstering their popular political appeal by patronizing the city's sacred temples and monasteries.[49] Cosimo wasted little time in following in his family's wake. His projects were so widespread that one can easily mistake them for a princely attempt to monopolize all the city's sacred space. However, this type of analysis ignores the subtle differences in various ducal projects, differences that represent Cosimo's attention to the tensions between public and private patronage. In some respects, he could not afford to concentrate his patronage in a single center, since sacred power in Florence, unlike Venice, was multipolar and thus spread out among the city's different neighborhoods.[50] However, that same multipolarity made arbitrary takeover of sacred space difficult. Centralizing sacred power in a city in which decentralized sacral power had been the norm could not be done easily; stamping one's arms on any given church lacked credibility, a point that Cosimo understood well. A short anecdote reveals his attitude. When the Arno overflowed its banks in 1547, the rising tides spared neither secular nor religious buildings. A number of the monks whose complexes lined the river had no choice but to wade through the sludge to the Palazzo Signoria to appeal for government aid. Cosimo obliged, but the occasion, which he used as a convenient way to needle Pope Paul III, reveals some of Cosimo's thoughts on sacred space. As one of his secretaries related to the official in charge of the project: "The more diligence and solicitude you use in rebuilding these monasteries, the more it will be appreciated by his Excellency, who laughing, has said to me that if he has these walls rebuilt, the monks will need to put his arms on them and make a memory of this ruin just like Paul III does on every building that he constructs."[51] Making light of that particular pope was common sport in Cosimo's court, but the text is illuminating for the offhanded attitude it reveals. Like Florence, Rome's sacred landscape also had multipolar elements, and Cosimo knew that arbitrarily marking every project with his personal coat of arms could actually make him look foolish and overreaching.

Thus, the duke's exigencies were mutually contradictory. As a private citizen and a Medici, he had a tradition of private patronage to uphold; as a prince and representative of the city, his aims had to be more widespread. Such a situation required a deft touch. Fortunately he had a strategy, one that had been successful on other occasions: he played different roles at different times, acting as a personal patron in some churches and a ducal patron in others. Indeed, he was no stranger to this game of chameleon-like persona shifts; referring to his tendency to vary his personality according to the occasion, his court whispered about the young Cosimo that he "dukes and undukes himself at will."[52] He duked and unduked himself as a patron as well, using a style of personal patronage only in those sacred spaces where Florentine traditions supported his legitimate personal claims: neighborhood and familial churches. He kept his own personal presence largely out of public projects by directing and funding them in traditional ways.

In neighborhood churches, citizen patronage dictated a legitimate personal use of sacred space. Neighborhood mattered, and neighborhood churches were a focal point of neighborhood pride. Thus, it is not surprising that Florentine patrons generally preferred to place their most important projects in their own local neighborhood churches.[53] This is borne out by a quick survey of the record books of the Franciscans of Santa Croce, the Benedictines of le Murate, and the Augustinians of San Jacopo tra il Fosse, who win this honor for no other reason than they were all in the same part of the city, and they all kept some of the era's tidier records. Between 1555 and 1580, Florentines made a total of forty-two major bequests to these three monasteries.[54] Some were entirely monetary; others were grants of property. Most of them carried the duty of performing masses for a deceased soul. However, almost all of them reveal similar patterns of patronage, since thirty-six of the donors (80 percent) can be demonstrably linked to the respective monastery by ties of family or neighborhood.[55] Moreover, one of the remaining six patrons was Giovanna d'Austria, the wife of Francesco I, who as a foreigner could not have been expected to know or respect traditions of citizen patronage. Though these bequests were somewhat more modest than the major artistic pieces commissioned by the duke, the patterns were the same: people donated to monasteries to which they had geographical or familial ties. When Cosimo set about patronizing his own sacred spaces, the pattern had already been neatly laid out for him.

One of Cosimo's first real personal projects involved considerable restorations in San Lorenzo. For this project he chose Jacopo Pontormo, the artist who had so indelibly immortalized Cosimo's namesake in a 1520 portrait. This was only Cosimo's first step in putting his own highly personal claim on San Lorenzo. When the new sacristy was completed, Cosimo staged a public translation of the bodies of Lorenzo and Giuliano dei Medici into their current tombs there. While he was commissioning Pontormo to paint the sacristy, he was planning with the sculptor Bandinelli the great statue of his father, Giovanni delle Bande Nere, on the base of the basilica's front steps.[56] Though his favored sculptor's agonizing lethargy robbed Cosimo of seeing this completed in his lifetime, he was able to hang some of the standards won at Scannagallo up on San Lorenzo, in triumphant symbiosis with his ancestral sacred space.[57] He also personally commissioned Bronzino's *Martyrdom of San Lorenzo,* which, unlike Pontormo's *Last Judgment,* survives to this day. This was not the only personal element of Cosimo's relationship with San Lorenzo. In 1550, the Opera of San Lorenzo consented to offer up masses for Cosimo's parents, free of charge.[58] In all these cases, then, he was only patronizing space on which he had an indisputable claim. Not only was San Lorenzo in the Medici's traditional San Giovanni quarter, but it was just across the street from the Medici family palace. Indeed, San Lorenzo was the

Medici church par excellence; the family had paid for the construction of much of it out of their own purses and over the
years had made considerable endowments and bequests.[59] Thus,
the San Lorenzo commissions did little more than put Cosimo's
mark on a space to which he already had indisputable ties of
family, neighborhood, and tradition.

Cosimo courted the same highly personal relationship with
the monastery-and-church complex of Santissima Annunziata.
Another important shrine in the San Giovanni quarter, this
monastery lay on the axis leading out from the city center and
into the traditional Medici lands of the Mugello. Like San Lorenzo, the Annunziata had been heir to a long history of Medici
patronage. Both Cosimo the Elder and his son Piero had reserved cells among the Servites, and in the mid-fifteenth century, Piero dei Medici had commissioned Michelozzo to design
a sumptuous home there for the miraculous image of the Virgin
Mary. Michelozzo did not disappoint, producing the plans for
the baldachin under which the image still stands to this day.[60]
Over the intervening years, Medici patrons had littered the space
with ex votos, and unlike their Dominican neighbors down the
street, the Servite friars had done nothing to lose the goodwill
of their patrons.[61] Indeed, in 1498 the Servites had been among
the most anti-Savonarolan elements of the city, even loaning
siege ladders to the angry mob that sacked San Marco and took
Savonarola prisoner.[62]

Thus Cosimo had rightful historical, religious, and political
ties to this Florentine shrine as well, ties that he cultivated in
markedly personal ways. He made at least one highly theatrical
procession to the Annunziata, but Cosimo and Eleonora left more
permanent signs of their presence in this sacred space as well.
To the Medici ex votos already in Annunziata the duchess
added her own, a finely carved silver bust given in thanks for
the numerous times she had had recourse to the Madonna.[63] A
list of votive offerings compiled in the seventeenth century also

mentions a bust of Giovanni delle Bande Neri, which we might reasonably assume was placed there by Cosimo.[64] Cosimo appeared even more explicitly and personally; Santissima Annunziata was one of the few places where he felt no qualms displaying his own image. In 1560 he allowed Alessandro Allori to include his likeness in the Annunziata commission *The Expulsion of the Money Changers*.[65] In 1569 Cosimo commissioned a statue in his own image and likeness to fill a niche in the Annunziata's Chapel of Saint Luke, which was to house the new confraternity of artists.[66] Moreover, though Cosimo's move out of the Medici palace may have severed his local ties, his court and artists maintained a lively presence in the local church. Ugolino Grifoni, the sons of Agnolo Niccolini, and his favorite Sforza Almeini were all among those who had houses nearby.[67] Vasari actually lived in the convent for a time, and the tourist who is so inclined can still discover in the Annunziata the tombs of a number of important officials and artists, including the secretary Angelo Marzi Medici, the writer G. B. Tedaldi, the painter Giovanni Stradano, the treasurer Thomasso dei Medici, and the sculptors Baccio Bandinelli and Giovambattista Giambologna.[68] The remains of Cellini and Pontormo are there as well, enjoying in death the rest their various neuroses denied them in life. Thus, long after Cosimo moved out, his court continued to provide a vital connection to the Annunziata neighborhood.

If Cosimo left signs of his personal dominance in churches to which he had legitimate ties as a citizen patron, quite different were the projects undertaken in the Florentine cathedral, Santa Croce, and Santa Maria Novella, spaces to which he could not lay such historically valid personal claims. Unlike San Lorenzo, the cathedral had been built with public rather than private funds.[69] Cosimo acted accordingly. Under Bandinelli's influence, Cosimo's first cathedral project consisted in little more than transforming the wood choir into a more suitably eternal marble, for the choir had been built on the designs of Brunelleschi, an artistic hero of the republic.[70] Rather than snatch control of the Duomo outright, Cosimo chose to work through the traditional republican entity, the Opera del Duomo, whose compliance he rather heavy-handedly secured in 1540. The funding for the projects in the cathedral continued to come from the Opera's traditional revenues, though privately the entity was largely hemmed in by Bandinelli's caprice.[71] Thus Cosimo directed the project through a traditional entity and funded it with traditional means. Moreover, despite Bandinelli's claim that Cosimo's projects were designed to leave his eternal memory in the city's major church, the duke's presence in the form of *stemma* or personal imagery is noticeably lacking in all of the extant major works undertaken in the cathedral, including the remains of Bandinelli's choir,[72] the large Bandinelli altar statues, and Vasari's *Last Judgment* in the cupola. The observer searching for Cosimo's likeness in the cathedral will search in vain, for he well knew the differing protocols for public and private projects.

He completed the huge renovations to Santa Croce and Santa Maria Novella in the same way, though with an entirely different program in mind. In this case, the ideas for the renovations percolated out of Trent rather than out of Bandinelli's imagination. Tridentine architecture stressed laic participation in the Eucharist, but from a liturgical standpoint, the walling of the cathedral choir had only further cut the laity off from the mass. Thus the post-Tridentine projects went in a wholly different direction, as Cosimo commissioned Vasari to remove the rood screens and redesign the side chapels for use as more intimate liturgical settings.[73] In many ways, the physical renovation of these two buildings was a visible representation of church reform, and the timing of the project was no accident. It certainly was not just by chance that Cosimo restructured the city's most important Franciscan church on Tridentine lines in the same year that the Franciscan general synod met in Florence to reform the order itself along the same lines. Indeed, one might speculate that the renovation projects were meant to be read as

visual representations of Cosimo's own work in helping to reform the order.

Cosimo had been attempting to reform both the conventual
Dominicans and the Franciscans for years. In the 1550s, he
spent considerable energy in getting his own confidant appointed protector of the Dominicans of Santa Maria Novella
before he finally gave up and handed control over to the Observant Dominicans.[74] He spent even more energy cajoling the Franciscan cardinal protector as well. In 1544, he brought the protector of the order, Cardinal Carpi, to Tuscany to help reform the
monasteries.[75] When that measure failed to get the business of
reform done, Cosimo continued to complain to Carpi, urging
him in no uncertain terms to elect a general who would "re-
press the insolent lust, sodomies and sacrileges these religious
commit."[76] Cosimo knew just the man: his own confidant Raf-
faelo Sannini,[77] whom he had already foisted on the order in the
role of Tuscan provincial.[78] This particular project failed, so
Cosimo had wait on his reform until 1565, when the general
synod met in Florence and redrew their constitution, remedy-
ing, at least on paper, many of the faults he had spent years
complaining about.[79] Thus, these architectural projects gave
visual expression to his very popular interventions in church
reform.

In both cases, Cosimo chose to work through the churches'
respective *operae,* although in both cases he had denuded these
churches of their independence, giving Vasari a free hand to im-
pose uniformity on the hodgepodge of familial chapels that had
grown up over the years. Cosimo's hand was certainly a little
heavier now, but he did give the displaced families the right to
fund the construction of the new chapels. Many took the offer
with less than a whimper. Some bowed out, their places taken by
the duke's own favorites, but even the new men were well
matched to locations where their families had historical ties. For
instance, Alessandro Strozzi got the rights to a chapel in Santa
Maria Novella, a longtime Strozzi church in the traditional Strozzi

quarter. The duke's physician Andrea Pasquali also got a chapel in the Dominican church, right above the spot where his family held a tomb.[80] When a branch of the Serristori family declared that they could not pay for the new chapel in Santa Croce, their rights were transferred to Averardo Serristori, a member of another branch of the family and the duke's ambassador to Rome.[81] Thus Cosimo's personal marks were largely absent from these projects as well; though he demolished familial chapels, he assuaged feelings by keeping them in familial hands. In this he was following historical precedent; the last major renovation of Santa Croce had also been accomplished with a combination of private and public funds.[82]

Two other sacred spaces will round out this discussion and bring the pertinent dichotomy to the fore. The first project was legitimized on the grounds of neighborhood, the second on familial ties. Indeed, neighborhood alone was sufficient grounds for patronage, and new houses meant new neighborhoods. When Eleonora's already frail health took a turn for the worse in the late 1540s, Cosimo, in search of more salubrious air, used her private fortune to purchase the old Pitti Palace on the other side of the Arno. From there on out, Cosimo began to cultivate ties with the Oltrarno's most important monastery-and-church complex, Santo Spirito. My research found no hint of a relationship between Cosimo and Santo Spirito before the move, but after the move he seems to have quickly taken to his new neighborhood church. For instance, in 1553 he sought a new confessor among the monks in Father Girolamo Cardenas.[83] In 1565 Cosimo sponsored and attended a *sacre rappresentazione* of the Annunciation in the church.[84] In the same year he made a personal donation to refurbish the interior.[85] Of course, none of this was beyond the pale of acceptable private citizen patronage, since Santo Spirito was his new neighborhood church.

As already mentioned, neighborhood was not the only tradition relevant to citizen patronage. Familial ties served just as well. Few sacred spaces were as tightly bound to Cosimo's court as the convent of the Santissima Annunziata detto Murate, which was situated near the old city walls on the Via Ghibellina, nowhere near the centers of Cosimo's private power. Nevertheless, le Murate was on the court rolls for monthly payments by 1558, and Eleonora funded the rebuilding of the nuns' refectory in 1560.[86] One of Bronzino's portraits of Cosimo even found its way into the convent's collection.[87] Clearly, he had decided to cultivate ties to this convent, but what would have drawn him to such close ties with a convent so distant from his base of power? For starters, the Medici bank had financed the sisters' move to the Via Ghibellina in the fifteenth century.[88] This gave the Medici their in(In the mid-fifteenth century, Lorenzo had made several important bequests to the monastery, even leaving an ex voto offering to the monastery in return for the Virgin's intercession with his gout.[89] The offering was reputedly an image of himself, suggesting that Cosimo's own portrait found its way into the Murate church in deliberate imitation of the Magnificent.) Moreover, Cosimo's family tree included more than just his Medici ancestors. His paternal grandmother, Caterina Sforza, had patronized le Murate years before, bequeathing 2,000 gold florins to the monastery in exchange for the nuns' gifts, prayers, and favors, one of which included hiding her jewels and children in safekeeping during her revolt against the Borgia. Later, Caterina received permission to keep a cell in the cloister at her personal disposal.[90] However, more recent familial ties were probably more important. Before being married off to Henri of Valois, young Catherine dei Medici had been deposited in le Murate as a lay sister to receive protection and education. It is quite possible that Cosimo's patronage of the convent grew out of his desire to appease her. Her grateful memories of a childhood spent in the cloister paid off for the monastery when she became queen of France, and she apparently chose to do her giving through Cosimo. Records show Cosimo ordering alms of grain for the monastery on her behalf in 1548.[91] The timing coincides with her accession to the throne, a moment when Cosimo sought to use his consanguinity with her to effect a rapprochement with the French.[92] Thus his patronage of le Murate was shrewd, falling under traditional and more common patronage patterns but also furthering his international diplomatic interests. Like most of his projects, it was adroitly done. He kept his public projects outwardly public, and he kept his private projects only where tradition dictated they belonged.

Sacred Ritual

The tension between public and private power was played out not only on the grounds of sacred space but also on the battlefield of sacred rituals. Florence was no stranger to the overlap, as citizens and governments traditionally used religious festival to celebrate civic identity.[93] Like other Italian communes, the feast of the city's patron saint was the most important civic celebration of the year. In Florence's case, this was the Feast of Saint John the Baptist on June 24. The Feast of the Annunciation on March 25 remained important as well, since this was the day on which Florentines traditionally celebrated the new year. Cosimo utilized the commune's language of sacral-political ritual and took limited control over the regulation of liturgical time. At the same time he manipulated them both, molding them into a celebration of his own personal power without completely forsaking the meanings with which republican observers imbued them. Quite predictably, he was careful not to push his control too far, for accommodation was the key to mastering the hands of sacred time as well.

Cosimo's first ritual acts served to underscore the consensual nature of his new power. For instance, eschewing the escort offered by his father's veterans, the young Medici scion chose to enter Florence as a simple citizen at the service of the republic. His subsequent actions only served to underscore this subservience to the traditional languages of republican ritual, even if his intentions in this regard were not always successfully fulfilled. One of his first ritual obligations was to carry out the funeral for his deceased predecessor. In this case, he had two choices: give Alessandro either a sumptuous funeral designed to emphasize his royal status or a private funeral that would distance Alessandro's regime from Cosimo's own. In this case it seems that Cosimo would have preferred the latter, as his government repeatedly postponed the funeral obsequies for two months after the assassination. By March, the imperial agents in the city, Cardinal Cibo and Alessandro Vitelli, would brook no more dithering and took matters into their own hands. On March 6, the imperial guard moved the body from the old sacristy to the new sacristy with a triumphant pomp. When the funeral was held one week later, the imperial guard who arranged the obsequies had Alessandro's likeness reproduced in wax, clothed in the ducal garb, and placed on a litter.[94] The presence of this wax figure was doubtless meant to imitate, as the Medici's Este contemporaries were doing in Ferrara, the double funeral accorded the sacral kings of the French.[95] At the point of death, the monarch's two bodies (biological and mystical-political) were separated and the mortal one interred in the casket while the symbol of the ever-living mystical-political entity (represented by the wax figure) remained above in order to symbolize its enduring quality and thus the legitimate continuation of power.[96] In this way, the double funeral was a ritual designed to navigate the tensions between the monarch's dual nature as both mortal man and immortal head of the immortal body politic.

Neither Vitelli nor Cibo seemed particularly concerned about the fact that this ritual would aggravate Florentine sensibilities, though its dynastic implications could not have been lost on the Florentine audience. Thus it is telling that the impetus for Alessandro's funeral did not come from Cosimo's camp, for they certainly understood that dynastic claims such as the one embodied in the double funeral did not graft easily onto the body metaphor traditions of republican Florence. As explained in Chapter 1, the apotheosis of Cosimo rarely implied that he somehow represented the entire polity in his own body or that as head of the polity he suffused the body politic with divine charisma. Cosimo always downplayed the extent to which he portrayed himself as the head of the mystical Florentine body. For good reason. Florentines had been cutting off the metaphorical political heads of tyrants in their art and literature for several decades.[97] To be the "head" of the metaphorical Florentine body politic was a dangerous proposition. Thus, Cosimo did not usually employ the body metaphors so potent in the rest of early modern Europe. This helps explain why he dithered for two months rather than burying Alessandro right away, for he had apparently not yet found a way to reconcile the exigencies of preparing a funeral for his predecessor that properly spoke to both imperial and Florentine audiences. Eventually, the imperials, who had the possession of the fortress and the city's cache of arms, simply presented Cosimo with a fait accompli. Lacking the power to preempt the funeral, he did manage to undercut the extent to which it could be read as a double funeral on the French model. He accomplished this with his simple presence.[98] In the French tradition, the heir could not be present at the double funeral because his presence would disrupt the fiction that the old king lived on, thus presenting the audience with the awkward presence of two "living" kings in the same place.[99] The imperial agents in Florence may have forced the regal funeral on a reticent duke and unapproving Florence, but they could not force either the duke or the Florentines to impute the original underlying ritual meanings to the act.[100] With his presence, Cosimo signaled that he would forgo the type of ritual that would suggest his power descended by hereditary right rather than by election from the senate.[101]

Cosimo's marriage to Eleonora de Toledo gave the young duke another chance to portray a subdued picture of his dynastic claims. This began with Eleonora's entrance into the city, which could have followed several established processional Florentine paths designed to establish dominance over the city's various sacral centers. Florence's sacred topography, unlike that of many other Italian cities, was organized around a set of competing and centrifugal centers, so many ritual entries, such as episcopal entries, the occasional sojourns of Our Lady of Impruneta, and the triumphal entry of Leo X in 1515, processed throughout several of the city's different sections, with the implicit message that the power of the entrant crossed the border lines of neighborhoods.[102] Eleonora's entry route made rather more limited claims. She did not make a tour of the city's sacred spaces like Leo X; she was not received, like foreign dignitaries usually were, at the Piazza Signoria; and she did not make a circumambulation around the old walls, as her successor duchess would do in 1565. Entering at Porta Prato and proceeding to the Arno via Borgo Ognissanti, Eleonora's route was limited to a detour through Canto Carnesecchi and Canto Tornaquinci before heading straight to the Piazza San Giovanni and a tour of the cathedral. From the cathedral square, Eleonora and her escort made their way up Via Nunziata to San Marco. From there they progressed down the Via Larga to their final destination, the Medici palace.[103] Indeed, Eleonora deviated from a direct path to the Medici palace in only three ways: a north turn at the Via Tournabuoni, a stop at the cathedral, and a detour around the northern part of the San Giovanni quarter. The latter is completely explainable with reference to private Medici exigencies alone: she was simply visiting the traditional Medici neighborhood, and her presence there, much like Cosimo's patronage of the same sacred spaces, was more a gesture of familial and neighborhood devotion than civic subservience. Nor was her presence at the cathedral problematic; she was after all a foreign princess, and as Giambullari noted, she was received at the cathedral with the ceremony "usually given to such High Princesses."[104] Why then did Eleonora's retinue turn up the Via Tournabuoni? Aside from the considerable aesthetic reasons, this detour may have been designed to send a message specifically to the Strozzi and their partisans, since the turn up the Via Tournabuoni would have taken the procession directly past the Palazzo Strozzi.[105] Given Cosimo's recent history with the Strozzi, this may have been designed to signal the prince's dominance over this one house. However, given the options, Eleonora's route overall made rather limited claims about the new ducal couple's public dominance.

Cosimo's literati also struck a surprisingly balanced tone in their use of festival apparatus, managing to accomplish the difficult task of speaking to the concerns of their two audiences: one foreign and imperial, the other local and republican. Indeed, both audiences expected Cosimo to make a splendid impression right from the start, for even the Florentines found their own sense of honor bound up with the presence of noble foreign dignitaries.[106] To this end, Eleonora was greeted by a procession of the city's nobles, who escorted her into the city through a set of triumphal arches. The arches bore a panoply of *imprese,* each one designed with propagandistic intent, mostly to associate the Medici with the nobility of the Hapsburg emperors. However, insofar as these very publicly displayed *imprese* celebrated Medici history, they quite plainly foregrounded Cosimo's own father, Giovanni delle Bande Neri.[107] As Cosimo must have certainly known, Giovanni was a highly popular figure in Florence. More important, unlike Cosimo the Elder and Lorenzo the Magnificent, Giovanni was not associated in the Florentine mind with the Medici's history of attempts at political hegemony. Not until the procession reached the far more limited and private setting of the cortile of the Medici palace did the figures of Cosimo the Elder, Lorenzo the Magnificent, and the other ruling figures of Medici history make their appearances, with the obvious dynastic overtones that such representations would evoke.[108] Thus, Cosimo modulated his use of Medici history to send two different messages: the first a muted but more wide-ranging public message centered on the figure of Giovanni, the second a far more dynastic message centered on Lorenzo and Cosimo but limited to a more restricted circle and more private space.

Moreover, Cosimo's literati were able to use the traditional wedding feast to borrow key elements from Florence's most important civic/religious celebration: the Festival of San Giovanni. For instance, at a central moment in the wedding festivities, the avatars of Florence's dominions appeared in succession, promising future fecundity in both their own land and in the loins of the betrothed. In token of the promise, each of the goddesses laid representations of their bountiful agricultural dowries at the feet of the couple.[109] The avatars of the dominion were not meant to represent pagan gods in a pagan sense but to represent the people and the land, their products a symbolic representation of the tribute of the territories. The foreign observer might have missed the obvious civic significance, but Florentines themselves most certainly would have called to mind a similar moment during the Festival of San Giovanni in which the subject communes offered to the dominant city their own banners, food, and wax torches, laid at the feet of Florence and John the Baptist.[110] Over time, Cosimo would seek to appropriate this powerful symbol of Florentine domination in a more direct way by receiving the tribute of independently created feuds during the San Giovanni festival itself.[111] In this ritual, the Florentine republic had assumed the role of keeper of the dominion's treasures, indeed, the keeper of empire itself. The associations must only have been heightened, because in a nod to civic tradition, the wedding fell just before the June celebrations of the San Giovanni festival.[112] Thus the poetically pagan pageantry effected the symbolic transfer of sacral power; Cosimo made himself the new keeper of empire by vaguely inserting a personal and quasi-feudal element into the public rituals of Florentine empire.[113]

Closely tied to the regulation of sacred ritual was regulation of sacred time, which Florentine governments had long been battling over as a way to express evolving forms of political power.[114] As part of his self-fashioned identity as the protector of Catholic tradition, Cosimo wasted little time in tightening up his own legislation on sacred time, making sure that no man's "little reverence and fear of the great and omnipotent God" would bring "dishonor and public scandal on the Christian religion."[115] The ban on work had far-reaching implications: peasants were not allowed to seed the land, work their fields, or transport agricultural goods; merchants were not allowed to buy or sell; and bodegas, artisans, and bankers were obliged to close. Few exceptions were made, but there was some accommodation. Candlemakers were allowed to sell votive candles, while doctors and apothecaries could keep their shops open. One of the most important accommodations to popular sensibilities was that destitute artisans were allowed to work in their shops as long as they kept the windows tightly shut.[116] The new law proposed few novelties; the secular power had long used coercion to keep the Sabbath holy, but as with his other legislation, Cosimo's promulgation of the law meant he was about to get serious in prosecuting it. It also sent a clear message about the duke's role in defending sacred time.

However, transforming defense of sacred time into control of sacred time was a trick for no mean political conjurer, since all sorts of limitations boxed the duke in. He could not, for instance, simply invent his own religious feasts. The timing of feast days was out of his control, so despite their civil associations, it would have been difficult to use the Roman calendar alone to celebrate Medici power. However, the *feste,* or religious feasts, were closely linked to a more distinctly civil phenomenon, the *feria.*[117] *Ferie* primarily involved a prorogation of certain courts and the suspension of private and/or public debts. This occasion was a little like a civic holiday before such a thing existed and before such a word would have even been entirely intelligible. The *feria* was the civil authority's preferred mode for honoring religious feast days, but Cosimo's government extended the imaginative uses to which the *feria* could be put beyond the limits of the Roman calendar. For instance, in times of economic distress, governments might create *ferie* in order to temporarily lift crushing burdens of debt from the backs of the peasantry.[118] Only greedy and unpopular creditors could protest a move like that, but Cosimo was prepared to use the *feria* for less altruistic reasons as well. Already in 1539, the supreme magistrate used a *feria* to make a sort of holiday out of Cosimo's accession to the throne.[119] Cosimo's minions added a few touches of their own to this new civic holiday by holding a solemn mass in the cathedral and lighting an appropriately modest fireworks display.[120] The day may not have technically been a religious feast, but any observer would have certainly felt that it was, for the *feria* and mass mimicked the more properly religious feast days, while the fireworks display conjured up images of the Festival of San Giovanni. Thus did defense of sacred time become control, and thus did control become utilization.

When Cosimo regulated the celebration of *ferie* in legislation, his own holiday was officially enshrined in Florentine life. Moreover, the new calendar showed a marked favoritism toward Medici feasts. For instance, though Cosimo declared several *ferie* null and void, the ascension of the Medici pope Clement VII was not among them. Moreover, if Clement was one of only three popes who did not lose their status, it is no surprise that Cosmus and Damian, the traditional Medici saints, were also among those who did not lose civic recognition of their own day.[121] Thus, Cosimo was able to thrust the traditional protector saints of the Medici house, as well as himself and his line, into the ranks of protector saints of the Florentine populace along with such local heroes as Saint Romulus of Fiesole, San Donnino, Saint Giovanni Gualberto, and San Zenobius.[122] Cosimo also used the *feria* to celebrate political triumphs, for example his victory of Scannagallo, the treaty of Chateau-Cambresis, and the victory over the Turks at Lepanto.[123] Of course, he did not invent the political use of festival time; the last Florentine republic had created its own peculiar republican festival celebrating the expulsion of the Medici.[124] However, Cosimo refashioned the government's protection of sacred time for his own political needs, inventing and preserving a number of quasi-personal holidays.

Indeed, sacral time and sacral festival could be made to serve political ends, but Cosimo well understood the limits that hemmed in his control. A 1537 case from Figline reveals his rapid learning curve. The men and the community of Figline held an annual procession in honor of a relic that they believed to be a piece of the true cross. Like most similar processions, this was both a religious and a civic ceremony, and the community of Figline and the brothers from the monastery that owned the relic were locking horns in a bitter struggle over precedence in the procession. Cosimo was well aware that this admixture of civic and religious passion was a powder keg destined to ignite violent altercations on the street, so he ordered the procession postponed. As a salve to religious scruples, the pious Cosimo suggested that "in exchange of the procession, the community ask and multiply with their prayers toward the divine goodness that God accept with open arms and receive in his most holy grace everyone who seeks him with contrite and humble heart."[125] However, Cosimo quickly thought better of the idea, and one day later he wrote again belaying the order and allowing the procession.[126] Someone was giving him good advice, for it is not hard to imagine how quickly the duke himself could have become the target of Figline's rancor. He gave a similar nod to the people's penchant for imbuing sacred festival with civic meaning on his visit to Rome in 1560. When asked by Alessandro Strozzi at what point they might leave Rome, Cosimo responded that they could not do so until after the Feast of Saint Peter, writing: "the Feast of Saint Peter is beginning in the middle of the month in which you say you want to leave, and if you leave so close to the time of the festival, it will seem that you don't care about it, and you are fleeing that day which is so celebrated in that city."[127] Indeed, Cosimo well understood the power and meanings of religious-civic festivals.

Thus did Cosimo shrewdly utilize the ritual vocabulary of Florence and take control of its sacred calendar, celebrating his own personal power in forms that Florentines would find familiar and eschewing those they might find offensive. As always, he was self-regulating, understanding the extent to which his subjects would accept his control, backing off at prudent moments, and regulating his intervention to send acceptable messages. Thus, his control over sacred time followed his usual pattern: defense, insinuation, control, and accommodation.

Sacred Power: Indulgences and Miracles

Sacred office may very well have been the most lucrative element of sacral tradition, sacred space may have been the most visible, and sacred time the most controllable, but none of these was the most important. That palm went to sacred power: the indulgence and the miracle. The first flowed through the hierarchical channels of the church and guaranteed the penitent sinner remission of the temporal punishment of sins. The indulgence could be won in this life, or the price would have to be paid in the next, either through the prayers of those left below or in the torments of purgatory. On the other hand, miracles sometimes skirted the hierarchical structures of the church, putting the believer in direct contact with the supernatural. Cosimo wasted little time in monitoring the instances of both forms of sacred power in his realm.

From the first, Cosimo took indulgences under his own personal care. Only three months after his election, he instructed Chiarissimo dei Medici to give every aid to the jubilee proclaimed by the prior of the Incurables, "because from such a meritorious work one is able to do much for the salvation of all those who seek it."[128] From the beginning, Cosimo's line on indulgences was in strict conformity with Catholic doctrine. Moreover, as with indulgences, so with the indulgence's concomitant partner, masses for the dead, which early modern Catholics almost always commissioned with the thought of quickening their passage up the mount of purgatory. In 1540 the pope interdicted Florence over the disputed collection of a tithe, and Cosimo boldly claimed that all his priests would prefer to remain under interdiction rather than hand over a single scudo to Rome.[129] However, as All Saints and All Souls Day approached, he panicked and decided instead to attempt to accommodate his policies to public opinion. As Cosimo's bravado faltered, so did his confident expectation of his subjects' support. Because All Souls Day included ceremonies for the dead, the interdict opened up dangerous ground, since it meant that a number of Florentines would simply lose the masses commissioned for their dead relatives. Cosimo wrote to his ambassador in Rome, Averardo Serristori: "It seems appropriate, and my duty to remind the pope that we are now near the solemnity of All Saints and the ceremonies of the dead need to take place."[130] When the bull came through, Cosimo asked Serristori to rush it to Florence so that the suspension could be published in time.[131] However, because the pope's hackles were once again raised against the duke, Cosimo received neither the immediate suspension nor the dispensation for All Saints, a fact that left him unpopular with his people and furious with the pope.[132]

From that point on, Cosimo took more care. Both in 1545 and 1546, he asked his ambassador to get the pope's personal confirmation of the cathedral's traditional indulgence on the Feast of the Annunciation.[133] Even under an unfriendly pope, Cosimo respected the power of the indulgence. With friendly popes he was downright obsequious. In April 1560, Cosimo proclaimed a *feria* for the indulgences attached to the crusade.[134] In December of the same year he proclaimed a *feria* for eight whole days, strongly recommending that his population take advantage of the indulgence offered for the reopening of the Council of Trent. The text read:

> We are aware how much clemency and charity moves the most beatific and Holy Vicar of God on Earth, Pope Pius IV, to give the treasures and graces of the Most Holy Church liberally to faithful Christians. Since we must provide the opportunity for every person to freely and without impediment enrich themselves of so particular a gift of indulgence . . . their lordships publicly proclaim and give notice that they have made and created a *feria* for the city of Florence only. . . . Next Sunday, solemn processions will be held in the city, and we exhort every person to prepare themselves to follow it devoutly according to the order of the bull in order to gain such an indulgence. We also exhort all to pray to God with all their heart for the conservation, augment, and greatness of the true and living faith.[135]

Cosimo himself set the example. In Rome at the time, he made the procession with the barefooted pope from Saint Peter's to Santa Maria Sopra Minerva.[136] Cosimo closed the bodegas down for another Florentine jubilee in 1564; this indulgence was given to those who would visit the seven major churches of Florence.[137] He did it again for the holy year of 1565 and again in 1566 for an indulgence proclaimed for the Knights of Malta.[138] Florentines got the opportunity to win more indulgences in 1571, this time to celebrate the fact that Christendom's princes had set aside their differences just long enough for one military action against the Turks.[139]

Cosimo's protection of the indulgence fit tidily into the prevailing ideology of secular government and its duty toward its subjects' salvation, but as always, protection also meant control. Before any edicts concerning indulgence could be nailed to the church doors, they had to pass through the hands of Cosimo's own auditor. In practical effect, it seems that petitions to proclaim indulgences were almost never denied. Indeed, Cosimo's single dispute is the exception that proves the rule. In the century-long search for revenue to fund the building of Saint Peter's, Julius III had awarded all unfulfilled pious bequests to be applied to the Fabrica di San Pietro. He had also deputed agents of the Fabrica to go rifling through old wills to find them. When the agents of the pope pressed Cosimo to open up Tuscan wills to their deputies, Cosimo respectfully but firmly declined, refusing his aid to the agents of both Julius III and Paul IV.[140] His arguments were rather telling. Apart from the predictable protestations of the poverty of the *patria*, he felt that his subjects might find it irritating to see their bequests sent away from their local monasteries and to Rome instead. He thus did not want it "to be a reason that people might refrain from similar good works." On that note he bragged: "Here in Tuscany, the zeal of religion is conserved, perhaps more so than in other states, and I do not want it to diminish at all."[141] Cosimo thus argued, rather paradoxically, that the deputies could not fulfill the pious bequests of the dead because they were simply too important. Indeed, even if Florentines professed obedience to Rome, that obedience did not imply that they loved seeing their treasures go south. Thus the accord Cosimo finally reached with Pius IV in 1562 stipulated that only a fifth of such *lasciti* were to go to Rome, with a third of that fifth staying in Tuscany for the benefit of its native temples.[142] This time it was Rome pushing for a quick expedition so that they could publish the indulgences associated with spontaneous apparition before the Feast of All Saints.[143] With that, Cosimo ordered all Florentine notaries to present their wills so that the Roman auditors could free those souls "perhaps still racked in the pains of purgatory."[144]

Thus Cosimo quite readily went along with most of Rome's indulgences. However, his deference raises the question: why protect the indulgence, the very item that had set so many fires of reform in the north? No doubt the factors were many. Cosimo's own language suggests a personal belief in the Catholic doctrine of merit.[145] He also was desperate to win the goodwill of Rome and his own bishops. However, other evidence suggests the explanation very well may lie elsewhere, in his own population's enduring belief in purgatory and consequent enduring appetite for indulgences. This should not surprise; purgatory held a special place in Florentine culture as the central piece of the most popular theological work of the age: Dante's *Divine Comedy*. The importance of Dante's masterpiece transcended the literate world, for his peculiar vision of heaven, hell, and the space between had even been inscribed onto the walls of the cathedral in 1465. Moreover, the shades populating Dante's literary masterpiece had been unequivocal in begging prayers from the living for their speedier passage up the holy but tortuous mountain.[146] Nor did Dante's acceptance of prayers for the dead give way to significant challenges in the leap from trecento to quattrocento. If anything, the voice of Archbishop Antoninus had been even more insistent, remarking that under the commandment of honoring father and mother, pious believers needed "to make sure that they have given the bequests made to the churches and other pious places at the due time if their parents are dead. And if he or she had not done it, they can be called murderers of the souls of the parents, taking away from them due suffrage, which is not without great sin."[147] In one sense the Reformation had cast the bishop's assertion in grave doubt by throwing down the gauntlet against the whole business: works, purgatory, masses for the dead, and especially indulgences. However, in another way, the Reformation had only made belief in purgatory stronger by sealing it as a mark of Catholic identity. One controversialist's sermon, published at the request of Alessandro Strozzi, illustrates the point. Although the author reportedly was on the cutting edge of Italy's reform movement, this apparently did not extend so far as to deny purgatory, indulgence, and the efficacy of prayers for the dead.[148] Though the first half of the sermon denigrated man's works with a passion that ultimately landed its author in front of the Inquisition,[149] the conclusion left no doubt on what side of the confessional divide it proposed to fall, ending on a crescendo of doctrinal purity: "Since Christ is so rich and so just and has no need of his merits, which de jure must follow his works, we can ask for them ardently, and with them we can remedy our miseries. We can ask for his bloody sweat, his hunger in the desert, his difficulties in prayer . . . and all that he suffered for us at the end of his life. Moreover, (speaking piously) if we are negated this, we can shake and break down the gates of heaven with tears and cries, asking for what is ours, although he would never deny them since he is most trustworthy."[150] Violent yet pious metaphor thus expressed, Fra Andrea exhorted his flock to continue to make their pious bequests. If this acceptably Catholic view on indulgences came from one of Italy's reformers even before the Council of Trent's decree on justification, we can easily imagine what the hard-liners said.[151] Moreover, as the leaders of the Protestant movement were either chased underground or out of Italy in the 1540s, one message on indulgences came to predominate.[152] In fact, the Reformation probably made the point a more important theme than it otherwise would have been.

Was Cosimo paying attention to his subjects' view on purgatory and indulgences? To gauge their continuing popularity, he would have only needed to mark how many flocked to the churches where the indulgences were being promulgated. The historian does not share that luxury; for the modern investigator, testaments are the only remaining clue that speak the language of personal belief, since Italian Protestants by the mid-1540s were exceedingly careful with whom they openly shared their religious opinions. Open professions of Protestant ideas would have only sent one on an unpleasant exile to Geneva or an even more unpleasant visit to the local inquisitor. However, apart from the 3 lire tax that went directly into the cathedral's coffers, no one could compel the dead. Testators could show their religious preferences by choosing to have masses or prayers said for them and/or by choosing to commend their souls to the Virgin Mary and the saints. The first action showed an active belief in purgatory and a rejection of the Protestant doctrine of *sola fide*. The second showed an affirmation of Catholic identity.

Of course, analyzing testaments is not without its difficulties. In the first place, testators did not have total authorial control over their wills, since the exact words were usually dictated by notaries, who often relied on rote notarial lingo. However, just as Sam Cohn has noted in his study of Sienese testaments, sixteenth-century Florentine notarial books frequently contained diverse formulae.[153] Thus, it seems likely that testators found some space in their wills to express personal religious sentiments, even if the religious attitudes of the testators were not the only and sometimes not the primary concern of testaments.[154] For instance, testators might use any number of bequests to support family members living in monasteries, to leave their memory in local churches, and even to subvert the social order.[155] Nonetheless, there would be little reason to request prayers or masses after death unless one sincerely adhered to traditional Catholic beliefs on purgatory.[156] Moreover, many testators specified that the mass be performed quickly after their death, presumably because they envisioned a temporal connection between the realms of earth and purgatory.[157] Thus, it seems reasonable to assume that requests for prayers and masses, as well as gifts prefaced with the phrase *in rimedio animae*, imply at least a basic familiarity and belief in the Catholic doctrine of purgatory. One might reasonably assume that this corresponded to Florentines' appetite for indulgences, since indulgences and masses for the dead performed essentially the same function.

Of course, we do not have any nontestamentary evidence of the religious opinions of the vast majority of testators, so it might be useful to test these assumptions against the wills of contemporaries whose religious views can be established on the basis of other evidence: in this case, Bartolommeo Panciatichi, Niccolò Machiavelli, and Benvenuto Cellini. Panciatichi, one of the duke's own secretaries, certainly harbored Protestant opinions. He wasn't apparently very secretive about them either, as he was arrested, inquisited, and found guilty of heresy in 1552. Only Panciatichi knew how much sincerity there was in his forced abjuration, but the will he had crafted two years earlier fits the profile of a man convinced of the doctrine of *sola gratia*. He left no money for masses, no money to any monastery, and no instructions for his heirs' prayers. Moreover, he commended his soul only to God, leaving out the traditional invocation of the Virgin Mary. Seemingly, Panciatichi did not expect to make it to heaven with pious bequests. Of course, this did not imply an absence of real charitable impulse. He did leave money to dower impoverished noble girls, but he gave no indication that he expected to reap any merit from this act; the formula *pro rimedio animae* is conspicuously absent from any section of his testament. The absence of any bequests designed to speed his soul through purgatory corresponds to what we know of his *sola gratia* beliefs.[158] On the other hand, Niccolò Machiavelli's will confirms the picture of a man whose political philosophy reveals him to be relatively unconcerned with the hereafter, for Machiavelli was most likely "unconcerned with religion in an emotional sense."[159] In due form, Machiavelli left no money to pious causes, no money for masses, no instructions for prayers, and did not invoke the Virgin.[160] Whereas Panciatichi had left alms to pious causes, presumably on the grounds that the true Christian ought to be charitable for the honor and love of God alone, Machiavelli did not. It was a fitting last testament for a man whose political philosophy was scandalously less concerned with the hereafter than those of any of his contemporaries. In the final case, Cellini's will shows very different preoccupations, for his autobiography reveals a deep, almost hysterical attraction to Catholic forms of piety.[161] He most certainly believed in the doctrine of expiation and the intercession of the saints, and thus, despite a wild youth—or perhaps because of it—he left a considerable sum of money for masses and orations in his honor, as well as an anniversary mass in the baptistery of San Giovanni. The sums were by no means negligible.[162] Though these three examples do not prove that bequests for masses and testamentary preambles are infallible guides to deciphering religious affiliation, they do support the premise that the making of a will could be an occasion for expressing individual religious preference.

Thus, the wills of Florentines can be used as a window into popular piety. Studied from this angle, Cosimo's protection of the indulgence appears as a winning policy, since belief in purgatory seems to have remained a constant of Florentine spirituality, unlike, for instance, patterns of piety in neighboring Siena. This may help to explain why Cosimo aimed his support for indulgences primarily at the citizens of Florence itself. For instance, Cosimo's 1560 *feria* was created for Florence alone, and the 1564 *feria* was celebrated for those who would receive an indulgence by visiting the major Florentine churches. Why favor Florence in this regard when so many other laws had been designed to favor cities in the dominion? By targeting Florence rather than Siena, Cosimo may have been following his own population's lead. In Siena, reformed opinion was rife, and Cosimo knew it; consequently, the latter part of the sixteenth century produced a marked decline in the percentage of testators requesting masses in Siena.[163] On the other hand, Florentines continued to bequeath masses and the office of the dead at a rate substantially unchanged throughout the decades in question, this over and above the funeral mass, which the overwhelming majority of testators left to their heirs' discretion. In Siena, requests for masses did not recover from the lows of the midcentury until after a papal visitation stimulated interest among the lower classes at the end of the sixteenth century, suggesting that Counter-Reformation piety in Siena took hold as a dialogue between the established ecclesiastical church and interested laymen among the lower classes. In contrast, on the eve of the Reformation, Florence already had a more lively culture surrounding intercessory masses,[164] and analysis of sixteenth-century Florentine wills suggests that requests for prayers and masses neither tailed off nor grew with any remarkable change over the course of the five decades in question. A sampling of over fourteen hundred wills notarized in Florence between 1520 and 1569 shows that nearly half of all Florentine testators requested masses or prayers for their souls during the 1520s. If we include those testators who preceded other types of bequests with the phrase *in rimedio animae,* the number of testators actively affirming belief in purgatory climbs to 54 percent. The number changed very little across the decades; in the 1530s, it was at 49 percent. At the height of Protestant activity in the 1540s, the sample actually shows the highest percentage of testators asking for masses and prayers: almost 52 percent. In the 1550s and 1560s, the percentage stayed around 50 percent. If we add those testaments that did not request prayers but used the formula *pro rimedio animae,* we find the same consistency. The constancy of these wills suggests that Florentine interest in indulgences remained largely unchanged during Cosimo's reign (Figure 6.4).

What, exactly, do these numbers mean? Did Protestantism affect just a few, or did proindulgence literature cancel out its effects? My view tends toward the former. For it is clear that an overwhelming majority of the populace continued to self-identify as Catholics, even if they didn't all request masses for their souls (Figure 6.5). Though the very rich could often afford seemingly

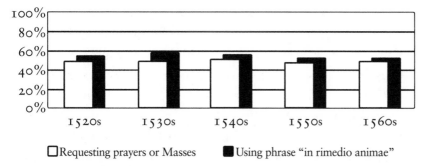

FIGURE 6.4. Percentage of testators demonstrating belief in Purgatory. (Courtesy of Daniel Lewis.)

endless bequests for masses, it seems that the office of the dead may have been out of some testators' price range. The going rate appears to have been 2 scudi, roughly equivalent to three weeks' wages for a skilled artisan.[165] This impression is confirmed by the fact that the percentage of those identified as nobles, and presumably more able to afford such luxuries, requested masses at a rate appreciably greater than that of the general population, at 61 percent (Figure 6.6). At any rate, the traditional invocation of the Virgin Mary marked most testators out as probably Catholic and, at the minimum, not strongly attached to Calvinist or Lutheran doctrines. Normally the formula ran something like this: "the testator humbly and devoutly commends his/her soul to omnipotent God, his most glorious mother the Virgin Mary, and the entire court of the celestial paradise."[166] Though it was standard testamentary formula, it did not need to be included. The formula could be varied at will and was occasionally omitted, as has been noted in the cases of Panciatichi and Machiavelli. The formula could also be expanded to include a range of individuals' protector saints. If one counts requests for masses, for prayers, or for offices and traditional Marian preambles as evidence of Catholic identity, the number of Catholics in sixteenth-century Florence stands at least 93 percent of the total testating population. That number steadily and slowly increased, from 92 percent at the outbreak of the Protestant movement in the 1520s to 98 percent by the end of the period. This is in marked contrast to similar trends in, for example, Munster, which saw considerably more confessional change. In 1536, Munster's testators used the traditional Catholic invocation of Mary in more than 60 percent of cases, and that number shrank to almost zero by the end of the century.[167] Thus, it seems that the continuing popularity of the indulgence was simply one piece of a more diffuse process of Florentine Catholic self-identification. Cosimo's ever more active support of the indulgence followed his population's own lead. Indulgences simply remained an essential aspect of popular piety as the Florentine mind became ever more rooted in the triumphant Catholicism of the Counter-Reformation.

Indulgences were fairly uncomplicated. Rome loved to give them, Florentines loved to get them, and all Cosimo had to do was get out of the way. However, the other great manifestation of sacred power, the miraculous intercession of the Virgin, was more difficult to handle. The Virgin's habit of making unexpected appearances on Tuscan soil could skirt the hierarchy and undermine political authority in potentially explosive ways. Thus, the prudent prince moved swiftly to take oversight of one of Tuscany's most potentially explosive miracles. In 1536 the Virgin Mary had appeared to a shepherd girl in the small commune of Combarbio, just outside Anghiari. The local bishop examined the matter, declared the apparition authentic, and approved the cult. Within months, votive offerings were pouring in, miracles were being reported, and the walls of a shrine were quickly appearing near the location of the apparition. Combarbio was quickly becoming a hot spot of intense local piety.

When the political events of 1537 unfolded, the men of Anghiari and the Virgin of Combarbio both had strong opinions to offer the new duke. Anghiari voiced its opinion by offering the commune as a base of activity for the republican rebels.[168] Our

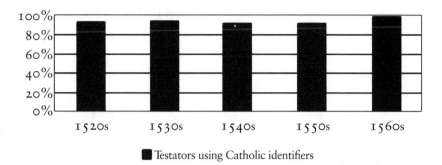

FIGURE 6.5. Percentage of testators using Catholic identifiers.
(Courtesy of Daniel Lewis.)

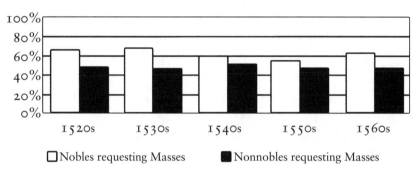

FIGURE 6.6. Comparison of nobles and nonnobles requesting masses.
(Courtesy of Daniel Lewis.)

Lady voiced her opinion by miraculously freeing a nun from prison and giving her a message to take to Cosimo: "unite the city and live in peace and the fear of God, or a great scourge is prepared for Florence."[169] Cosimo could not let the Virgin's threats go ignored, nor could he let such a politically explosive apparition continue to go unchecked in such a politically explosive region. As usual, scandal gave him his opening. When a question arose over appropriations of bequests, he took swift and immediate regulatory action, ordering his local vicar to make an exact account of all donated alms and forbidding anyone to proceed with church construction without his consent.

He also asked his vicar to provide him with more detailed information on the apparition itself. What miracles had been reported? Which were true? Which were false? How were alms distributed? How did the Virgin manifest herself? Most important, was the devotion born out of a true spirit of charity, or was there something sinister behind it?[170] Eventually, Cosimo found a more efficient means of surveillance by cajoling the community to make the church the preserve of the politically quiescent Carmelites.[171] His attention to popular piety, however, prevented him from giving free play to his natural skepticism and mistrust; he also instructed his vicar to "communicate this our letter with men that live there, but do it so as not to alter anyone in their devotion or good mind and so that no scandal arises." The pattern of accommodation and control again appears. Cosimo wanted oversight, but the last thing he wanted was to set his own government up against the Virgin in the popular mind or to shake the peoples' faith in the manifestation of the divine.

Cosimo found a way to turn his surveillance of the miraculous to his own account in other ways, quietly abetting politically useful manifestations of the miraculous against more ambivalent ones. For instance, he clearly favored the image of the Annunziata in its silent duel with Our Lady of Impruneta by privileging the latter more properly Medicean image at the expense of the more ambivalent former. Both images had long and storied histories, and both had important places in Florence's economy of the miraculous. However, only the Annunziata was unambiguously Medicean. According to legend, the Madonna of Santa Maria Impruneta had been painted by Saint Luke and then buried by San Romualdo, the semilegendary bishop of Fiesole, in the fourth century. Its impressive origins were accompanied by an equally impressive rediscovery, the sort of miraculous dramatics at which medieval historians excelled. Having made a start in walling their church, locals returned every morning to find, like Penelope's suitors, that the work had been inexplicably undone over the night. Taking this as an omen that they were building in the wrong spot, they loaded a mule with supplies and sent him on his way, electing to build the church wherever he might stop. As the reader may guess, the mule fortuitously chose the very spot at which Romualdo had hidden Saint Luke's image centuries before. The Impruneta legend was born. The image made its first appearance in Florence during the plague year of 1354 and from that point on had been repeatedly carried into the city in order to ward off plague, pestilence, drought, war, and flooding.[172] In Florentine minds, the Impruneta was the most important symbol of the Virgin's special protection of the city.

The miraculous image of the Annunziata was a close second, sporting a more colorful history and a rival list of miracles. Though of more recent vintage, the Annunziata's origins were comparably dramatic. Having agonized over how to depict the Virgin's face, a thirteenth-century Servite monk had fallen asleep in front of his half-finished painting. On waking, he found the Virgin's face miraculously completed. Word spread quickly, and miracles followed in due course, the first of which undoubtedly was one of the more memorable. The Virgin reportedly blanched a local women's suspiciously dark-skinned baby in order to spare the unfortunate matron the wrath of her (white) husband. As such stories spread, the image quickly became a locus for the city's plethora of miracle seekers.[173]

In these respects, there was not much to commend one Madonna over the other. They played complementary roles in Florentine life: one the focus of personalized devotions, the other the city's preferred heavenly advocate in times of general crisis. However, there was one important difference between the two Madonnas: the Annunziata was an undisputedly Medicean totem, and the Impruneta was not. Whereas the Virgin of the Annunziata was Cosimo's neighborhood miracle worker, whose cult resided near the traditional Medici power base, the Impruneta spent most of its days on the peripheries of Florence, dangerously out from under the government's thumb. Whereas the Medici had indisputable claims to the Annunziata, the Impruneta was in Buondelmonte territory. Most of the canonries belonged to Buondelmonte clients, and the interior space of the Impruneta's shrine was practically littered with testaments to that family's control.[174] Though Cosimo's first archbishop of Florence was both a Buondelmonte and Medici supporter, as a clan, the Buondelmonte family had not always been Medici stalwarts; for instance, earlier in the century Zanobi Buondelmonte had been chased into French exile for plotting the Medici's overthrow.[175] Whatever the case, one thing was certain: the Impruneta was definitely outside Cosimo's personal control. It was not entirely clear whose side she was on anyway. In 1526 when the Medici had brought the image into the city to protect themselves against the citizens, the Virgin showed her displeasure, at least in the eyes of republican observers, by ruining the procession with a thunderstorm.[176] Moreover, the last Florentine republic did its part to transform the miraculous virgin into a more forcefully anti-Medicean image. During the republicans' three short years in power, they had brought the image into the city no less than three times before finally electing to house the icon in the city permanently, this of course to keep the Virgin's protection close at hand against the city's Medicean besiegers.[177]

Given the recent history, Cosimo probably acted prudently in privileging the Annunziata over the Impruneta. Of course, he was wise enough not to show the less favored image any outright hostility. Control always involved accommodation. To that end, he allowed the image to be carried into the city in its traditional function of rain totem, when he had to deal with his first drought in 1538. The Madonna apparently obliged the city with the expected precipitation, so when a summer's worth of bad storms swelled the banks of the Arno in 1547, Cosimo brought the Impruneta in again, showing her the reverence that the miraculous image had come to expect from the city's leaders. Reports even suggested that as the duke watched the procession from a window in the Palazzo Signoria, the sight of the city's piety brought tears to his eyes.[178] However, we cannot ignore the marked contrast between Cosimo's palpable reluctance to bring the Impruneta into the city's walls vis-à-vis the quick reaction the city normally showed when disaster loomed. The Virgin made her short journey to the city only after a whole summer of dangerous rains, after the Arno had already flooded twice, and after local processions near the sanctuary had failed.[179]

Indeed, Cosimo's reluctance to turn to the Impruneta is striking when viewed in the light of the city's history. Between 1432 and 1529, the republic brought the image into the city at least forty-one times, and the longest gap between visits was eleven years.[180] On the other hand, after the processions surrounding the 1547 flood, Cosimo never let the Impruneta into the city again, allowing twenty-seven years to lapse without a visit. It was not for lack of crises. A number of bad harvests might have occasioned processional devotions with the Impruneta, but he did not call for her, not even when the starving poor were dropping dead in the streets. The war with Siena should have certainly brought the Virgin within the city walls, but he did not call for it then, not even when Piero Strozzi's bold military tactics struck right into the heart of the Florentine dominion. Cosimo did not call for the Impruneta when the Arno jumped its banks in 1557, cascading into the city and wreaking general havoc. He did not call for the image after foiling an assassination plot in 1559.[181] And when the 1556 drought prompted some of the Capponi family to beg for the image, he gruffly scribbled on the bottom of the request: "let them have a procession on the mountain."[182]

Of course, it looked very bad to ignore the Virgin's succor forever. By 1562, some were starting to mutter about the prince's lack of devotion, but by then he had a new plan, one that would demonstrate his support for popular piety without recourse to the Impruneta. That year an unusually intense drought not only threatened the harvest but seriously affected the drinkable water supply. This time the hungry bellies were accompanied by thirsty mouths, which cried out for a supplicatory procession, and this time Cosimo complied. However, instead of the Impruneta he allowed a different company to bring in a different image, the Madonna della Quercia, who was thus given the Impruneta's honors of making the rains come.[183] Discovered in an oak tree in 1520 just outside the Porta Pinta, the miraculous image had first attracted the attention of the populace by healing an incurable. Again, word went around the city. Again, supplications and money poured in. A confraternity was formed to build the church in 1520, and Michelangelo was appointed the architect in 1523. The completed church, now destroyed and lost to history, was consecrated by the visiting Franciscan bishop of Bitonto in 1552. During those forty years, the importance of the image grew considerably. Indeed, by 1561 the company had grown so big that they were forced to construct a new building in which to meet.[184] Cosimo was certainly aware of the growing devotion to this image and deftly chose this burgeoning cult to replace that of the Impruneta. Indeed, the Madonna della Quercia was a smart choice. The Quercia had a legitimate Florentine history but had never been caught explicitly preferring popular government to the Medici. Moreover, its devotion was growing, quickly becoming an essential feature of local popular piety. Thus, Cosimo was able to associate his own house with an image rapidly growing in popularity while lending his own authority to this growth, thereby sanctioning a devotion to which he was almost certainly tied by patronage bonds.[185] This was control over sacred power exercised with an acute sensibility to popular attitudes.

Unlike Cosimo, later Medici did not completely ignore the Impruneta, so posterity conveniently chose to forget this abnormal policy of his. However, there is little doubt that the canons of the Impruneta knew exactly what end of the stick their image was getting. The Madonna della Quercia was brought into Florence in September 1562 and was credited with the rain that followed its return to its church outside the Porta Pinta. This new policy represented a considerable financial loss for the Impruneta, as it dried up the votive offerings that had inevitably poured into the Impruneta's coffers following any successful Florentine procession. Small surprise then that a short three weeks after the Quercia made its debut in Florence, the Impruneta shot back with its own miracle. A *ricordi* from 1562 explains: "I remember how in the year 1562, it did not rain from the first of March to the fifth of October, and the rivers became ditches. All the wells around the parish dried up. By chance, under Monte Santa Maria, a vein of water was found near to our parish, and all the people came for water, and the water was named the water of Santa Maria because it came from the Monte Santa Maria. Many who were ill with fever drank of this water and were healed as soon as they drank. Praised be to the glorious Virgin Mother, our Advocate."[186] The discovery of a miraculous nearby well may have salvaged prestige, but the Impruneta's next entrance into Florence had to wait on a new duke. The Medici would not call on the Impruneta again until 1581, having shut it out of the city for an unprecedented thirty-seven years.[187] All this stands in marked contrast to Cosimo's devotion to the cult of the Annunziata. For instance, on the Annunziata's special feast days he made exceptions to his rigid *feria* laws, allowing the sale of the little votive lights with which true believers festooned the church.[188] It was to the Annunziata and its local cult that Cosimo directed the attention of visiting dignitaries.[189] Perhaps most important, it was the aid of that Virgin whom Cosimo sought in times of war.

After his armies had crushed Piero Strozzi's forces during the war with Siena, Cosimo staged a wickedly ingenious set-piece of sacral power. Bearing olive branches of peace, the messengers brought him the news of his victory over Strozzi in the Piazza Santa Trinità, a location undeniably in the heart of local

Strozzi power and directly adjacent to the Strozzi's neighborhood church. From there he made his way directly to the Annunziata, to his own sacred space and special protector, remaining on his knees in thanksgiving before the image for nearly half an hour.[190] After long years, Cosimo's Madonna had finally delivered Piero Strozzi into his hands, and she was duly rewarded with his votive thanks.

Conclusion

Defense, insinuation, control, accommodation: these four strategies consistently marked Cosimo's policy toward popular piety. In this way, he was able to make local expressions of sacred power his own, planting his own practice of ruler sacrality firmly in the ground of local tradition. In his handling of sacred office, patronage of sacred space, and policy toward rituals, festivals, miracles, and indulgences Cosimo traveled a well-trodden path, winning control and insinuation by showing keen sensitivities to popular piety and custom. Just as the rhetorical aspects of his sacral monarchy consistently referenced Florentine intellectual tradition, his practical exercise of sacral power consistently referenced the traditional assumptions of sacred Florence.

Conclusion

Early modern historians of political sacrality have satiated our historical appetites on a limited range of issues. They have relentlessly pursued genealogies of political thought through space and time, examined the transformation of sacral politics into modern secular polities, and analyzed the relationships between political propaganda and political exigencies. However, political mythologies were not just a matter of old ideologies meeting new political exigencies. They also involved old ideologies integrating—and failing to integrate—with basic habits of thought. "Great oaks from little acorns grow," wrote the great *Annales* historian Marc Bloch, "but only if they meet favorable conditions of soil and climate."[1] As I have attempted to show, these conditions were not just political, but cultural and religious as well. When the historian does not account for these deep-seated assumptions, it is very difficult to view political propaganda in anything but the most cynical terms. However, it is hard to see how a credible program of legitimation could have succeeded if it consisted of nothing more than the cynically conceived maxims of intellectual elites. Rather, Cosimo's experience suggests that successful propaganda sat on a rock of shared local axioms and cultural tropes.

Cosimo was indeed able to present himself as a terrestrial god and a divine monarch, but only because Florentine thought was already comfortable with the idea of terrestrial divinity. He was also successful in projecting his divine right claims, but only because in Florence (as elsewhere) everything was part of the divine plan. He may have arisen to save Christian virtue for Christian politics, but only because Machiavelli had left a shattered moral system begging for proof of its own utility. He may have achieved divine status as an ecclesiastical patron, but only because that is exactly what his subjects wanted him to be. He may have achieved divine status as a religious reformer, but only by tapping into the undying popularity of his nemesis, Savonarola. Finally, he may have wrangled control over Florentine sacral traditions, but only because he was a shrewd compromiser, playing on the traditional desires and expectations of his subjects. Indeed, Cosimo was successful largely because he and his mythmakers seem to have known just what the soil and climate of Florentine culture would bear.

Indeed, in contrast to a view of Cosimo as a "divine right" absolutist, this study suggests that even in the creation of his ducal mystique he was quite consciously hemmed in by Florentines' traditional assumptions about the relationship between the sacred and the political. Even though these assumptions were largely forged in a republican past, many of them could be channeled to help underscore his message of personalized monarchy. At other times, they clearly limited the scope of the rhetoric. For instance, in Renaissance Florence, the divine power was still immanently located in physical hot spots, no spot hotter than man himself. Cosimo was able to tap into this idea to achieve an apotheosis that might have been considered idolatry in other polities. At the same time, Florentine traditions limited the forms this apotheosis could take. Even in ducal Florence, power might ultimately come from God, but on the rhetorical level it still flowed through the republic. Thus, Cosimo had to be far more circumspect in both his expressions and his practice of power than some of his more secure contemporaries and near contemporaries, like the Valois kings of France, the Sforzas of Milan, and the Este dukes of Ferrara.

Thus, Cosimo's experience throws light on a pair of other relevant issues. First, the Florentine experience gives the lie to the larger links that the historian Paul Monod has elucidated between Catholic reform and desacralization, at least in this one context. That the Protestant Reformation rapidly accelerated the desacralization of monarchical institutions is probably beyond doubt. Yet, while it is to be expected that the similar social changes wrought by the Protestant and Catholic Reformations would end in similar political effects, this does not seem to be the case for sacral monarchy. The current scholarly trend, which seeks to point out the similarities between the two reformations, often overlooks the profound differences between Catholic and Protestant theology and thus fails to take into account the profound differences in the worldviews of the men and women shaped by those theologies. Religion did continue to help people organize reality, and the mere fact that Cosimo was neither theologian nor saint does not mean that his policies were religiously apathetic. Rather, he and his literati were steeped in local religious tradition, a Florentine Catholic humanism that reinvested individuated objects and people with sacral power in ways Protestant thought did not. Thus, in the Catholic Reformation's reaffirmation of human virtue, Eucharistic transformation, saintly intercession, and personal cooperation with grace, the Florentine religious climate engendered a worldview that was substantially distinct from that of the Protestant Reformation yet formed the essential matrix on which Cosimo could impress his version of sacralized monarchy.

Finally, Cosimo's Florentine stage raises a host of difficult issues for tidy categorizations of religion, democracy, republicanism, and monarchy. Cosimo's monarchy did radically transform some of the structures of power in Florence, yet elements of republicanism lived on in surprising ways. Thus, Cosimo's case speaks against the assumption that the sacralizing elements of monarchical thought always led in authoritarian directions. Not only did consensual elements of power remain rhetorically important, the practice of sacral power in Florence remained rooted in a dialectic (uneven though it was) between ruler and ruled, while the propaganda of sacral monarchy remained rooted in a parallel dialectic between author and audience. This resulted in a blending of monarchical and republican traditions simultaneously grounded in both sacred and secular elements. In short, Medicean Florence points to the importance of consensual aspects of sacral monarchy over and above its traditional association with absolutism.

By way of an addendum, we may add one lesson for today. In times of political instability, laying hold of the rhetoric of legitimacy cannot be overlooked. It can mean the difference between peaceful succession and revolution, stability and chaos, success and failure. Moreover, the keys that legitimize that rhetoric are often found one step removed from the political realm, in localized assumptions that are drunk in by local populations like the local air. Cosimo's propaganda worked because the wily young duke and his even wilier client-scholars took heed of this fact, never straying too far from policies and ideologies that would make sense to Florentines. They pushed sacral monarchy right up to the limits Florence would bear and then pushed no further. Consequently, Cosimo may have begun in blood, but he ended as a god.

Appendix

Sources and Abbreviations

Notes

Acknowledgments

Index

Appendix: Glossary of Names

GIOVAMBATTISTA ADRIANI   Former republican who fought against the Medici during the siege. Later he sought Cosimo's favor and was reconciled to the regime. He sat in the Florentine Academy and held a chair as a reader in rhetoric at the Studio of Pisa. Cosimo named him an official historian, and he wrote *Istorie de'suoi tempi* and a panegyric biography of Cosimo.

> Source: Albertini, Rudolf von. *Firenze dalla repubblica al principato: Storia e coscienza politica*. Turin: Giulio Einaudi editore, 1970.

FRANCESCO ALTONI   Master fencer and longtime servant of the Medici house. He planned to dedicate a fencing treatise called *Monomarchia* to the duke, and in the said dedication he claims to have known Cosimo from childhood. It is likely that Altoni served with Giovanni delle Bande Nere and even possible that he served as Cosimo's fencing instructor.

> Source: Altoni, Francesco. *Monomachia: Trattato dell'arte di scherma*, ed. Alessandro Battistini, Marco Rubboli, and Iacopo Venni. Rome: Il Cerchio Iniziative Editoriali, 2007.

SCIPIONE AMMIRATO   Born in Lecce; studied law at the University of Naples and was in the patronage network of the reforming churchman Girolamo Seripando. He moved to Florence in 1569 and under Cosimo's patronage wrote a history of Florence. While in Florence he was active in the Academy of the Alterati, for which he produced his anti-Machiavellian work *Discourses on Cornelius Tacitus.*

> Source: Cochrane, Eric. *Florence in the Forgotten Centuries: 1527–1800; A History of Florence and the Florentines in the Age of the Grand Dukes.* Chicago: University of Chicago Press, 1971.

BACCIO BALDINI   Scholar and reader in medicine in the Studio of Pisa. For a time, he served as Cosimo I's *protomedico.* He wrote several panegyrics in praise of Cosimo, as well as tracts on medicine, fate, and an unpublished tract on clemency that he dedicated to Cosimo I.

> Source: Inghirami, Francesco. *Storia Toscana.* Vol. 12. Fiesole: Poligrafia Fiesolana, 1843.

OTTAVIO BANDINI   As a young man, one of many Florentines who gave funeral orations in praise of Cosimo I. He later became a cardinal.

> Source: Merola, Alberto. "Ottavio Bandini." In *Dizionario Biografico degli Italiani,* vol. 5, 712–718.

COSIMO BARTOLI   Polymath and descendant from a Florentine family of longtime Medici clients; served as Cosimo I's ambassador to Venice. His *Discorsi historici universali* was dedicated to Cosimo, and he was one of three authors whom Cosimo commissioned to translate Boethius's *Consolation of Philosophy* into Tuscan.

> Source: Bryce, Judith. *Cosimo Bartoli (1503–1572): The Career of a Florentine Polymath.* Geneva: Libraire Droz, 1983.

FABIO BENVOGLIENTI (B. 1518)   Sienese jurist who settled in Rome during the Farnese papacy. He had ties to the literary circles in

Florence, and in addition to writing several poems on the deaths of various members of Cosimo's family, he penned an unpublished work on Augustus that he dedicated to Cosimo.

Source: De Angeli, Luigi. "Fabio Benvoglienti." In *Biografia degli Scrittori Sanesi.* Siena: Rossi, 1824.

BENEDETTO BETTI Florentine writer of the sixteenth-century. His primary literary legacy was his description of Cosimo's funeral in 1574, along with the eulogy he produced for it.

Source: Negri, Giulio. "Benedetto Betti." In *Istoria degli scrittori Fiorentini.* Ferrara: Pomatelli, 1722.

VINCENZO BORGHINI Florentine Benedictine and Cosimo I's choice as the rector of the Hospital of the Innocents. He was a major figure in the cultural circle of Cosimo, who held him in very high regard. Beyond producing his *Discourses on the Origin of Florence,* he worked closely with Cosimo's favorite, Giorgio Vasari, to produce the *inventione* for a number of commissions.

Source: Gavitt, Philip. "Charity and State Building in Cinquecento Florence: Vincenzio Borghini as Administrator of the Ospedale degli Innocenti." *Journal of Modern History* 69 (1997).

ANTONIO BRUCIOLI (1498–1566) Florentine republican who was expelled from Florence by the Medici in 1522 and again during the final Florentine republic. Though he never returned to Florence, he worked in Cosimo's employ from 1538 on, acting as a spy in Venice. He dedicated at least two works to Cosimo, who compensated him for at least one of them.

Source: Spini, Giorgio. *Tra Rinascimento e Riforma: Antonio Brucioli.* Florence: La Nuova Italia Editrice, 1940.

GIOVANBATTISTA CAPPONI Descendant of a client house of the Medici. He held several offices under them, including membership in the Florentine senate, *commisario* of Pisa, *commisario* of Pistoia, and superintendent of the grand ducal possessions. It is likely this last post that prompted him to write his *Spechietto della inclita Città di Firenze et dominio,* which he dedicated to Duke Cosimo.

Source: Medici Archive Project, "Giovanbattista Capponi," http://documents
.medici.org/people_details.cfm?personid=3093.

BERNARDO DAVANZATI   Though his father fought for the last Florentine republic, suffering proscription and loss of goods, Davanzati himself returned to Cosimo's Florence, where he became an active member in the Florentine Academy, over which he was eventually elected consul. He is primarily known for his work in economics. This study cites his *Oration on the Death of Cosimo,* which he delivered to the Academia dei Alterati.

Source: Zaccaria, Raffaella. "Davanzati, Bernardo." In *Dizionario Biografico degli Italiani,* vol. 33.

ANDREA DAZZI   Florentine scholar and preceptor of Greek and Latin at the Studio of Florence; he later held the chair of poetry and rhetoric at the University of Pisa. He dedicated a long praise poem to Cosimo.

Source: Grendler, Paul. *The Universities of the Italian Renaissance.*
Baltimore: Johns Hopkins University Press, 2002.

LODOVICO DOMENICHI   One of the three scholars Cosimo called on to translate Boethius's *Consolation of Philosophy* and deeply embedded in the cultural world of Cosimo's Florence. Domenichi was tied to one of the major cultural power brokers in Florence, Paolo Giovio, whose selected letters Domenichi collected and published in 1560. He also worked closely with Cosimo's ducal press, Torrentino. Domenichi was also a Protestant who was arrested by the Inquisition in 1552. Though he was eventually found guilty, Cosimo was able to get his sentence mitigated.

Sources: Adorni-Braccesi, Simonetta. "La Riforma tra Lucca, Siena,
e Firenze." In *Storia della civiltà Toscana: Il Principato Mediceo,* vol. 3, ed.

Elena Fasano Guarini (Florence: La Tipografica Varese, 2007). Piscini, Angela. In *Dizionario Biografico degli Italiani,* vol. 40.

GIOVANNI FABRINI FIGLINE　It is likely that the Giovanni Fabrini di Figline is the same Giovanni di Feglini who renounced a benefice to Averardo Serristori's son in 1546. This would make him a client of one of Cosimo's most important ambassadors.

Source: ASFi, AGBE 4375 c. 23–25.

GIOVANBATTISTA GÈLLI　Son of a Florentine shoemaker; won a stipend from Cosimo as a reader in the Florentine Academy. He was deeply involved in several aspects of Cosimo's cultural policy. He dedicated several works and poems to Cosimo and was a key player in Cosimo's takeover of the Florentine Academy. Gèlli was also responsible for the *stanze* recited at the wedding of Cosimo and Eleonora.

Sources: D'Alessandro, Alessandro. "Il mito dell'origine 'aramea' di Firenze in un trattatello di Giambattista Gelli." *Archivio Storico Italiano* 138 (1980). Piscini, Angela. "Gelli, Giovan Battista." In *Dizionario Biografico degli Italiani,* vol. 53. De Gaetano, Armando. *G. B. Gelli and the Florentine Academy: The Rebellion against Latin.* Florence: Olchski, 1976.

PAOLO GIOVIO (1483–1552)　Longtime Medici client, historian, and archbishop of Como. He was one of the most important cultural arbiters in ducal Florence, where he lived from 1549 to his death. He dedicated his major work, *History of his Times,* to Cosimo. When he died in 1552, Cosimo allowed him to be buried in San Lorenzo, the Medici family church.

Source: Zimmerman, T. C. Price. *Paolo Giovio: The Historian and the Crisis of Sixteenth-Century Italy.* Princeton: Princeton University Press, 1995.

GIOVAN BATTISTA GUALANDI　Cistercian monk who was involved in several translation projects. Not much can be said about his connection to Florentine literary circles beyond the fact that he was in Cosimo's ecclesiastical patronage network. Ostensibly for these benefits, he dedicated his *Dialogue of the Best Prince* to Cosimo in 1561.

Source: ASFi, AGBE 4378c. 283 (November 27, 1549).

TORQUATO MALASPINA   Poet, member of the Academy of the Alterati, and knight of Saint Stephan. Cosimo's son, Ferdinand I, employed him as a diplomatic ambassador. He was given the task of delivering Cosimo's eulogy to Cosimo's crusading order, the knights of Saint Stefano.

Source: Trucchi, Francesco. *Poesie Italiane inedited di dugento autori.* Prato: Guasti, 1847.

NICCOLÒ MARTÈLLI   Florentine merchant and longtime Medici client; dedicated a number of praise poems to the Medici dukes and other members of the Medici family. He was an original member of the Academia dei Umidi and remained in the academy after its takeover by the Duke. Cosimo eventually named him podesta of Impruneta.

Source: Stumpo, Elisabetta. "Martelli, Niccolò." In *Dizionario Biografico degli Italiani,* vol. 71.

DOMENICO MELLINI   Secretary and confidant to Cosimo and a member of the Florentine Academy. He wrote a number of tracts describing Medici festivals.

Source: Zimmerman, T. C. Price. *Paolo Giovio: The Historian and the Crisis of Sixteenth-Century Italy.* Princeton: Princeton University Press, 1995.

FILLIPPO JACOPO NÈRLI (1485–1566)   Longtime Medici client and holder of numerous important posts and offices in the dominion under Cosimo. Nerli's *History of Florence* culminated in the advent of Cosimo.

Source: Ciccaglioni, Giovanni. "Nèrli, Filippo." In *Dizionario Biografico degli Italiani,* vol. 73.

BERNARDO PUCCINI Served as an architect, *proveditore* of the Uffizi, and military engineer during Cosimo's war with Siena. He wrote an oration for Cosimo's court on Cosimo's death, but it is unlikely that it was ever delivered.

Source: Lamberini, Daniela. *Il Principe difeso: Vita e opere di Bernardo Puccini.* Florence: Giuntina, 1990.

LUCIO PAOLO ROSELLO Padovan jurist and Protestant with links to Cosimo's court. Rosello has increasingly become a figure of interest and contested meaning in modern historiography. Among other things, he was an active figure in Venice's evangelical circles and a creative plagiarist of Agostino Nifo (who in turn plagiarized from Machiavelli).

Sources: Martin, John Jeffries. *Venice's Hidden Enemies: Italian Heretics in a Renaissance City.* Berkeley: University of California Press, 1993; Anglo, Sydney. *Machiavelli: The First Century, Studies in Enthusiasm, Hostility and Irrelevance.* Oxford: Oxford University Press, 2005. Rosello, Lucio Paolo. *Il ritratto del vero governo del Prencipe (1552): Edizione critica a cura di Matteo Salvetti.* Ed. Matteo Salvetti. Milan: FrancoAngeli, 2008.

LIONARDO SALVIATI Member of the Florentine Academy who was named by Cosimo a knight of San Stefano.

Source: Brown, Peter Melville. *Lionardo Salviati: A Critical Biography.* Oxford: Oxford University Press, 1974.

BERNARDO SEGNI (1504–1558) One of the few former republicans who can be shown to have joined Cosimo's circle entirely for pragmatic reasons. Segni's unpublished *History of Florence* painted a very unflattering picture of Cosimo. Nevertheless, he cultivated a relationship with Paolo Giovio, dedicated a number of his translations to Cosimo, and served the ducal government in a number of capacities.

Source: Gentile, Michele Lupo. *Studi sulla storiografia Fiorentina alla corte di Cosimo I de'Medici.* Pisa: Tipografia Successori FF. Nistri, 1905.

GABRIELLE SIMEONI (1509–1572)   Poet and antiquarian with ties to Pier Francesco Riccio. Simeoni dedicated a number of praise poems to Cosimo.

Source: ASFi, Med. f. 1175c. 16 (August 24, 1549).

LORENZO STROZZI   Former republican, close collaborator with Machiavelli, brother to Filippo Strozzi, and uncle to Cosimo's archenemy Piero Strozzi. Lorenzo Strozzi's dedication of his tract *Treatise on Patience* to Cosimo is a little difficult to explain. Despite the fact that Cosimo had Lorenzo arrested during the days preceding the battle of Montemurlo, he appears to have made his peace with the duke, settling in to live quietly in Cosimo's Tuscany and making an offering of his work to Cosimo as a patron. Indeed, Lorenzo did not overtly blame Cosimo for his brother's death in his *Life of Filippo Strozzi*. In that work, Filippo appears as a man who was forced against his reason and will to attack Cosimo's Florence, and Cosimo does not appear as a major force behind Filippo's imprisonment, torture, and death. Rather, Cardinal Cibo, Piero Strozzi, and the Holy Roman Emperor come off as the villains. Thus, Lorenzo probably dedicated his tract to Cosimo in order to prove his loyalty to the new regime.

Source: Strozzi, Lorenzo. *Le vite degli uomini illustri della casa Strozzi.* Florence: Landi, 1892.

BENEDETTO VARCHI (1503–1565)   Perhaps the most famous and celebrated of the literary figures who found their way to Cosimo's court. Varchi was a virulent republican who nevertheless made peace with Cosimo after falling out with the Strozzi. Varchi was given several honorific posts by Cosimo, as well as the Villa di Topaia.

Source: Pirotti, Umberto. *Benedetto Varchi e la cultura del suo tempo* (Florence: Olschki, 1971).

GIORGIO VASARI (1511–1574)   Painter and architect; most famous for his literary contributions to the discipline of art history. He was a frequent and close collaborator with Cosimo, who assigned him many of the most important artistic commissions in Florence, including the decoration of the Duomo's ceiling, the program for the Piazza Signoria, and the renovations of Santa Croce and Santa Maria Novella.

Source: Rubin, Patricia Lee. *Giorgio Vasari: Art and History.* New Haven: Yale University Press, 1995.

Sources and Abbreviations

Archivio di Stato Firenze (ASFi)
    AGBE   Auditore dei Giurisidizione e Benefici Ecclesiastici
    CRS   Compagnie Religiosi Soppresse da Pietro Leopoldo
    CRSF   Corporazioni Religiosi Soppresse da Governo Francese
    Man.   Manoscritti
    Med.   Mediceo del Principato
    Misc.   Miscellanea Medicea
    MS   Magistrato Supremo
    NA   Notarile Ante Cosimiano
    Otto   Otto della Guardia et Balia
    PS   Practica Segreta
Archivio Segreto Vaticano (ASV)
    Farnese   Carte Farnesiane
    Segr. Stato, Principi   Segretario di Stato, Principi
Biblioteca Nazionale Centrale Firenze (BNCF)
    B.R.   Banco Rari
    Magliabecchiana
    Palat.   Fondo Palatino
    F. Guic.   Fondo Guicciardini
    Fondo Nazionale
Biblioteca Laurenziana (BL)
    Medicea Palat.   Medicea Palatina
    Pluteus
Biblioteca Marucelliana (BM)
    MS   Manoscritti
Biblioteca Riccardiana (BR)
    MS   Manoscritti

Notes

Prologue

1. Benedetto Varchi, *Storia fiorentina*, vol. 3 (Florence: Successori le Monnier, 1888), 185.
2. Cosimo Bartoli, *Discorsi historici universali di Cosimo Bartoli gentilhuomo, et accademico Fiorentino* (Venice: Francesco Franceschi Senesi, 1569), 311–312.
3. The events surrounding the murder of Alessandro and the election of Cosimo can be found, with little variation, in a number of secondary sources. The most authoritative contemporary account is Benedetto Varchi's *Storia Fiorentina*, composed under Medici patronage by one of the most illustrious scholars of the day. The study of Cosimo's government has long taken as a key secondary text Riguccio Galluzzi's *Istoria del Granducato di Toscana sotto il governo della casa Medici a sua Altezza Reale il Serenissimo Pietro Leopoldo: Principe Reale d'Ungheria e di Boemia Arciduca d'Austria, Granduca di Toscana* (Milan: Ristampa Anastica, 1974), 1–17. Nearly forty years ago, Eric Cochrane's eminently readable *Florence in the Forgotten Centuries: 1527–1800; A History of Florence and the Florentines in the Age of the Grand Dukes* (Chicago: University of Chicago Press, 1971) gave the English language its first real historical treatment of the period. For an examination of Lorenzo's own motivations analyzed through a hermeneutic of "humanistic vengeance," see Nicholas Scott Baker, "Writing the Wrongs of the Past: Vengeance, Humanism, and the Assassination of Alessandro de' Medici," *Sixteenth Century Journal* 38 (2007); for the role of Alessandro's race, see John K. Brackett, "Race and Rulership: Alessandro de' Medici, First Medici Duke of Florence," in *Black Africans in Renaissance Europe*, ed. T. F. Earle and K. J. P. Lowe (Cambridge: Cambridge University Press, 2005).
4. See Lorenzino dei Medici, "Apologia," in *Apologia e lettere*, ed. Francesco Ersparmer (Rome: Salerno Editrice, 1991), 35.

5. Cochrane, *Florence,* 15.

6. Varchi, *Storia fiorentina,* 183.

7. Ibid., 37.

8. Cochrane, *Florence,* 31.

9. Between 1494 and 1530, Florence changed governments four times. This latest attempt at Medici rule had been in place since 1530, when the newly humbled Pope Clement VII and Charles V joined forces to crush the last Florentine republic.

10. The Florentine senate was the body of aristocrats known as the Senato dei Quarantotto, the Senate of the Forty-Eight.

11. For an analysis of the motivations of the duke-makers, see Marcello Simonetta, "Francesco Vettori, Francesco Guicciardini and Cosimo I: The Prince after Machiavelli," in *The Cultural Politics of Duke Cosimo I de' Medici,* ed. Konrad Eisenbichler (Aldershot: Ashgate, 2001), 1–8. For a more in-depth look at Guicciardini's and Vettori's political philosophies and how they played into their decision to elect Cosimo, see Furio Diaz, *Il granducato di Toscana: I Medici: Storia d'Italia,* vol. 11, ed. G. Galasso (Turin: UTET, 1976), 31–38.

12. The most thorough and accessible analyses of Cosimo's childhood come from two twentieth-century biographers, whose opinions of the man are diametrically opposed. Cecily Booth's work was meant to clear "the suspicions that blackened Cosimo's name." Cecily Booth, *Cosimo I: Duke of Florence* (Cambridge: Cambridge University Press, 1921). Roberto Cantagalli's biography portrays Cosimo as somewhat of a Machiavellian monster. Roberto Cantagalli, *Cosimo I: Granduca di Toscana* (Milan: Mursia editore, 1985).

13. Giorgio Spini, *Cosimo I e l'indipendenza del principato mediceo* (Florence: Valecchi Editore, 1980), 20–21, and Danilo Marrara, *Studi giuridici sulla Toscana medicea: contributo alla storia degli stati assoluti in Italia* (Milan: Dott. A. Giuffrè Editore, 1965), 20.

14. As with all colorfully told stories, this one has its doubters, but she probably said something to that effect. See Ernst Breisach, *Caterina Sforza: A Renaissance Virago* (Chicago: University of Chicago Press, 1967), 103.

15. For an extended discussion of the evolution of class tensions in medieval and early modern Florence see John Najemy, *A History of Florence 1200–1575* (Oxford: Blackwell, 2006). Recently, much work has been devoted to Cosimo's incorporation of the Tuscan region into a territorial state, a development for which Cosimo is generally applauded. Even generations of anti-Medicean historians have grudgingly admitted that the Medici in general and Cosimo in particular treated the Florentine dominion in a much more evenhanded manner than the Florentine republic had. Indeed, much of the recent analysis of Cosimo's rule has studied this dynamic of territorial state-building, focusing on the extent to which Cosimo was able

to centralize the structures of juridical and legal power. See especially Elena Fasano Guarini, *Lo stato Mediceo di Cosimo I* (Florence: Sansoni Editore, 1973); Jean Boutier, Sandra Landi, and Oliver Rouchon, eds., *Florence et la Toscane XIVe XIXe siècles: Les dynamiques d'un état italien* (Rennes: Presses Universitaires de Rennes, 2004), and William J. Connell and Andrea Zorzi, eds., *Florentine Tuscany: Structures and Practices of Power* (Cambridge: Cambridge University Press, 2004). Giovanni Benadusi has taken a non-Florence-centered approach, viewing the process from the perspective of local elites in the small commune of Poppi, who used their roles in the newly centralized political structure to secure their political, cultural, and economic ascendancy over their local society. See Giovanna Benadusi, *A Provincial Elite in Early Modern Tuscany: Family and Power in the Creation of the State* (Baltimore: Johns Hopkins University Press, 1996).

16. Cosimo's stratagems for centralizing political power have been widely studied in this century. The hares were set running at the beginning of the century by Antonio Anzilotti, who focused on Cosimo's reorganization of existing bureaucratic structures, which enabled him to directly control all aspects of government. Antonio Anzilotti, *La costituzione interna dello stato Fiorentino sotto il duca Cosimo I de'Medici* (Florence: Francesco Lumachi, 1910). On the reform of penal law as a centralizing feature of Cosimo's governance see also Guarini, *Lo stato,* 24–47. Furio Diaz has noted his repressive legislation; Diaz, *Il granducato,* 106. A long line of anti-Medicean historians have attributed Cosimo's success to his efficient liquidation of irreconcilable enemies, a claim that is all the more believable since we find it in the mouth of one of his many panegyrists. Mario Matasilani, *La felicità del serenissimo Cosimo Medici gran duca di Toscana* (Florence: Alla Stamperia di loro Altezze: Appresso Giorgio Marescotti, 1572), 39. Others have noted his ability to persuade former republicans to join rather than oppose his new government, Cochrane, *Florence,* 27–32. Marcello Fantoni has argued that the Medici used courtly ceremonial as means of political power, a use that signficantly predates similar political ritual at Versailles. Marcello Fantoni, *La corte del granduca: Forma e simboli del potere mediceo fra Cinque e Seicento* (Rome: Bulzoni Editore, 1994), 131. R. Burr Litchfield has written, with a longer chronological focus, on the monarchy's successful co-optation and the transformation of Florence's urban mercantile patrician class into an agency of ducal government. R. Burr Litchfield, *Emergence of a Bureaucracy: The Florentine Patricians, 1530–1790* (Princeton: Princeton University Press, 1985).

17. This, for instance, was the verdict of both of the ambassadors sent to Florence by the Republic of Venice. See *Relazioni degli Ambasciatori Veneti al Senato,* vol. 3, ed. Arnaldo Segarizzi (Bari: Gius. Laterza et Figli, 1916), 128 and 198.

18. It seems that the antagonism between old and young was an old theme in Florentine political life. See Richard Trexler, *Public Life in Renaissance Florence* (Ithaca: Cornell University Press, 1980), 392–393.

19. Najemy, *History of Florence,* 450.

20. Marc Jurdjevic has argued that the Valori family tenaciously clung to its republican past by reappropriating memories of familial involvement with events and characters of the republican era well into the sixteenth century. See Mark Jurdjevic, *Guardians of Republicanism: The Valori in the Florentine Renaissance* (Oxford: Oxford University Press, 2008).

Introduction

1. See Sergio Bertelli, *The Kings's Body: Sacred Rituals of Power in Medieval and Early Modern Europe,* trans. R. Burr Litchfield (University Park: Pennsylvania State University Press, 2001).

2. The most influential expression of this idea was formulated by Leonardo Bruni, the classic exposition of which is in Hans Baron, *The Crisis of the Early Italian Renaissance: Civic Humanism and Republican Liberty in an Age of Classicism and Tyranny* (Princeton: Princeton University Press, 1966), 1–71. See also Girolamo Savonarola, *Trattato di Frate Ieronimo Savonarola circa il reggimento e governo della città di Firenze* (Florence: Elibron Classics, 2006).

3. See these seminal studies on Medici governance in the fifteenth century: Nicolai Rubinstein, *The Government of Florence under the Medici: 1434–1494* (Oxford: Clarendon Press, 1997); Dale Kent, *The Rise of the Medici: Faction in Florence, 1424–1434* (Oxford: Oxford University Press, 1978); Arnaldo D'Addario, *La formazione dello stato moderno in Toscana: Da Cosimo Vecchio a Cosimo I de'Medici* (Lecce: Adriatica Editrice sal, 1976); and Paula Clarke, *The Soderini and the Medici: Power and Patronage in Fifteenth-Century Florence* (Oxford: Clarendon Press, 1991).

4. See Donald Weinstein, *Savonarola and Florence: Prophecy and Patriotism in the Renaissance* (Princeton: Princeton University Press, 1970); Lorenzo Polizzotto, *The Elect Nation: The Savonarolan Movement in Florence 1494–1545* (Oxford: Clarendon Press, 1994); and Lauro Martines, *Fire in the City: Savonarola and the Struggle for the Soul of Renaissance Florence* (Oxford: Oxford University Press, 2006).

5. On the last Florentine republic, see the highly readable Cecil Roth, *The Last Florentine Republic, 1527–1530* (London: Metheun, 1925), and the less ideologically committed J. N. Stephens, *The Fall of the Florentine Republic, 1512–1530* (Oxford: Clarendon Press, 1983).

6. On the relationship of Florence to modern republicanism, the most seminal studies are, of course, J. G. A. Pocock, *The Machiavellian Moment: Florentine Political Thought and the Atlantic Republican Tradition* (Princeton:

Princeton University Press, 1975), and Baron's *Crisis of the Renaissance.*

7. This study will rely primarily on three categories of source ɪ first can broadly be categorized as published and unpublished ɪ terials, including sermons, plays, devotional works, and theo.......ɪ ɪɪea-tises. All of them date from the sixteenth century. All of them were either produced by Tuscans or religious related to Florentine culture in some way. Some of the religious authors had relationships with the Medici, but most did not. They are primarily used to uncover patterns of thought in contemporary Florentine religious culture. The second type of source can be broadly defined as panegyrical literature. These published and unpublished biographies, funeral orations, and dedications were written primarily to glorify Cosimo and to support the Medici government. I refer to the authors of these tracts variously as literati, mythmakers, and panegyrists. Again, the authors vary in personal history, importance, and closeness to the regime, but they are bound together by the fact that each of these works was generally either directly commissioned by the Medici or written for Cosimo with the hope of securing patronage, favor, or financial gain. In total, they provide a snapshot into the type of propaganda that arose from a certain cultural milieu, rather than a centrally organized campaign of propaganda. The details of each writer's relationship to Cosimo can be found in the appendix. The final set of sources consists of archival sources, including letters, diaries, petitions, wills, and government documents. These are largely used to test the extent to which external propaganda resonated with the assumptions apparent in the internal conversations of the government and among the populace.

8. A practice performed by the French kings until the eighteenth century and the English until the seventeenth, most famously brought to the consciousness of the scholarly community in Marc Bloch's classic work *The Royal Touch: Sacred Monarchy and Scrofula in England and France,* trans. J. E. Andersen (London: Routledge and Kegan Paul, 1973).

9. A rather late homage by Lionardo Salviati to the Knights of San Stefano on the occasion of Cosimo's coronation is the exception that proves the rule in this case. Lionardo Salviati, *Orazione del Cavalier Lionardo Salviati intorno alla coronazione del Serenissimo Cosimo Medici Gran Duca di Toscana* (Florence: Sermatelli, 1570), unpaginated.

10. See especially Dennis Romano, *The Likeness of Venice: A Life of Doge Francesco Foscari* (New Haven: Yale University Press, 2007), 49–50.

11. The Bolognese Matasilani was an exception. See Matasilani, *La felicità,* 16–17.

12. For instance, Cosimo's counterparts in Britain alternately traced their lines to King Arthur, Brutus, and the Trojans. See Keith Thomas, *Religion and the Decline of Magic* (New York: Scribner, 1971), 416–417. The Hapsburgs

also traced their genealogy to the Trojan Aeneas. See Marie Tanner, *The Last Descendant of Aeneas; The Hapsburgs and the Mythic Image of the Emperor* (New Haven: Yale University Press, 1993), 98.

13. At Cosimo's funeral oration, Scipione Ammirato, who later wrote his own genealogy of the Medici, remarked that he took pleasure in knowing that "non da straniere, e barbare Provincie egli tragga la sua origine, come (non so con quanta prudenza sia con lor pace detto) molti si sogliono gloriare; ma dalla nostra Christiana antichissima, e sopra tutte le altre nobilissima Italia, et delle Regioni, et Paesi di quella della Toscana." Scipione Ammirato, *Oratione di Signore Scipione Ammirato in morte del Cosimo I dei Medici* (BNCF, Magliabecchiana XXVII c. 104), 39r–39v. Similar sentiments were expressed by his *protomedico*, Baccio Baldini, who noted that the Medici had "not come from other parts, but here from the first beginning were born, nurtured, and raised, always recognizing Tuscany as their own mother" (non d'altronde venuti, ma in essa insino dal suo primo principio nati, et in quella nutriti et allevati, la riconobbero sempre com lor propria madre); Baccio Baldini, *Orazione fatta nella Accademia Fiorentina: In lode del Serenissimo Sig. Cosimo Medici, Gran Duca di Toscana, gloriosa memoria* (Florence: Bartolommeo Sermartelli, 1574), unpaginated.

14. Cochrane, *Florence,* 62–64; Francesca Fiorani, "Maps, Politics, and the Grand Duke of Florence: The Sala della Guardaroba Nuova of Cosimo I de'Medici," in *Renaissance Representations of the Prince: Basilike Eikon,* ed. Roy Eriksen and Magne Malmanger (Rome: Edizioni Kappa, 2001), 87. Henk van Veen, "Republicanism in the Visual Propaganda of Cosimo I de' Medici," *Journal of the Warburg and Courtauld Institutes* 55 (1992), 200–209; Bram Kempers, *Painting, Power, and Patronage: The Rise of the Professional Artist in the Italian Renaissance,* trans. Beverley Jackson (London: Allen Lane Penguin Press, 1987); Michael Sherberg, "The Accademia Fiorentina and the Question of Language: The Politics of Theory in Ducal Florence," *Renaissance Quarterly* 56 (2003), 26–27; and Jonathan Davies, *Culture and Power: Tuscany and Its Universities, 1537–1609* (Leiden: Brill, 2009).

15. As Elena Fasano Guarini has argued, some of the main ideologues of republican Florence, such as Guicciardini and Machiavelli, were never so strictly attached to republicanism as has been thought; on the other hand, republican ideals were only slowly and gradually transformed into full support for monarchy among historians and political thinkers of the ducal period. See Elena Fasano Guarini, *Repubbliche e principi: Istituzione e pratiche di potere nella Toscana granducale del '500–'600* (Bologna: Mulino, 2010).

16. See Jurdjevic, *Guardians,* 1–17.

17. For examples of this approach see Bertelli, *King's Body;* Peter Stacey, *Roman Monarchy and the Renaissance Prince* (Cambridge: Cambridge Uni-

versity Press, 2007); Ralph Giesey, *The Royal Funeral Ceremony in Renaissance France* (Geneva: E Droz, 1960); Bloch, *Royal Touch;* Giovanni Ricci, *Il principe e la morte: Corpo, cuore, effigie nel rinascimento* (Bologna: Mulino 1998); and Susanna Pietrosanti, *Sacralità medicee* (Florence: Firenze Libri, 1991).

18. Great examples of this type of study include: Robert Zaller, "Breaking the Vessels: The Desacralization of Monarchy in Early Modern England," *Sixteenth Century Journal* 29 (1998), 757–778; Dale van Kley, *The Religious Origins of the French Revolution: From Calvin to the Civil Constitution, 1560–1791* (New Haven: Yale University Press, 1996); Paul Monod, *The Power of Kings: Monarchy and Religion in Europe, 1589–1715* (New Haven: Yale University Press, 1999); Richard C. McCoy, *Alterations of State: Sacred Kingship in the English Reformation* (New York: Columbia University Press, 2002); and Christopher Elwood, *The Body Broken: The Calvinist Doctrine of the Eucharist and the Symbolization of Power in Sixteenth-Century France* (Oxford: Oxford University Press, 1999). There have been some departures from this paradigm. Stephen L. Collins, *From Divine Cosmos to Sovereign State: An Intellectual History of Consciousness in the Idea of Order in Renassaince England* (New York: Oxford University Press, 1989), examines desacralization without much reference to religious transformations at all. Moreover, a recent edited volume has questioned the extent to which monarchy was desacralized in the later early modern period. Michael Schaich, introduction to *Monarchy and Religion: The Transformation of Royal Culture in Eighteenth Century Europe*, ed. Michael Schaich (Oxford: Oxford University Press, 2007).

19. See especially Charles Trinkaus, *In Our Image and Likeness: Humanity and Divinity in Italian Humanist Thought* (Chicago: University of Chicago Press, 1970), and Richard Trexler's monumental *Public Life in Renaissance Florence*. See also Timothy Verdon and John Henderson, eds., *Christianity and the Renaissance: Image and Religious Imagination in the Quattrocento* (Syracuse: Syracuse University Press, 1990). For a fine historiographical treatment, see David Peterson, "Out of the Margins: Religion and the Church in Renaissance Italy," *Renaissance Quarterly* 53, no. 3 (2000), 835–879. However, the master narrative continues to situate Christian humanism decidedly north of the Alps all too often. Burckhardt laid out his areligious vision of the Renaissance in part 6 of his classic work; see Burckhardt, *The Civilization of the Renaissance in Italy*, trans. S. G. C Middlemore (New York: Harper and Row, 1958), 426–516. See also the introduction to Renée Neu Watkins, *Humanism and Liberty: Writings on Freedom from Fifteenth-Century Florence*, ed. and trans. Renée Neu Watkins (Columbia: University of South Carolina Press, 1978), 6, and George Holmes, "Renaissance Culture," in *The Oxford Illustrated History of Italy*, ed. George Holmes (Oxford: Oxford University Press, 2001), 93–95.

While acknowledging the Renaissance urge to incorporate the pagan into the Christian, Harry Hearder still posits the idea of a "secular Renaissance"; Hearder, *Italy: A Short History,* 2nd ed. (Cambridge: Cambridge University Press, 2001), 106. See Stevie Davies, *Renaissance Views of Man* (Manchester: Manchester University Press, 1978), 16. Even the new editions of R. R. Palmer, *A History of the Modern World* (New York: Knopf, 2002), through which many students continue to get their metanarrative of Western history, still make the dichotomy. See Chapter 2.

20. For instance, an examination of religion's impact on political culture is lacking in the excellent works of H. C. Butters, *Governors and Government in Early Sixteenth-Century Florence: 1502–1519* (Oxford: Clarendon Press, 1985); Niccolai Rubinstein, *The Government of Florence under the Medici;* Clarke, *Soderini and the Medici,* and Konrad Eisenblichler, ed., *The Cultural Politics of Duke Cosimo I de' Medici* (Aldershot: Ashgate, 2001). Notable exceptions are Dale Kent, *The Patron's Oeuvre: Cosimo de'Medici and the Florentine Renaissance* (New Haven: Yale University Press, 2000), and Peter Francis Howard, *Beyond the Written Word: Preaching and Theology in the Florence of Archbishop Antoninus, 1427–1459* (Florence: Olschki, 1995). The inertia permitting this trend probably derives its legacy from a pair of magisterial figures: Hans Baron and J. G. A. Pocock. Baron's work posited Florence as the cultural nursemaid to a secular civic ideal, a dramatic break from medieval theological models of politics and history. See especially, Baron, *Crisis,* 156–157. Picking up on this secular rendering, J. G. A. Pocock argued that Florentine "civic humanism" had been transmitted to Cromwellian England and thence to the early American republic, thus preparing the basis of the modern republican secular state. See Pocock, *Machiavellian Moment,* 8. More recently, an excellent set of essays have begun to question Baron's monolithic interpretation; see *Renaissance Civic Humanism: Reappraisals and Reflections,* ed. James Hankins (Cambridge: Cambridge University Press, 2000).

21. See Henk van Veen, *Cosimo I and His Self-Representation in Florentine Art and Culture,* trans. Andrew McCormick (Cambridge: Cambridge University Press, 2006), 165–166; Maria Lupi, "Cosimo de'Medici, Domenico Bonsi, e la riforma della chiesa a Trento," *Rivista di storia della chiesa in Italia* 36 (1982), 26; Massimo Firpo, *Gli affreschi di Pontormo a San Lorenzo; Eresia, politica, e cultura nella Firenze di Cosimo I* (Milan: G. Einaudi, 1997), 311; Cantagalli, *Cosimo,* 18; and Marrara, *Studi giuridici,* 58–59. A recent edited volume studying Cosimo's cultural politics tellingly does not include any essays concerning the impact of religion on political culture, even though the editor surely cannot be accused of indifference toward the topic. See Eisenblichler, *Cultural Politics of Duke Cosimo I de' Medici.* Those few scholars who have taken the question seriously, like Arnaldo d'Addario and Giorgio Spini, have largely confined themselves to

studies of the institutional relationship between the ducal government and the local and international organs of church power. See D'Addario, *La formazione dello stato moderno* and Spini, *Cosimo I.*

22. Paul F. Grendler, "Man Is Almost a God: Fra Battista Carioni between Renaissance and Catholic Reformation," in *Humanity and Divinity in Renaissance and Reformation: Essays in Honor of Charles Trinkaus,* ed. John W. O'Malley, Thomas M. Izbicki, and Gerald Christianson (Leiden: Brill, 1993), 227–228.

23. Monod, *Power of Kings,* 7 and 36, and 53, where he writes: "Sacred monarchs . . . could find little consolation in reformed religion, of whatever variety." Monod locates this opposition to sacral monarchy primarily among Spanish Jesuits.

1. The Familiarity of Terrestrial Divinity

1. On the relationship between Vasari and Cosimo, see Patricia Lee Rubin, *Giorgio Vasari: Art and History* (New Haven: Yale University Press, 1995).

2. For more on the tondo, see W. Chandler Kirwin, "Vasari's Tondo of Cosimo with His Architects, Engineers, and Sculptors in the Palazzo Vecchio: Typology and Reidentification of Portraits," *Mitteilungen des Kunsthistorischen Institutes in Florenz* 15 (1971), 105–122.

3. Cited in Charles Davis, "Frescos by Vasari for Sforza Almeni, 'Coppiere' to Duke Cosimo I," *Mitteilungen des Kunsthistorischen Institutes in Florenz* 24 (1980), 154.

4. Ernst Kantorowicz, *The King's Two Bodies: A Study in Medieval Political Theology* (Princeton: Princeton University Press, 1957), 3.

5. Stacey, *Roman Monarchy,* 81.

6. See H. I. Marrou, "L'Idée de Dieu et la Divinité du Roi," in *The Sacral Kingship: Contributions to the Central Theme of the VIIIth International Congress for the History of Religions* (Leiden: Brill, 1959).

7. In this, the sixteenth century was deeply indebted to the type of rhetoric that Trinkaus has identified as an essential feature of quattrocento humanism. See especially 171–322.

8. Cited in Howard, *Beyond the Written Word,* 209: "bonum commune reipublicae est quoddam divinum."

9. The most famous example of Cosimo as Augustus is Vincenzo Danti's statue of Cosimo, now in the Bargello Museum. Danti's statue was originally on the arch that leads from the Uffizi to the Lungarno. See Roger Crum, "Cosmos: The World of Cosmo: The Iconography of the Uffizi Façade," *Art Bulletin* 71 (1989), 237–253. For Cosimo as Apollo, see Paul William Richelson, *Studies in the Personal Imagery of Cosimo I de' Medici, Duke of Florence* (New York: Garland, 1978), 35–45, and Gabrielle

Langdon, *Medici Women: Portraits of Power, Love, and Betrayal from the Court of Cosimo I* (Toronto: University of Toronto Press, 2006), 76.

10. I am here following Susanna Pietrosanti's interpretation of the event. Pietrosanti, *Sacralità medicee*, 57–58.

11. Kurt Forster, "Metaphors of Rule: Political Ideology and History in the Portraits of Cosimo I de' Medici," *Mitteilungen des Kunsthistorischen Institutes in Florenz* 15 (1971), 79–81.

12. Maria Ann Conelli, "Boboli Gardens; Fountains and Propaganda in Sixteenth Century Italy," *Studies in the History of Gardens and Designed Landscapes* 18 (1998), 300–316; and van Veen, *Cosimo*, 106–112.

13. See Langdon, *Medici Women*, 25 and 72–77.

14. Figline's work was a translation of a work by Francesco Patritius, which the translator had found insufficiently monarchical. Thus, he added his own first chapter on the sacrality of princes. Giovanni Fabrini di Figline, chapter 1 of *Il sacro regno del vero reggimento, e della vera felicità del principe* (Venice: Comin di Trino di Montferrato, 1547), 4–5: "Noi confessiamo, che sia un solo Iddio: a la cui simiglianza è in terra il Principe, e perciò per tale risembranza de la divina maestà, e per mantenere la sua memoria, dico, che i Principi sono necessari in terra, che rassembrino la potenza divina."

15. Cited in Michel Plaisance, *L'Académie et le prince: Culture e politique à Florence au temps de Côme Premier et de François de Médicis* (Rome: Vecchiarelli Editore, 2004), 260–261: "in loro il sommo Iddio riverire."

16. Antonio Brucioli, "Del Giusto Principe," in *Dialogi*, ed. Aldo Landi (Naples: Prismi, 1982), 209: "A chi non sa che il governo d'uno giusto e buono principe passa tutti gli altri governi di che si ha cognizione, avendo più conformità a quello d'Iddio sopra l'universo mondo." For Brucioli's long path from republican to exile in France, to unsuccessful courter of ducal favor, see the biography by Giorgio Spini, *Tra Rinascimento e Riforma: Antonio Brucioli* (Florence: La Nuova Italia Editrice, 1940).

17. Delmo Maestri, "La 'letture' di Giovan Batista Gelli sopra la Commedia di Dante nella cultura fiorentina dei tempi di Cosimo I de' Medici," *Lettere Italiane* 26 (1974) 3–24.

18. Giambattista Gelli, "Dedicazione," in *La circe* (Florence, 1550), 5–6: "obligati de rendere honore a Iddio . . . debbono in quell modo che è sanno e posson migliore honorare sempre i loro principi . . . i veri simulacri et le veri imagini d'Iddio."

19. Matteo Saminiati, *Discorso nel quale con chiarissime et facilissime ragioni si mostra la fallacia di tutte l'heresie che in questi tempo travagliono tanto la Cristianità* (BL Medicea . . . Palat. CXLIV), 13r: "a la cui persona rappresenti in Terra la Maiesta, et grandezza del suo fattore; che la Monarchia sia tale tutti ad una voce confessono, e, si pruova chiarissime prima dalla proportione, e similitudine che ella tiene col governo indotto da Dio,

per il reggimento del Cielo, del quale quello che più participa non si può negare che non sia piu nobile, e piu perfetto di tutti gli altri." Sanminiato was a Lucchese who, among other things, gave a funeral oration in the Duomo for Archbishop Altoviti. See Vincenzo Borghini, *Discorsi di Monsignore Don. Vincenzo Borghini,* pt. 2 (Florence: Appresso Pietro Viviani, 1755), 591.

20. Patritius wrote that subjects need to obey their princes because there is nothing more similar to God "than a prince, or a principate." Patritius, *Il sacro regno del vero reggimento, e della vera felicità del principe,* trans. Giovanni Fabrini di Figline (Venice: Per Comin di Trino di Monferrato, 1547), 188. On Vergerio, see Baron, *Crisis,* 133–134. Castiglione had argued in 1528: "Just as in heaven, the sun and moon and other stars show the world as in a mirror some likeness of God, so on earth a much liker image of God is found in those good Princes who love and revere him." Baldassare Castiglione, *The Book of the Courtier,* trans. Leonard Eckstein Opdycke (Hertfordshire: Wordsworth Classics of World Literature, 2000), 247. On Giles of Rome, see J. H. Burns, *Lordship, Kingship, and Empire: The Idea of Monarchy, 1400–1525* (Oxford: Clarendon Press, 1992), 57. Erasmus had drawn his version of the argument from Xenophon. Desiderius Erasmus, *The Education of a Christian Prince,* trans. Neil M. Chesire and Michael J. Heath (Cambridge: Cambridge University Press, 1997), 1. Moreover, the theme had been recently advanced by a number of Spanish writers as well; for that context, see Antonio Feros, "Vicedioses pero humanos, el drama del Rey," *Cuadernos de Historia Moderna* 14 (1993), 103–131.

21. Giovanni Fabrini di Figline, "Dedicazione," in *Il Sacro regno del vero reggimento, e della vera Felicità del Principe,* trans. Giovanni Fabrini di Figline (Venice: Domenico and Giovan Battista Guerra, 1569), iii: "acciochè leggendolo, come in vivo, e chiar cristallo ci vegga tutte quelle sue Sante virtù, che le ha donato il cielo, e che ella ha ampliate con la sua prudenza."

22. Bernardo Segni, "Dedicazione," *Trattati dei governi di Aristotile* (Florence: Lorenzo Torrentino, 1549), 8: "No si negar però che dio Ottimo non l'habbia fatto grande dimostatione di favore, per haverla collocata sotto à quello governo medesimo, col quale egli governa et amminstra questo universo."

23. For Segni's career, see Michele Lupo Gentile, *Studi sulla storiografia Fiorentina alla corte di Cosimo I de' Medici* (Pisa: Tipografia Successori FF. Nistri, 1905), 19–24. For the harsh critique of Cosimo in his privately composed history, see 82.

24. Leonardus Ginus, *Pro Travalliatorum Academia gratulatio.* (BNCF, Magliabecchiana XXVII c. 16), 36r: "qui tanquam mortales Dii omnibus presint, comuniterque omnia administrent."

25. Torquato Malaspina, *Orazione in lode del Gran Duca Cosimo del Signore Marchese Torquato Malespina Cavaliere di Santo Stefano recitata nella Chiesa de Cavalieri vi. Aprili MDLXXVIII* (BNCF, Magliabecchiana XXVII c. 104), 200r: "il governo d'un solo à quello d'Iddio simigliante."

26. Michel Capri, *Canzone di Michel Capri al Serenissimo Cosimo Medici Gran Duca di Toscana* (Florence: Bartholomeo Sermartelli, 1570), ii: "Somigliandosi per cosi fatta guisa (in un certo modo) a'l Celeste, e divino Monarca, gran Padre de l'increato, et glorioso suo splendore; a cui gradisce i grandi, e piccioli lumi, che da noi suoi tributari di quore (per honorarlo) accesi se li vengano."

27. Prete Francesco Da Trivigi, *Canzone all'Illustrissimo et Eccelenissimo. Signore, Cosimo de Medici Duca di Fiorenza et di Siena* (Florence: Torrentini, 1565), 4: "Et se à Vostra Signore parrà (come forsi à molti altri pare) che questa sia stata troppo alta, et animosa impresa al mio basso, et debole ingegno, ella si ramenti che sempre in tutti i secoli, Il creator del tutto si compiacque: grandemente, d'esser lodato, et fatto conoscere da rozi, et bassi ingegni, per la bocca de'quali, egli manifestò al mondo gli altissimi secreti della sua immensa divinità."

28. Giorgio Vasari, *Le vite de' più eccelenti pittori, scultore, e architettori,* ed. Rosanna Bettarini (Florence: Sansoni, 1966), 7: "Accetti dunque Vostra Eccellenza illustrissima questo mio, anzi pur Suo, libro delle Vite degli artefici del disegno, et a somglianza del grande Iddio più all'animo mio et alle buone intenzioni che all'opera riguardando, da me prenda ben volentieri non quello che io vorrei e doverrei, ma quello che io posso."

29. Da Trivigi, *Canzone,* 5: "De l'alma mia d'affetto ogn'hor si calda / Ch'è fatta à l'opre tue tempio sacrato / Ond'è lo mio intelletto arso, e'nfiammato / De'merti lor cui raggio altro non scalda / Per cui sfavilla, e vede chiaramente / Il ben del Sommo Dio visibilmente / Come in Cristallo il sol limpido, et terso / Per te vagheggia il bel de l'universo." I have chosen to maintain the rhyme schemes for these poems in the translations.

30. See Plaisance, *L'Académie et le prince,* 75–76.

31. Niccolò Martelli, sonnet 43 in *Cento sonnetti a Cosimo dei Medici* (BR, MS. 3910): "Quanta vede del Ciel larga pietade / Chi mira il mio gran' Cosmo e'l suo Reale / Chiaro, aspetto divin che e tanto e tale' / Che maggior ben non ha la nostra etade."

32. Ibid., sonnet 62 and sonnet 77.

33. Ibid., 37–38.

34. Anonymous, "La dignità di l'Huomo, prima delle sue miserie," in *Sermoni raccolti* (BNFC, Fondo Nazionale II. III. 413), 58v: "La compositione del'huomo è la più admirabile opera che Iddio habbia fatto." The same type of juxtaposition can be seen in Lorenzo Davidico, *Anatomia dei vitii* (Florence, 1550), 300–303.

35. The author lifted the sentiment directly from Petrarch. See Trinkaus, *In Our Image,* 194.

36. Anonymous, "La dignità," 57r–59r.

37. Cited in Frances A. Yates, *Giordano Bruno and the Hermetic Tradition* (Chicago: Chicago University Press, 1991), 23.

38. Jacobus Antoninus Ferrari, *Apologia sive disputatio pro Ilustrissimo Cosmo Medice Florentiae Respublicae Duce Thusciaeque L'arthe ad Pium IIII massimum Pontificis Sanctis* (BM, MS. c. XLV), 51r: "dixit hominem esse animal honorandum, et mirabile ad imaginem Dei formatum."

39. Yates, *Giordano Bruno*, 2.

40. Marsilio Ficino, *Platonic Theology*, vol. 1, ed. James Hankins with William Bowen, trans. Michael J. B Allen and John Warden (Cambridge, Mass.: Harvard University Press, 2001), 8–11.

41. A full treatment of both Platonism and Hermeticism in Cosimo's court has yet to be written, but there are some general outlines in Judith Bryce, *Cosimo Bartoli (1503–1572): The Career of a Florentine Polymath* (Geneva: Libraire Droz, 1983) and Alessandro D'Alessandro, "Il mito dell'origine 'aramea' di Firenze in un trattatello di Giambattista Gelli," *Archivio Storico Italiano* 138 (1980), 339–389.

42. Genesis 1:26.

43. In addition to the many other citations mentioned in this chapter, see Lorenzo Strozzi, *Trattato di pazienza* (BNCF, Magliabecchiana XXXV c. 106), 13v; Lorenzo Davidico, *Trattato della commvnione induttiuo a frequentar quella : Intitolato fiamma d'amor divino, qual contiene diuersi notabili passi utilissimi da sapere* (Florence, 1550), 3v; Simone Portio, *Modo di orare Christianamente con la espositione del Pater Noster: Fatta da M. Simone Portio Napoletano*, tradotto in lingua Fiorentina da Giovam Batista Gelli (Florence, 1551), 39, 52, and 72; Davidico, *Anatomia*, 108r; Fabrini, *Il sacro regno*, 13v; Anonymous, *I gradi della vita spirituale* (BNCF, Magliabecchiana XXXV c. 70), 34r; and Dolciati, *Prediche diversi* (BNCF, Magliabecchiana XXXV c. 107), 35v.

44. Angelo Bettini, *Preparazione alla festa di Santo Domenico fatta dal Angelo Bettini alle monache di S. Domenico di Lucca* (1540) (BNCF, Magliabecchiana XXXV c. 72), 110v: "offendendo l'homo spesso se medesimo guastando in se la Divina ymagine pel peccato."

45. And this because God created only man in his likeness: "Dio alla sua sembianza creò, e cio sono gl'huomini solamente." Lelio Bonsi, "Sermone per doversi recitare il Giovedi Santo," in *Cinque lezioni di Monsignore Lelio Bonsi lette da Lui publicamente nella Accadamia Fiorentina, Aggiuntovi un breve trattato della cometa. E nella fine un sermone sopra l'Eucarestia da doversi recitare il giovedi Santo del medesimo Autore* (Florence: Giunti, 1560), 107r.

46. Fra Andrea da Volterra, *Trattato utile del Reverendo Frate Andrea da Volterra sopra la disputa della gratia, et delle opere predicato in Firenze nella chiesa di Santo Spirito l'anno M.D.XLIII* (Florence: ad instantia Bene Gionti, 1544), 6v.

47. Anonymous, "La dignita," 58v: "nella mirabile compositione del'huomo più che nella gran fabrica del cielo, e più che nella forza degl'elimenti, e che in tutto l'ordine dell'universo, ci, è rappresentata l'eccellenza del suo sapere: ma si vede ancora, come in chiarissimo specchio, il medesimo essere di Dio, et gli altri secreti della sua divinità, et Trinità, parte di questo viddero li antichi savi con la luce naturale, poiche contemplando cio Mercurio Trimegisto disse che gran miracolo era l'huomo, nel quale cose grandi si vedevano: et Aristotile credette che l'huomo fosse il fine à chi tutte le cose riveriscono."

48. Francesco Vieri, *Breve compendio della dottrina di Platone in novello che ella è conforme alla fede nostra* (BNCF, Magliabecchiana XXXIV c. 17), 26v: "e se bene Platone nel Timeo pone oltre al padre del Mondo, più Dij, questo viene, perche egli stima, che siano Dij per participazione di natura spirituale, et eterna, e per similitudine di bontà, e per potere godere della paterna eredità; così la divina scrittura dice, che per Giesù Christo ci è dato podestà di farci Dij, e figliuoli di Dio, per similitudine di vita quaggiù, e poi per fruitione dei beni paterni."

49. Vieri, *Breve compendio,* 8v: "è la più conforme alla christiana e divina; come di ciò ne fà ampissima testimonianza Agostino santo, uno dei primi teologi, della nostra santa e Catolica chiesa, nella sua opera della città di Dio." See also Cesare Vasoli, "Agostino e la Cultura Umanistica Toscana fra Trecento e Quattrocento," in *Gli umanisti e Agostino: codici in mostra,* ed. Donatella Coppini and Mariangela Regoliosi (Florence: Edizioni Polistampa, 2001), 40.

50. Augustine, *Augustine: Later Works,* selected and trans. with introduction by John Burnaby (Philadelphia: Westminster Press, 1955), 86–87.

51. Trinkaus, *In Our Image,* cites several humanists who make the argument, including Valla, 156; Facio, 218; and Brandolini, 299–302. The idea was raised by Salutati as well. See Coluccio Salutati, *De Fato et Fortuna,* ed. Concetta Bianca (Florence: Olschki, 1985), 9–11. See also Fra Girolamo Savonarola, *Prediche del reuerendo padre fra Gieronimo da Ferrara per tutto l'anno nuouamente con somma diligentia ricorrette* (Venice: Giouanni Antonio di Volpini, 1540), 33v–35r.

52. Dolciati, *Prediche diversi,* 33v: "nella creatura rationale la quale è l'huomo anchora più expressamente si truova la imagine della sancta trinità. Perilche volendo esso iddio creare quello, dixe quelche è scripto nel genesi al primo capitolo. Cioe, facciamo l'huomo ad imagine et similitudine nostra. La quale imagine si può considerare in tre modi. Prima chome è formata naturalmente. Et quanto a questo dice el padre sancto agustino nel libro della trinità. Benche la mente nostra non sia di quello natura della quale è iddio: ivi pero si debbe cerchare la immagine di quello: di cui nessuna chosa è migliore. Hor l'anima nostra è una chosa sola, et ha tre potentie: delle quelli luna non e l'altra: cioe la memoria, l'intellecto, et la voluntà."

53. Anonymous, "La dignità," 58r: "nessuna cosa è che cosi bene rappresenti l'altra, come fa l'huomo Iddio, et massimo nell'anima, laquale è incorrutti-bile, immortali, simplicissima senza compositione alcuna, et tutta in un es-sere, come è Iddio, et in questo esser la tre potenze, con le quali rappresenta Santissima Trinità."

54. Anonymous, *Prediche e sermoni parte Latini e parte volgari e altre materie sacre* (BNCF, Magliabecchiana XXXV cod.128), 31r:"sia la mia immag-ine, et adornella con tre potentie: memoria, intellecto, et voluntà."

55. Domenico Mellini, *Trattato di Domenico Mellini intitolato visione di-mostratrice della malvagita del carnale amore* (Florence: Giunti, 1566), 61–62: "Ella [the soul/anima] dal superno Rè delle Stelle è stata creata Spiri-tale et eterna à sua imagine, con tre potenze in un'essenza, si come esso è un'essenza et un solo et vero Dio in tre Persone, l'una dall'altra realmente distinte. Queste potenze sono l'Intelletto . . . la Volontà . . . et la Memoria."

56. In both the Latin and the Italian, a philosophical distinction can be made between intellect (*intellectus, intelletto* or *intelligenza*) and reason (*ratio, ragione*). Intellect equates with understanding, and reason with a discur-sive search for understanding starting from understood premises. Thus, properly speaking, humans only shared intellect with God and not reason, since there was no intelligible way to speak of God "searching" for under-standing. But for our purposes the distinction was not always pertinent.

57. Baccio Baldini, *Panegirico alla clemenza di Baccio Baldini allo Illustrissimo Signore Cosimo dei Medici Duca di Firenze* (BL, Pluteus XLII cod. 31), 14r: "vivono secondo l'intelletta, per cui solamente l'huomo si congiunge con Dio."

58. Simone Portio, *Se l'huomo diventa buona o cattivo volontariamente*, tra-dotta in volgare per Giovann Batista Gelli (Florence: Torrentino, 1551), 31: "se il senso è superato, e mandato per terra, et regna l'intelletto, che l'huomo libero al tutto da esso senso diventa come affermono i Platonici, quasi che uno Dio."

59. Ibid., 31–33: "la natura de l'huomo è stata chiamata divina, per essere stata dotata de l'intelletto, ilquale e immisto, e divino, et pero quegli che vivono secondo esso intelletto non meritono di essere chiamati puri huo-mini, ma amici di Dio, et congiuntissimi a quello."

60. Francesco Cattani da Diacceto, *Homelie del Reverendo Monsignore Fran-cesco Cattani da Diacceto Canonico Fiorentino et Protonotario Apostolico* (Florence: Torrentini, 1559), 33: "l'huomo è in potenza ad ottener' la sci-enza de beati, che consiste nel veder Iddio, et a cio è ordinato come a suo fine, per esser' la ragionevol' creatura capace di cotal cognitione in quanto che l'è ad imagine di Dio." The same argument can be found in another preacher of some reknown, who was learned in the classics himself but not entirely favorable to classical civilization. See Paradiso Mazzinghi, *Sermoni e cose ascetiche* (BNCF, Magliabecchiana XXXV c. 13), 16v.

61. Reverendo Cornelio Musso, *Predica del Reverendo Monsignore Cornelio Vescovo di Bitonto fatta in Trento il Giorno di San Donato l'Anno MDXLV. Per l'allegresse, che si fecere venuta la nuova, ch'era nato il primogenito del Principe di Spagna figliuolo di Carlo Quinto Imperadore* (Venice: Gabriel Giolito de Ferrari e Fratelli, 1553), 3v: "Il sommo Padre dell'humana natura, che per farci superiori a tutte le spetie de gli animali, ci diede quella parte divina della ragione; per farci pari o almeno simili alli angeli."

62. Lodovico Domenichi, "Dedicazione," in *Severino Boetio de conforti philosophici,* trans. M. Lodovico Domenichi (Florence: Torrentino, 1550), 5r: "La Sapienza, è Scienza delle cose divine, et humane, nellaquale si contiene la communanza di Dio, et degli huomini." The passage is a paraphrase of Cicero, *De Officiis,* trans. Walter Miller (Cambridge, Mass.: Harvard University Press, 1913), 156.

63. Giovanni Bernardo Gualandi, *De Optimo principe dialogus* (Florence: Torrentino, 1561), 115: "philosophari, res quidem divina est. Homini aut (Augustino teste) nulla est philosophandi causa, nisi ut beatus existat."

64. See Gualandi, *De Optimo,* 71 and 171.

65. Baccio Baldini, *Discorso dell'essenza del fato, e delle forze sue sopra le cose del mondo: e particolarmente sopra l'operazioni de gl'huomini* (Florence: Sermatelli, 1578), 15: "Platone athenieses, filosofo di tanta riverenza appresso gli antichi, che egli fù da loro et meritamente nominato divino."

66. Filippo Sassetti, *Oratione in laude di Monsignore Lelio Torelli, fatta, et recitata nell'Accademia Fiorentina da M. Filippo Sassetti Accademico, detto tra gli Alterati l'assetato* (BNCF, Magliabecchiana XXVII C. 104), 162r: "mirando la sospesa imagine del padre della ragione Monsignore Lelio Torelli."

67. Vasari, *Vite,* 11. See also Ficino's admiration for the arts of mankind in Trinkaus, *In Our Image,* 482–483.

68. Gualandi, *De Optimo,* 115.

69. Vieri, *Breve compendio,* 3v: "ogni suo atto, et ogni sua specolazione dee essere finalmente indirizzata al culto divino, di quel Signore dal quale habbiamo ricevuto così questo preziosissimo dono della Filosofia, come ogni altro bene."

70. Baldini, *Discorso,* 23: "la volontà si come libera è propria dell'huomo, et è una forma et una perfezione che l'huomo hà da Dio, et dalla natura, perciohe egli è hùomo, et è questo quel dono per il quale nelle sacre lettere si legge che Dio volendo creare l'huomo disse, Facciamo l'huomo à immagine et simiglianza nostra, perciohe si come Iddio è libero, et non può essere violentato ne sforzato da cosa alcuna, così la volontà et il libero voler del l'huomo non può esser sforzato da cosa alcuna."

71. Pico della Mirandola, "Oratio Dignititatis Hominis," www.thelatinlibrary .com/mirandola/oratio.shtml (accessed December 15, 2008): "O summam

Dei patris liberalitatem, summam et admirandam hominis foelicitatem! Cui datum id habere quod optat, id esse quod velit. Bruta simul atque nascuntur id secum afferunt (ut ait Lucilius) e bulga matris quod possessura sunt. Supremi spiritus aut ab initio aut paulo mox id fuerunt, quod sunt futuri in perpetuas aeternitates. Nascenti homini omnifaria semina et omnigenae vitae germina indidit Pater. Quae quisque excoluerit illa adolescent, et fructus suos ferent in illo. Si vegetalia planta fiet, si sensualia obrutescet, si rationalia caeleste evadet animal, si intellectualia angelus erit et Dei filius. Et si nulla creaturarum sorte contentus in unitatis centrum suae se receperit, unus cum Deo spiritus factus, in solitaria Patris caligine qui est super omnia constitutus omnibus antestabit."

72. Anonymous, "La dignita," 58v: "l'huomo ha in se la natura di tutte le cose, così la libertà du essere cioche gli piace: se sta in otio, è, come pietra, se si da alla carne, è, come animal bruto, et se vuole, è, fatto Angiolo per contemplare la faccia del padre, et, è, in suo arbitrio farsi cosi eccellente, che sia numerato fra quelli à chi Dio disse, Iddij sete voi."

73. Baldini, *Discorso,* 29: "se egli con la libertà della volontà sua vince le sue cattive inclinazioni naturali, è sopra Fato, et del tutto padrone di se stesso, et simigliante à Dio, ma se egli si lascia vincere alle sue cattive inclinazioni naturali et ubbidisce à quelle, diviene servo del Fato et perde da se stesso la libertà della volontà sua et si riduce da se stesso nel medesimo grado nel quale sono gli animali senza ragione."

74. Baldini, *Panegirico,* 9r: "liberato per le vertù purgative da tutte la pertubationi riscevendo dentro di se per i sensi le forme delle cose naturali risguardando poi se medesimo a simiglianza di Dio le intende."

75. Giambattista Gelli, "Dedicazione," in *Modo di orare christianamente con la espositione del Pater Noster: fatta da M. Simone Portio Napoletano,* tradotto in lingua Fiorentina da Giovam Batista Gelli (Florence, 1551), 5: "(Virtu) inalza gli huomini sopra la conditione humana, et fagli participare del divino."

76. Patritius, *Il sacro regno,* 25v: "il sommo bene sia Iddio, et egli essere autore di tutti i beni, e che il fine de l'huomo non è altro, se non per similtudine accostarsi à Dio, ilche solo può fare con le virtue, la onde bene dissero gli stoici, che tra Dio e buoni era una amicitia generata da la virtù."

77. See respectively, Frosino Lapini, *Esposizione non meno utile che dotta sopra l'orazione del Signore tratta dal Concilio Coloniese* (Florence: Torrentino, 1562), 3: "ordinò alla beatitudine la sua creature, la quale essa creata haveva à imagine, e simiglianza sua," and Davidico, *Anatomia,* 301v: "Pur l'imagine in noi di Dio ricerca che viviamo da Dei in terra."

78. Savonarola, *Trattato,* 5: "quasi come uno Dio in terra."

79. Cornelio Musso, *I tre libri delle prediche del Reverendissimo Mons. Cornelio Musso, Vescovo di Bitonto* (Venice: Giolito, MDLXXVI), 196: "Che si come Iddio, quando prese il confortio dell'humana natura, non estrinsecamente

non in apparentia, non in opinione, ma veramente in se stesso tolse la carne, e l'anima dell'huomo; cosi il Giustificato, se diventa figliuol d'Iddio per adottione, è essaltato al confortio della natura Divina, e deificato."

80. This was the charge brought against Fra Carioni, whom Grendler has identified as a major link between Renaissance and Counter-Reformation. See Grendler, "Man Is Almost a God," 242–243.

81. Admittedly not a Tuscan, but the reforming bishop was read in Florence and widely influenced Counter-Reformation thought. Scipione Ammirato was actually an employee of Seripando before arriving in Florence. See Cochrane, *Florence*, 137–138.

82. Girolamo Seripando, "Terza Predica," in *Prediche sopra il Paternostro* (BR, MS. 1410), 30v–31r: "gli heroi ò simidij venerati et tanto celebrati da gli antichi, come superiori à gl'altri huomini . . . aduncerto grado di divinità, come si scrive d'Ercole, et di Romulo, et altri, non asseguirno tanti honori, et tante laudi, ne per nobilità ne per grandi richezze', ma per opere maravigliose fatte in beneficijo non delle case et famiglie loro, ma di tutta la generatione humana et per l'altezza delle virtù hèroice, con le quali si levorno da terra, et alzorno sempre la conditione comune de gli altri huomini."

83. Gelli, "Dedicazione," *Di Modo di Orare*, 5: "per ilche è sono da i Gentili chiamati Semidei, o Heroi, et da i Cristiani, Santi, et beati."

84. John 1:12. Among the frequent contemporary referenences to John, see Bettini, *Preparazione*, 7r, and Anonymous, "Il Giorno del Circunscisione," in *Sermoni raccolti* (BNFC, Fondo Nazionale II. III. 413), 45r–51r. See also Galatians 4:4–7.

85. Anonymous, *I gradi*, 2v: "Idio pelli meriti del Salvatore figlol suo vi ha donato cose grandissime, e pretiosi doni, accioche per questo doventiate consorti e partecipi della divina natura."

86. Diacceto, *Homelie*, 12: "Diciamo che noi siamo particolarmente suoi figliuoli, per haverlo ricevuto mediante la fede, et ubidienza: et egli ne ha conceduta particolare potenza di divenir suoi figliouli mediante la grazia dell'adozione."

87. See Antonino, *Opera di Santo Antonino Arcivescovo Fiorentino utilissima et necessaria alla instruttione delle sacerdote et di qualunche devota persona la quale desidera sapere bene confessarsi delli suoi peccati* (Venice: Giunti, 1536), 34v; Anonymous, "La dignità," 58v–59r; Frate Girolamo Quaino, *Predica fatta in Udine nella Chiesa Maggiore la Prima domenica dello Advento, l'anno MDLV, sopra la Epistola Corrente, nella quale si tratta della preperazione a vita eterna, et della temperantia* (Venice: Arrivabene, 1555); Mellini, *Trattato*, 53; Portio, *Modo di Orare*, 28 and 50–52; Lapini, *Esposizione*, 9r–17v; Davidico, *Anatomia*, 79v; Strozzi, *Trattato*, 15r; Ambrosio Catarino Polito, *Trattato de la giustificatione de l'huomo nel cospetto di Dio, secondo la pura dottrina de lo Evangelio* (Rome: Cartolari, 1544), 44v and 52v; Fra Andrea, *Trattato*, 12r; Petrus Canisius,

Somma della dottrina Christiana, tradotta dalla Latina nella lingua volgare da Messer Angelo Divitio da Bibbiena (Genoa: Belloni, 1561), 7v and 79r. Canisius's important catechism was translated into vulgar Florentine by one of Cosimo's own secretaries, Angelo Dovitio.

88. Lorenzo Davidico, *Trattato,* 20v.

89. Anonymous, "Predica del Santissimo Sacramento delle Eucharistica," in *Sermoni raccolti* (BNFC, Fondo Nazionale II. III. 413), 6r: "Questo cibo è spirituale, celeste, et divino. perche è cibo dello spirito nostro, et degnamente pigliandolo ci fa tutti spirituali, celesti, et divini . . . in questo santissimo sacramento communicò tutto se stesso."

90. Bonsi, "Sermone," 105r: "qual cosa puo desiderarsi piu oltra, che diventare una stessa cosa con Giesu Christo? Conciosia, che non è dubbio nessuno che mediante questa grazia, e comunicazione del corpo, e sangue del Signore in lui stesso ci transformiamo."

91. Ibid., 109v: "mangerami, e non tu mutarai me in te, ma si bene trasmutarai te in me."

92. See John O'Malley, *The First Jesuits* (Cambridge, Mass.: Harvard University Press, 1993), 154–155.

93. For example, Davidico, *Trattato,* 14r.

94. Ibid., 14r. For more on Davidico, see Massimo Firpo, *Nel labirinto del mondo: Lorenzo Davidico fra santi, eretici, et inquisitori* (Florence: Olschki, 1992).

95. Anonymous, "Dell Confessione," in *Sermoni raccolti* (BNFC, Fondo Nazionale, II, III, 413), 2r. In the Italian, the "luoghotenente," and Ambrosio Catharino Polito, *Trattato nuovo utile, et necessario de l'institutione de la Confessione sacramentale introdotta da Christo, et de la necessita, convenientia, e frutti di quella, Et del modo del confessarsi con la sufficiente essaminatione* (Rome: Contrado del Pellegrino, 1554), 12r–13v: "si ricerca che sia considerativa de la presentia di Dio, et che a lui si pensi far la confessione, et non a huomo puro, ma a Dio prima et dipoi a quello che tien la persona sua in quel atto particolarmente." This conceit was even extended to the guardian father of confraternities. Eisenblichler notes that the guardian father was "seen as the agent of God." Konrad Eisenblichler, *The Boys of the Archangel Raphael: A Youth Confraternity in Florence, 1411–1785* (Toronto: University of Toronto Press, 1998), 100.

96. See O'Malley, *First Jesuits,* 136–145.

97. Frate Archangelo, *Apologia pro Illustrissimo Domino Johanne Pico Mirnadulae, contra Petrum Garsiam Epsicopum Usselensum* (BL, Pluteus LIV c. 16), 39r–39v: "Deus Deorum dominus locutus est. Unus tum est Deus per essentiam, multi autem per participationem: Quo sens alibi dixit idem vates, dicens: Ego dixi, Dii estis, et filii excelsi omnes. Quod exponens Christus, dixit: Dii estis, ad quos sermo Dei factus est. Nam denuo (ut Jacobus ait) genuit nos verbo veritatis sunt et Dii per participationem, et per chrisma

divinitatis; iuxta illud Johannis: Dedit eis potestatem filios Dei fieri, et Dii per virtutes excellentiam, ut ait Aristo in Ethicis. Et sic dicunt, quia vicem Dei tenent; sicut iudicibus in Exodo."

98. Anonymous, "La dignità," 58v: "accioche per tale imagine si potesse conoscer, chi l'havesse fabricato." The argument comes from the first book of Pico's *Heptaplus*. See Paul Oskar Kristeller, "The Dignity of Man," in *Renaissance Concepts of Man and Other Essays* (New York: Harper and Row, 1972), 16.

99. Fabrini, *Il sacro regno,* 4v–5r: "ogniuno puo vedere, che il principato ha più simiglianza col regno celeste di tutti gli altri governi, lasciato da Dio in terra à simiglianza de'l celeste coro, accioche si conosca tra noi mortali molto maggiormente la sua grandezza, e potenza incomprensibile."

100. See, for instance, Girolamo Savonarola, *Triompho della croce di Christo: Della verita della fede Christiana* (Venice: al segno della Speranza, 1547), 4: "To come to the knowledge of invisible things, we have need of the visibile, because all of our knowledge begins from our senses." "A noi bisogna per le cose visibili, venire in cognitione delle invisibili, perche ogni nostra cognitione comincia dal senso."

101. Vieri, *Breve compendio,* 22r: "Non si può salire alla cognizione della Divina Maestà, in questa vita, se non per similtudine di queste cose create."

102. Dante, *Paradisio,* trans. Allen Mandelbaum (New York: Bantam Books, 1984), canto 3. Mellini, *Trattato,* 55: "per le Creature visibili l'huomo conosce l'nvisibili,"

103. Mellini, *Trattato,* 48–49: "La forma poi è quella perfezione, la quale dà veramente l'essere alla bellezza, et quasi ne corpi humani la dipigne, et questo è un raggio della divina bontà: et uno splendore, che sceso da quella, et sopra la materia preparatagli per ottima disposizione spiegandosi, fa d'ogni intorno lucente et vago quel fiore, quella vivacità, et quella grazia, laquale egli medesimo ne volti humani, et in tutte l'altre cose produce. et questa bellezza provoca, et rapisce à se le cose tutte, che hanno facultà di intendere et di conoscere, accioche per benifizio di lei elleno siano fatte di essa divina bonta partecipi: in che è la vera et ultima loro perfezione. Nella qual bellezza, et ne' quai beni non bisogna fermarsi, come in ultimo termine di felicità. conciosia che dalla bellezza, et bontà delle cose di quà giù sia necessario innalzarsi con l'intelletto à quel sommo bello et primo amato da tutte le cose et desiderato: et di queste servirsi come di scala, che ne conduca alla contemplazione del loro facitore."

104. The idea of beauty as an effluence of the divine was a Platonic concept, drawn from the Phaedrus.

105. Flaminio Nobili, *Trattato dell'amore humano composto, et donato ha gia molti anni da M. Flaminio Nobili all'Illustrisimo et Eccellentissimo Signore Prencipe di Firenze et di Siena* (Lucca: Busdraghi, 1562), 25r–25v: "A questo Divino Amore non sò già quanto necessaria scala sia la bellezza,

donnesca; percioche il considerare i miracolosi, et pur ordinati effetti della Natura, i muovimenti stabilito del Cielo, il vigor della luce, la perfettione dell'universo, mi pare molto più sicuro strada per condurci alla cognition dela Somma Bellezza."

106. Francesco Visdomini, *Tutte le prediche et homelie* (Venice: Giordano Ziletti, 1574), 95v: "per rogala di naturale imitatione scoprono l'esser di Dio con l'esser suo, et le innumberabili et infinite sue vertù col picciolo sembiante et vestigio ch'esse ne servano, accioche per esse, come per la scala visibile, possano gli fortunati contemplatori ascendere a conoscer parte delle invisibili vertù divine, come (per esempio) la sua bellezza nel sole, la forza nel fuoco, la dolcezza nell'aria, la stabilità nella terra, et brievemente come sù in Cielo in Dio solo si conoscono perfettamente le creature, cosi qua giù, come meglio si può nelle creature si scopre la vertù del creatore."

107. For instance, the reaffirmation of icons based itself largely on the same epistemology. See Domenico Basilio Lapis, *Epistola Responsiva Domni Basiliij de Lapis Monachi ordinis cistercien, in quoddam epistolium fratris Bernardini de Senis de purgatorio libero arbitrio* (BNCF, Magliabecchiana XXXIV c. 6.), 28r.

108. See Alison Brown, "Platonism in Fifteenth-Century Florence and Its Contribution to Early Modern Political Thought," *Journal of Modern History* 58 (1986).

109. Sebastiano Gentile, "Ficino e il platonismo di Lorenzo," in *Lorenzo de' Medici. New Perspectives,* ed. Bernard Toscani (New York: Peter Lang, 1993), 28–35.

110. See, for instance, the prologue to the legislation setting up the Pisan studio. Lorenzo Cantini, ed., *Legislazione Toscana*, vol. 1 (Florence: Albizziana da S. Maria in Campo, 1800), 195–196. For Cosimo's patronage of the Pisan studio, see Giovanni Cascio Pratilli, *L'università e il principe: gli studi di Siena e di Pisa tra Rinascimento e Controriforma* (Florence: Olschki, 1975). On the ducal press, see Antonio Ricci, "Lorenzo Torrentino and the Cultural Program of Cosimo I de' Medici," in *The Cultural Politics of Duke Cosimo I de' Medici,* ed. Konrad Eisenbichler (Aldershot: Ashgate, 2001), 103.

111. Fiorani, "Maps, Politics, and the Grand Duke," 74.

112. Francesco Vossilla, "Cosimo I, lo Scrittoio del Bachiacca, una Carcassa di Capodoglio e la Filosofia Naturale," *Mitteilungen des Kunsthistorischen Institutes in Florenz* 37 (1993), 381–395.

113. Alfredo Perifano, *L'Alchimie à la cour de Côme Ier de Médicis: Savoirs, culture, et politique* (Paris: Honoré Champion Éditeur, 1997), and Suzanne Butters, *The Triumph of Vulcan: Sculptors' Tools, Porphyry, and the Prince in Ducal Florence* (Florence: Olschki, 1996), 241–248.

114. For an example of the linkage of Cosimo's name, the medical profession, and the healing of the body politics see Da Trivigi, *Canzone*, 9; Martelli, sonnet 6 in *Cento sonnetti,* and Deborah Parker, "The Poetry of Patronage: Bronzino

and the Medici," *Renaissance Studies* 17 (2003), 234. Cosimo was not the first to use the play on the Medici name to make himself the "doctor of the state." See Kent's discussion of the elder Cosimo in *Patron's Oeuvre*, 119. Moreover, Renaissance theorists would have certainly imbibed the analogy of medic/governor from both Seneca and Cicero; see Stacey, *Roman Monarchy*, 57–58. For Christ as medic, see Anonymous, "Il Giorno del circumscisione," 59v; Dolciati, *Prediche diversi*, 29r–29v; and Fra Andrea, *Lezioni et sermoni* (BNFC, Fondo Nazionale II, I, 32, Ex Magliabecchiana XXXV cod. 125), 225.

115. Butters, *Triumph of Vulcan*, 44–48.

116. Cited in Perifano, *L'alchimie*, 85: "un cortesia veramente degna d'essere usata da Principi grandi, sì come quella che gli rende più che alcun'altra cosa simiglianti à Dio. perciochè ei fanno a gli huomini in questa guisa il maggior benfitio che sia quasi possibile far loro, rendendo o conservando a quegli la loro sanità senza la quale eglino non possono veramente godere niuno di quei doni che Iddio ottomo e grandissimo ha dato loro."

117. Cited in ibid., 86.

118. Annette Finley-Crosswhite argues that Henri IV intentionally drew on the traditional French royal custom of touching for scrofula in order to bolster his metaphorical position as the healer of the body politic. Finley-Croswhite, "Henry IV and the Diseased Body Politic," in *Princes and Princely Culture, 1450–1650*, vol. 1, eds. Martin Gosman, A. A. MacDonald, and Arie Johan Vanderjagt (Leiden: Brill, 2003).

119. It may seem strange to claim that alchemy was both more "magical" and more "scientific," but nevertheless that is the case. This is because, at least to Ficino, magic was little more than the manipulation of the occult forces of nature. See Yates, *Giordano Bruno*, 62–83.

120. Andrew C. Minor and Bonner Mitchell, eds., *A Renaissance Entertainment: Festivities for the Marriage of Cosimo I, Duke of Florence, in 1539* (Columbia: University of Missouri Press, 1968), 230.

121. Ammirato, *Oratione*, 51r: "non humano ma Divino Principe." See also Ottavio Bandini, *Orazione funerale di Monsignore Ottavio Bandini Fiorentino, Da lui fatte, e recitata il di XIX di Giugno 1574, nell'esequie del Serenissimo Cosimo de Medici primo Grand Duca di Toscana*, tradotto dalla Lingua Latina da Francesco Falconcini (Florence: Giorgio Marescotti, 1574), unpaginated: "Non poteva questa divina, et immortal vertù star più nascosta."

122. Benedetto Betti, *Orazione funerale di Benedetto Betti. Da Lui publicamente recitata nelle essequie del Serenissimo Cosimo Medici, Gran Duca di Toscana* (Florence: Giunti, 1574), unpaginated: "considerandole in quel modo che comporta la debolezza del mio ingegno, non so, con qual nome io debba chiamarlo, che io non dica molto meno di quel che merita il suo valore, se gia io non imiterò quelli antichi Lacedemonii, i quali quando am-

miravano grandemente qualche personaggio, lo chiamavano et reputavano divino: la qual cosa se fu detta per qualche ragione, in que' tempi, di molti grandi Heroi, ragionevolmente si potrà ella dire anche del Serenissimo Gran Duca: Però che quelli furono ammirati particolarmente per una qualche virtù, ma questi le haveva tutte in se raccolte di maniera, che l'animo suo pareva che fusse il proprio albergo delle virtù, che son dette Heroiche et divine."

123. For Cosimo as Augustus, see all of Matasilani, *La felicità,* and Girolamo del Vezzo, "Canzone," in *Rime diverse sopra la morte del Serenissimo Granduca di Toscana* (BNCF, Magliabecchiana XXVII c. 104), 110r; Fabio Bentovoglienti, *Vita d'Augusto intitolato al'Illustrissimo et Eccelentissimo Signore Cosimo de Medici Duca di Fiorenza e di Siena* (BL, Pluteus XLII c. 26); and Paola Corrias, "Don Vincenzo Borghini e l'iconologia del potere alla corte di Cosimo I e di Francesco I de' Medici," *Storia del'arte* 81 (1994), 172. For Cosimo as Camillus, see Janet Cox-Rearick, *Dynasty and Destiny in Medici Art: Pontormo, Leo X, and the Two Cosimos* (Princeton: Princeton University Press, 1984); 251; and Forster, "Metaphors of Rule," 93. As Camillus as a type for the anti-French Cosimo, see Andrea Dactii, *Poemata,* (Florence: Torrentino, 1549), 14. For Cosimo as Apollo and Hercules, see Richelson, *Studies in the Personal Imagery,* 37 and 79–92, respectively.

124. See Richelson, *Studies in the Personal Imagery,* 109–112; Graham Smith, "Cosimo I and the Joseph Tapestries for the Palazzo Vecchio," *Renaissance and Reformation* 6 (1982), 183–196; Francesco Vieri, *Orazione di M. Francesco Vieri cognominato il Vieri nella morte del Serernissimo Granduca di Toscana* (BNCF, Magliabecchiana XXVII c. 104), 9v; and Marcia Hall, *Renovation and Counter-Reformation: Vasari and Duke Cosimo in Sta Maria Novella and Sta Croce, 1565–1577* (Oxford: Clarendon Press, 1979), 5.

125. Vieri, *Orazione,* 2r: "il quale per beneficenza, e per tutte le virtù era divino, et per vera, e somma Religione santissimo."

126. See Niccolò Martelli, sonnet 17 in *Cento sonnetti,*; Betti, *Orazione;* Ginus, *Pro travalliatorum,* 31v; G. B. Adriani, "Orazione di Monsignore Giovanni Batista Adriani fatto in Latino all'essequie del Serenissimo Cosimo de Medici granduca di Toscana," in *Scritti varii editi ed inediti di G. B. Adriani e di Marcello suo figliuolo* (Bologna: Commissione per i testi di lingua, 1968), 1771, and Cantini, *Legislazione,* vol. 1, 277 and 313; vol. 2, 151.

127. Fabrini, *Il sacro regno,* 111r: "se noi consideriamo bene la cosa, noi vedremo, che sarà come un secondo Iddio, e conosceremo, che come Iddio volse co'l suo sangue ricomperare, e liberare il suo popolo eletto, così il principe mandato da Dio, con pensieri, con affanni, con disagi, e con continovi pericoli di morte libera la republica da tutti i flagelli, che le soprastanno, e la gastiga, e correggie, mettendola in quella via, che la conduca a la gloria celeste. Talche noi diremo quel, che dice Esiodo, che'l principe sia compagno di Dio. e perciò come Iddio ordina a l'anime beate il luogo in

cielo, così il principe à quello le conduce per quelle vie, che piacciono à esso Dio. la qual cosa stando così non voglio dire gia, che si debba chimare uno Iddio in terrra, come chiamava il Senato Romano il loro imperadori, quando s'erano portati gloriosamente in qualche importante fatione."

128. Timothy Verdon, "Immagini della Controriforma: L'iconografia dell'area Liturgica de Santa Maria del Fiore," in *Atti del VII Centenario del Duomo di Firenze: La Cattedrale come spazio sacro,* vol. 2, pt. 2, ed. Timothy Verdon and Annalisa Innocenti (Florence: Edifir, 2001), 524–525.

129. Samantha Kelly, *The New Solomon: Robert of Naples (1309–1343) and Fourteenth-Century Kingship* (Leiden: Brill, 2003),

130. Gregory Lubkin, *A Renaissance Court: Milan under Galeazzo Maria Sforza* (Berkeley: University of California Press, 1994), 71.

131. Matteo Casini, *I gesti del principe: La festa politica a Firenze e Venezia in età rinascimentale* (Venice, 1996), 55.

132. Monod, *Power of Kings,* 23.

133. See Romano, *Likeness of Venice,* 49–50. In his model of apotheosis by virtue, Cosimo more closely resembled the fourteenth-century Angevin king Robert of Naples, another cadet heir with legitimacy issues. For Robert's apotheosis by virtue, see Kelly, *New Solomon,* 117–118.

134. On apotheosis in the rest of Europe, see Monod, *Power of Kings,* 36.

135. Boethius, much admired by Renaissance philosophers, had even claimed that since supreme goodness and supreme happiness were identical with God, "each happy individual is therefore divine." Boethius, *The Consolation of Philosophy,* trans. Victor Watts (London: Penguin, 1999), 71.

136. All the saints but especially the often-cited Augustine usually won the honors.

137. ASFi, Med. 1070c. 296r (November 5, 1543). Lorenzo Pagni to Pier Francesco Riccio.

138. Ferrari, *Apologia,* 6r.

139. Baldini, *Discorso,* 15.

140. Vasari explicitly defended the title in *Vite,* 26–27. According to Deborah Parker, this is how Bronzino thought of Michelangelo as well. Parker, *Bronzino: Renaissance Painter as Poet* (Cambridge: Cambridge University Press, 2000), 71.

141. Richard Trexler, *Church and Community, 1200–1600; Studies in the History of Florence and New Spain* (Rome: Edizioni di Storia et Letteratura, 1987), 222.

142. ASFi, Med. 1070c. 133r (December 4, 1542). Giovanni Conti to Pier Francesco Riccio.

2. Divine Right Rule and the Providential Worldview

1. ASFi, AGBE 4378c. 283 (November 27, 1549): "Stimo Iddio habbi così voluto mi dia in mano, à causa non rovini in tutto."

2. ASFi, Med. 210c. 72v–73r (April 28, 1559): "ben crediamo al certo che per salute di quello, et per voluntà di Dio sia venuta sotto la nostra mano, dove che secondo il nostro costume, prevalerà la justitia ad ogni passione, et affetto particolare, ne lasceremo suffocare chiunche vorra viver bene dalla potenza et ingordigia altrui."

3. Marrara, *Studi giuridici*, 27: "senza tener conto del tenore e della stessa esistenza dell'atto di investitura, già nel 1557 aveva dichiarato di avere ricevuto direttamente da Dio 'l'imperio e dominio' del nuovo stato, ritenendo, pertanto, di non doverlo considerare subordinato ad altri che a se stesso."

4. ASFi, Med. 211c. 28r–28v (August 5, 1559): "Poiche è piaciuto à Dio et alla benignità del Re Cattolico di mettermi nell'intero posseso dello stato di Siena." Emphasis mine.

5. ASFi, Med. 24, c.145r–146v (July 12, 1556): "mai o trovato che in ogni sorte di principato non vi sia qualche limitatione . . . non ci'è pare esser assoluto certe maggior che in tutti li altri perche è fondato da dio, in che nella carità nella povertà nella pace queste sono limitationi oneste . . . quanto alla pace sia davver ogni sorte di limitation per far lutta li cristiani e tener la guerra contro alli infideli queste sono limitatione voluntarie introdotte dal verbo di dio le quali Sua Santità la da abrucciare."

6. And little different from a long tradition of Christian and humanist thinking.

7. See Glenn Richardson, *Renaissance Monarchy: The Reigns of Henry VIII, Francis I, and Charles V* (London: Hodder Arnold, 2002), 20–24.

8. Giovambattista Gelli, "Dedicazione," in *Tutte le lettioni* (Florence, 1551), 1: "infra tutti i ben fortunati regni, et felicissime città, la nostra con tutti gli huomini suoi, può et debbe al pari di qualunche altra si voglia, ringratiare Iddio; et gloriarsi di haver dopo tanti, et tanti suoi travagli, riscevuto da esso, donatore di tutti i beni, per principe, la Illustrissimo et Eccellentissimo Signore Vostra"

9. Lucio Paolo Rosello, *Il ritratto del vero governo del prencipe dal'essempio vivo del gran Cosimo de'Medici* (Venice: Giovan Maria Bonelli, 1552), 3: "il stato che gli ha dato Iddio." See also 10r: "la cui buona sorte, et espressa providenza di Dio l'ha di privato (benche nobilissimo cittadino) levato alla Ducale degnità." For more on Rosello, see John Jeffries Martin, *Venice's Hidden Enemies: Italian Heretics in a Renaissance City* (Berkeley: University of California Press, 1993), 81.

10. Francesco Altoni, "Dedicazione," in *Monomachia ovvero arte di scherma* (BNCF, Fondo Nazionale II, III, 315), 1r–1v: "Dio la chiamassi all'altissimo grado en quale la si trova."

11. Frate Archangelo, *Apologia,* 2v: "Nam quibus in ramis tutius nidulari poterant. Aut quo patrocinio adversus cavillantes (si qui forte sunt) protegi? Tu in omni Italia literarium senatum unus amplecteris, atque foves; namque sive id fato, sive divina providentia fiat; multis ab hinc a'vis

Mediceo sanguini proprium fuit, et quodamodo peculiare, atque haereditarium bonorum literarum suscipere patrocinium, atque ingenijs favere. Necesse est aut idem sempre esse, quod sempre idem fuit."

12. ASFi, Med. 183c. 289r–292v (n.d.). In this author's opinion, the most likely candidates for the authorship of this letter seem to be Vincenzo Nobili, future *depositario generale,* or Vincenzio Bovio: "Havendo la divina essentia nella felicissima et per consequens fecundissima genitura et natività di Vostra Eccelentia et in si tenera età *afflatu divino* in expectato et senza alchuno humano obstaculo promossa et insignita al supremo grado del principato di questa sua Città et Stato."

13. Vincenzio Fedeli, *Relazioni degli ambasciatori Veneti al senato,* vol. 3, ed. Arnaldo Segarizzi (Bari: Gius. Laterza et Figli, 1916), 129: "il signore Iddio permise che fossero sottomessi ad un prencipe solo: il che finalmente è ritornato in beneficio di tutti; perché ora, con la presenza del tremendo prencipe e spaventevole, tutte le cose sono tornate a' suoi primi principi. E tanto è il terrore delle severe e subite esecuzioni e tanto è potente ed esecutivo il braccio della sua giustizia (che tocca tutti gli ordini, senza rispetto di persona alcuna), che, se bene stanno soggetti con infinito rammarico e cordoglio, stanno però in pace ed in quiete, né piú si sente disordine né pertubazione alcuna fra loro, avendo il signor Iddio cavato da tanti detestandi mali questo bene: che ciascuno sta sicurissimo nello stato suo, purché stia ne' termini dell'obbedienza."

14. Ibid., 135: "Il che ho voluto dire, ché questa elezione par fusse fatta per sola volontá divina, perché poi né al popolo, né al Stato, né a Cesare piacque."

15. Marucelli, *Cronaca Fiorentina,* ed. Enrico Coppi (Florence: Olschki, 2000), vi.

16. Ibid., 5.

17. Ibid., 3: "Volse Iddio, amatore della nostra città, che questi non levassero romore, anzi inspirati da Dio andorno pianamente al Cardinale Cybo."

18. Ambrosio Catarino Polito, *Discorso del Reverendo Padre Frate Ambrosio Catharino Polito, Vescovo di Minori. contra la dottrina et le profetie di Fra Girolamo Savonarola* (Venice: Ferrarij, 1548), 44r: "Et vedi che alla fine à questo si sono poi accordati, et Iddio l'ha favorito. Benche non voglio però, che niuno mi reputi partigiano di stato alcuno . . . piacerami sempre quello stato, ò in Fiorenza, ò in altra Città, il quale sarà giusto et farà giustitia." Emphasis mine.

19. This point of view has been put forth more recently by Gary Ianziti, *Humanistic Historiography under the Sforzas: Politics and Propaganda in Fifteenth-Century Milan* (Oxford: Oxford University Press, 1988), 1–3.

20. Lelio Bonsi, "Lezzione quinta di Lelio Bonsi, sopra quei versi di Dante, nel settimo canto dell'Inferno, che trattano della fortuna," in *Cinque lezioni di Monsignore Lelio Bonsi lette da lui publicamente nella Accadamia Fioren-*

tina, Aggiuntovi un breve trattato della cometa. E nella fine un sermone sopra l'Eucarestia da doversi recitare il Giovedi Santo del medesimo autore (Florence: Giunti, 1560), 84.

21. Augustine of Hippo, *The City of God*, trans. Gerald G. Walsh, Demetrius B. Zema, Grace Monahan, and Daniel Honan and ed. Vernon J. Bourke (New York: Image Books, 1958), 99–118.

22. Vieri, *Breve compendio*, 50r: "Dio hà così diligente providenza di noi, che insino i capelli del capo nostro gli sono noti; e che non cade una passera in terra, senza la volontà del padre celeste." And 50r–50v: "Se il padre eterno provvede insino à gli uccelli, tanto piu provederà à noi, che siamo tanto piu nobili." The quotes are from Matthew 10: 29–30.

23. Bonsi "Lezzione," 86rv.

24. Ibid., 89r–90v: "La sentenza dei sacri Teologi, si come ella è senza alcun dubbio piu vera, e piu certa di tutte l'altre, cosi è ancora piu breve, e piu agevole, percioche essi togliendo del tutto di tutte le cose il caso, e la fortuna, riducono tutti gl'effetti di tutte le cagioni nella podesta di Dio, e nella providenza divina: dimaniera, che se bene considerati alcuni effetti secondo noi, e quanto alle cagioni particolari, pare che si possano chiamar fortunevoli, e casuali: considerati non dimeno secondo Dio, e quanto alla cagione universale, si vede manifestamente, che procedeno con grandissimo ordine, e da sapienza infinita: E che è quelli, il quale sappiendo, che Dio non solo ha cognizione, ma cura di tutte le cose non solo celesti, e sempiterne, ma mondane, e corrottibili, non dico in universale secondo le spezie, ma particolarmente ancora, e in quanto agl'individui, non conosca insiememente, che, non che altro, ne pure una foglia si muove senza la saputa, e voglia di lui?"

25. Baldini, *Discorso*, 9: "Significano ultimamente i Toscani per questa parola fato, l'assoluta et libera volontà di Dio ottimo, et grandissimo, et la providenza che egli hà di tutto questo universo."

26. Giovanni Gualandi, *De vero iudicio ac providentia Dei, ac ipsius gubernatione rerum mundi* (Florence: Torrentinus, 1562).

27. Cited in Cox-Rearick, *Dynasty and Destiny*, 287.

28. Davidico, *Trattato*, 28: "ha tanta providentia sopra ciascuno di noi, come se altra cura non havesse."

29. In addition to the other examples cited in this chapter, see Strozzi, *Trattato*, 44; Lapini, *Esposizione*, 3; Visdomini, *Tutte le prediche*, 29; and Seripando, "Terza Predica," 10r.

30. Vieri, *Orazione*, 2r: "la Divina Providenza, non solo per Signore begnissimo ci haveva dato, ma ancora per amorevole, giusto, e prudentissimo Padre, e difensore potentissimo nostro, e della sua Chiesa santa liberamente donato."

31. Fabrini, *Il sacro regno*, 1r: "Chi con puro cuore, e perfetta fede crederrà, che'l sommo, et immortal fattore di ciascheduna cosa creata . . . (come

negar non si puo) governi, regga, e disponga tutto l'universo, non dubiterà
ancora che (quasi come sue membra) non disponga a'l bene, et ordini à ciascheduna repubblica che egli ama, quel governo, et ordine di vivere di
tempo in tempo, che conosce sufficiente à mantenerla."

32. Salviati, *Orazione,* 9: "Di che la virtù argomento, la fortuna di questo Principe rende testimonianza, la qual fortuna sopr'alla cura delle terrene cose
sempre della Divina Providenza è ministra." Others, like Betti and Giurgi,
also used the language of providence to explain Cosimo's divine right. See
Betti, *Orazione,* unpaginated, and Tommaso Giurgi, *Oratione di Giugurta
Tomasi Academico Travagliato da lui publicamente recitata nell'Academia
il di nove di gennaro* (BNCF, Magliabecchiana XXVII c. 16), 5v.

33. Augustine, *City of God,* 45.

34. Gualandi, *De vero Iudicio.*

35. Baldini, *Discorso,* 41–42: "et avvengono i mali in questo universo senza
che Iddio ne sia cagione, anzi gli usa alla conservazione et al ben'esser
dell'universo."

36. Strozzi, *Trattato,* 56.

37. Ibid., 1.

38. Three translations were produced: one by Varchi, one by Domenichi, and
one by Bartoli. Each bore dedications to Cosimo.

39. The notebooks, or *zibaldone,* were collections of handwritten passages
copied down from favorite authors. See Kent, *Patron's Oeuvre,* 88.

40. For the sacred play as an educative feature of Florentine life, see Lorenzo
Polizzotto, *Children of the Promise: The Confraternity of the Purification
and the Socialization of Youths in Florence: 1427–1785* (Oxford: Oxford
University Press, 2004), 78–86.

41. Anonymous, *La rappresentazione di Abataccio* (BNCF, B.R. 179.1), 1r: "O
Voi che siate vaghi di sapere / le occulte cose esecreti di Dio / et giudicate
col falio vedere / et parvi quel che e bene tal volta rio / perche nascose son
le cose vere / voi la giustitia mettete in oblio / voi vedrete oggi se voi state
attenti / come alqui dobbiamo star contenti."

42. Marucelli, *Cronaca,* 147: "gran mormoratione del principe per tutto il
mondo. Niente di meno, bisogna accordarsi con la volontà di Dio che a
qualche fine comporta simil cose, et così segue et chiunque vuol mangiare
bisogna che paghi."

43. Cosimo I, *Lettere* (Florence: Vallecchi, 1940), 183: "L'attione mondane son
tali che ogni giorno, secondo che è la volontà del gran motore, si muovu-
ono hor in piacere et hora in dispiacere di noi altri corpi imperfetti. Ma
egli, che non può errare, dispone di noi et della vita e della morte in quel
modo che all sua gran bontà piace. Et sempre debbiamo pensare che sia a
benefitio nostro."

44. Ibid., 190: "Consolati adunque et ringratia Dio di ogni suo voler, servilo et
pregalo che ti indirizzi conforme al voler suo, et che ti dia consolatione di

questi successi, sì come egli solo lo può fare. Nè io certo ho trovato in questi casi altra consolatione che quella che Dio m'ha data."

45. On the death of his daughter, the duchess of Ferrara, see ASFi, Med. 213c. 50r (May 4, 1561); on the death of his son Piero see ASFi, Med. 10c. 167r–168r (June 8, 1547); on the death of Cardinal Savello's father ASFi, Med. 194c. 76r–76v (July 19, 1551); on the death of Cardinal Santiquattro ASFi, Med. 185c. 156v–157r (October 23, 1544); and to Agnolo Niccolini on the occasion of the death of that minister's son ASFi, Med. 196c. 16v (November 17, 1551).

46. Strozzi, *Trattato*, 21r and 14r: "per cio che stolta cosa è constrastare alla voluntà di Dio, sappiendo egli massimamente eleggere il tempo meglio per noi. . . . chi ne mormora pare che nieghi la providenza et bontà sua." One wonders if Cosimo recognized the perversity of requesting this tract from Lorenzo, since Cosimo had been primarily responsible for the death of Lorenzo's own brother.

47. Benedetto Varchi, *Orazione funebre per Maria Salviati* (BNCF, Fondo Nazionale II, IV, 1, 8), 120v: "fra le dolcezze sue, è di vero sicome, i buon sudditi si devono contentare et riscevere lietamente, tutto quello che piace à i principi, et Signori loro, cosi i signori e principi buoni, i quali senza alcun dubbio è Vostra Eccelentia debbono riscievere lietamente et contentarsi di tutto quello, che a Diò piace."

48. For more on Cosimo's political use of masculinity, see Nicholas Scott Baker, "Power and Passion in Sixteenth-Century Florence: The Sexual and Political Reputations of Alessandro and Cosimo I de' Medici," *Journal of the History of Sexuality* 19 (2010), 437–457.

49. Fabrini, *Il sacro regno*, 7r: "Quanto sia vera tale oppenione di tanto poeta, brevemente ve lo voglio provare. Iddio è savissimo, conosce le cose future, come le presenti, e passate; di piu giustissimo, e immutabile; e tutte le cose, che sono, sono per volontà sua. Se dunque tutte le cose seno per sua volontà, et egli giusto, e savio, e immutabile, et havendo sempre avanti gli occhi il futuro, come il presente, e passato, ne seguita, che ancora quello, che egli ordina, che venga di tempo in tempo, non possa esser altramente, che egli ha ordinato, ne stare meglio, ne si possa mutare, ne da altri, ne da lui stesso; perche se altri lo potesse mutare, sarebbe da piu di Dio, e se egli lo mutasse, sarebbe mutabile, et di più non giusto, ò almeno non savio. non giusto; perche, se egli l'havesse ordinato giustamente, lo caverebbe di quella giustitia, non savio, perche, se egli lo rimutasse per non l'havere ordinato bene, sarebbe segno, che malamente egli havesse veduto."

50. Bartoli, *Discorsi,* 321: "Imparino adunque i Principi a governare prudentemente per via della virtù della bontà et della clementia non deviano però dall justizia, i loro sudditi; piuttosto che per la via delli vizij della malignità o crudeltà; et i privati a viver quieti alla volontà di dio, senza ilquale non

hanno i principi le supreme potestà loro." On Bartoli's role in Cosimo's takeover of the Academy, see Plaisance, *L'Académie et le prince,* 80–86.

51. Cited in van Veen, *Cosimo,* 29.

52. See for instance, Peter Blickle, "Social Protest and Reformation Theology," in *Religion, Politics, and Social Protest: Three Studies on Early Modern Germany,* ed. Kaspar von Greyerz (London: Allen and Unwin, 1984).

53. The idea that the king's relationship with the divinity was essential to the food supply is the famous thesis of the early anthropologist James Frazer. See the reprinted Frazer, *The Golden Bough: A Study in Magic and Religion* (London: Oxford University Press, 1994). Though discredited in some fields, it has gained traction in medieval studies of both the pre-Christian Germans and Celts. See J. M. Wallace, Hadrill, *Early Germanic Kingship in England and on the Continent* (Oxford: Clarendon Press, 1971), 8, and Bernhard Maier, "Sacral Kingship in Pre-Christian Ireland," *Zeitschrift fur Religions- und Geistesgeschicte* 41 (1989), 12–32.

54. Cited in Rory McTurk, "Sacral Kingship in Ancient Scandanavia: a review of some recent literature," *Saga-Book: Viking Society for Northern Research* 19 (1975), 139: "If they get no rain, they blame me; if they get no sunshine, the do likewise. If hard times befall them—whether hunger, or pestilence, or whatever it may be—I always have to take the blame for it. It is as if they did not realize that I am a human being, and no god."

55. Baldini, *Discorso,* 13–14. The matter of intelligences remained in dispute.

56. Savonarola, *Prediche,* 1.

57. Eusebius of Caesarea, *The History of the Church,* trans. G. A. Williams (London: Penguin Books, 1989).

58. Savonarola, *Prediche,* 7r–8r.

59. Visdomini, *Tutte le prediche,* 34v: "Non può con honor suo più tolerar Iddio, Vero è, che mal volentieri et contra ogni sua intentione (parlando all'humana . . .), pur è forza mostrar anco quanto può la giustitia, e la vendetta."

60. Dolciati, *Prediche diversi,* 38r.

61. Anonymous, *Prediche,* 80r.

62. On prodigies, portents, and prophecies in the early part of the century, see Ottavia Niccoli, *Prophecy and People in Renaissance Italy,* trans. Lydia G. Cochrane (Princeton: Princeton University Press, 1987), 29–32.

63. Mazzinghi, *Sermoni,* 14r: "El magno et vivente idio Nostro Signore in la sua infallible spia ha in tal ordine del principio del mondo insino adesso observato cioe che quando alcuna immutatione et innovatione ha voluto far a noi mortali alchun segno innanzi permecter acio le gente et populi alla penitentia si disponghino." For Mazzinghi's employment, see ASFi, MS 7c. 144r–144v (October 26, 1542).

64. Mazzinghi, *Sermoni,* 14r–14v: "quando idio volse la regal Città di Jerusalem per Tito et Re Spasiano destruer et aniglar avanti per maximi terrori et

celesti segni a penitentia quelli provocar volse: si come Iosepho storico *de Bello Judaico* et Eusebio Cesariense nella *Ecclesiastica historia* . . . scrivano una stella in forma di coltello sopra la città per uno anno et le comete conxitial fiamme arder furno viste star, la luna per 12 nocte continuemente pati l'eclipse, le porte del tempio di maximo carico et peso nella mezza nocte per se stesse s'aprisono nel 21 giorno di magio nello occaso del sole il Carri di homini armati con le arme combacter insieme furno visti et moltri altri per iquali no si volsono convertir, onde fu la gran mortalità et fame et peste et angoscie grande patirno et la Città fu totalmente eradicata."

65. Anonymous, *La rappresentazione di Santa Agata* (BNCF, B.R. 179. 9), 68r: "O Quintiano no vegian chiaramente / c'ha torto ai dato a Agata tormenti / et ciasucno di noi si ne dolente / et sianne assai turbati et malcontenti / se non ti vai condio subitamente / sareno i sensi tua star dolenti / a tua cagion tanti tremuoti vengono / et tutto el popolo in paura tengono."

66. See Anonymous, "Dell confessione," 2v.

67. Cox-Rearick, *Dynasty and Destiny,* 148–149.

68. Marucelli, *Cronaca,* 108: "Hor Voi, Principe illustre et honorato / per il cui gran valor Firenze bella / tutti obliando e suoi passati danni / felice et lieta hor si posa in pace / seguite pure il cominciato stile / perché chi teme primeramente Iddio / rivolta gl'occhi e le sue leggi honora / come voi fate, glorioso e lieto / felice fine conduce sempre ogni sua impresa."

69. Adriani, "Orazione Funebre," 156: "avendo egli fidanza in Dio e nella buona conscienza sua, si sbrigò sempre da ogni pericolo, vinse spesso i nimici."

70. Gabrielle Symeoni, *Le III parte del campo dei primi studii* (Venice: per Comino da Trino di Monferrato, 1546), 6v: "Non temer già di morte, affanno, o duole / Ch'à giusta impresa d'ogni buon Signore / favorisce l'etterno et sommo Dio."

71. Salviati, *Orazione,* 9: "mà sacrosanto." And "la fortuna di questo Principe rende testimonianza."

72. Vieri, *Breve Compendio,* 5v: "che il Lor Principe è, con la pietà congiunto, con quel Signore che è Signore de' Signori: e Re de' Rè, e dal quale ci viene ogni aiuto, ne' pericolosi casi, et ogni bene, in questa presente vita."

73. ASFi, Med. 204 c. 21v (August 9, 1554): "Victoria che Dio Nostro Signore ci ha dato."

74. ASFi, Med. 182 c. 79v–80r (August 1, 1537): "ne pigliate quel contento et conforto faciamo noi di qua col renderne devotissime gratie alla bontà divina dalla quale procede ogni gratia et dono."

75. ASFi, Med. 23 c. 276r–279r (December 10, 1552): "dal indie ne son venuti una quantità quasi incredibile, onde si conosce che Dio vuole aiutarlo et percio Sua Santità lo deve fare ancor essa."

76. Matasilani, *La felicità,* 2–13: "Segni veramente mandati da DIO."

77. The Capricorn was associated with imperial imagery because it was the zodiacal sign of both Augustus and Charles V. See Josephine von Hennenberg, "Two Renaissance Cassoni for Cosimo I de' Medici in the Victoria and Albert Museum," *Mitteilungen des Kunsthistorischen institutes in Florenz* 35 (1991), 115–132. For the Capricorn motif at the Villa Castello, see Forster, "Metaphors of Rule," 91.

78. It had been a favorite motif of Leo X. See Charles Stinger, *The Renaissance in Rome* (Bloomington: Indiana University Press, 1998), 298. Indeed, the idea of the eternal spring at least goes back in Florentine culture to Dante, who adorned the top of the Mountain of Purgatory with his garden of earthly delights. See Dante, *Purgatorio,* trans. Robert Hollander and Jean Hollander (New York: Doubleday, 2003), cantos 27–31.

79. Matasilani, *La felicità,* 9r–9v.

80. Ibid., 4–6.

81. Bettini, *Preparazione,* 6r–7r: "cioe gia è passato l verno e la pioggia s'è partita e se ne andata et nella nostra terra sono apparsi i fiori che significano la rinovatione del tempo il qual tempo del veno piovoso et freddo nel qual nessuno poteva adoperarsi ci ha pel suo advenimento tolto via il sol della iustitia Christo iddio nostro et col suo appropinquarsi et riscaldar la terra de nostri cuori ci ha rinovata la stagione et ridotta la florida primavera nella qual tutte le cose cominciano a germinare et li fiori ci danno speranza de subsequenti frutti i quali oderiferi et fiameggianti dimostrono la rinovatio del homo vecchio et sono in noi la fragarantia et il decore della celeste gratia." On Bettini's Savonarolanism, see Polizzotto, *Elect Nation,* 410.

82. Mazzinghi, *Sermoni,* 8v: "io sono sotoposto alla tua potentia del diavolo et non sapeva il tuo santissimo nome; alor legava le nube no lasciando pinguere, et gli arbori non davano illoro fructo, et andava per le gregge delle pecore et incontinente, si dissertavano i pesci del mare legava che non potevano andare per illoro sentiere et tucto per mia lectitia. Ma ora signor mio, ò cognosciuto il tuo sancto nome et sono pentito della multitudine della mia peccati et nella gratia tua voglio sempre permanere et tue comandmenti sempre voglio ubidire orando adimandando grate che tu me conceda il tuo sancitissimo amore el quale è sempiterno bene; et per la tua misericordia ti prego che tu rompa che garni delle nube siche discenda la piova sopra la terra, gli arbori dieno illoro fructo, et le femine pasturischono sansa alcuna macula et succiano l fanculli el lacte delle lore madre."

83. For quattrocento examples, see Trexler, *Public Life,* 347–354.

84. Marucelli, *Cronaca,* 32: "Addì 24 di gennaio 1543 occorse a ore diciasette incirca un grandissimo eclessi nel sole, il qual durò un'ora e mezzo del che molti furono che, per tale ecipse, stettero ammirati perché fu di tal sorte che quasi non si scorgeva un huomo da l'altro e io in verità fui uno di

quelli, per non sapere et non pensare che cosa fussi questa così spaventosa, ma solo poi pensavo che altro non fussi che segni grandi mandati dal grande Iddio acciò che noi tutti scellerati ci riducessimo a nuova vita perché assai cose si vedeva et si veggono in simile età, da fare molti maggiore segni apparire nel cielo che questi, massime la sfacciata et inutile Italia, et tutto con ordine del magno Dio, acciò che siamo apparecchiati quando verrà il flagello."

85. Benvenuto Cellini, *The Autobiography of Benvenuto Cellini,* trans. John Addington Symonds (Garden City, N.Y.: Garden City, 1927), 162.

86. Ibid., 18.

87. Ibid., 29.

88. Ibid., 315.

89. Giuliano dei Ricci, *Cronaca, 1532–1606* (Naples: Riccardo Ricciardi Editore, 1972), 20: "Et sè cognosciuto dalli effetti che Nostro Signore Dio non manca mai di soccorrere alli suoi quando più sono abbandonati di ogni aiuto humano, et quando più le cose sono desperate all'hora vi mette la sua sanctissima mano; di che ne fa fede lo Spirito Santo per bocca del propheta David."

90. Anonymous, "Diario fiorentino di anonimo delle cose occorse l'anno 1537," *Archivio Storico Italiano* 106 (1958), 557: "augurio dei grandissime cose."

91. Bernardo Segni, *Storie fiorentine* (Augusta: D. R. Mertz e G. J. Majer, 1723), 271: "stimavano i popoli che tanti segni disusati e rari non fussono venuti a caso, e che e' dovessono significar qualche gran rovina."

92. Agostino Lapini, *Diario fiorentino di Agostino Lapini dal 252 al 1596* (Florence: Sansoni, 1900), 103: "venneno grandissimi terremoti qui in Firenze; ma maggiormente a Scarperia che in altro luogo, e per tutto il Mugello; dove rovinorno assai case, et vi morirno di molta gente. Et in questo tempo cominciorno le compagnie de' contadini, che sono vicine a Firenze, a venire ogni anno a visitare pricissionalmente La Nunziata, e seguitano et seguiteranno per memoria di detti tremoti, per placare l'ira di Dio."

93. Cecilia Hewlett, *Rural Communities in Renaissance Tuscany: Religious Identities and Local Loyalties* (Turnhout: Brepols, 2008), 163–164.

94. Cited in Eisenblichler, *Boys of the Archangel,* 176–177.

95. Ricci, *Cronaca,* 31: "Piaccia à Dio che habbino havuto fine qui e non guardi a' peccati nostri degni di maggior gastigo."

96. Martelli, *Cento sonnetti,* 21: "Quando'l Sol devea piu di nebbie folte / Esser condenso, et l'aer di ogni intorno / Piogge versar come nel Capricorno / Al' breve di suol fare spesse et molte / Per miracol del Ciel fur via disciolte / Le negre humide nubi et s'allargorno / Dalla fronte solar che più bel giorno / Non apre al'hor che al giel le forz' ha tolte / Ch'apperse'l di Signor' che fusti eletto / Al'honorato Seggio, e Tal fien sempre / in memoria, dei secol'

che verrano / Per mostrar sol che al humane tempre / Nostre soggiunse anco il voler perfetto / Di quel che muove il Cieli."

97. Da Trivigi, *Canzone,* 8: "Quel divin Lume, che'l suo raggio porge / Acciò, che luce in Ciel, ciò, che qui splende / Occhio vago di lui, che'l tutto affrena / Che fia qual'è, qual fu, et move, e'ntende / Ogni voce, ogni moto, ch'ode, et scorge / Per te la fronte sua liete, et serena / Ha di splendor più, ch'anzi ingombra, et piena / tal, che pallustre huomor, o nube oscura / Più non la copre, o tenebroso velo."

98. Minor and Mitchell, *Renaissance Entertainment,* 196.

99. Domenico Mellini, *Raccolto delle feste fatte in Fiorenza dalli Illustrissimi et Eccellentissimi Nostri Signori e padroni il Sigore Duca, et Sigore Principe di Fiorenza, et di Siena, nella venuta del Serenissimo Arciduca Carlo d'Austria per honorarne la presenza di sua Altezza* (Florence: Giunti, 1569), 4v.

100. Symeoni, *Le III parte,* 4r: "di serpi velenose, et Lappe / Occuperan (la Dio mercede) i luoghi / Fior, frondi, herbe, ombre, antri, onde, aure soavi. / Hor si ch' in vece di brinate et gielo / Piover vedrassi una si grata manna / Sul terren Tosco, che faranno à gara / Di chi ne sparger à piu larga copia / Cerer, o Bacco, Pan, Pomona, o, Pale."

101. Girolamo Baccelli, "Canzone," in *Rime diverse sopra la morte del Serenissimo granduca di toscana* (BNCF, Magliabecchiana XXVII c. 104), 75v: "Apparia d'ogn'intorno il ciel sereno, Quando in un tratto aspra, e ventosa pioggia / In disusata foggia / Fe crescer l'onde, e'l fiume irato, e pieno / la bell'opra disperse, io venni meno."

102. Michel Capri, "Canzone," in *Rime diverse sopra la morte del Serenissimo Granduca di toscana* (BNCF, Magliabecchiana XXVII c. 104), 87r: "ben tel mostraro ancor l'oscure, et adre / Stelle, e le nubi, ch'oscuraro il Sole . . . Che del morto Gran Cosmo il Ciel si duole."

103. Cosimo Aldana, "Canzone," in *Rime Diverse sopra la morte del Serenissimo Granduca di toscana* (BNCF, Magliabecchiana XXVII c. 104), 96r–97r: "Piena d'un gran dolor l'alma Natura / In van si duol, si affligge, e si lamenta / Contro del ciel, di morte e di Fortuna . . . ; Ascondi Apollo, i tuo bei raggi ardenti; Vestiti, o ciel di tenebroso horrore."

104. See also del Vezzo, "Canzone," 108r, and Cosimo Gacci, "Canzone," in *Rime diverse sopra la morte del Serenissimo Granduca di Toscana* (BNCF, Magliabecchiana XXVII c. 104), 102v.

105. Giurgi, *Oratione,* 5r–5v. When he was in his villa practicing agriculture "senti in un' subbito, per volere di Dio che già cominciava ad operarsi per la salute nostra, quasi novello Numa chiamarsi a tanto Imperio, anzi (per meglio dire, quasi nuovo David esservi mandato da Dio, come prima li havevano augurato le piante de le sue possessioni che in cosi fredda stagione contra il corso di natura miracolosamente fiorirono, per divina providenza come si puo credere che per questo mezzo accennava al Gran Cosmo

che nel fiorire de la sua piu verde eta de voleva porlo in mezzo di questa provincia quasi lucente specchio, nel quale risguardando ciascuno, potesse regolarsi al bene operare." Matasilani also recorded the story about Cosimo's garden, Matasilani, *La felicità,* 28.

106. See Francis Oakley, *Politics and Eternity: Studies in the History of Medieval and Early Modern Political Thought* (Leiden: Brill, 1999), 54.

107. Cox-Rearick, *Dynasty and Destiny,* 255.

108. Ibid., 161.

109. For a discussion of this, see Thomas, *Religion and the Decline of Magic,* 136.

110. See Vieri, *Breve compendio,* 100r: "se bene dal Cielo si può predire, quello, à che l'huomo è inclinato, come da cagione remota, concorrono poi tante cagioni più prossime, che possono rendere fallace, quel giudizio, e massimamente intorno nostro, e dalla nostra volontà, che sono potenze libere."

111. ASFi, Med. 210c. 20r (February 13, 1559).

112. See Antoninus, *Opera,* 10r; Girolamo Savonarola, *Opera singolare del contra l'astrologia divinatrice* (Venice, 1536); and Giovanni Pico della Mirandola, *Disputationes Adversus Astrologiam Divinatricem,* 2 vols., ed. Eugenio Garin (Florence: Vallecchi Editore, 1946 and 1952).

113. Thomas Aquinas, *Summa Theologica,* 2–2, q. 95, art. 5.

114. Savonarola, *Opera,* 26.

115. Baldini, *Discorso,* 29: "L'animo dell'huomo adunque è contenuto da il Fato, percioche egli è congiunto col corpo del quale il Fato è signore, si come di tutti gli altri corpi." Even Savonarola, who took the strict anti-Augustinian line against prophetic astrology, nevertheless granted some approval to the idea that the stars influence life. Savonarola, *Prediche,* 1r–2r. Pico went a step further than Aquinas by rejecting even the idea that the stars influence the body. Pico, *Disputationes Adversus Astrologiam Divinatricem,* 4.11.

116. Marsilio Ficino, *Opera Omnia* (Basel: Henricpetrina, 1576), 569.

117. Galluzzi, *Istoria,* 169.

118. Raffaella Castagnola, "Un oroscopo per Cosimo I," *Rinascimento* 29 (1989), 125–189.

119. Cited in Trinkaus, *In Our Image,* 477.

120. Salutati, *De Fato,* 52: "si Deum vel Dei providentiam fati nomine nuncupemus . . . nullum inconveniens sit fato nostras subicere voluntates, non sic quod libertate priventur (nam tunc omnino essent), sed ut suorum actuum, quos 'Deus operator in nobis,' libere et ab omni compulsionis necessitate secure causa sint et agenti Deo libere cooperentur, a quibus solis actus, quorum coefficientis cause sunt, voluntaris appelamus."

121. Savonarola, *Triompho,* 15r–15v: "Le cose irrationabili, sono mosse da Dio, al fin loro per instinto naturale, piu tosto condutte et menate da altri, che da medesime governate. Ma l'huomo che ha libero arbitrio, puo haver

di se medesimo providentia, et pero è cosi mosso da Dio al suo fine, che anchora muove se medesimo operando insieme con Dio. Adunque appartiene à l'huomo, cercar con ogni studio, e diligentia il suo ultimo fine, alqual è stato ordinato dalla divina providentia e I debiti mezzi da pervenir à quello . . . la divina providentia, mediante le virtu morali, move tutti gli huomini, iquali per haver il libero arbitrio, sempre move liberamente. Et pero se saranno consentienti alla motione della divina providentia, senza dubbio per I debiti mezzi perverrano al lor desiderato fine."

122. Baldini, *Discorso*, 39: "tutti questi effetti sian condotti al fine loro dalla propria natura de gli huomini in quanto elle è dritta ma non forzata dalla divina provedenza."

123. When claims were made that Cosimo was to be like a new Augustus, this was not to emphasize the event's ineluctability but to emphasize that "fate," that is, God acting through nature, had given Cosimo the natural virtues necessary to rule. Consider, for instance, the appeal that Giurgi made to Cosimo's Capricorn ascendant: "One can see clearly the prudence of this unconquered prince, since he has judged that it is very good to favor this ascendant that he had common with Augustus (Capricorn), which made him, by the will of God, fortunate and pacific, since he would otherwise have been by his nature most bellicose." Giurgi, *Oratione*, 6r: "si può chiaramente vedere che se la prudenza di questo invitto principe, non havesse giudicato che è sommamente bene di favorire quello ascendente che egli hà comune con Augusto, il quale lo fa per volere di Dio fortunato et pacifico, egli sarebbe stato per natura bellicosissimo."

124. This was a rather distinct debate from the one more commonly associated with the Reformation: that is the debate on faith and works.

125. Claudia Bareggi, "Giunti, Doni, Torrentino; tre tipografie fiorentine fra Repubblica e Principato," *Nuova Rivista Storica* 58 (1974), 322.

126. Polito, *Trattato*, 42–50; and Lapis, *Epistola*, 26v–27r.

127. *Canons and Decrees of the Council of Trent*, trans. Rev. H. J. Schroeder, O.P. (Rockford, Ill.: Tan Books, 1978), 31–32.

128. Italians tended to use the word "Luterani" as a pejorative for all Protestant reformers.

129. Davidico, *Anatomia*, 78r: "benche Dio faccia il tutto in ogni cosa, niente di manco non esclude, perho le cause seconde, anzi come si vede per esperientia, per le seconde cause ordinariamente fa tutte le cose."

130. Lapis, *Epistola*, 24v–27v: "ille qui fecit te sine te non tamen salvabit te. Dei opus est vocare, hominum vero credere vel non creder quod in voluntate liberi arbitrij ponere est nec minus in evangelio dicitur . . . iure dicendum liber arbitrium etiam in bonis operibus aliquid operari."

131. See Musso, *I tre libri:* "Iddio muove ogni cosa soavemente, secondo le nature loro. L'huomo è animal rationale, e di libero arbitrio: però è mosso liberamente. Bisogna, che egli, quando è mosso, da se si muova. Non è un

tronco, ne è un sasso: è huomo. Operi da huomo, consenta, ò dissenta. Se dissente, non riceverà mai la gratia: perche Iddio non isforza gli huomini. Se consente, gia n'è fatto degno da Dio, et la riceve."

132. Visdomini, *Tutte le prediche*, 35v–36r: "Operando Iddio come causa universale qua giù ciò che si fa, quantunque dal lato suo non faccia alcuna cosa necessariamente, come quello che tutto opera colla santissima, potentissima, et liberalissima sua voluntà, per rispetto però di molte cause seconde concorrenti secondo la loro natura che non è vertibile, et (come dice l'Angelico dottore Tomaso) modificando il generale influsso che dall prima causa deriva, si può dire che molti effeti necessariamente emergono, come il calor del fuoco, il corso de'fiumi, il lume del sole, la propagation de gli animali, la vita delle piante; Ma quanto opera Iddio nell'huomo, per esser l'una, et l'altra causa libera, che (come dissi) non è voluntà senza libertà, l'effetto segue senza alcuna sorte di necessità pienamente libero, et contingente; non volendo Iddio a modo alcuno romper l'ordine posto dalla sua creatione in le sue creature, per loquale debbe (con debito della sua benignità, quale chiamano i Teologi debito di promessa) conservar l'huomo libero, et far che liberamente operi, et liberamente, giungi al suo fine."

133. Ibid., 44v: "piace a Dio, et piace anche a loro."

134. See ASFi, Med. 37c. 154r (November 2, 1555).

135. Paolo Giovio, *Lettere volgari di Monsignore Paolo Giovio da Como vescovo di Nocera*, ed. Lodovico Domenichi (Venice: Giovan Battista et Marchion Sessa, 1560), 32–33: "E gran sengo, e piu che chiaro e manifesto, che l'animo di Vostro Eccelletissimo come dritto e giusto nelle publiche e private attioni del temperato governo, e religiosa vita è molto caro e acccepto a Nostro Signore Iddio poi che havendo fatto prova della risoluta costanza e patienza sua col levarle al paradiso l'agno immaculato assai tosto, ha voluto ristorarla e espiarle ogni reliquia del dolor della carne col dono de si bel fanciullo nato senza molestia della felicissima Signoria."

136. For Nerli's connection to the Medici see Rudolf von Albertini, *Firenze dalla repubblica al principato: storia e coscienza politica* (Turin: Einaudi, 1970), 320, and Michele Lupo Gentili, *Studi sulla storiografia Fiorentina alla corte di Cosimo I de' Medici* (Pisa: Nistri, 1905), 65. He was, in fact, Cosimo's uncle. Filippo Nerli, *Comentarij de' fatti civili occorsi dentro la città di Firenze dall'Anno MCCXV al MDXXXVII* (Augusta: David Raimondo Mertz, 1728), 298.

137. On the dangers of traveling in Italy, see Jean Delumeau, *Vie economique et sociale de Rome dans la second moitie du XVI siecle* (Paris: E. de Boccard, 1957–59), 1–115.

138. ASFi, Med. 2c. 34r (September 24, 1537): "a dio è piaciutore condurvi salvi in Nizza."

139. ASFi, Med. 10c. 128r–128v (May 18, 1547): "a dio piace dar buona ventura, poi che s'intende il camino esser in Germania pericoloso molto."

140. David Gentilcore, *Healers and Healing in Early Modern Italy* (Manchester: Manchester University Press, 1998) 1–13.

141. ASFi, Med. 1170c. 162 (February 19, 1543): "gratia di Dio speriamo per la prudenza de medici."

142. ASFi, Med. 37c. 145r (undated, 1555): "che a dio Nostro Signore piaciuto far seguir."

143. ASFi, Med. 191c. 47r (May 13, 1549): "havendo a usare la dote mi ha pregato che io il raccomandi alla Signore Vostro reverendo et illustrissima del quale officio, non mi parendo potere manchare, per stare ne servitii mia. Priego Vostro Signore reverendo che poi che è stata voluta di Dio che si casi con la detta Damigella, le piaccia favorirlo che consequisca la dote che mi dice essere in mano del sopradetta Marchessa."

144. ASFi, Med. 37c. 107 (May 26, 1555): "Con tutto che nella parte Imperiali sien state quelli gran divisioni et controversie che per letteri vostri et d'altri habbiamo inteso et che queste si possa dire che habbino causato la elettione del Cardinale di Napoli al Pontificato, noi la reconosciamo nondimeno da la prima causa che è Nostro Signore Dio et speriamo di lui quelle sante opere a benefitio universale de Christani conservatione dela Santa Chiesa et exaltatione dela Religione et fede nostra che la vita et le sante opere sue hanno promesso."

145. Reinhard Bendix, *Kings or People: Power and the Mandate to Rule* (Berkeley: Univeristy of California Press, 1978), 3–18.

146. John Neville Figgis, *Divine Right* (Cambridge: Cambridge University Press, 1922), 5–6.

147. I am following here Oakley's analysis of Ullman.

148. On this point, Koenigsberger writes: "In contrast to the emperors, kings, and princes of early modern Europe, no republican regime claimed to be dei gratia, instituted and justified by the will of God." Helmut Koenigsberger, "Republicanism, Monarchism, and Liberty," in *Royal and Republican Sovereignty in Early Modern Europe: Essays in memory of Ragnhild Hatton* (Cambridge: Cambridge University Press, 1997), 44. In this, he was surely missing Savonarola's Florentine republic. See also Mack Holt, *The French Wars of Religion: 1562–1629* (Cambridge: Cambridge University Press, 1995), 78–79.

149. van Veen, *Cosimo*, 5.

150. See Oakley, *Politics and Eternity,* 54. Glenn Burgess has attempted to de-link absolutism and divine right in the context of English monarchy. Glenn Burgess, "The Divine Right of Kings Reconsidered," *English Historical Review* 108 (1992), 837–861.

151. Luca Mannori, "Il pensiero storico e giuridico-politico," in *Storia della civiltà Toscana: Il principato mediceo,* vol. 3, ed. Elena Fasano Guarini (Florence: La Tipografica Varese, 2005), 324–327. Such an appeal to the popular will would last long into the ducal period.

152. See Umberto Pirotti, *Benedetto Varchi e la cultura del suo tempo* (Florence: Olschki, 1971): 6–13.
153. Cantagalli, *Cosimo,* 94.
154. Cited in Pirotti, *Benedetto Varchi,* 15: "Mandovi parte di quel che voi avete a avere da me, e appuntatemi debitore del restante."
155. Varchi, *Storia fiorentina,* 200.
156. The voice of the people is the voice of God.
157. Ferrari, *Apologia,* 29v–30r: "qui suae primae institutionis rectitudine et iustitia imperandi aliis tantumdem Principibus, praestaret hic sermo verus est, et omni acceptatione dignus, quem probat authoritate legis Christi nostri dicentis furem et latronem esse eum, qui non intrat per ostium in (olile?) ovium, introeuntem vero per ostium, verum forem Pastorem, sed ingressus per ostium formans Pastorem non est aliud quem justa dei vocatio Principum ad principatus per illos, qui ius vocandi ad illos habent."
158. Ibid., 30v.
159. Rosello, *Il ritratto,* 10–11: "La vera elettione è quella, che si fa da gli animi non violentati, non corrotti, ma liberi, come in vero si vede essere avvenuto nel Duca Cosimo . . . e se vogliamo essaminare questa elettione da I notabili, e virtuosi successi di quella, vederemo che furono da piu alta potentia governati gli animi di coloro che fecero cosi santa elettione."
160. Carmen Menchini, "I panegirici di Cosimo de'Medici: tra retorica e storia," in *Nunc alia tempora, alii mores: storici e storia in età postridentina. Atti del Convengo internazionale Torino, 24–27 settembre 2003* (Florence: Olschki, 2005), 346.
161. Ammirato, *Oratione,* 41r: "Liberamente fatta . . . quasi divina providentia approvata."
162. Daniela Lamberini, *Il principe difeso: Vita e opere di Bernardo Puccini* (Florence: Giuntina, 1990), 409: "Cosimo, la quale fu dato al mondo da Dio . . . ponendo in cuore a quei cittadini che tenevano in mano la somma autorità della repubblica di eleggere lui."
163. Adriani,"Orazione Funebre," 33: "quasi divinamente corse loro agli occhi il lume e la chiarezza di questo nobile giovenetto della istessa famiglia de' Medici, il qual solo pareva che potesse sanare le piaghe della sua patria." Emphasis mine. Adriani is also using the traditional wordplay on the Medici name, which means physicians as well.
164. Davanzati, *Orazione fatta Dal Bernardo Davanzati alla morte di Cosimo I* (BNCF, Magliabecchiana XXVII c. 52), 5v: "tanto stupendo successo non si dee riconoscere ne da gli iddij de Greci ne dalla fortuna Romana, ma dal benigno volere del grande Iddio benedetto, che lui' ne fece degno, o vero dal suo giudicio non errante, che scelse forse questo huomo piacciuto al suo cuore, et a si grande fortuna l'alzò, per mirabile modi, accioche egli con mirabil virtù, due popoli governasse."

165. Ibid., 4r–4v: "cosi naturalmente ancora si faceano i re di quegli eroici tempi, quando i popoli eleggeano spontaneamente, colui che gli altri avanzasse di meriti, o di virtù sue."

166. Ibid., 3v: "nel diciottesimo anno essendo venuta (come volle colui, che di tutte le cose divine et umane è ottimo dispositore) la morte del Duca Alessandro, tutti gli occhi si voltarano al Signore Cosimo, e subito egli fu dal Senato fatto capo, e poi duca della republica fiorentina."

167. Giovambatista Capponi, *Spechietto della inclita città di firenze et suo dominio* (BL, Pluteus LXII c. 24.), 1v: "Quando si ritrovava uno che in tal consideratione (the ability to live by natural laws) excedassi dicevono quelli esser dii, ne mancho lo credevono quando conosciuto havessino uno più che l'altro havessi ritrovato altra cosa abenificio dalla humana natura."

168. Ibid., 2v: "tanto che doppo longo tempo vengono aun tale individuo, che dicevono quelllo esser uno dio et più che li altri meritare di esser exaltati, et come capo sopra li altri quello preponevono, quando per lor medemi conoscevono la unita et monarchia esser cosa unica et divina."

169. Rosello, *Il ritratto*, 26v–27r: "quando se ne truova alcuno tanto compiutamente fornito [with virtues] che sono rari discesi, che tal huomo è nato ad esser Prencipe. Sappiamo troppo bene, che que'primi Prencipi furono eletti solamente per fame di virtù, poi che i popoli senza aspettare alcuno particolar premio, ò pena, eleggevano ciascuno quello, che reputave piu atto à mantenere la pace commune. Et nel vecchio testamento habbiamo, che il popolo di Dio non confidandosi di saper per se stesso far' elettione di Prencipe giusto, et saggio, lo chiedeva à Dio."

170. Varchi, *Storia Fiorentina*, 205–206.

171. Betti, *Orazione*, unpaginated: "poteva a ragione giudicarlo nato, non à privatamente vivere, ma à regnare, et reggere ampissimi popoli et stati. Come si conobbe, essendo egli molto giovanetto, per divino consiglio, eletto, et assunto unitamente da suoi cittadini, dopo la acerba morto del Duca Alessandro, al governo di questo stato."

172. Vieri, *Orazione*, 4v: "questo huomo nato per governare la più fiorita parte d'Italia tanti anni così bene."

173. Ibid., 2r–4v: "fatto Duca, Capo, Signore della Republica Fiorentina, da suoi Cittadini stessi."

174. Malaspina, *Orazione*, 199v: "volere divino, et per merito, et prudenza loro, et per la benivolenza de'sudditi, et per lo forte, et potere stato."

175. See Michael Enright, *Iona, Tara, and Soissons: The Origin of the Royal Annointing Ritual* (Berlin: de Gruyter, 1985).

3. Rescuing Virtue from Machiavelli

1. Lapini, *Diario*, 109.

2. Goro Stendardi, *Antiche famiglie patrizie di Firenze in Malta e in Santo Stefano* (Florence: Zannoni Editore, 1995), 246.

3. See *ASFi, Manoscritti* 166c. 14v.

4. Gaetano, *La stirpe de' Medici di Cafaggiolo: Saggio di ricerche sulla trans-missione ereditaria dei caratteri biologici,* vol. 2. (Florence: Nardini, 1986), 30–31.

5. Especially Booth, *Cosimo,* 2.

6. Cantagalli, *Cosimo,* 18; van Veen, *Cosimo,* 165–166; Pieraccini, *La stirpe,* 13–14; Michele Lupo Gentile, *La politica di Paolo III nelle sue relazioni colla corte Medicea* (Sarzana: Lunense, 1906), iv.

7. See Menchini, "I panegirici," 352.

8. For a more generally European discussion, see Robert Bireley, *The Counter-Reformation Prince: Anti-Machiavellianism or Catholic Statecraft in Early Modern Europe* (Chapel Hill: University of North Carolina Press, 1990).

9. For the English reception of Machiavelli see Felix Raab, *The English Face of Machiavelli: A Changing Interpretation 1500–1700* (London: Routledge and Kegan Paul, 1964); for the French, see Albert Cherel, *La pensée de Machiavel en France* (Paris: L'artisan du Livre, 1935). On the reluctance to use Machiavelli's name, see Sydney Anglo, *Machiavelli: The First Century, Studies in Enthusiasm, Hostility and Irrelevance* (Oxford: Oxford University Press, 2005), 178–179.

10. See Cochrane, *Florence,* 124.

11. Giovambattista Busini, *Lettere di Giovambattista Busini a Benedetto Varchi sopra l'assedio di Firenze* (Florence: Gaetano Milanesi, 1861), 84.

12. Cited in Anglo, *Machiavelli,* 166–167.

13. Varchi, *Storia fiorentina,* 200: "empia veramente e da dover essere non solo biasimate ma spenta, come cercò di fare egli se stesso dopo il rivolgimento dello stato, non essendo ancora stampato."

14. Ibid., 201.

15. As demonstrated by Sydney Anglo, Rosello's tract was almost completely plagariazed from Agostino Nifo, who was himself deeply concerned with Machiavelli's problems and questions. Anglo, *Machiavelli,* 42–85.

16. Ibid., 83.

17. Rosello, *Il ritratto,* 16: "Se tutto fussero buoni, ogniuno terrebbe cari i beneficij hauuti dal Prencipe, e così à lui meglio riusirebbe l'esser amato, che temuto. Ma poi che veggiamo chiaramente esserci piu huomini cattivi, che buoni, piu ingrati, che riconoscenti de'beneficij, piu leggieri, che stabili, piu simulatori, che veraci, piu infideli, che fedeli, e che la maggior parte ama piu tosto l'utile proprio, che quello del Prencipe, promettando largamente, et attenendo nulla, ò poco, sembra che il timore de'popoli giovi piu al Prencipe, che l'amore."

18. Bryce, *Cosimo Bartoli,* 282.

19. Cochrane, *Florence,* 123–124.

20. Brian Richardson, "*The Prince* and Its Early Italian Readers," in *Niccolò Machiavelli's "The Prince": New Interdisciplinary Essays,* ed. Martin Coyle (Manchester: Manchester University Press, 1996), 33–35.

21. Francesco Inghirami, *Storia Toscana,* vol. 12 (Fiesole: Poligrafia Fiesolana, 1843), 165.

22. Bryce, *Cosimo Bartoli,* 303.

23. Richardson, *"The Prince,"* 25.

24. For a discussion of the explicitly political nature of preaching on virtues and vices in fifteenth-century Florence, see Howard, *Beyond the Written Word,* 170–174. In the most public instance, the cardinal and theological virtues were translated onto the less famous south doors of the baptistery by Andrea Pisano in 1330. Gloria Fossi, *Arte a Firenze* (Florence: Giunti, 2006), 52.

25. See Mellini, *Raccolto.*

26. Quentin Skinner, *The Foundations of Modern Political Thought,* vol. 1 (Cambridge: Cambridge Unviersity Press, 1978), 126.

27. Antoninus had prefaced his discourse on them with the admission that they had been treated of "not just (by) the Holy Doctors, but also the philosophers, rhetoricians, and poets." Antoninus, *Opera,* 65: "Della quale non solamente parlono gli dottori santi, ma anchora li philosophi, rethorici, et poeti."

28. Dolciati, *Prediche diversi,* 34r: "moral virtues make man perfect in human civility." This was very much a Savonarolan ideal; see Polizzotto, *Children of the Promise,* 6.

29. Bettini, *Preparazione,* 101v. He wrote that the life of man should aim to "rafernarli da gli imperi de desiderij bestiali et altri disordinate passioni. Cominciarono a dimostra la via per la qual noi sia passati delle virtudí non conoscendo pero a qual piu alto fine è caminassero che a in viver civile et pacifico in questo mondo."

30. Howard, *Beyond the Written Word,* 197–201. See also Cesare Vasoli, "Movimenti religiosi e crisi politiche dalla Signoria al Principato," in *Idee, istituzioni, scienza, ed arti nella Firenze dei Medici,* ed. Cesare Vasoli (Florence: Giunti Martello, 1980), 47.

31. Thus, Cosimo's promotion of his own natural virtue was not, as one recent historian has claimed, a significant shift away from the model of "divine governance" and toward a traditional republican stance of *buon governo,* van Veen, *Cosimo,* 54. Rather, it was an attempt to reconcile the two: that is, to prove that divine governance was good governance.

32. Ginus, *Pro travalliatorum,* 34v: "Propterea nimirum; quod quemadmodum divinitus dominatum dari hominibus certo sciunt; sic te (quantam homini licet) Dei quam simillimum esse conspiciunt. Ut summa cura, summa sapientia, summa iustitia, summa pietate, orbem ille universum administrat; sic vigilitantissimum, sapientissimum, iustissimum et maxima pietate insignem tui te omnes agnoscunt et experiantur."

33. See for instance Musso, *I tre libri,* 7: "Iddio . . . non solo ha, ma è somma, e perfetta pace."

34. The dissenting voices here are Sebastian de Grazia and Maurizio Viroli. See Sebastiano de Grazia, *Machiavelli in Hell* (Princeton: Princeton University Press, 1989), and Maurizio Viroli *Machiavelli's God,* trans. Anthony Shugaar (Princeton: Princeton University Press, 2010).

35. Skinner, *Foundations,* 138.

36. Felix Gilbert, *Machiavelli and Guicciardini: Politics and History in Sixteenth Century Florence* (Princeton: Princeton University Press, 1965), 179. On this question, see also Harvey Mansfield, *Machiavelli's Virtue* (Chicago: University of Chicago Press, 1966); Paul Rahe, introduction to *Machiavelli's Liberal Republican Legacy,* ed. Rahe (Cambridge: Cambridge University Press, 2006), xxii; and Shelley Burtt, *Virtue Transformed: Political Argument in England, 1688–1740* (Cambridge: Cambridge University Press, 1992), 66.

37. Niccolò Machiavelli, *Il Principe,* ed. Giorgio Inglese (Turin: Einaudi, 1995), 102–104.

38. Ibid., 103: "uno uomo che voglia fare in tutte le parte professione di buono, conviene' che ruini in fra tanti che non sono buoni. Onde è necessario, volendosi uno principe mantenere, imparare a potere essere non buono."

39. Ibid., 118: "hassi a intendere questo, che uno principe e massime uno principe nuovo, non può osservare tutte quelle cose per le quali gli uomini sono tenuti buoni, sendo spesso necessitato, per mantenere lo stato, operare contro alla fede, contro alla carità, contro alla umanità, contro alla religione . . . non partirsi dal bene, potendo, ma sapere entrare nel male, necessitato."

40. Ibid., 108–115. See also Niccolò Machiavelli, *Discorsi di Nicolò Machiavelli, sopra la prima deca di Tito Livio,* ed. Giorgio Inglese (Milan: Rizzoli, 1996), 112–113.

41. Machiavelli, *Il Principe,* 118.

42. Machiavelli, *Discorsi,* 528.

43. Machiavelli, *Il Principe,* 109: "Debbe pertanto uno principe non si curare della infamia del crudele per tenere e' sudditi sua uniti e in fede."

44. Savonarola, *Trattato,* 6.

45. Cantini, *Legislazione,* vol. 1, 313: "Advertendo l'Illustrissimo, et Eccellentissimo Signor Duca di Firenze, qualmente gli Huomini de moderni tempi si astengono dal male operare pel timore, che gl'hanno delle pene, che per alcuna virtù, o altro rispetto che gli muova."

46. ASFi, Med. 183c. 289r–292v (undated, 1539).

47. Augustine, *City of God,* 88–89.

48. Capponi, *Spechietto,* 4r: "el modo di conservare la humana et politica conversatione sanza la quale tutte la monarchia et le republiche, regni imperii non civile conversatione ma veri latrocini certamente sarebbono."

49. See Richelson, *Studies in the Personal Imagery,* 47; and Pietrosanti, *Sacralità medicee,* 86.

50. ASFi, Med. 182c. iv (January 15, 1537) and ASFi, Med. 182c. 59r–59v (June 15, 1537): "sopra ogni altra cosa desiderate et venerato atteso esser il principale fundamento de ogni summo bene et tanto piu accetta à nostro signore Idio."

51. Fedeli, *Relazioni,* 137–140.

52. See Gualandi, *De Optimo,* 52.

53. ASFi, Med. 24c. 97 (December 27, 1555): "anzi sendo io risolutissimo che quando mio figlio non tenessi la vita che conviene a buon prete non solo di lascialo seguitare in tal profession ma del tutto rimuoverlo."

54. The claim made by Cantagalli that the imprisonment of Bandini was a Machiavellian move used to punish the unfortunate ambassador for attempting to ransom the life of Filippo Strozzi years earlier does not fit Cosimo's own stated sentiments, nor would it have followed the advice of Machiavelli, who cautioned princes not to wait on administering justice but have all the bloody business done at once.

55. Fedeli, *Relazione,* 140.

56. Most modern treatments have made this out to be a Machiavellian move par excellence; a salve to Pius V in order to get crowned grand duke. However, this assumes that Carnesecchi's guilt or innocence was all the same to a religiously tolerant Cosimo. However, the idea that Cosimo was religiously tolerant is rather anachronistic, and Carnesecchi was undoubtedly guilty of heresy. Thus, the obvious and often overlooked explanation for Cosimo's deliverance of Carnesecchi was that he simply came to believe that Carnesecchi was guilty. Indeed, in 1566, when Carnesecchi was finally found guilty, inquisitors had found the proverbial smoking gun they had lacked before, indisputable proof of Carnesecchi's guilt culled from the personal letters of the recently deceased Giulia Gonzaga. See Camilla Russell, *Giulia Gonzaga and the Religious Controversies of Sixteenth-Century Italy* (Turnhout: Brepols, 2006), 202–203.

57. Cited in Anzilotti, *La costituzione,* 126: "Ciò ci dà causa prima a pensar che voi stimate poco l'onor nostro, che consiste in far giustizia egualmente; e inoltre gran carico a voi, per doversi dir da ognuno che per essere essa causa con il nostro maiordomo voi non la spediate, anzi ci andiate con respetto per fare giustizia a chi l'ha. . . . E ricordatevi termina in causa, che tocchino à nostri servitori spedirle di qui innanzi con più prestezza . . . facendo giustizia a chi l'ha, senza respetto."

58. Gualandi, *De Optimo,* 53: "sic iste iustissimis aeterni Dei legibus conformari studeat."

59. Ibid.: "omnium legum est inanis censura (augustino teste) nisi Divinae legis imaginem."

60. Malaspina, *Orazione,* 198r–198v: "Molto più avventurosi quelli che si reggono con buone, et dritte leggi, et alto si debbono con somme lodi levare gli Autori di esse; onde à gran ragione furono da gli antichi figliuoli degli

Dii appellati, percioche in cio l'huomo si rende più à Dio simigliante, il quale è d'ogni ordine, et d'ogni dirittura principio."

61. ASFi, Med. 10, 334r–335r (July 29, 1547): "Habbiamo risposto alli giorni passati assai largamente à M. Bernardo vostro Fratello, sopra li medesimi capi che si contengono anche nella lettera vostra de vi di Settembre. Però con questa vi diramo solamente; che così come non ci siamo mai lassati ne lasseremo vincere di cortesia et d'amorevolezza da quelli, che ci hanno fidelmente servito et obbedito: così ancora ci è parso che convenga alla dignità dell'ufficio nostro di procedere con giustizia contra li altri, che sprezzate le divine et humane leggi. Hanno cerco di offendere non solamente noi loro signore, ma ancora la patria et li congiunti suoi, come fece Alberto vostro fratello, alla persona del quale havendo iddio Nostro Signore in quello atto, che sceleramente commetteva, dato quella pena che meritava. Dimostrò ancora à noi quanto dovessimo con ragione fare contro alla sua memoria, quale essendo per ciò giustamente dannata nè vengono in consequentia applicati al nostro Fisco li beni et substantie sue."

62. *Galluzzi, Istoria*, 145–146. For Machiavelli's quip see Machiavelli, *Il Principe*, 111–112: "above all, the prince needs to keep his hands off his subject's goods because a man will sooner forget the death of his father than the loss of his patrimony." "Ma sopratutto astenersi da la roba di altri; perché li uomini sdimenticano piú presto la morte del padre che la perdita del patrimonio."

63. See especially Stacey, *Roman Monarchy*, 145–147.

64. As Cosimo remarked, the Duke of Piombino does no justice, and his people "live like beasts." Cosimo I, *Lettere*, 86.

65. Gualandi, *De Optimo*, 47. The quote from Cyprian reads: "Iustitia Regis pax est populorum, tutamen patriae, immunitas plebis, munimentum gentis, cura languorum, gaudium hominium, temperies aeris, serenitas maris, terrae foecunditas, solatium pauperum, haereditas filiorum, et sibimetipsis spes futurae beatitudinis."

66. Ammirato, *Oratione*, 48v: "il potere di giorno, et di notte liberamente andare per questo Dominio; il non trovare che ti dia noia, et che il tuo camino ti impedisca, e t'intralci, il poter goder de' tua beni, e del tuo havere senza temer del Soldato, del Cortigiano, del Giudice, et del Notaio, il non ti far bisogno, nonche con danari, et con favori, ma ne pure con le piacevoli apparenze d'honori, et di servitù di comprar la tua ragione, et il tuo diritto."

67. Brucioli, "Del Giusto Principe," 227.

68. Gualandi, *De Optimo*, 18: "Regnum a gente in gentem transfertur propter iniustitias et iniurias."

69. Bernardo Puccini, *Oratione nella funerabile pompa del Serenissimo Cosimo dei Medici Gran Duca di Thoscana di Bernardo Puccini, agli Illustrimi Signori honorati Gentilhuomini della corte.* (Magliabecchiana 27: 13),

4v: "elle havesse per compagna la Giustitia anzi per guida, et per signora, avenga che nulla gioverebbe che la prudenza vedesse le cagioni per le quali i regni et le signorie si rebbono ó caggiono, se la giustitia non le ritenesse ó scacciasse, accio ragionevolmente, giustamente, et legittimamente si viva."

70. Rosello, *Il ritratto,* 14v: "Se mi citaste sei cento esempij, non mi potreste persuadere, che la crudeltà fosse piu atta à conservare i regni, che la clementia e se vorrete discorrere per le historie, vi trovarete pochi, a' quali sia riuscito bene usare crudeltà, come avvenne à Cambise, et à Silla."

71. Stacey, *Roman* Monarchy, 60, 105, and 156

72. Brucioli, "Del Giusto Principe," 212–213: "E che pertanto anche questa sia sicura e giusta dominazione ne è chiaro e manifesto segno che da' loro popoli successivamente sono constituiti re e da quegli amati, e ancora perché volentieri a quegli si sottopongono i cittadini, né si possono, sanno o vogliono reggere altrimenti senza una tale dominazione, essendo giá assuefatti a obedire e a essere governati. E questi due solamente si possono con vero nome di principe chiamare, e tutte l'altre specii di dominazioni perpetue sono ingiuste tirannidi." For Brucioli's repeated and unsuccessful attempts to woo Cosimo's favor, see Giorgio Spini, *Tra Rinascimento e Riforma: Antonio Brucioli* (Florence: La Nuova Italia Editrice, 1940).

73. Rosello, *Il ritratto,* 19v: "Quando il Prencipe non ingiuria i soggetti, non rapisce i loro beni, et fa il tutto evidenti ragioni, coloro, che bramano di viver quietamente, l'amano di cuore; et gli scelerati non hanno di che dolersi, ma non può esser odiato, poi che non fa cosa alcuna, che lo possa render odioso, e tuttavia è temuto, poi che non perdona à delinquenti."

74. Gualandi, *De Optimo,* 105–106: "Nihil efficacius regnum tuetur, ac stabile tenet, nihil melius, nihil aptius ad veram civium benevolentia conciliandam, atque diutissimè retindendam, ispa clementia."

75. Bartoli, *Discorsi,* 321: "et questo gli riuscirà ogni volta che essi si risolveranno di volere essere piu amati che temuti, e che essi si ricorderanno di havere ad essere benigni piu che severi padri de loro popoli; perche dallo amore che ei porteranno a sudditi, nascerà il desiderio che eglin'haran di beneficarli, et dal desiderio la azione, della quale nascerà lo universale amor de popoli verso di loro, et il desiderio della salute, et felicita di quella."

76. Giovanbatista Cini, *Orazione recitata da Giovanbatista Cini nell'Accademia Fiorentina publicamente nel morte di Messer Francesco Campana* (BNCF, Magliabecchiana XXVII c. 2), 9r–9v: "dicendo che se e nimici col temerlo l'havevano in odio, che gl'amici amandolo spererebbono da lui ogni bene, ricordandogli spesso l'opinione, del'animo che haveva sopra questo Julio Cesare, il quale piu tosto volse procacciarsi grandezza, perdonando a color che l'havevevvano offeso, che perseguitandogli (come harebbe potuto) vendicarsi di tutte l'ingiurie."

77. Baldini, *Panegirico,* 5v: "Da questo cosi alta vertù adunque son conservati i regni, et le provincie, percio che giudicandosi per lei benignamente questo

gli non malignamente peccano, si viene a render gli animi de i soggeti divo-
tissimi verso i principi loro."

78. Bartoli, *Discorsi,* 321: "Et se bene di Pandolfo et de gli altri che furon presi
fu fatto quel che voleva il debito della iustizia; perdonò nondimeno Signore
Eccelentia et a beni di Pandolfo rilasciandoli a figliuoli, et alla roba di alcuni altri, con la sua solita clementia, gastigando piu tosto con clementia
che con rigidità, quegli che havevano errato."

79. Bentovoglienti, *Vita d'Augusto,* 1v: "esso quanto fu in maggior grandezza,
tanto piu fu temperato e benigno: cosi ella quanto é stata in maggior fortuna, tanto ha usato piu belli atti di clementia e di bontá."

80. Ibid., 9r: "è stato da rei temuto, e da buoni amato come giustissimo."

81. Davanzati, *Orazione:* "Lasciò La guardia di sua persona, e solo an-
dosi per la citta, come vero e legittimo Re, guardato dalla benivolenza de
suoi."

82. Rosello, *Il ritratto,* 15v: "ad ogni modo la clementia dee vincere la crudeltà,
altramente il Prencipe non si rassomiglierebbe à Dio, di qui egli è imagine
viva, poi che veggiamo quanta pietà usa Dio verso di noi peccatori, le cui
colpe ci rendono degni della morte eterna."

83. Gualandi, *De Optimo,* 105–106: "Fieri nequit clementem Principem, ab
omnibus non amari. Cum enim hanc induit, talem se civibus praebet, quales
(ut aiebat seneca) sibi Deos esse peroptat."

84. Baldini, *Panegirico,* 6v: "come dicono i Platonici, divenga per lei, simile a
Dio."

85. Bartoli, *Discorsi,* 291: "Ne doverebbe un Principe pensare ad altro che
ad ordinarsi et portarsi non altrimenti verso i suoi sudditi che in quella
maniera, nellaquale ci vorrebbe che Dio si portassi verso di lui, et se ei volessi che Dio fussi implacabile verso i suoi errori, fino all'ultima sua rovina,
di calo egli. Oltre a che non sarà ne fu mai Principe alcuno si grande che
possa essere del tutto sicuro dalla ira di Dio; et se Dio non punisce subito
gli errori, et i difetti de gli huomini, anzi è benigno et si lascia placare, non
è egli piu ragionevole che un Principe che non è altro che un huomo, per-
doni ancora egli a gli errori de gli huomini? et eserciti con animo posato,
benigno, et tranquillo lo Imperio, et la auttorità sua?"

86. For examples of this see Antonino, *Opera,* 3r–4r. Strozzi, *Trattato,* 36r.
Mazzinghi, *Sermoni,* 3r. Dolciati, *Prediche diversi,* 38v. Anton Francesco
Grazzini, *Tre Preghi Sulla Croce* (BNCF, Magliabecchiana XXXV cod. 44),
10r–10v and 18r; Fra Andrea, *Trattato,* 16r–17v; Anonymous, "Dell Con-
fessione," 1v–2r; Anonymous, "Predica del Santissimo Sacramento," 13–14;
Gualandi, *De vero Iudicio,* 85 and 43; Diacceto, *Homelie,* 102–103; Polito,
Discorso, 8v; and Musso, *I tre libri,* 162. The ubiquity of the motif even
extended to legal tracts; see Sebastianus Medicius, *Tractatus de Legibus et
Statutis* (Florence: Torrentin, 1569), 23–24. The reconciliation of the apparent contradiction was not only a Christian dilemma; early humanists had

been well aware that the same problem had troubled Roman authors as well. See Stacey, *Roman Monarchy,* 34 and 155.

87. Rosello, *Il ritratto,* 19v: "veggiamo il Duca Cosimo portarsi in guisa, che i suoi lo temono, ma non gli portano odio. Si come Iddio, et il padre, il quale è temuto, et non però odiato. Et questo gli riesce mantendo una clemente, et severa giustizia."

88. Salviati, *Orazione:* "si giusto nella clemenza, ò si clemente nella giustizia" that his clemency and justice were "anzi divine, che humane vertù."

89. ASFi, Med. 208, c. 98r–98v (October 19, 1558): "Io non ho mai denegata la gratia à quei miei cittadini, che col pentirsi delli errori passati, me l'hanno domandata, eccetto pero ad alcuni, che voluntariamente hanno voluto peccare, et ricorrere di poi quando non hanno potuto far altro."

90. ASFi, Med. 182c. 250r–250v (March 13, 1538): "Noi ci satisferemo et contenteremo sempre cha la giustitia habbi il suo debito et honorato luogho purche lei sia sempre accompagnata con qualche honesta et giustificata misericordia et pietà." See also ASFi, Med. 183c. 9v–10r (May 22, 1538), informing his vicar "non si escha del dritto corso della debita iustitia accompagnata dalla misericordia."

91. ASFi, Med. 182, 261r: "quia misericordia Domini plena est terra mossi alle prece efficace."

92. ASFi, Med. 10, c. 226r–231v (June 25, 1547): "Non lasserò anco di ricordare con debito reverentia (havendosi à venire al' castigo de delinquenti) che la Maesta Sua, lassando quella città in la solita liberta, ò vero mettendola in subiectione, nell'un caso et nell'altro debbia più presto pendere nella clementia et nella gratia che nel'rigore della justitia, poi che la cosa é tanto invecchiata, non dico gia di lassare impuniti e' delicti e demeriti loro piu gravi, ma fare il castigo in manco numero che si pùo, et non nella moltitudine, perche il castigo di pochi oltre che sara exemplare alli altrj, e fara star ognuno in timore, almeno non inciterà l'odio universale, et di poi la remissioni et la gratia di molti genererà amore nelli animi loro verso di quella."

93. Machiavelli, *Discorsi,* 91–94.

94. Ibid., 91–101.

95. My interpretation of Machiavelli on religion here follows most closely those of Anthony Parel and Mark Hulliung; see, respectively, Mark Hulliung, *Citizen Machiavelli* (Princeton: Princeton University Press, 1984), and Anthony J. Parel, *The Machiavellian Cosmos* (New Haven: Yale University Press, 1992).

96. Machiavelli, *Il principe,* 381: "Avendoci la nostra religione mostro la verità e la vera via, ci fa stimare meno l'onore del mondo: onde I Gentili, stimandolo assai, ed avendo posto in quell il sommo bene, erano nelle azioni loro più feroci. . . . E se la religione nostra richiede che tu abbi in te fortezza, vuole che tu sia atto a patire più che a fare una cosa forte. Questo modo di

vivere, adunque, pare che abbi renduto il mondo debole, e datolo in preda
algi uomini scelarati."

97. Machiavelli, *Discorsi,* 91–101.
98. Religion was considered a virtue, in that it was a subset of justice, in this
   case, rendering God his due.
99. Gualandi, *De Optimo,* 77: "Vestram igitur militiam non damnamus, alioqui
   reprobandus bellicosississimus David, Regius vates, Deo summe charus."
100. Ibid., 79: "Suscipienda igitur sunt bella . . . ob hanc causam, ut fine iniuria
   in pace vivatur. Ceterum bellum iustum est, quod ex edicto geritur, de re-
   bus repetundis, aut propulsandae iniuriae cause."
101. Machiavelli, *Discorsi,* 309. Machiavelli scholars have subjected Machiavelli to a thorough search of his preference for war over peace, and
   whether or not his statements can be taken to mean a rejection of the just
   war tradition. The most complete exposition of this point is in Michael
   Hörnqvist, *Machiavelli and Empire* (Cambridge: Cambridge University
   Press, 2004), 88–91.
102. Machiavelli, *Discorsi,* 112–113.
103. G. B. Adriani, "Vita di Cosimo dei Medici," in *Scritti varii editi ed inediti di
   G. B. Adriani e di Marcello suo figliuolo,* ed. Adolfo Bartoli (Bologna:
   Commissione per i testi di lingua, 1968), 114; and Ammirato, *Oratione,*
   45r–46r.
104. ASFi, Med. 10c. 40r–44v (April 18, 1547).
105. ASFi, Med. 323c. 43r–43v (September 21, 1549).
106. See ASFi, Med. 323c. 66r (February 12, 1550). ASFi, Med. 323c. 103r
   (May 29, 1550). ASFi, Med. 323c. 121v–122r (May 4, 1552).
107. ASFi, Med. 323c. 91v–92r (February 10, 1551).
108. ASFi, Med. 24c. 145r–145v (July 12, 1556).
109. Besides his aforementioned refusal to intervene in 1547, Cosimo had
   readied himself to come to Siena's aid in 1544. ASFi, Med. 5c. 513r–519r
   (March 26, 1544).
110. ASFi, Med. 323 91v–92r (Feb 10, 1552).
111. This letter was in response to a request for a safe-conduct. ASFi, Med.
   202c. 46r–46v (February 7, 1554): "Certificandolo che il fin nostro dela
   guerra non è altra che liberarli dalla oppressione et servitù di Franzese che
   sotto professo di liberar li stati se le fanno proprii et di tengon in continua
   guerra."
112. Booth, *Cosimo,* 141–142.
113. ASFi, Med. 199c. 60v (March 2, 1552): "Mi dispiace bene che non sia in
   facultà mia di provedere, che li soldati Caesarii non venghino à predare et
   far danni come scriviano che fanno, nel dominio loro, perche trovandosi
   con le forze, che gli è noto, non posso io prohibirli che non lo faccino.
   Come per se stesse lo possano considerare, et volessi dio, che fusse in poter
   mio di poterci provedere, perche cognoscerebbeno in questa si come hanno

potuto cognoscere in tutti le altre actioni mie, ch io ho desiderato sempre di fargli benefitio."

114. Cosimo I, *Lettere*, 157: "con nostro molto dolore abbiamo inteso la ruberia che l'exercito del marchese ha fatto in Casole, da cui neanco la casa di Dio è andata esente. Noi non vogliamo queste iniquità: quando l'exercito può dare il sacco, le chiese hanno essere rispettate, et il primo che averà ardire di fare insulto a chiese, monisteri, spedali, e altri tali luoghi, noi vogliamo che paghi la pena di tanta sua malvagità con la perdita del capo."

115. Giurgi, *Oratione*, 6v: "Vedete come a tempo conobbe l'occasione di combattere, et conchiudete da questo che se per mantenimento dela pace li convenisse guerreggiare, egli mostrarebbe che non cede a Pirro."

116. Ibid., 7r: "egli conformandosi col' volere di Giesucristo, all'hora solamente s'e lasciato indurre a prender guerra, che per opra di seditiosi ribelli hà veduto turbarsi nelo stato suo la pace et la giustitia."

117. Puccini, *Oratione*, 4v: "mai operò contra a suoi nimici per altra cagione che per haver pace."

118. Puccini, in fact, never recited the oration, and it remained in manuscript until 1990.

119. Baldini, *Orazione*, unpaginated: "veggendo che i pensieri della pace, i quali egli haveva più tempo . . . et ne haveva tenuti più volte trattati, non havevano più luogo."

120. Malaspina, *Orazione*, 196v.

121. Baldini, *Orazione:* "cognoscendo questo Gran' Principe non per altro doversi far la guerra, se non per haver la pace, essendo ancora nella città di Mont Alcino, rimasti alquanti de i nimici, deliberò con la clemenza, et con la bontà sua vincerli più tosto che l'armi."

122. Bandini, *Orazione:* "La quale guerra egli con tanta prudenza, et senno governò, che non meno si fece amare da' nemici, che da' suoi, ne meno si fece temere da suoi, che da nemici, talmente che condussse la cosa à quel felice fine, il quale da ognuno era sommamente sperato, et desiderato."

4. Prince or *Patrone?* Cosimo as Ecclesiastical Patron

1. Roberto Bizzocchi, *Chiesa e potere nella Toscana del quattrocento* (Bologna: Il Mulino, 1987), 59–63. See also Gene Brucker, *Renaissance Florence* (Berkeley: University of California Press, 1983), 76.

2. See David S. Peterson, "State-Building, Church Reform, and the Politics of Legitimacy in Florence, 1375–1460," in *Florentine Tuscany: Structures and Practices of Power*, ed. William Connell and Andrea Zorzi (Cambridge: Cambridge University Press, 2000).

3. There were occasions of both treachery and territorial dispute. The papacy was certainly complicit in the Pazzi conspiracy to assassinate Lorenzo, and

the fourteenth-century War of the Eight Saints was fought over territorial disputes. On the relationship of the Medici to the papacy, see George Holmes, "How the Medici Became the Pope's Bankers," in *Florentine Studies: Politics and Society in Renaissance Florence,* ed. Niccolai Rubinstein (Evanston, Ill.: Northwestern University, 1968). Partner does note that there was usually friction over taxation. See Peter Partner, "Florence and the Papacy," in Rubinstein, *Florentine Studies,* 401.

4. Bizzocchi, *Chiesa e potere,* 165–167.

5. For Cosimo's relationship with Paul III see Spini, *Cosimo I;* Gentile, *La Politica;* and Antonietta Amati, "Cosimo I e i frati di San Marco," *Archivio Storico Italiano* 81 (1923), 225–277.

6. The classic exposition of this dynamic is Paolo Prodi, *The Papal Prince; One Body and Two Souls: The Papal Monarchy in Early Modern Europe,* trans. Susan Haskins (Cambridge: Cambridge University Press, 1987).

7. Thomas James Dandelet, *Spanish Rome, 1500–1700* (New Haven: Yale University Press, 2001), 216. Dandelet argues that Spain practiced a form of soft imperialism in Rome through the implicit threat of violence and the judicious handling of the patronage system.

8. Michael Jacob Levin, *Agents of Empire: Spanish Ambassadors in Sixteenth-Century Italy* (Ithaca: Cornell University Press, 2005), 143–150.

9. One recent scholar has made the claim that Cosimo tacitly allowed a crypto-Valdensian movement to operate largely unfettered in his territory during the first twenty years of his rule. The argument stands on the idea that Cosimo was making a veiled antipapal statement. Firpo, *Gli affreschi.* Whatever Cosimo's actual knowledge of this group's heterodoxy (and there is no direct evidence he knew anything about their religious persuasions), he tried very hard not to break with the papacy or submit the church to his direct control. See Niccolò Rodolico, "Cosimo I e il concilio di Trento," *Archivio Storico Italiano* 122 (1964), 8.

10. Melissa Merriam Bullard, *Lorenzo il Magnifico: Image, Anxiety, Politics and Finance* (Florence: Olschki, 1994), 135; and Najemy, *History of Florence,* 267.

11. See especially Kent, *Rise of the Medici,* 26–30.

12. Trexler, *Public Life,* 27.

13. Kent, *Patron's Oeuvre,* 134–138.

14. Cited in ibid., 135.

15. Cited in Kent, *Rise of the Medici,* 49.

16. Varchi, *Orazione,* 125r: "senza fine devete piu tosto, et di notte et di giorno pregarla devotemente che ella si come fa qui sicurissimo porto à tutte le vostre tempeste intercedendo per voi, et impetrando, non pure pieta e perdono ma gratia ancora et favore dal suo unico et illustrioso figluolo sempre dunque bisogno, cosi ora certissimo soccorso alle vostre colpe, et d'ovunque bisogni e sempre interceda per voi et v'impetri su nel Regno del Cielo, non

solamente favore et gratia, ma perdono e pietà dal santissimo et unico figlio di Dio."

17. ASFi, AGBE 6076c. 63r (August 16, 1565): "Sendo vacata la pieve di Stia per la morte di quel piovano et spettandose Vostra Eccelenza Illustrissima il fare elettione di nuovo Rettore à chi si cometta quella cura, per essere patronato di quella, come la debbe sapere. Io non confidando punto in alcuna particolar merito o alcun sofficientia che non ne so conoscere alcuna in me, ma solo nella benignità sua la quale è stata sempre naturale a quella Illustrissima casa et nella bontà d'Iddio il quale è potente fare soprabbondare come in tutti gli altri ancora in me, che gratia e sofficientia. Recorro humilmente à suplicarle della presente gratia."

18. See, for instance, ASFi, Med. 197c. 39r (March 25, 1552) and ASFi, Med. 201c. 117v (April 28, 1554).

19. ASFi, Med. 5c. 628a–628b (March 28, 1546).

20. ASFi, Med. 197c. 69r (April 28, 1552): "e gia stato costa quattro mesi senza haver mai potuto conseguirne il fine, per i molti favori (dice lui) che vengono fatta all'adversario suo familiare del Reverendo Cardinal Trani."

21. The list is much larger, but for a sampling of cases see ASFi, Med. 23c. 82 (September 30, 1552); ASFi, Med. 23c. 294r–294v (December 10, 1552); ASFi, Med. 37c. 153r (November 1, 1555); ASFi, Med. 183c. 97v (September 13, 1538); ASFi, Med. 185c. 156r (October 23, 1544); ASFi, Med. 188c. 25r–25v (April 30, 1548); ASFi, Med. 191c. 52v (May 22, 1549); ASFi, Med. 194c. 122v (September 26, 1551); ASFi, Med. 196c. 14v (November 13, 1551); ASFi, Med. 196c. 28r (December 2, 1551); ASFi, Med. 196c. 80r–81v (January 24, 1552); ASFi, Med. 197c. 13v (February 27, 1552); ASFi, Med. 199c. 46v (February 17, 1553); ASFi, Med. 202c. 64v (February 20, 1554); ASFi, Med. 204c. 49r (October 6, 1554); ASFi, Med. 207c. 131r (August 6, 1558); ASFi, Med. 208c. 35r (February 27, 1558); ASFi, Med. 208c. 105v–106r (November 14, 1558); ASFi, Med. 210c. 4r (January 5, 1559); ASFi, Med. 211c. 42v (June 22, 1560).

22. See ASFi, Med. 192c. 92v (December 17, 1549); ASFi, Med. 195c. 119v–120r (October 28, 1551); ASFi, Med. 196c. 28v (December 2, 1551); ASFi, Med. 196c. 35r (December 9, 1551); ASFi, Med. 197c. 29v (March 16, 1552); ASFi, Med. 198c. 119v (September 19, 1552); ASFi, Med. 199c. 124r (May (misdated as June) 5, 1553); ASFi, Med. 199c. 138v (June 4, 1553); ASFi, Med. 199c. 153v–154r (June 30, 1553); ASFi, Med. 201c. 175r (July 1, 1554); ASFi, Med. 203c. 39r (November 20, 1553); ASFi, Med. 206c. 127v (November 18, 1557); ASFi, Med. 208c. 83v (September 21, 1558).

23. Baglioni's presence in Cosimo's army is well attested in the secondary literature, as it sparked a violent feud with Paul III when Baglioni put himself at the head of Paul's Perugian rebels. Stefano Colonna was the *luoghotenete generale* of Cosimo's army from 1541 to his death in 1548; the Col-

onna family continued as allies during the war of Siena in the 1550s; see Adriani, "Vita di Cosimo," 67. See also Graham Smith, "Bronzino's Portrait of Stefano Colonna: A Note on its Florentine Provenance," *Zeitschrift für Kunstgeschichte* 40 (1977), 265–269. For notes on Giovanfrancesco da Bagno, see G. B. Adriani, *Istorie de' suoi tempi* (1583; Prato: Frattelli Giachetti, 1824), vol. 4, 65. For Giovan Battista Savelli, see Marucelli, *Cronaca*, 132.

24. Count Troilo di Rossi of San Secondo had married Bianco Riario Sforza, daughter of Cosimo's paternal grandmother, Caterina Sforza. Cosimo was second cousins once removed with the three Cybos: Caterina, Cardinal Innocenzo, and Lorenzo, the Duke of Ferentillo, who had married into the Malaspina family of Massa-Carrara. The Cybos' mother, Maria Maddelena dei Medici, and Cosimo's maternal grandmother, Lucrezia dei Medici, were both daughters of Lorenzo the Magnificent.

25. On the first matter, see ASFi, Med. 192c. 131r (March 9, 1550). On his supplication to Cardinal Carpi see ASFi, Med. 195c. 47v (June 25, 1551).

26. See ASFi, Med. 202c. 6v–7r (September 20, 1554).

27. ASFi, Med. 197c. 78v (April 24, 1552).

28. ASFi, Med. 23c. 66r–67r (September 30, 1552).

29. ASFi, Med. 212c. 99v (June 3, 1560).

30. On Bernardo Camaiani, see ASFi, Med. 189c. 75r–75v (November 24, 1548). Cosimo also intervened for a *criato* of his house named Neri da Volterra, ASFi, Med. 207c. 132v (October 21, 1558); for the nephew of Cardinal Poggio, ASFi, Med. 23c. 363r (December 28, 1552); for Conti Alamano, vassal of the pope and creature of the Medici house, ASFi, Med. 23c. 251r (November 22, 1552); and for an unnamed *criato*, wanting a dispensation to hold ecclesiastical benefices although he was a convicted murderer, ASFi, Med. 210c. 9r (January 14, 1559).

31. ASFi, Med. 197c. 26v (March 13, 1552).

32. ASFi, Med. 23c. 375r (December 31, 1552); ASFi, Med. 196c. 38rv (December 16, 1551); ASFi, Med. 197c. 25v (March 11, 1552); ASFi, Med. 201c. 13r (September 5, 1553).

33. To cite one example out of many, Cosimo tried to get benefices that had been left in deposit for the young Alessandro dei Medici, future archbishop of Florence and future Pope Leo XI, before he had come of legal age, notwithstanding the council's prohibition. ASFi, Med. 201c. 110r–110v (April 19, 1554).

34. ASFi, Med. 23c. 317r–317v (December 12, 1552).

35. See for instance ASFi, Med. 195c. 107r (October 12, 1551).

36. In his early days, Cosimo helped his client the bishop of Arezzo to resign his bishopric to his relative. See ASFi, Med. 2c. 14r (August 28, 1537). Cosimo intervened to help Cardinal Guidiccioni resign the bishopric of Lucca to his underage relative Alessandro. ASFi, Med. 189c. 57r (November 7,

1548). He similarly tried to help the archbishop of Siena renounce to a relative, ASFi, Med. 212c. 74r (May 16, 1560).

37. ASFi, Med. 188c. 58r–v (May 24, 1548); ASFi, Med. 194c. 50r–51v (April 10, 1551).

38. For examples see ASFi, Med. 23c. 102 (October 1552); ASFi, Med. 23c. 368r (December 30, 1552); ASFi, Med. 208c. 104rv (November 10, 1558); ASFi, Med. 4c. 84r–85v (July 1540); ASFi, Med. 182c. 158r (November 26, 1537); ASFi, Med. 192c. 119r (February 26, 1550); ASFi, Med. 195c. 151v (June 5, 1552); ASFi, Med. 212c. 41r (April 28, 1561).

39. These were the biggest favors of all, and Cosimo could not assure anything for anybody. Cosimo intervened unsuccessfully for his client Archbishop Colonna, ASFi, Med. 195c. 106v–107r (October 12, 1551), and for Don Ferrante Gonzaga, ASFi, Med. 201c. 103rv (April 8, 1554). He successfully secured cardinalships for the archbishop of Messina, ASFi, Med. 195c. 108v (October 14, 1551); Roberto Nobili, ASFi, Med. 202c. 17rv (December 26, 1553); his own sons Giovanni, ASFi, Med. 212c. 2r (February 13, 1560), and Ferdinand, as well as his functionary Agnolo Niccolini. As for the papacy, Cosimo was instrumental in both Julius III's election (see ASFi, Med. 323c. 52r [November 15, 1549]) and Pius IV's election. See Diaz, *Il granducato,* 186.

40. Frederic J. Baumgartner, *Behind Locked Doors: A History of the Papal Elections* (New York: Palgrave MacMillan, 2003), 101–185.

41. See Dandelet, *Spanish Rome,* 216.

42. For the importance of the banking interests in the early Medici's ecclesiastical policies see Holmes, "How the Medici," and Bullard, *Lorenzo,* 169.

43. Bullard, *Lorenzo,* 82–83.

44. For the Medici/Toledo power block, see Carlos José Hernando Sánchez, "Naples and Florence in Charles V's Italy: Family, Court, and Government in the Toledo-Medici Alliance," in *Spain in Italy: Politics, Society and Religion 1500–1700,* ed. Thomas James Dandelet and John A. Marino (Leiden: Brill, 2006), 155–171.

45. Konrad Eubel, Wilhelm Gulik, Stefan Ehses, and Patrick Gauchat, *Hierarchia Catholica,* vol. 3 (Monasterii: Sumptibus et typis librariae Regensbergianae, 1898), 25.

46. See ASFi, Med. 37c. 331r (December 27, 1555); ASFi, Med. 196c. 13rv (November 12, 1551); ASFi, Med. 185c. 45v (May 5, 1544); ASFi, Med. 185c. 64r (May 14, 1544); ASFi, Med. 189c. 54r (November 1, 1548); ASFi, Med. 192c. 19r (October 9, 1549); ASFi, Med. 192c. 131r (March 9, 1550); ASFi, Med. 195c. 65v (July 9, 1551); ASFi, Med. 195c. 106v (October 12, 1551).

47. Marucelli, *Cronaca,* 132.

48. ASFi, Med. 207c. 131v (August 6, 1558). Giulio della Rovere, the cardinal of Urbino, was the great-grandson of Ercole I d'Este, duke of Ferrara.

49. Langdon, *Medici Women,* 148–168.

50. Orsini was the child of Guido Ascanio's sister, Francesca di Bozio Sforza.
51. ASFi, Manoscritti 166c. 13r.
52. Sforza's mother was Paul's daughter, Costanza Farnese.
53. For examples see ASFi, Med. 24c. 54r–54v (undated, 1555); ASFi, Med. 37c. 38r (November 18, 1553); ASFi, Med. 189c. 7r–7v (May 2, 1555); ASFi, Med. 187c. 57r (November 7, 1548); ASFi, Med. 191c. 51r (March 17, 1548); ASFi, Med. 202c. 11v–12r (April 8, 1549); ASFi, Med. 202c. 23v (January 6, 1554); ASFi, Med. 206c. 30v–31r (January 22, 1554); ASFi, Med. 206c. 91v (June 22, 1557); ASFi, Med. 208c. 142v (December 28, 1557); ASFi, Med. 208c. 90v (September 30, 1558).
54. Charles Perkins, *Tuscan Sculptors* (Oxford: Longman, 1864), 254.
55. See Trexler, *Public Life,* 131–158.
56. ASFi, Med. 10c. 28r (April 21, 1547).
57. Giovio dedicated his *History of Illustrious Men* to Cosimo and was also in Alessandro Farnese's circle in Rome.
58. ASFi, Med. 2c. 14r (August 28, 1537). On the loan to the Minerbetti bishops see Carol Bresnahan Menning, "Loans and Favors, Kin and Clients: Cosimo dei Medici and the Monte di Pieta," *Journal of Modern History* 61 (1989), 493–495.
59. On Camaiani's role at Trent, see Hubert Jedin, "La politica conciliare di Cosimo I," *Rivista Storica Italiana* 62 (1950), 345–374.
60. Scipione Ammirato, *Vescovi di Fiesole, di Volterra, e d'Arezzo del Signore Scipione Ammirato,* reprinted from the Florentine edition of 1637 (Florence: Arnaldo Forni Editore, 1984), 188.
61. Giuseppe Cappelletti, *Le chiese d'Italia* vol. 21 (Venice: Antonelli, 1870), 447.
62. ASFi, Med. 24c. 97r–97v (December 27, 1555). Cosimo's appeals to Paul were, of course, to little avail.
63. Marrara, *Studi giuridici,* 60, and Lapini, *Diario,* 142.
64. See ASFi, Med. 1170c. 378 (April 11, 1543).
65. Cardinal Burgos's presence in Florence in 1543 is attested numerous times in the filza ASFi, Med. 1170. When Paul made his way through Tuscany to meet the emperor in Nice in 1537, Cosimo's ambassadors unsuccessfully tried to get him to come through Florence but were stymied by the brothers of Monte Uliveto, who got him to go by their monastery instead, thus leading toward Fucecco and away from Florence. The matter of a papal visit was one not only of diplomacy but also of prestige. See ASFi, Med. 331c. 6r (March 31, 1538). Even after their most heated exchange, that of the San Marco controversy, Cosimo tried to get Paul to come to Tuscany in 1546. ASFi, Med. 8c. 111r (October 18, 1546).
66. See "Elizabeth: November 1560, 21–30," Calendar of State Papers Foreign, Elizabeth: 1560–1561, vol. 3 (1865), pp. 401–416, http://www.british -history.ac.uk/report.aspx?compid=71877, accessed 10 July 2013: "The

Duke of Florence has departed from Florence to Sienna and thence to Rome, which he entered with much pomp in rich apparel, with above 1,000 horses and 400 arquebusiers for his guard. He is lodged in the Pope's palace and entertained with all kinds of banquetting. The Duchess also is there, and daily plays with the Cardinals and others; they write that this week past she lost 6,000 crowns. The Duke is daily at least two hours alone with the Pope in consult. Most men judge his being the letter is from an English ambassador in Rome here will breed no purpose. Mr. Pasquin and "Morphero" talk at liberty with schedules upon each corner "non sine quare lupus ad urbem" (not without asking why the wolf [Cosimo] is in the city [Rome])."

67. ASFi, Med. 24c. 344r (December 24, 1552).

68. ASFi, Med. 192c. 55v (September 14, 1559): "etiam con incomodo della Duchessa."

69. See Cantini, *Legislazione*, vol. 1, 186–187. The process was in the hands of a magistrate, the auditor of jurisdiction and ecclesiastical benefices, who answered directly to the duke. See Elena Taddei, "L'Auditorato della giurisdizione negli anni di governo di Cosimo I de'Medici: Affari beneficiali e problemi giurisdizionali," in *Potere e strutture nella Toscana del '500,* ed. Giorgio Spini (Florence: Olschki, 1980).

70. On Carpi's ecclesiastical posts, see Eubel et al., *Hierarchia,* 23–24.

71. For instance, it is certain that Carpi held at least one benefice in the diocese of Arezzo. ASFi, ABGE 4375. See also a letter Cosimo sent on behalf of the *schalco* of Cardinal Carpi to the commissary of Castrocaro on two vacant benefices. ASFi, Med. 182c. 81r (August 4, 1537). And ASFi, Med. 197c. 48r (March 31, 1552).

72. ASFi, Med. 182c. 95v (September 7, 1537).

73. See ASFi, Med. 185c. 145v (July 26, 1544); ASFi, Med. 323c. 31r (May 24, 1549).

74. ASFi, Med. 194c. 115r–115v (September 14, 1551).

75. ASFi, Med. 212c. 70v (May 15, 1560).

76. For the mutual links of favors that bound the two together see ASFi, Med. 182c. 81r (August 4, 1537); ASFi, Med. 182c. 95v (September 7, 1537); ASFi, Med. 183c. 186v (January 25, 1539); ASFi, Med. 185c. 78v–79v (May 23, 1544); ASFi, Med. 185c. 145v (July 26, 1544); ASFi, Med. 194c. 27r (March 20, 1551); ASFi, Med. 194c. 28v (March 21, 1551); ASFi, Med. 195c. 47v (June 25, 1551); ASFi, Med. 212c. 110r–110v (June 16, 1560); ASFi, Med. 323c. 31r (May 24, 1549). ASFi, Med. 210c. 48v (April 1, 1559).

77. Averardo Serristori, *Legazioni di Averardo Serristori ambasciatore di Cosimo I a Carlo Quinto e in corte di Roma (1537–1568),* comp. and ed. Luigi Serristori (Florence: Felice le Monnier, 1853), 135.

78. See Sánchez, "Naples and Florence," 166.

79. See, respectively, ASFi, ABGE 4375 c. 296 (August 6, 1546) and ASFi, ABGE. 4375 c. 2 and 63. The same cases make it clear that Cosimo's aid did not extend to subverting justice for del Monte's gain. See also ASFi, ABGE 4378 c. 324. This is a plaintive note from Lorenzo Fuggini, whom Cosimo has clearly strong-armed into settling his dispute with the del Montes over Santa Maria di Ambra.

80. ASFi, Med. 5 c. 633r–634r (April 20, 1546).

81. Julius later made Cosimo's ambassador the bishop of Fiesole. See Jedin, "La politica conciliare," 364; and Ammirato, *Vescovi*, 54.

82. ASFi, Med. 10 c. 263r (July 6, 1547).

83. Galluzzi, *Istoria*, 112.

84. Sánchez, "Naples and Florence," 171.

85. ASFi, Med. 183 c.104r (September 20, 1538).

86. See ASFi, Med. 652 c. 20r (January 21, 1540) and ASFi, Med. 652 c. 77r–77v (November 12, 1540).

87. ASFi, Med. 182 c. 198r (January 12, 1538).

88. For the point of view that Cosimo was a *sola politica* thinker see Lupi, "Cosimo," 26; Firpo, *Gli affreschi*, 311; Marrara, *Studi giuridici*, 58; Cochrane, *Florence*, 60; and Cantagalli, *Cosimo*, 77.

89. See ASFi, Med. 182 c. 80v (August 4, 1537).

90. For similar telling expressions see ASFi, Med. 182 c. 1v (January 15, 1537); ASFi, Med. 182 c. 169r (November 12, 1537); ASFi, Med. 182 26v–27r (March 11, 1537); and ASFi, Med. 182 46r (May 5, 1537).

91. Marucelli, *Cronaca*, 46 and 112–115.

92. ASFi, Med. 212 c. 118v–119r (June 30, 1560): "Non s'inganano punto le signori à credere, ch'io sia acerrimo persecutore delli Heretici, tanto è il zelo che ho sempre havuto, et haverò verso la santa fede cattolica et quella santa sede. Ringratiole dell'avviso, che mi danno con la loro di 23 del passto per illuminarmi delle opinioni erronée, che vanno pullulando in Siena, et delle provisioni, che le penserebbeno di farvi; ma perche in simili luoghi non sarebbe maraviglia, che le passione particolari ó qualche ambitione cercassero per nuocere altrui far di sinistre inventione, desidererei si come scrissi alle settimane passate, che le signori reverendi discendesser meco à quel che particolare, perche oltre al conoscere qual sia la mente mia contra simili rebelli della fede di Cristo, provederei per avventura di tal remedio, che le non haverebbino in ciò fatica, nè molestia alcuna; nondimeno l'havere à, procedere al buio in cosa tanto importante non mi pare, che si debba fregiar persona massime nobile, et honorata senza buon fondamento."

93. The most detailed secondary work on Cosimo's *auto-da-fè* is Gustavo Bertoli, "Luterani e anabattisti processati a Firenze nel 1552," *Archivio Storico Italiano* 154 (1996), 59–122.

94. It seems that the pope personally assured the Venetian ambassador of Cosimo's commitment. See ibid., 64. The pope supplied credential letters to

the master of the Sacred Palace later in the same year. ASV, Index Brevia-
rum, *Giulio III,* 123.

95. Cosimo, for instance, won Piero Guicciardini a spot as a *collaterale* of the
Campodoglio, a civic judgeship in Rome. For the request see ASFi, Med.
194c. 35v (March 28, 1551). The thank you note for the successful bid is in
ASFi, Med. 196c. 79r. Cosimo also got his client the bishop of Pavia the
governorship of Rome. ASFi, Med. 196c. 28r (February 12, 1551). He also
got Giovanni Maria Pichi the job of *potestaria* of the Iesu, see ASFi, Med.
195c. 108v (October 14, 1551); Pichi's election is mentioned in a letter
from Cardinal Burgos to Cardinal del Monte in ASV, *Segr. Stato, Principi*
20c. 595 (September 27, 1552). For other successes see ASFi, Med. 199c.
138v (June 4, 1553); and ASFi, Med. 199c. 153v–154r (June 3, 1553). For
favors in litigation, see ASFi, Med. 194c. 19r (June 23, 1551); ASFi, Med.
194c. 36r (March 28, 1551); ASFi, Med. 194c. 114v (September 14,
1551); and ASFi, Med. 196c. 24v (November 30, 1551).

96. ASFi, Med. 5c. 511r–511v (March 25, 1544).

97. ASFi, Med. 192c. 136v (March 11, 1550).

98. On Lorenzo, see Bullard, *Lorenzo,* 143. ASV, *Segr. Stato, Principi* 17c. 115
(October 13, 1552): "La christianissima Regina tenendo per fermo che la
intercessioni mia appresso Vostra Santità habbia à poter molto."

99. ASFi, Med. 323c. 100r–101r (Maggio 1551): "ci faria danno il vedersi che
Sua Santità la stringessi per nostro ordine perche in fatto non vogliamo
stringerla ma solo ricordar e informare Sua Santità del tucto accio da padre e signore, pigli quelli expedienti li parranno a proposito."

100. Eubel et al., *Hierarchia,* 25.

101. ASFi, Med. 194, 8r (March 3, 1551): "Se il Commendator Regnisso (al
quale la Signore Vostro Illustrissimo et Reverendo mostra particulare af-
fectione) non m'havesse imputato per poco religioso, o per dir meglio, per
Lutherano, non harei fatto il resentimento che ho fatto con esso lui."

102. This is, at least, what he implied to Burgos in the same correspondence.

103. ASFi, Med. 195c. 79v (July 21, 1551): "perche qui dove ordinariamente è lo
inquistori si riconoscano simili errori se alcuno lo accusa può venire da esso,
che sendoli non sol permessa da me, ma dato ogni favore, per potere castigar
chi erra, si farà il simile contra di lui, se si troverà che in lui sieno heresie."

104. ASFi, Med. 196c. 93v–94r (February 9, 1552).

105. A sentiment shared by Philippe Castagenetti, "Les Princes et les institutions
ecclésiastiques sous les grands-ducs Medicis," in *Florence et la Toscane
XIVe XIXe siècles: Les dynamiques d'un ètat italien,* ed. Jean Buotier, Sandra Landi, and Oliver Rouchon (Rennes: Presses Universitaires de Rennes,
2004), 305.

106. Cited in Booth, *Cosimo,* 160.

107. ASFi, Med. 201c. 103r–103v (April 8, 1554): "haver gran fede che la inter-
cessione nostra gli habbia molto à giovare in disporre Sua Santità à farlo
questo benefitio."

108. ASFi, Med. 37c. 157r (November 2, 1555): "io non sappi, come à questi tempi corra il mio inchiostro à quella corte."

109. From: "Mary: January 1556," Calendar of State Papers Foreign, Mary: 1553–1558 (1861), pp. 201–206,www.british-history.ac.uk/report.aspx ?compid=70428, accessed 10 July 2013. It was, for instance, in 1555 that Paul IV deprived the duke's soldier Giovanfrancesco da Bagno of his castle. See Adriani, *Istorie*, vol. 5, 99–100.

110. ASFi, Med. 208c. 126r–126v (December 18, 1558) and ASF, Med. 212c.100v (June 3, 1560).

111. ASFi, Med. 208c. 68v (August 28, 1558).

112. Cited in Anzilotti, *La constitutione*, 190–191: "l'esempio dell'Inquisizione che usa la Spagna, mostra quanto la sia perniciosa e detestabile, poichè l'abbraccia ogni cosa."

113. ASFi, Med. 210c. 20r (February 13, 1559): "Veduto quanto scrivete al concino circa il commissario dell'Inquisitione, ci contentiamo che egli possa con editti, et altro esseguire contra li libri prohibiti, che trattano della religione, et cose sacre, ò di Magia, incanti, geomantia, chiromantia, Astrologia giudicaria, et simile altre materie, sendo noi stati sempre osservanti della religione, et persecutore acerrimo di cotali delinquenti, ma considerando al danno poi di molti particolari senza profitto alcuno delle ordinationi di Sua Santità vogliamo che si sospenda, sino á nuovo precetto di Roma, la esecutione delli altri libri, etiam de medesimi Auctori prohibiti, purche non trattino di religione ò fede."

114. ASFi, Med. 210c. 33v (March 11, 1559): "si facesse piu dimostratione che effetti."

115. Valerio Marchetti, *Gruppi ereticali Senesi del Cinquecento* (Florence: La Nuova Italia, 1975), 165 and 232, and ASFi, Med. 210, 65r (April 20, 1559).

116. For the promise to extradite to Cardinal Alessandrino, see ASFi, Med. 208c. 134r (December 24, 1558). For the order for his immediate release see ASFi, Med. 210c. 20v (February 14, 1559).

117. ASFi, Med. 210c. 11v (January 21, 1559) and ASFi, Med. 210c. 44v (March 30, 1559).

118. ASFi, Med. 207c. 138v (June 2, 1559).

119. Though as Adriano Prosperi notes, by this time very few Florentines clung with any intensity to the religiously heterodox ferment of the 1540s and 1550s. Adriano Prosperi, "L'inquisizione Fiorentina dopo il Concilio di Trento," *Annuario dell'Istituto storico italiano per l'etá moderna e contemporanea* 37–38 (1995), 97–124.

120. Juan Polanco, *Epistolae et commentaria p. Joannis Alphonsi de Polanco e Societate Jesu; addenda caeteris ejusdem scriptis dispersis in his monumentis, quibus accedunt nonnulla coaeva, aliorum auctorum, illis conjunctissima,* vol. 1 (Rome: Monumenta Historica, 1961), 34.

121. See Marchetti, *Gruppi ereticali*, 162–164 and 196.

122. Ignatius of Loyola, *Monumenta Ignatiana, ex autographis vel ex antiquioribus exemplis collecta. Series prima. Sancti Ignatii de Loyola Societatis Jesu fundatoris epistolae et instructiones* (Madrid: Typis G. Lopez del Horno, 1903–11), 458–459.

123. Galluzzi, *Istoria,* 366.

124. Polanco, *Epistolae,* vol. 2, 179.

125. Diego Lainez, *Lainii monumenta; Epistolae et acta patris Jacobi Lainii, secundi praepositi generalis Societatis Jesu,* vol. 1 (Madrid: Typis G. Lopez del Horno, 1912), 63–64.

126. *Epistolae mixtae, ex variis Europae locis ab anno 1537 ad 1556 scriptae Monumenta Historica Societatis Iesu,* vol. 1 (Madrid: A. Avrial, 1898–1901), 336–337.

127. Ignatius, *Monumenta,* 717: "Su Excelencia tocó otro capítulo, diciendo que estas cosas nuevas son peligrosas, y que aun cuando algunos sean buenos en la Compañia, no lo son todos. Y habló de ciertas ocurrencias de Pistoya y de otras cosas que Marcos Bracci le había dicho de Roma, es á saber, nosotros quitábamos las mujeres á sus maridos."

128. Polanco, *Epistolae,* vol. 2, 41.

129. Ibid., vol. 3, 213.

5. Cosimo and Savonarolan Reform

1. It seems that the anti-Medicean conspirator Boscoli had had this in mind when plotting his revolt against the Medici. See Butters, *Governors and Government,* 211.

2. On this point, the Savonarolans may well have been right; even one modern historian has noted that up to the time of the last Florentine republic, moral legislation was the main difference between Florentine popular government and Medici government. Stephens, *Fall of the Florentine Republic,* 215.

3. Najemy, *History of Florence,* 390.

4. See Roberto Ridolfi's widely accepted debunking in Roberto Ridolfi, *The Life of Girolamo Savonarola,* trans. Cecil Grayson (New York: Knopf, 1959), 50.

5. Weinstein, *Savonarola and Florence,* 153–156.

6. Despite the best efforts of certain parties to squash this, the agitation would last throughout the sixteenth century. Cosimo himself complained to the pope about it in 1545. ASFi, Med. 6, 282v–283v (October 15, 1545). Archbishop Alessandro dei Medici forbade Savonarola's cult later in the century, as his cause for canonization became a major fault-line in the post-Tridentine church hierarchy. Miguel Gotor, *I beati del Papa: Santità, inquisizione, e obbedienza in età moderna* (Florence: Olschki, 2002), 1–23.

7. An image that is perhaps truly behind Savonarola's popularity in nineteenth-century Italy and his fame in modern historiography, especially his characterization in Pasquale Villari, *La storia di Girolamo Savonarola e de' suoi tempi* (Florence: Successori le Monnier, 1887–88).

8. Varchi, *Storia fiorentina,* 195: "che Firenze non solo ricuperebbe la sua antica libertà ma la si goderebbo in eterno con tutte quelle grazie e felicità che al popolo fiorentino erano state da Dio per la bocca di lui profetate e promesse."

9. See Polizzotto, *Elect Nation,* 420–432.

10. ASFi, Med. 6, c. 2r–3r (April 1, 1545): "e' frati pigliano e' fanciulli e' quali sono apena natj e gli fanno fratj" (the *frate* seize the children that are barely born and make them brothers).

11. ASFi, Med. 6, c. 2r–3r (April 1, 1545). He instructed his ambassador Averardo Serristori to "go to the feet of our Lord Paul III and ask him on behalf of us that he be content to grant to us, by way of papal brief or any other way that is pleasing to His Holiness, the authority to stipulate that brothers of any sort, observant or conventual, or monks, not be able to accept anyone who is not over the age of seventeen, and that any that have been given the habit but have not yet reached that age or taken their vows be sent back to their mother and father's house." "Andiate a piedi di nostro Signore et per parte nostra lo preghiate che sia contento concedercj, o per via di breve o per altro modo che più piacessi a Sua Santità con autorità che noi potiamo vietare che frati di nessuna sorte così osservanti come conventuali o monaci non possino accettar nessuno che non passi la età di 17 annj, et che tutti quelli che egli hanno vestiti in sino adosso che non aggiungono a questa età se già e non havessino fatto professione gli mandino a casa de' padri et delle madri loro."

12. Amati, "Cosimo I e i frati," 244–245.

13. Ibid., 246.

14. ASFi, Med. 6c. 282v–283r (October 14, 1545).

15. ASFi, Med. 6c. 257r–258v (September 21, 1545) and ASFi, Med. 6c. 282v–283r (October 14, 1545).

16. As the reader will recall, Anthony was the prior of San Marco, archbishop of Florence, and a canonized saint.

17. Cosimo I, *Lettere,* 95.

18. ASFi, Med. 6c. 257r–258v (September 21, 1545): "The usage that has been in the convent of San Marco, from that bad seed of Savonarola, goes on today, that is, in mixing themselves with the affairs of the state." "La usanza che è stata nel convento di Santo Marco da quall mala semenza in qua di fra Girolamo vadino ancora mescolandoci qualche cosetta dello stato."

19. ASFi, Med. 6c. 280r–281v (October 23, 1545): "Noj habbiamo mandato via e' frati di Santo Marco per e' mali comportamenti loro, i quali a me

non nocevano per via di religione, ma per la quiete di questo stato, et se io non gli havessi mandati gli manderei via di nuovo, perchè oltra che nelle cose di stato si debbe far così, io gli ho mandati via, perchè stavano in un convento di casa nostra, del quale noj non solamente gli possia cacciare a posta nostra ma lo potiamo abrusciare ogni volta che ci tornassi bene, che forse haveremo fatto meglio, acciocchè quella aria non infetti tutti quelli altri che per lo avenire vi debbeno habitare."

20. Cited in Amati, "Cosimo I e i frati," 251: "Farete liberamente intendere a Sua Santità che, nelle cose di Stato, non solo non havrò respetto a'frati, ma se e' cardinali ne daranno cagione gli impiccherò per la gola senza farne una minima parlata."

21. ASFi, Med. 6c. 280r–281v (October 23, 1545). Referring to the claim that he sheltered heretics, Cosimo claimed: "We are amazed at the rumors that His Holiness follows so atrociously toward us as you wrote us and it seems to us that the matter no longer proceeds for zeal of religion, but by the desire of His Holiness with this occasion to show his ill will toward us. He knows well that at other times we have even sent heretics to Rome, which has not been done by some others; for instance the Duke of Ferrara, who is the pope's own vassal, has done exactly the contrary. Not only has he not given heretics into the hands of His Holiness, he has kept them in his state." "Noi ci maravigliamo che e' romori di Sua Santità seguitino così atrocemente verso di noj come voj ci scrivete e ci pare che la cosa horamaj non proceda per zelo di religione ma per volerci Sua Santità con questa occasione mostrare la mala mente sua verso di noj, che sa ben Sua Santità che noi gli haviamo mandati gli eretici altre volte sino a Roma, il che da altri che da noi non gli è stato fatto, anzi che dal Duca di Ferrara, che è suo feudatario gli è stato fatto il contrario, che non solo non gli ha dato nelle mani a Sua Santità ma gli ha tenuti contro sua voglia nel suo stato."

22. ASFi, Med. 6c. 316 (October 31, 1545): "non lassando cosa alcuna nella città et nello stato mio, nella quale non volessino metter le manj, mantenendo del continuo nelli animj di detti lor seguacj et delli altrj cittadinj ancora quello intenso desiderio che hanno sempre hauto di stare sotto l'ombra et patrocinio della corona di Francia et di governare la città a populo. Di maniera che se io non ci havessi fatta opportuna et presta provisione, era in brevi per seguirne scandolo et disordine di importantia, et questa ultima cagione fu quella che mi sforzò a levargli di quel monasterio, havendo prima cerco di di farcj provisione et di darcj remedio col mezzo de' loro generalj et protector."

23. Amati, "Cosimo I e i frati," 253.

24. Firpo, *Gli Affreschi,* 332.

25. Amati, "Cosimo I e i frati," 269.

26. In 1548, he let the issue drop in order to ask that the taxes on the University at Pisa be used for the construction of the Florentine church in Rome. ASFi, Med. 9, c. 425 (February 22, 1548).

27. Savonarola, *Prediche*, 12r: "Io vi dico, che Dio vuole, che lo facciate, io ve lo dica un'altra volta, Dio vuole vedere giustitia, et vuole che tu punisca e bestemmiatori, e giucatori, e sodomitti, e tutti quelli che sono contrarii a lui, et al suo governo. Io ti dico. che vuole Dio, che siano puniti, et il buono reggimento è punire e cattivi, e levare via e sodomitti, e scelerata della terra tua." See also 115r–118v, 128r, 132r–v, 148v, 160v.

28. Rachel Erlanger, *The Unarmed Prophet: Savonarola in Florence* (New York: McGraw-Hill, 1988), 119.

29. Stephens, *Fall of the Florentine Republic*, 215.

30. Anonymous, *Diario Fiorentino di 1537*, 556.

31. Cantini, *Legislazione*, vol. 1, 210. July 8, 1542: "Considerato la Eccellentissimo et Illustrissimo Sigore Duca, et li suoi Magnifici Consiglieri, esser molto necessario a ciascheduno Stato, oltra qualunque altra opportuna provisione ordinar per le sue Città, et Dominio, che li vitii al tutto si spenghino, quelli massime che sogliono provocar a ira el sommo et onnipotente Dio: Et conoscendo che la bestemmia e peccato che più offende sua Maiestà che li altri, dal quale procedono nel mondo turbolentie, et inopinati flagelli: et volendolo al tutto stirpare, parendo modo congruo l'accrescere la pena a tali delinquenti da poi che le persone non si son corrette in virtù delle Leggi insino a quì fatte. Le quali imponevano piccola pena, ma più tosto dimenticare del iuditio divino, con lo andare perseverando nel vitio. Però col parere di più savi, et prudenti Cittadini hanno nello infrascritto modo proveduto."

32. Cosimo did "sometimes excuse the corporal punishment and make the blasphemer pay the monetary fine: "Qualche volta ha levato la pena corporale et fatto pagare la pecuniaria." Cited in William Connell, "Sacrilege and Redemption in Renaissance Florence: The Case of Antonio Rinaldeschi," *Journal of the Warburg and Courtauld Institutes* 61 (1998), 74.

33. On Florentines' reputation for sodomy, see Erlanger, *Unarmed Prophet*, 25. For an example of the embarassment that Savonarola's intransigence on the matter creates for modern hagiographers, see Pierre Van Paassen, *A Crown of Fire: The Life and Times of Girolamo Savonarola* (New York: Scribner's, 1960), 179.

34. Erlanger, *Unarmed Prophet*, 119.

35. Ibid., 2.

36. Cantini, *Legislazione,* vol. 1, 211–212: "Atteso la Eccellenza dell'Illustrissimo Signor Duca, et li suoi Magnifici Consiglieri, qualmente nelli tempi preteriti le persone si sono poco guardate dal nefando vitio della Sodomia rispetto alle piccole pene imposte dalle Leggi insino a quì ordinate: Et volendo al tutto estinguerlo, per la grande offesa che se ne fa al sommo, et onnipotente Iddio, et al dishonore che ne resulta nell'universale, et massime a chi preposta alla cura, governo, et reggimento de popoli, et che nella sua Città et Dominio si viva col timore di sua immensa Maiestà, et con la debita

honestà, quale si ricerca al politico vivere. Per tanto mossi da dette, et altre urgenti iuste et ragionevoli cause. Hanno col parere di più savi et prudenti Cittadini nell'infrascritto modo provveduto."

37. Ibid., 212–213. This law on blasphemy was apparently renewed in 1549; see Marucelli, *Cronaca,* 102.

38. Antoninus affirmed that much of the population (wrongly he made sure to mention) did not consider prostitution a sin. Antoninus, *Opera,* 20v.

39. Polizzotto, *Elect Nation,* 351.

40. Philip Gavitt, "Charity and State Building in Cinquecento Florence: Vincenzio Borghini as Administrator of the Ospedale degli Innocenti," *Journal of Modern History* 69 (1997), 257–260.

41. Cantini, *Legislazione,* vol. 2, 322.

42. Ibid., vol. 4, 184–185.

43. Ridolfi, *Life of Girolamo Savonarola,* 128.

44. Polizzotto, *Elect Nation,* 351.

45. Gilbert, *Machiavelli and Guicciardini,* 71.

46. Booth, *Cosimo,* 123.

47. John Brackett, *Criminal Justice and Crime in Late Renaissance Florence, 1537–1609* (Cambridge: Cambridge University Press, 2002), 117.

48. Ibid., 137.

49. For the former, see Trexler, *Public Life,* 350. In regard to the latter, see Diaz, *Il granducato,* 135.

50. Civil governments often argued that blasphemy and sodomy provoked civil disaster because they brought down the wrath of God. Thus, they argued, they were in the competency of the civil authority to adjudicate. See Elena Fasano Guarini, "Produzione di leggi e disciplinamento nella Toscana granducale tra Cinque e Seicento," in *Disciplina dell'anima, disciplina del corpo e disciplina della società tra medioevo ed età moderna,* ed. Paolo Prodi and Carla Penuti (Bologna: Società editrice Mulino, 1993), 671. Such a view seems to have been widespread throughout not only Italy but Europe as well. See Paul Grendler, *The Roman Inquisition and the Venetian Press, 1540–1605* (Princeton: Princeton University Press, 1977), 26. The confusion existed in Milan as well, see Domenico Sella, *Lo stato di Milano in età Spagnola* (Turin: UTET, 1987), 69. It was on these grounds that Luther himself justified civil interference in blasphemy cases, James M. Estes, *Peace, Order, and the Glory of God: Secular Authority and the Church in the Thought of Luther and Melanchthon, 1518–1559* (Leiden: Brill, 2005), 44–45. For the Florentine context, see Najemy, *History of Florence,* 244–245.

51. Gualandi, *De vero Iudicio,* 43–45.

52. Martines, *Fire in the City,* 151; and Polizzotto, *Elect Nation,* 251–252.

53. ASFi, Med. 5c. 377r–379r (November 17, 1543).

54. See Marucelli, *Cronaca,* 22; ASFi, Med. 1070c. 317 (October 16, 1543).

55. ASFi, Med. 5c. 355r–356r (November 16, 1543): "sforzato io dalla osservantia delle leggi et dal honor di Dio, il qual faccendomi ogni giorno tanto gratie non vorrei irritare, havendo da poi che fu fatta questa santa legge mandato per il medesimo conto della soddomia meglio che xii poveri huomini in galeria non posso ne debbo irritare Dio con non gastigare ancora li nobili et ricchi. Fammi male insino al anima che sia tocco à vostro signore reverentia et à me questa mala sorte, per trovarci si nel medemo errore ancora Giovanni Bandini . . . conforte vostro signore haver patientia et poi che Dio ordine tutto per il meglio crederche così ancora habbia ordinato questo et conformarsi con la voluta sua."

56. ASFi, Med. 355r–356r (October 16, 1543): "che io ho habbi fatto pigliar contro la mia voglia, ma havendolo più volte admonito, non ho voluto dare conto a dio dei peccati d'altri, maxime havendo fatto mettere in galea, molti poveri et mediocri per il medesimo peccato, secondo il tenore delle leggi notissimo a Ciascuno."

57. According to Parenti, such accusations had helped add to the unpopularity of the Soderini government of the early sixteenth century. For the charge, see Butters, *Governors and Government*, 57.

58. Cited in Pieraccini, *Le stirpe*, 13: "Direte a M. Bernardo Carnesecchi, che si ricordi, che i nostri consigli sono voleri, e quelli, che ci si oppongono li reputiamo nostri avversari. I poveri vogliamo soccorrergli, nè vogliamo che gli manchi il pane; sono in più numero de' ricchi, e meritano da noi anche per nostro interesse molto riguardo."

59. ASFi, Med. 182c. 81r–81v (August 5, 1537).

60. Gavitt, "Charity and State Building," 262.

61. For the *Spedalingo degli innocenti*, see ibid., 240–246; for the magistrate of pupils, see ASFi, Misc. 27/III c. 905 (1544).

62. Erlanger, *Unarmed Prophet*, 173–175.

63. Roth, *Last Florentine Republic*, 64.

64. Cantini, *Legislazione*, vol. 1, 320–326. Henk van Veen cites the 1562 sumptuary laws as evidence that after 1559, Cosimo, trying to appear as a republican prince, had no problem utilizing Savonarola's legacy. While Van Veen is certainly correct about the utilization of Savonarola, his thesis posits a temporal split that doesn't exist and ignores the fact that Cosimo's sumptuary legislation dates back to 1546, the very height of the Savonarolan controversy. Van Veen, *Cosimo*, 160–161.

65. Pieraccini, *Le stirpe*, 13.

66. Cellini, *Autobiography*, 326–328.

67. Carol Bresnahan Menning, *Charity and State in Late Renaissance Florence: The Monte di Pietà of Florence* (Ithaca: Cornell University Press, 1993), 22.

68. Stefanie Siegmund, *The Medici State and the Ghetto of Florence: The Construction of an Early Modern Jewish Community* (Stanford: Stanford University Press, 2006), 51–52.

69. In April 1545 Cosimo submitted all contracts of usury and the strange names under which such illicit contracts went to the authority of the Florentine *Otto di Guardia et Balia,* fixing harsher penalties and increasing supervision. For his legislation against shops that stayed open on holy days, see Cantini, *Legislazione,* vol. 1, 253–255.

70. For an in-depth study of the Monte, see Bresnahan Menning, *Charity and State.*

71. Siegmund, *Medici State,* 171–200. Siegmund argues that the real reason for the ghettoization of Tuscany's Jews was neither Jewish moneylending nor Cosimo's attempts to ingratiate himself with the pope but an attempt to rationalize the space of the early modern Tuscan state.

72. Though this old view, based largely on the testimony of the disaffected Cavalcanti, has been somewhat modified, the Medici did seem to have developed a reputation as populists. The Savonarolan republic was certainly frightened of the Medici's popularity with the poor. See Martines, *Fire in the City,* 178.

73. Savonarola, *Prediche,* 117: "se fussino buoni li principi, et li prelati, e faria bene tutto il mondo. O tepidi, o cattivi principi e sacerdoti, o Sammaria, voi siete causa di questo male." Savonarola's opinion resonated nicely with the concerns of the Counter-Reformation, which also proceeded largely on the assumption that a reform of religious would trickle down to a general reform of the laity. See especially Wietse De Boer, *The Conquest of the Soul: Confession, Discipline, and Public Order in Counter-Reformation Milan* (Boston: Brill, 2001).

74. Marucelli, *Cronaca,* 43.

75. Cosimo would come to the defense of his nuns over the stricter reforms imposed by Trent. See Silvia Evangelisti, "'We do not have it, and we do not want it': Women, Power, and Convent Reform in Florence," *Sixteenth Century Journal* 34 (2003), 677–700. Given the concerns of the *deputati,* it does not seem, as Evangelisti argues, that the difference between the Tridentine reforms and Cosimo's reforms was that Tridentine reforms prescribed active enclosure (disallowing nuns from leaving the monastery) while Cosimo did not. Cosimo's *deputati* were concerned about nuns leaving the monastery even before the Tridentine decrees of 1565. See ASFi, ABGE 4889C. 127r–127v (September 25, 1559) and ASFi, ABGE 4889c. 36r (August 12, 1546). Rather, the dispute probably concerned the strictness of the active enclosure, and whether it would be required for all convents.

76. On Savonarola's attempts to enclose female monastics see Tamar Herzig, *Savonarola's Women: Visions and Reform in Renaissance Italy* (Chicago: University of Chicago Press, 2008), 42.

77. See Craig Monson, *Nuns Behaving Badly: Tales of Music, Magic, Art, and Arson in the Convents of Italy* (Chicago: University of Chicago Pres, 2010), 8 and Elissa Weaver, *Convent Theatre in Early Modern Italy: Spiri-*

tual Fun and Learning for Women (Cambridge: Cambridge University Press, 2002), 14–15.

78. Weaver, *Convent Theatre*, 14.
79. Ibid., 24.
80. ASFi, ABGE 4889c. 7r (April 12, 1545).
81. Cosimo's own *deputati* were not above proceeding against a convent on the basis of rumor and innuendo. See ASFi, ABGE 4889c. 4r–5r (January 9, 1545).
82. See for instance, ASFi, ABGE 4889c. 1r–5v.
83. On the prior of Ortignano's house see ASFi, ABGE 4889c. 26v (March 17, 1545). The *deputati* remarked: "the nuns can do little that cannot be seen from said house." "Poche cose possono far quelle monache che non sieno viste di detta casa." On the scandalous nuns of Santucce see ASFi, ABGE 4889c. 129r–129v (September 3, 1559).
84. Gaetano Greco, "Controriforma e disciplinamento cattolico," in *Storia della civiltà Toscana: Il principato Mediceo,* vol. 3, ed. Elena Fasano Guarini (Florence: La Tipografica Varese, 2004), 242.
85. See ASFi, Med. 188c. 83r–83v (August 9, 1548).
86. See ASFi, Med. 24c. 99r (December 27, 1555).
87. Arnaldo D'Addario, *Aspetti della Controriforma a Firenze* (Rome: Minstero dell'Interno pubblicazioni degli Archivi di Stato, 1972), 344.
88. For examples see ASFi, Med. 187c. 49r–49v (March 17, 1548), when he asked the general of the Franciscans to approve of the punishment of three monks from Santa Croce who refused to end their commerce with the neighboring female monasteries, or ASFi, Med. 188c. 58r–58v (May 24, 1548), thanking the general of the Augustinians for allowing the bishop of Cortona to punish a number of friars whom Cosimo had arrested.
89. ASFi, Med. 197c. 33r–33v (March 20, 1552): "a correggere et reformare quei defetti et mancamenti che potessino esser in essa."
90. ASFi, Med. 199c. 142v–143r (June 12, 1553): "Havendo noi inteso esser morto, Il generale dei Frati de Servi, che era Aretino, et desiderando che tal grado non esca dei padri nostri di quella Religione di Thoscana, et che particularmente ne fussi honorato, Il convento nostro dela Anuntiata, per esser luogo tanto celebrato et il qual gia infiniti anni sono, non ha mai havuto quella dignità in casa. Ci siam mossi a scrivervi la presente perche siate con Nostro Signore et con il protetter di essa Religione che intendiamo essere Il Reverendo Santa Croce (at this time Marcello Cervini), per operare che il grado si dia a frati nostri di Thoscana, supplicando santissima et signore reverentia à honorare il convento dela Nuntiata condurlo al Venerabile padre Antonio Zacheria nostro Fiorentino, persona molto religiosa di buon governo, litterata et di exemplari costumi et dela quale si pùo fermamente sperare atteso le buone qualità sue et quella Religione ne habia a

esser universalmente contenta et sodisfatta farete adunque l'officio con ogni caldezza et efficacia."

91. For Cosimo's aid to the bishop of Arezzo see ASFi, Med. 182c. 30r–v (March 20, 1537). For a sample of some other examples of Cosimo's interventions, see ASFi, Med. 182c. 169r (December 11, 1537); ASFi, Med. 182c. 266v–267r (April 8, 1538); ASFi, Med. 182c. 252r (July 8, 1539); ASFi, Med. 194c. 50r–51r (April 10, 1551); ASFi, Med. 183c. 254v (July 10, 1539). Even later correspondances are full of general admonitions to work in concert with the ecclesiastical authorities. For instance, see ASFi, Med. 210c. 66r (April 20, 1559).

92. ASFi, Med. 206c. 103v (October 10, 1557): "non deveno esser in miglior conditione che li laici, onde egli si ha da coreggere et non patir che quelli che hanno a esser exemplo d'ogni obedienza et buon costume faccino il contrario."

93. ASFi, NA 21405c. 21 (November 1551).

94. On this account Savonarola wrote: "In the end, all the governments of Christian men need to be ordered to that beatitude which has been promised us by Christ." Savonarola, *Trattato,* 32: "tutti li governi delli uomini cristiani debbono essere ordinati finalmente alla beatitudine a noi da Cristo promessa." This, of course, derives from his Thomistic education. See Thomas Aquinas, *On Kingship: To the King of Cyprus,* trans. Gerald Phelan (Westport, Conn.: Hyperion Press, 1979), 63–67.

95. When writing to the podesta of Prato and ordering him to lend the secular arm in a scandal involving some monks, Cosimo warned him to proceed with such caution in discovering the defects of the nuns, writing, "One does not need to hear fables being told to the people and taking away their soul and devotion to those who are well disposed to serve the divine goodness and to be a nun." In this case, then, propaganda took a back seat to religion. ASFi, Med. 183c. 151v–152r (November 1538): "non si habbi ad intendere. se fussi possibile per alchuno quale ne possa incaricare et renderli monasteri predetti col discoprire e defecti et mancamenti loro fabula al populo et torre lo animo et devotione à chi fussi ben disposta servire a sua bontà divina et monacarsi."

96. Betti, *Orazione,* unpaginated: "di questo, ne sono testimonii i monasterii delle sacre vergini, egl'altri luoghi, che al culto divino sono dedicati, i quali sono stati fabricati, mantenuti, ornati, restaurati, et aiutati dalla somma pietà di questo Principe. Non è egli noto, che egl'ha fatto spessissimo volte l'uficio di vigilantissimo et amorevolissimo Pastore, nutrendole, e procurando, che ne fusse tenuta diligentissima cura? Io intesi, non ha molto tempo, da un Reverendo Religioso, che egli haveva vedute le lettere intere di mano del Gran Duca scritte à chi haveva la cura de' Monasterii, posti nelle piu lontane parti del suo Stato: Nelle quali appariva la rara bontà, anzi (lo dirò pure) la santità di questo Principe."

97. Weinstein, *Savonarola and Florence,* 27–66.
98. Andre Chastel, *Art et Humanisme à Florence au temps de Laurent de le Magnifique* (Paris: Presse Universitaires de France, 1961), 69–71.
99. Gualandi, *De Optimo,* 33: "Erant [the Tuscans] inquit in supplicijs deorum magnifici, domi verò pauci."
100. Cited in van Veen, *Cosimo,* 184.
101. Ingrid Rowland, *The Scarinth of Scornello: A Tale of Renaissance Forgery* (Chicago: University of Chicago Press, 2005), 67.
102. ASFi, Med. 5c. 628a–628b (March 28, 1546).
103. Van Veen, *Cosimo,* 162–166.

6. Defense of the Sacred

1. By 1537, one of the most outstanding examples of this trend was the Spanish monarchy, which had won wide-ranging patronage rights with the *Patronato Real.* See Elliott, *Imperial Spain, 1469–1716* (New York: Saint Martin's Press, 1964), 89–92. The other outstanding example was the king of France, who had won similar patronage rights in 1516 with the Concordat of Bologna. See R. J. Knecht, *The Rise and Fall of Renaissance France, 1483–1610* (Malden, Mass.: Blackwell, 2001), 94–96. As Paolo Prodi has shown, the pioneer of the movement toward singular control over secular and ecclesiastical governance was the papal monarchy, which had an easier time accomplishing this feat because it already held the reins of both spiritual and temporal authority in its own hands. Prodi, *Papal Prince.*
2. In England, this dynamic has been studied by McCoy, *Alterations of State,* 23–54, and in Spain by Monod, *Power of Kings,* 58–59. Nearer to home, the papal monarchy had patronized sacred space in Rome intensely since the end of the Great Schism. For an in depth analysis, see Stinger, *The Renaissance in Rome,* 222–234 and 264–283.
3. See especially Bertelli, *King's Body,* and Bloch, *Royal Touch.*
4. See Martines, *Fire in the City,* 85–110.
5. In this case Cosimo was at a serious disadvantage vis-à-vis other early modern monarchs. Cosimo had to accommodate the wishes of local communities because Italians often elected their own pastors; in this, they seem to have been exceptional, as the custom of election had largely died out in northern Europe. See Denys Hay, *The Church in Italy in the Fifteenth-Century* (Cambridge: Cambridge University Press, 1977), 24.
6. ASFi, AGBE 4377c. 306r–307r (October 27, 1548): "più presto per combatter che per elegger il nuovo prete."
7. Ibid.: "a molti incognito del tutto."
8. The Auditor of Jurisdiction and Ecclesiastical Benefices was a magistracy set up and given a special mandate by Cosimo to hear cases involving ecclesiastics. See Anzilotti, *La costituzione,* 119–129.

9. The numbers come from ASFi, AGBE 4375.

10. Cantini, *Legislazione,* vol. 1, 186–187: "avendo noi per esperienza veduto quali disordini, e scandali, che alcune volte sono intervenuti per conto dei Benefizi vacati per Morte, o per qualunque altra si voglia cause ci è parso a proposito avvertire, e provvedere per quanto si può, che per l'avvenire non ne seguan più, e che si osservi le antiquate costituzioni perciò firmate tra la Sede Apostolica, e questa Città, disponenti: che se ne prenda la Possessione in nome di chi rappresenta questo stato per restituirla dipoi a chi canonicamente, e di ragione sarà giudicato spettarsi, e tor l'animo a qualunque presumersi armata mano, o per forza intrudervisi."

11. In 1466 the Florentine republic had argued: "If the authority of the magistrate is not interposed on the possession that is sought, it often happens that great disputes arise, and controversies lead to the taking of arms and bloodshed." "Nisi interposita auctoritate magistratus possessiones petantur, sepenumero fit ut magnae rixae oriantur et ad arma et sanguinem contentiones prorumpant." Cited in Bizzocchi, *Chiesa e potere,* 119.

12. ASFi, Med. 182c. 100r (September 7, 1537); ASFi, Med. 183c. 12r (May 24, 1538); ASFi, Med. 183c. 44v (July 6, 1538); ASFi, Med. 183c. 47r–47v (July 11, 1537); ASFi, Med. 183c. 53r–53v (July 26, 1537).

13. See ASFi, Med. 183c. 242r (June 14, 1539).

14. On clerics in Cosimo's court and his use of benefices, see Taddei, "L'Auditorato," 29–75.

15. From the years 1546–1559, ASFi, AGBE filze 4375–4388.

16. ASFi, Med. 1170c. 76r (December 7, 1552): "non sappai chi meglio li potessi far gratia di benefitii che il cardinale di burgos et don francesco et che lui era duca et li duca non danno benefitii ne entrate ecclesiastiche."

17. ASFi, Med. 194c. 52v (April 11, 1551): "io non potrò esser imputato d'alcune violentia, ò d'haver messo la mano nelle cose ecclesiastiche con propria autorità et senza espresso ordine di Sua Beatitudine."

18. See Michele Ansani, "La provista dei benefici (1450–1466): Strumenti e limiti dell'intervento ducale," in *Gli Sforza, la Chiesa Lombarda, la corte di Roma: Strutture e pratiche beneficiarie nel ducato di Milano (1450–1535),* ed. Giorgio Chittolini (Naples: Liguori Editori, 1989), 46–74.

19. For a sampling of such cases, see ASFi, Med. 182c. 100r (September 7, 1537). ASFi, Med. 183c. 12r–12v (May 24, 1538). ASFi, Med. 183c. 69v–70r (August 9, 1538). ASFi, Med. 183c. 205r–205v (April 1, 1539). ASFi, Med. 183c. 276v (August 5, 1539). ASFi, Med. 183c. 280v (August 12, 1539). ASFi, Med. 195c. 30r (June 17, 1551). ASFi, Med. 195c. 78v (July 21, 1551). ASFi, Med. 208c. 74v (September 3, 1558). ASFi, Med. 208c. 93r (October 4, 1558).

20. ASFi, AGBE 4376c. 136–138 (July 28, 1547) and ASFi, AGBE 4376c. 274 (September 27, 1547).

21. Hewlett, *Rural Communities,* 19–20.

22. ASFi, AGBE 4379c. 191 (February 13, 1550) and ASFi, Med. 208c. 77v (September 4, 1558).

23. See ASFi, AGBE 4377c. 151 (July 28, 1548); and ASFi, AGBE 4377c. 222 (September 11, 1548).

24. See the Calamecca case below.

25. According to Bizzocchi, this had been an operating principle as far back as the fifteenth century; Bizzocchi, *Chiesa e potere*, 138.

26. For the relations between Calamecca and Florence, see Hewlett, *Rural Communities*, 62–70.

27. ASFi, AGBE 4377c. 222 (September 11, 1548): "non gia che noi non lo conosciamo degnissimo di tal cosa, ma per essere stato alli servizi vostri, non vogliamo che homo del mondo posse pensare che noi castigiamo e nostri preti diocesani per darli a prete vostri domestici."

28. The first five years for which such records were kept.

29. See Figure 1.

30. For example, before sending a Servite named Basilio to Prato in 1538 to read in logic, he sent letters to the community asking for their opinion of the man and what they thought of his appointment. See ASFi, Med. 183c. 17v–17r (May 30, 1538).

31. ASFi, Med. 201c. 81v–82r (March 11, 1554): "Intendo che pare molto aspero alli nostri Cittadini d'Arezzo che la prime dignita et offitii della Cathedrale Aretina sieno exercitate da persone forestiere et non sono idoneè, ne accette loro, et parendomi che io molta ragione sene dolglino ancorche io gia dua volte habbia recero de la cause che é tra Nicolo Gamarrini di Arezzo et un nipote del Vescovo di Lucera sopra il primierato di essa Cathedrale si accomodi tra essi convenientemente non ho possuto mancare (illegible) la terza volta con pregar la Santità Vostra che sia contenta far opera quel Vescovo si disponga ad acettar una pensione honesta, et lassar goder pacificamente il primierato al Gammurrino, poiche ve è riseduto gia vente mese et satisfa molto al universale di quel Clero, et della Citta."

32. ASFi, Med. 201, c. 140 (May 28, 1554).

33. This was also a sine qua non and a standard promise to any community from whom Cosimo attempted to get a procuratorship. From ASFi, Med. 182c. 113v–114r (October 6, 1537).

34. For the license of possession see ASFi, AGBE 4350c. 404.

35. See ASFi, AGBE 4379c. 10. In 1542, Cosimo gave perhaps another two benefices to Camaiani in the Arezzo diocese. See ASFi, Med. 5c. 39r–40r (January 9, 1543).

36. ASFi, AGBE 4375c. 156 (May 29, 1546).

37. ASFi, AGBE 4384c. 570.

38. ASFi, Med. 185c. 141r (July 24, 1544).

39. ASFi, AGBE 5097c. 27 (October 30, 1554).

40. ASFi, Med. 182c. 92v–94r (August 27, 1537); ASFi, Med. 206c. 63r (November 14, 1556); and ASFi, Med. 185c. 149v (Undated, 1544).
41. ASFi, Med. 23c. 631r–631v (March 5, 1553).
42. ASFi, AGBE 4375c. 136–138 (July 28, 1546).
43. See for instance Alessandro Strozzi's renouncement of the church of San Piero di Sopra Vicino a Sancto Casciano, ASFi, AGBE 4376c. 459 (January 12, 1547); and Christopher Herrera's renouncement of a benefice in Arezzo, ASFi, AGBE 4379c. 370 (October 29, 1550).
44. Cosimo did convince Pandolfo Pucci, that is, before Pucci tried to kill him, to give the benefice of Tre Santi in Valdelsa to the brother of the dead rector, Piero dei Jacopo Medici. ASFi, Med. 197c. 64r (April 16, 1552); for another example, see ASFi, AGBE 4375c. 360 (September 6, 1546).
45. The number of benefices given to relatives and in-laws is probably quite a bit higher than that, but absent extensive genealogical tables, relatives related in the maternal line would be impossible to trace. The number is once again drawn from a five-year sample (1546–1550) of over a thousand benefices.
46. See ASFi, AGBE 4377c. 34.
47. ASFi, Med. 183c. 288r (August 21, 1539). Cosimo favored the career of young Alessandro dei Medici, future archbishop of Florence and later Pope Leo XI, who as the child of Bernardo Medici and Francesca Salviati was Cosimo's first cousin. As soon as Alessandro came of age, Cosimo went to lengths to get the benefices that had been reserved for him. ASFi, Med. 201c. 110r–110v (April 19, 1554). He also procured a benefice for the nephew of his client bishop Alessandro Marzi Medici, bishop of Assisi, ASFi, Med. 182c. 91r–91v (August 19, 1537). Cosimo also interceded for the uncle of his secretary, Martio dei Marzi Medici, the bishop of Marsico, in order to a restore a benefice to him. ASFi, Med. 182c. 215r–216v (January 30, 1537). For the bishop of Arezzo, see ASF, Med. 2c. 14r (August 28, 1537). Finally, for the bishop of Lucca, see ASFi, Med. 189c. 57r (November 7, 1548).
48. Edward Muir and Ronald Weissman, *The Power of Place: Bringing Together Geographical and Sociological Imaginations,* ed. John Agnew and James Duncan (Boston: Unwin Hyman, 1989), 100.
49. More specifically, as Richard Trexler points out, they had sought to associate themselves with the power of the sacred objects that those sacred spaces contained. See Trexler, *Church and Community,* 13–15.
50. Muir and Weissman, *Power of Place,* 81–88.
51. ASFi, Med. 1173c. 291 (August 8, 1547): "Et quanta più diligentia et sollicitudine ci si apporterà sarà all'Eccellentia sua [Cosimo I] tanto maggiormente grata, la qual ridendo, mi ha detto, "S'io fo rifare i muri alle monache ci doverranno metter la mia arme, et far memoria di questa ruina come fa fare Papa Pauolo a ogni fabrica che fa."

52. Fedeli, *Relazione*, 146.
53. For Florentines patronizing local churches see K. J. P. Lowe, "Patronage and Territoriality in Early Sixteenth-Century Florence," *Renaissance Studies* 7 (1993), 259.
54. In this case the word "major" means that these grants were large enough to be recorded in the monasteries' compilation books. This usually meant that the money either funded an endowment for perpetual masses or a construction project. The relevant bequests can be found in ASFi, CRSF 81, vol. 91; ASFi, CRSF, 92, vol. 128; and ASFi, CRSF 123, vol. 10.
55. At times, the familial or neighborhood connections between donor and monastery are plainly demonstrated in the *legati* books themselves. When they are not, the process of establishing connections between people who lived five hundred years ago and the places that they lived is of course, a tricky business, but one made easier by the 1562 census conducted by Cosimo. It is for this reason that I have chosen the years 1555–1580, since they allow me to place the proper names in the proper quarters. In each case, I have linked the person to the quarter of Santa Croce, either by his or her own name or the name of someone to whom he or she was related in the first degree. See Silvia Meloni Trkulja, *I Fiorentini in 1562: Descritione delle bocche della città et stato di Fiorenza fatta l'anno 1562,* ed. Silvia Meloni Trkulja (Florence: Bruschi, 1991).
56. Lapini, *Diario*, 124.
57. Ibid., 113.
58. Robert Gaston, "Liturgy and Patronage in San Lorenzo Florence, 1350–1650," in *Patronage, Art, and Society in Renaissance Italy,* ed. F. W. C. Kent and Patricia Simmons with J. C. Eade (Oxford: Clarendon Press, 1987), 128.
59. Ibid., 111–123.
60. Fossi, *Arte,* 149–150.
61. See Ferdinando Mancini, "Restauratione d'alcuni più segnalati miracoli della S.MA Nunziata di Fiorenza (transcription by Iginia Dini)," in *La SS. Annunziata di Firenze: Studi e documenti sulla chiesa e il convento,* ed. Eugenio Casalini, Iginia Dini, Renzo Giorgetti, and Paola Ircani (Florence: Convento della SS. Annunziata, 1978).
62. Martines, *Fire in the City,* 239–240.
63. Mancini, "Restauratione," 97: "testa fino al busto d'argento al naturale, di buon peso."
64. Ibid., 93.
65. Richelson, *Studies in the Personal Imagery,* 115.
66. Ibid., 113–114. All previous scholars have taken this to be Cosimo as Joshua.
67. Fantoni, *La corte del granduca,* 177–178.
68. Rubin, *Giorgio Vasari,* 98.

69. Brucker, *Renaissance Florence*, 32.

70. Verdon, *Immagini della Controriforma*, 522–523.

71. Louis Alexander Waldman, "Bandinelli and the Opera di Santa Maria del Fiore: Patronage, Privilege, and Pedagogy," in *Santa Maria del Fiore: The Cathedral and Its Sculpture; Acts of the International Symposium for the VII Centenary of the Cathedral of Florence, Florence Villa I Tatti, 5–6 June 1997*, ed. Margaret Haines (Fiesole: Edizioni Cadmo, 2001), 221–237.

72. What remains today of Bandinelli's choir is just the base of the original structure.

73. Hall, *Renovation and Counter-Reformation*, 7–13.

74. On Cosimo's intervention in Santa Maria Novella, see ASFi, Med. 199c.109v–110r (April 18, 1553). On the monks' replacement, see Lapini, *Diario*, 117.

75. ASFi, Med. 185c. 145v (July 26, 1544).

76. ASFi, Med. 323c. 31r (May 24, 1549): "poter reprimer la insolentie lussure, soddomie, et sacrilegii che in questo religiosi sono."

77. ASFi, Med. 194c. 115r–115v (September 14, 1551). Adopted from Alessandro's administration, Sannini had worn many hats for Cosimo already, functioning as a local inquisitor, a ducal informant, and an instrumental collaborator in carrying out the reforms of the female monasteries.

78. ASFi, Med. 182c. 35v–36r (April 11, 1537).

79. For instance, their commerce with women of ill repute, their scandalous association with female monasteries, their propensity for making novices of excessively young boys, and their habit of accepting more brothers than they could afford. Santa Sede, *Bullarium Romanum*, vol. 7, ed. Francisco Gaude (Augusta: Seb. Franco et Henrico Dalmazzo Editoribus, 1862), 401–422.

80. Hall, *Renovation and Counter-Reformation*, 16–27.

81. Ibid., 133.

82. Fossi, *Arte*, 422.

83. ASFi, Med. 207, c. 95v–96r (September 6, 1557).

84. Lapini, *Diario*, 151.

85. van Veen, *Cosimo*, 122–123.

86. ASFi, Med. 631 and K. J. P. Lowe, *Nuns' Chronicles and Convent Culture in Renaissance and Counter Reformation Italy* (Cambridge: Cambridge University Press, 2003), 135.

87. Ibid., 373.

88. Lowe, "Patronage," 264.

89. See F. W. Kent, *Lorenzo de'Medici and the Art of Magnificience* (Baltimore: Johns Hopkins University Press, 2006), 64–66, and Lowe, *Nuns' Chronicles*, 372.

90. Lowe, *Nuns' Chronicles*, 175–176.

91. ASFi, Med. 189c. 74v (November 11, 1548).

92. See Cosimo's painstakingly constructed letter to Catherine on her accession, ASFi, Med. 10c. 28r (April 21, 1547).

93. Heidi Chrétien, *The Festival of San Giovanni: Imagery and Political Power in Renaissance Florence* (New York: Peter Lang, 1994), 1–3.

94. See Cesare Paoli and E. Casanova, "Cosimo I de'Medici e I fuorusciti del 1537," *Archivio Storico Italiano* 11, ser. 5 (1893), 301–303. For an interpretation of the event, see Trexler, *Church and Community*, 231–232.

95. On the Este, see Ricci, *Il principe*.

96. The classic works on the double funeral and the theory of the king's two bodies are, respectively, Giesey, *The Royal Funeral* and Kantorowicz, *King's Two Bodies*.

97. Of course, the Florentine celebration of David as decapitator of Goliath and tyrant slayer was the most potent example, but the list could be extended. Especially in the commission of statues, the Medici themselves found it wise to associate themselves with the tyrant slayers David, Judith, and Perseus, ostensibly to ward off the criticisms that they were themselves in fact the tyrants. See Sarah Blake McHam, "Donatello's Bronze *David* and *Judith* as Metaphors of Medici Rule in Florence," *Art Bulletin* 83, no. 1 (2001), 32–47. Cosimo's choice of the Perseus statue was almost certainly designed to continue this tradition. See Cellini, *Autiobiography*, 317.

98. For a brief description of the funeral, see Domenico Moreni, *Pompe funebri celebrate nell'imperiale e real basilica di San Lorenzo* (Florence: Magheri, 1827), 47–48.

99. See Edward Muir, *Ritual in Early Modern Europe* (Cambridge: Cambridge University Press, 1997), 251–252.

100. For the manner in which similar political rituals might be imbued with contested meanings, see Edward Muir, "Representations of Power in Renaissance Italy," in *Italy in the Renaissance (1300–1550),* ed. John M. Najemy (Oxford: Oxford University Press, 2004), 227.

101. Such a maneuver would be consistent with the type of fictitious rituals Cosimo was letting play out on the more explicitly political plane, for instance by letting the senate create the *Otto di Practica* without his presence, though even foreign ambassadors knew Cosimo manipulated everything behind the scenes. See Paoli and Casanova, "Cosimo I de'Medici."

102. See Muir, "Representations," 240–242. On Episcopal processions, see Maureen Miller, "Urban Space, Sacred Topography, and Ritual Meanings in Florence: The Route of the Bishop's Entry," in *The Bishop Re-Formed: Studies in Episcopal Power and Culture in the Central Middle Ages*, ed. John Ott and Anna Trumbore (Aldershot: Ashgate, 2007), 240. On the *Impruneta*, see Trexler, *Public Life*, 355–358.

103. Minor and Mitchell, *Renaissance Entertainment*, 121–122.

104. Ibid., 122.

105. Though it may also be the case that this road was the widest and most attractive available.

106. For the ways Florentines had traditionally used the visits of foreigners to compensate for their lack of feudal honor, see Trexler, *Public Life,* 279–330.

107. Minor and Mitchell, *Renaissance Entertainment,* 118–121.

108. Ibid., 124–135.

109. Ibid., 223. The pagan flair of the pageant, no doubt, followed the typical contemporary poetic license in this matter. At any rate, the various goddesses were reinserted into a Christian framework by asserting their inferiority to the God of the universe. Apollo enjoined Cosimo: "And since they give you their pure and sincere hearts with their dearest and most beautiful dowries love them as a father, just and true. For their humble prayers above the stars will obtain from Him who governs the world and Heaven, life and issue and honor, with eternal peace."

110. Chrétien, *Festival of San Giovanni,* 38–39.

111. Casini, *I gesti del principe,* 257.

112. Kent, *Patron's Oeuvre,* 60, and Minor and Mitchell, *Renaissance Entertainment,* 100–101.

113. On the tensions between the civic/feudal and public/private elements of the the San Giovanni festival, see Trexler, *Public Life,* 218.

114. Casini, *I gesti del principe,* 153.

115. Cantini, *Legislazione,* vol. 1, 370–373, October 15, 1547: "Attendendo, che per li tempi passati li huomini li giorni festivi delle Domeniche, et altre Feste comandate dalla Santa Chiesa con poca riverentia, et timore del Magno, et Onnipotente Dio hanno consueto fare li loro esercitii, come li altri giorni di lavoro in massimo dishonore, et publico scandolo della Christiana Religione."

116. Ibid., 370–372.

117. In liturgical terminology, the term *feria* was often equated simply with a feast day. The equation of *feria* with feast day is currently lost in ecclesiastical terminology, but the original sense lives on in modern Italian in its meaning of holiday. In later liturgical terminology, *feria* came to refer to a weekday, in which sense it lives on in the modern Italian word for weekday: *feriale.* However, it is clear that the Tuscan government had neither of these religious meanings in mind in its legislation; a *feria* at this time and in this setting was a distinct category whose most distinct function was the prorogation of debt.

118. Cosimo, for instance, created *ferie* for this reason in 1550, 1554, and 1562.

119. ASFi, MS 5 c. 46r (January 7, 1540).

120. A letter from an unknown source to Ugolino Grifoni confirms that these quickly became traditional accoutrements of the festival of Cosimo's election. See ASFi, Med. 1070c. 14r–14v (January 9, 1542).

121. In any case, the supreme magistrate had already been granting Cosmus and Damian their *feria* on a year-to-year basis. ASFi, MS 5c. 16r (September 19, 1539).

122. On Cosimo's regulation of the *ferie* see Florentine Government, *Ferie nuovamente ordinate per Sua Eccellentia nella corte della merchantia di Firenze* (Florence: Bandito per Domenicho Barlacchi, 1542).

123. Cantini, *Legislazione,* vol. 3, 103–104 and 279–280.

124. Stephens, *The Fall of the Florentine Republic,* 219.

125. ASFi, Med. 182c. 51r (May 25, 1537): "in cambio d'essa, si supplichi et multiplichi con le orationi appresso la bonta divina atteso che ella gratamente accetta et riceve in la sua gratia sanctissima ciaschuno che col cuor contrito et humiliato la ricercha."

126. ASFi, Med. 182c. 51v–52r (May 26, 1537).

127. ASFi, Med. 212c. 72r (May 16, 1560): "che fatta la festa di San Piero si metta à camino, pero che da mezzo il mese come scrivete che doverebbe esser la partita, al detto tempo della festa come si breve spatio che poco importa, et parera che fugga quel giorno cosi celebre in quella città."

128. The local jubilee is not to be confused with the universal jubilee proclaimed by the pope, but it is clear that this jubilee must have ultimately rested on the Roman authority, as it seems to have included some sort of indulgence with it. ASFi, Med. 182c. 26v–27r (March 11, 1537): "ci sara grato non gli è ne manchiate a causa una tanto meritevole opera si possi tirare avanti per salute di tutti quelli che bramano la eterna salute."

129. Cosimo I, *Lettere,* 55.

130. ASFi, Med. 4c. 105r–108r (October 30, 1540): "mi è parso convenire al debito mio come già siàmo alla Solemnita di tutti e santi conseguentemente alla cerimonia da morti."

131. Ibid.

132. ASFi, Med. 4, c. 110r–112v (November 4, 1540).

133. See ASFi, Med. 5, 510r (March 8, 1544); and ASFi, Med. 5, 571r (March 2, 1544).

134. Lapini, *Diario,* 126–127.

135. Cantini, *Legislazione,* vol. 4, 105, December 22, 1560: "Atteso con quanta clemenza, e carità cristianamente si sia mosso il Beatissimo, e Santissimo Vicario di Dio in Terra Papa Pio Quarto a dare liberale a Fedeli Cristiani delli Tesori, e Grazie della Chiesa Santissima, e che perciò fa di bisogno provvedere che ciascuna persona possa liberamente e senza impedimento arrichirsi di tanto particolar dono dell'Indulgenza già pubblicata; Imperò Lor Signorie fanno pubblicamente bandire, e notificare a ciascuno come hanno fatto, e creato Ferie per la Città di Fiorenza solamente quanto all'esecuzioni personali et etiam per gli cessanti da dover cominciare domani che sarà il di 23 del presente, e per dover durare tutto detto Mese di Decembre, e però esortare ogni persona che Domenica prossima nel cui giorno si faranno per la Città Processioni solenni si disponga a seguirle dietro divotamente

secondo l'ordine della Bolla per conseguirne tanta Indulgenza, Supplicando Dio di tutto cuore per la conservazione, augumento, e grandezza della sua vera, e Santissima Fede."

136. Ibid., vol. 4, 106.

137. Ibid., vol. 5, 172.

138. Ibid., vol. 5, 187–188, and vol. 6, 8–9.

139. Ibid., vol. 7, 362–363.

140. On Paul IV, see Anzilotti, *La costituzione,* 188–189.

141. Cosimo respectfully declined in a letter to the papal nephew in 1551. See ASFi, Med. 194c. 25r–25v (March 18, 1551): "fussi per esser causa di far ritirar le persone da far simili buone opere"; "et ci si conserva il zelo della Religione, forse piu che nelli altri stati, il quale non vorrei che per cio si diminuisce punto."

142. ASFi, PS 6c. 186.

143. ASFi, PS 6c. 334.

144. Cantini, *Legislazione,* vol. 4, 339: "si trovano forse ancor astretti alle pene del purgatorio."

145. ASFi, Med. 182c. 1v (January 15, 1537); ASFi, Med. 182c. 169r (November 12, 1537); ASFi, Med. 182 26v–27r (March 11, 1537); and ASFi, Med. 182 46r (May 5, 1537).

146. Dante, *Purgatorio,* canto 3, verses 140–145.

147. Antonino, *Opera,* 16v: "se poi che sono morti, ha satisfatto alli lasciti fatti alle Chiese, ò ad altri luoghi pij, al tempo debito. Et quando non lo habbi fatto, tale si puo domandare homicidiario, dell'anime de suoi genitori, subtrahendo à quelli, li debiti suffragii, ilche non esenza grande peccato."

148. On Ghetti's heretical sermons in Venice, see Martin, *Venice's Hidden Enemies,* 88.

149. See Firpo, *Gli affreschi,* 229–232.

150. Fra Andrea, *Trattato,* 15r: "essendo Christo tanto riccho, et tanto giusto: et non havendo bisgno de suoi meriti, quali de iure debbano ricevere le sue operationi, dimandiamogli arditamente che con quegli suvvenga alle miserie nostre, et dimandiangli tutti i sudori suoi: et quel sudar del sangue, dimandiamogli la fame patita nel deserto, gli stenti fatti nell'orare . . . tutto quel che egli finalmente per noi ha patito, et piamente parlando, se egli ci negassi questo, noi potiamo percuotere et rompere il Cielo con le lachrime et gemiti, chiedendo quelch'è nostro: ma egli che e fidelissimo non ce lo potrà negare."

151. For examples of Tuscan religious writers' support of purgatory, see Anonymous, *Gradi,* 14v, Davidico, *Anatomia,* 80r–81v; Strozzi, *Trattato,* 36r, Visdomini, *Tutte le prediche,* 201–219; and Mellini, *Trattato,* 62–63.

152. On the expulsion of reformers from Italy, see Giovanni Romeo, *L'inquisizione nell'Italia Moderna* (Rome: Laterza, 2002).

153. Samuel K. Cohn Jr., *Death and Property in Siena* (Baltimore: Johns Hopkins University Press, 1988), 177.

154. On the other hand, some testators expanded on the preamble considerably, for example Agata, a farmer's wife, whose preamble invoked not only Mary but Peter, Paul, and John the Baptist as well. ASFi, NA filze 13631 (1528).

155. Indeed, many bequests to monasteries were, in fact, granted specifically to relatives; sometimes the relative was obliged to pray for the testator, but they were often not obliged to do anything, suggesting that the continued popularity of pious bequests to monasteries in Florence had much to do with kinship ties. See also Cohn, *Death and Property*, 103–105, and Giovanna Benadusi, "Investing the Riches of the Poor: Servant Women and Their Last Wills," *American Historical Review* 109, no. 3 (June 2004), 805–826.

156. See Trexler, *Church and Community*, 266–267.

157. On the other hand, an absence of requests for masses or a dearth of pious bequests may have had more to do with concerns to conserve the patrimony for universal heirs than with religious affiliation or sentiment. Cohn, *Death and Property*, 144–145.

158. Panciatichi's testament is found in ASFi, NA 16332c. 319r–321r. For another example, Camilla Russell found a similar lack of Catholic identifiers in the will of Giulia Gonzaga, also known for her *sola fide* beliefs. Russell, *Giulia Gonzaga*, 200.

159. The characterization is drawn from Raab, *English Face*, 46.

160. This is the second of Machiavelli's two testaments. ASFi, NA 3698c. 102r–105r.

161. For instance, when Paul III threw him into prison in 1539, he turned to his guardian angel, praying to God to let him know what sin he was "so sorely expiating." He even claimed to have witnessed a miraculous vision of the divine clemency, in which the Madonna and Child appeared along with Saint Peter, pleading his cause to God. See Cellini, *Autobiography*, 222–224.

162. Cellini had several testaments drawn up. See ASFi, NA 6762c. 44. His other testaments are in the same volume.

163. See Marchetti, *Gruppi ereticali*; George McClure, "Heresy at Play: Academies and the Literary Underground in Counter-Reformation Siena," *Renaissance Quarterly* 63 (2010), 1115–1207 and Cohn, *Death and Property*, 166–167.

164. Cohn notes that testators in Siena only began specifying the number of masses and distinguishing between the Mass of Saint Gregory and the Office of the Dead at the end of the sixteenth century. Cohn, *Death and Property*, 167. My analysis of Florentine wills suggests that Florentines had been doing these throughout the sixteenth century.

165. Richard Goldthwaite, *The Building of Renaissance Florence: An Economic and Social History* (Baltimore: Johns Hopkins University Press), 439.

166. In its full Latin: "In primis quidem anima sua omnipotenti deo, eius glorissime matrisque semper virginis marie, toti curia celestii paradisi, humilte, devote, comandavit."

167. Ronnie Po-chia Hsia, *Society and Religion in Munster, 1535–1618* (New Haven: Yale University Press, 1984), 180.

168. See ASFi, Otto 8 c. 14r (August 2, 1538).

169. Anonymous, *Diario Fiorentino di 1537,* 561: "unire la città e si vivessi pacificamente e con timore di Dio, altrimenti che grandissimo fragello era preparato sopra Firenze."

170. ASFi, Med. 182 c. 74r–75r (July 14, 1537).

171. ASFi, AGBE 4377 c. 102 (June 22, 1548).

172. Francesco Rondinelli, *Relazione del contagio stato in Firenze L'anno 1630 e 1633, con un breve ragguaglio delle Miracolosa Immagine della Madonna dell'Impruneta* (Florence: Giovanni Batista Landini, 1634), 250–258.

173. Mancini, "Restauratione," 86.

174. See N. Ugo Ceccherini, *Santa Maria Impruneta: Notizie storiche* (Florence: Ciardi, 1890).

175. In fact, he had previously been the rector of the Impruneta's shrine. For Buondelmonte as a Medicean, see Miller, "Urban Space, Sacred Topography," 246.

176. Trexler, *Public Life,* 69.

177. Roth, *Last Florentine Republic,* 76, 140, 162, and 204.

178. Rondinelli, *Relazione,* 268–275.

179. ASFi, MS 4307 c. 103r–104r (November 14, 1547).

180. Rondinelli, *Relazione,* 256–268.

181. Polizzotto, *Elect Nation,* 317.

182. ASFi, PS 2 c. unpaginated (April 29, 1556).

183. ASFi, Man. 14r, and Lapini, *Diario,* 134.

184. ASFi, CRS 1324 pt. 2, c. 43r–43v.

185. On the way those who associated themselves with sacred images simultaneously lent those images their own authority; see Trexler, *Church and Community,* 19. On the confraternity of Santa Maria Quercia and Cosimo's policies toward confraternities, see Ronald Weissman, *Ritual Brotherhood in Renaissance Florence* (New York: Academic Press, 1982), 190–199.

186. Cited in Ceccherini, *Santa Maria Impruneta,* 12: "Ricordo come l'anno 1562 il primo di marzo . . . stette sino a dì 5 d'ottobre 1562, che mai piovve tanto che li fiumi corressino, ne li fossati. Si secorono tutti li pozzi qui della pieve, e qui all'intorno; e per sorte si trovò una vena d'acqua sotto il Monte Santa Maria, appresso alla nostra Pieve, dove concorsone tutti li popoli per detta acqua, e si nominò detta acqua, l'acqua di Santa Maria,

per uscire da detto Monte Santa Maria, e di molti, che bevvono di tal acqua li quali avevano la febbre, subito bevuta, guarirono, a laude della gloriosa Madre Vergine Nostra Avvocata."

187. See Rondinelli, *Relazione*, 268–270.

188. Cantini, *Legislazione*, vol. 3, 226–235.

189. ASFi, Med. 1169c. 4 (October 19, 1539).

190. Lapini, *Diario*, 112–113.

Conclusion

1. Marc Bloch, *The Historian's Craft*, trans. Peter Putnam (New York: Vintage Books, 1953), 32.

Acknowledgments

I would like to take the opportunity to thank the many people who have given advice and encouragement to bring this book to fruition, foremost among them my advisor and mentor, Ronnie Po-Chia Hsia. I would also like to thank Brian Curran, A. G. Roeber, and Matthew Restall. This project could not have been completed without the generous funding of a Fulbright scholarship, as well as funding from Pennsylvania State University and institutional support from the Medici Archive Project. I would like especially to thank Edward Goldberg for his support of the project, from its inception (during my very first trip to Florence) to its conclusion. Thanks also to *Renaissance and Reformation/Renaissance et Réforme* for allowing me to republish portions of an article entitled "Cardinals, Inquisitors, and Jesuits: Curial Patronage and Counter-Reformation in Cosimo I's Florence," *Renaissance and Reformation/Renaissance et Réforme* 32, no. 1 (2009), in Chapter 4.

I would like to thank Tovah Bender, Adriano Prosperi, Gilberto Aranci, Alessio Assonitis, Jennifer Haraguchi, Philip Hnakovitch, Spencer Delbridge, Henry Tom, Clare Copeland, and Martha Ramsey for their comments and suggestions during the research and writing process. A special thanks to Kate Lowe for her kind and encouraging words to a young scholar on his first day in the archives.

The staff at the Archivio di Stato Firenze, the Biblioteca Nazionale, and Archivio Segreto Vaticano were extremely helpful in allowing me to carry out this project.

This book could not have been written without the support of my family. A special thanks to my wife, who moved halfway around the world so that I could do the research.

Thanks as well to the anonymous readers of the manuscript, whose many suggestions improved the final product greatly. Finally, I would like to extend a warm thanks to Harvard University Press, especially to Ian Stevenson for his support and guidance and to Edward Muir for his insights, expertise, and encouragement. This work owes a profound debt to them. All mistakes are my own.

Index

Absolutism, 11, 12, 53, 97, 135, 246
Anti-Machiavellianism, 11, 69, 105,
  106, 108–109, 113, 118, 120, 132
Antoninus, Saint, 19, 37, 87, 110,
  168, 183, 227
Aquinas, Thomas, 31, 49, 87
Aristotle, 22, 86, 91; in support of
  divinization of man, 28, 31, 40;
  reconciled with Christianity, 59–60
Astrology: to legitimize rulers, 71–73;
  compatible with Christianity,
  86–88; and fate, 88–89, 90
Augustine: powers of the soul, 28–30;
  used by Christian humanists, 30,
  32, 38; free will exercising virtue,
  33; on providentialism, 51, 59–60,
  62–63, 67; quoted by preachers,
  61; on evil, 63; used in sacred plays,
  64–66, 73; and Cosimo, 69, 101,
  115, 117; just-war theory, 126–127
Augustus, 49, 81; Cosimo compared
  to, 19–20, 46, 76, 122

Baglioni, Ridolpho, 140
Bronzino, 207, 213
Burgos, cardinal, 145, 148, 150, 197.
  See also Toledo, cardinal

Cellini, Benvenuto, 78–79, 181, 209,
  230–231

Dante, 41, 83, 90, 227
David, 39, 46, 72, 74, 84, 126
Delle Bande Neri, Giovanni, 4, 54,
  207, 209, 218
Divine right, 10, 55, 58, 96–97,
  102–103, 244; relationship with
  absolutism, 12; links with providentialism, 51–53, 61–62, 69, 84–85;
  legitimizing Cosimo, 53, 54, 57,
  99; astrology and, 86; linked to
  republicanism, 98, 102
Duomo, 160, 210, 257. See also
  Florentine cathedral

Eleanora, duchess. See Toledo, Eleonora

Fabrini, Giovanni, 22, 47, 61, 68–69
Feast of John the Baptist, 74, 214,
  219, 221
Ficino, Marsilio, 26–27, 28, 33, 43,
  44, 87–88
Florence, 11, 14, 19, 62, 204, 205, 225,
  231–233; Cosimo takes throne,
  1–7; republicanism, 8–9, 22, 97;
  impacted by the Renaissance, 14,
  22, 47–49; Cosimo as divine ruler
  of, 54–55, 57, 76, 84, 244–245;
  virtue, 109–110, 113; relationship
  with the papacy, 133–134, 224;
  patronage, 136, 157; relationship

Florence *(continued)*
with the Inquisition, 154, 158;
Jesuits, 160–161; religious reform,
171, 175, 189–190; and Santa
Maria Impruneta, 237, 241
Florentine Academy, 32, 43, 60, 69, 89
Florentine cathedral, 47, 151, 154, 184,
209–210, 217–218. *See also* Duomo
Fortune, 51, 54, 55, 100; ancient
philosophy, 59–60; legitimacy of
Cosimo, 62, 75, 85; relationship to
providence, 64, 74, 76, 79

Gelli, Giambattista, 21, 35, 36, 54, 69
Giovio, Paolo, 93, 106, 147

Index of Prohibited Books, 87, 105, 158

Julius III, pope, 128, 140, 142, 147,
148, 149, 152, 226

Loyola, Ignatius, 161

Machiavelli, Niccolò, 11, 114, 118,
244; influence in Florence, 105–107;
refutation of, 108; and virtue,
110–112; and Cosimo, 113, 115,
125; justice, 119; clemency,
120–122; religion, 125–126,
231–232; war and peace, 127
Medici, Alessandro, 121, 146, 166;
death of, 1–4, 57, 78, 100; funeral
of, 215–216
Medici, Cosimo the Elder, 5, 135, 136,
208, 218
Medici, Ferdinand, 20
Medici, Francesco, 67, 82
Medici, Giovanni, son of Cosimo,
104, 116, 147
Medici, Lorenzo, 43, 135, 163–165,
218–219; relationship with Rome,
155; Pazzi conspiracy, 169; protection of Jews, 181–182; support of
Santissima Annunziata, 213
Monte di Pietà, 147, 181, 182

Palazzo Vecchio (Signoria), 16, 19, 43,
74, 205, 239
Paul III, pope, 144, 150, 158; relationship with Cosimo, 134, 148, 151,
155–156, 168, 176
Paul IV, pope, 53, 96, 128, 141, 152,
154, 157–158, 226
Pius IV, pope, 140, 142, 147, 148,
152, 159, 225, 226
Pius V, pope, 6
Plato, 21, 41, 43; translation by
Ficino, 26–27; reconciled with
Christianity, 28, 33, 87; used to
support divinization of man, 31,
32; and Christian humanists, 59
Pontormo, Jacopo, 20, 207, 209
Providence, 57, 85, 94–95, 103; early
modern views, 51, 55; multicausal,
52, 86, 93, 96; election of Cosimo,
54, 61–62, 99, 102; reconciled with
Plato, 59; relationship to divine
right, 62–63, 69; in sacred plays,
64; as fortune, 75; relationship to
astrology, 88–89
Pucci, Antonio. *See* Santiquatrro,
cardinal
Pucci, Pandolfo, 122, 176–178

Salviati, Maria, 4, 137
Santa Croce, 109, 187, 203, 209–210,
212
Santa Fiora, cardinal, 145, 148, 157
Santa Maria Novella, 209–210, 211
Santiquatrro, cardinal, 150–151, 176
Santissima Annunziata, 2, 80, 187,
208–209; miraculous image, 236,
237–238; cult, 241
Savonarola, 9, 11, 39, 91, 115,
171–173, 175–178, 190–191, 208;
on terrestrial divinity, 29, 35;
criticized by Catharino, 57–58; on

causation, 70; on providentialism, 71–72; condemnation of astrology, 87, 89, 90; movement against Cosimo, 163–164, 165–167; at Lorenzo Medici's death, 165; brothers of San Marco, 168; appeasement by Cosimo, 170, 174, 179–180; scapegoating of Jews, 181–182; religious reform, 183–184, 188

Segni, Bernardo, 22, 79
Speculum principis, 106, 110
Strozzi, Alessandro, 96, 147, 148, 160–161, 186, 211, 223, 228
Studio of Pisa, 31, 43, 44, 88, 108

Toledo, cardinal, 144, 155–156, 157, 158, 161. *See also* Burgos, cardinal
Toledo, Eleonora, 67, 148, 175. 213; divinization of, 20; marriage to Cosimo, 144, 217–218; relationship to Diego Lainez,160; Jesuits and, 161; Santissima Annunziata, 208; health issues, 212, 217, 218

Toledo, Pedro, 161
Trent, Council of, 47, 90, 184, 186, 210, 225, 228

Varchi, Benedetto, 68, 95, 97–98, 101, 106–107, 137
Vasari, Giorgio, 19, 209; *The Apotheosis of Cosimo*, 16–17; dedication to Cosimo, 23; divinization of artists, 32; post-Tridentine projects, 210–211
Vecchio, Cosimo il. *See* Medici, Cosimo the Elder
Virtue, 10–11, 15, 63, 106, 121–122, 244–245; of Cosimo, 22, 48, 62, 64, 74, 100–102, 109, 123, 124; godliness of man, 30, 33, 36, 45–46, 49; relationship to free will, 35; reception of Eucharist, 38; relationship to fortune, 62; relationship to the natural world, 77–78; in Machiavelli, 105, 107, 111–112, 113, 131–132; Christian humanist, 109–111